D1527757

THE CLASSICS IN MODERNIST
TRANSLATION

Bloomsbury Studies in Classical Reception

Bloomsbury Studies in Classical Reception presents scholarly monographs offering new and innovative research and debate to students and scholars in the reception of Classical Studies. Each volume will explore the appropriation, reconceptualization and recontextualization of various aspects of the Graeco-Roman world and its culture, looking at the impact of the ancient world on modernity. Research will also cover reception within antiquity, the theory and practice of translation, and reception theory.

Also available in the series:

ANCIENT MAGIC AND THE SUPERNATURAL IN THE MODERN VISUAL AND PERFORMING ARTS
edited by Filippo Carlà & Irene Berti

ANCIENT GREEK MYTH IN WORLD FICTION SINCE 1989
edited by Justine McConnell & Edith Hall

CLASSICS IN EXTREMIS
edited by Edmund Richardson

FRANKENSTEIN AND ITS CLASSICS
edited by Jesse Weiner, Benjamin Eldon Stevens & Brett M. Rogers

GREEK AND ROMAN CLASSICS IN THE BRITISH STRUGGLE FOR SOCIAL REFORM
edited by Henry Stead & Edith Hall

HOMER'S ILIAD AND THE TROJAN WAR: DIALOGUES ON TRADITION
by Jan Haywood & Naoíse Mac Sweeney

IMAGINING XERXES
by Emma Bridges

JULIUS CAESAR'S SELF-CREATED IMAGE AND ITS DRAMATIC AFTERLIFE
by Miryana Dimitrova

OVID'S MYTH OF PYGMALION ON SCREEN
by Paula James

READING POETRY, WRITING GENRE
edited by Silvio Bär & Emily Hauser

THE CODEX FORI MUSSOLINI
by Han Lamers & Bettina Reitz-Joosse

THE GENTLE, JEALOUS GOD
by Simon Perris

VICTORIAN CLASSICAL BURLESQUES
by Laura Monrós-Gaspar

VICTORIAN EPIC BURLESQUES
by Rachel Bryant Davies

ONCE AND FUTURE ANTIQUITIES IN SCIENCE FICTION AND FANTASY
edited by Brett M. Rogers & Benjamin Eldon Stevens

THE CLASSICS IN MODERNIST TRANSLATION

Edited by
Miranda Hickman and Lynn Kozak

BLOOMSBURY ACADEMIC
LONDON • NEW YORK • OXFORD • NEW DELHI • SYDNEY

BLOOMSBURY ACADEMIC
Bloomsbury Publishing Plc
50 Bedford Square, London, WC1B 3DP, UK
1385 Broadway, New York, NY 10018, USA

BLOOMSBURY, BLOOMSBURY ACADEMIC and the Diana logo are trademarks of
Bloomsbury Publishing Plc

First published in Great Britain 2019

Cover image: Dawson, Manierre (1887–1969): *Meeting (The Three Graces)*, 1912 New York,
Metropolitan Museum of Art. Oil on canvas. 58 1/8 × 48 in. (147.6 × 121.9 cm). Gift of
Myra Bairstow and Lewis J. Obi, M.D., 2007 (2007.331) © 2017. Image copyright
The Metropolitan Museum of Art/Art Resource/Scala, Florence.

A catalogue record for this book is available from the British Library.

Library of Congress Cataloging-in-Publication Data
Names: Hickman, Miranda, editor. | Kozak, Lynn, editor.
Title: The classics in modernist translation / edited by Miranda Hickman & Lynn Kozak.
Other titles: Bloomsbury studies in classical reception.
Description: London : Bloomsbury Academic, 2019. | Series: Bloomsbury studies
in classical reception
Identifiers: LCCN 2018040924| ISBN 9781350040953 (hardback) | ISBN 9781350040977 (epub)
Subjects: LCSH: Classical literature—Translating. | Classical literature—Appreciation.
Classification: LCC PA3013 .C5984 2019 | DDC 880.09—dc23 LC record available at
https://lccn.loc.gov/2018040924

ISBN: HB: 978-1-3500-4095-3
          ePDF: 978-1-3500-4096-0
          eBook: 978-1-3500-4097-7

Series: Bloomsbury Studies in Classical Reception

Typeset by RefineCatch Limited, Bungay, Suffolk
Printed and bound in Great Britain

To find out more about our authors and books visit www.bloomsbury.com and sign up
for our newsletters.

CONTENTS

Contents

FIGURES

CONTRIBUTORS

Editors

Miranda Hickman is Associate Professor of English at McGill University in Montréal, where she focuses chiefly on modernist studies and modern poetry. Recent publications include essays on Wyndham Lewis (in *Wyndham Lewis*, Edinburgh, 2015) and the women painters of Vorticism (in *Vorticism: New Perspectives*, Oxford University Press, 2013). She is co-editor of *Rereading the New Criticism* (Ohio State University Press, 2012), editor and author of essays for *The Letters of Ezra Pound and Stanley Nott* (McGill-Queen's University Press, 2011), and author of *The Geometry of Modernism* (University of Texas Press, 2005). She has contributed chapters on T.S. Eliot, H.D., Mina Loy, Marianne Moore and Ezra Pound to the *Blackwell Companion to Modernist Poetry* (2014), *A History of Modernist Poetry* (Cambridge University Press, 2015) and Cambridge Companions to *H.D.* (2012) and *Modernist Women Poets* (2010). Her co-authored article with Lynn Kozak on H.D.'s early translations of Euripides will appear in the *Classical Receptions Journal* (2018). Current work includes a book in progress on women in cultural criticism in interwar Britain.

Lynn Kozak is Associate Professor of Classics at McGill University in Montréal. Current research focuses on serial poetics, from epic performance to new media forms, building on the monograph *Experiencing Hektor: Character in the* Iliad, published in 2016 by Bloomsbury Academic. Forthcoming work includes further work on H.D.'s translations of Greek tragic choruses (with Miranda Hickman), characterization and seriality in television procedurals and Homeric fandom. Recent creative work includes literal translations of Hrosvitha's *Sapientia* and Sophocles' *Oedipus Tyrannus*, adapted by Joseph Shragge, for Scapegoat Carnivale Theatre, and *Previously on . . . the* Iliad, a weekly serial performance sponsored by the Fonds de Recherche du Québec – Société et Culture of a new, partially improvised translation of the entire *Iliad*, that took place between January and August 2018.

Contributors

Gregory Baker is Assistant Professor and Director of the Certificate in Irish Studies in the Department of English at the Catholic University of America, Washington, DC. He holds an undergraduate degree in Classics (University of Chicago) and an MA and PhD in Comparative Literature from Brown University (English, Ancient Greek and Latin). His book in progress *Classics, Modernism and the Celtic Fringe* addresses the cultural history of classics and its impact on modernist literary revivals in twentieth-century Scotland, Ireland and Wales. Recent work includes the article '"Attic Salt into an Undiluted

Scots": Aristophanes and the Modernism of Douglas Young', in *Brill's Companion to the Reception of Aristophanes* (2016), and his annotated bibliography 'Classical Reception in English Literature, 1880–2000' is forthcoming in *The Oxford History of Classical Reception in English Literature (Volume 5)*, ed. Kenneth Haynes.

Marsha Bryant is Professor of English and Distinguished Teaching Scholar at the University of Florida. She has published extensively on modernism and modernist poetry (with articles on, among others, H.D., Auden, the modernist long poem and teaching modernist literature) as well as contemporary poetry. Her most recent book is *Women's Poetry and Popular Culture* (Palgrave Macmillan, 2013). With Mary Ann Eaverly, she has developed courses and museum exhibits focused on women's poetry; her co-authored article with Eaverly, 'Egypto-modernism: James Henry Breasted, H.D., and the New Past', appears in *Modernism/modernity 14.3* (2007): 435–53.

Massimo Cè holds a BA in Classics from Magdalen College, Oxford (2013) and an MA in Classics from Harvard University (2015). He is now pursuing his PhD in Classical Philology at Harvard, where he is currently completing a PhD on Homeric translation in antiquity.

Michael Coyle is Professor of English at Colgate University. Founder and first president of the Modernist Studies Association, he is author of *Ezra Pound, Popular Genres, and the Discourse of Culture* (Pennsylvania State University Press, 1995). Other publications include his chapter 'The Waste Land' in *A Companion to T.S. Eliot* (ed. David Chinitz, Wiley-Blackwell, 2009), *Broadcasting Modernism* (co-edited with Debra Rae Cohen and Jane Lewty, 2009), 'Pound and Race' (*Ezra Pound in Context*, 2010) and *Ezra Pound and African American Modernism* (National Poetry Foundation, 2001). Current research focuses on modernist poetry, critical theory and jazz.

Sara Dunton pursued an award-winning career in interior architecture before completing her doctorate in English at the University of New Brunswick (2016), with a focus on modernist literature. Her research addresses H.D.'s engagement with the visual arts, use of ekphrasis and fascination with Pre-Raphaelite artists. The recipient of a Social Sciences and Humanities Research Council Canada Graduate Scholarship for doctoral studies, she has presented papers on both Mina Loy and H.D. at several international conferences, and has published essays in both *Paideuma* (2013) and *H.D. and Modernity* (2014).

Mary Ann Eaverly is Professor and Chair of Classics at the University of Florida. She is author of *Archaic Greek Equestrian Sculpture* (University of Michigan Press, 1995) and *Tan Men/Pale Women: Color and Gender in Archaic Greece and Egypt, a Comparative Approach* (University of Michigan Press, 2013). With Marsha Bryant, she has co-authored several articles on H.D.'s work, including most recently 'Excavating H.D.'s Egypt' in *Approaches to Teaching H.D.'s Poetry and Prose* (MLA, 2011). Her current research project is a study of the iconography of the female nude in Archaic Greek art. The winner of several university teaching awards, she has taught in Rome and Paris and excavated in Greece, Israel, Cyprus and Spain.

Contributors

Leah Flack is Associate Professor of English at Marquette University, Wisconsin. Working in comparative modernism, classical reception studies and Irish literature, she has published *Modernism and Homer: The Odysseys of H.D., James Joyce, Osip Mandelstam, and Ezra Pound* (Cambridge University Press, 2015). She has also published in *Modernism/modernity* and the *James Joyce Quarterly*, and edited collections in classical reception studies and Irish literature. Current projects include *James Joyce and Classical Modernism* (Bloomsbury Academic, forthcoming 2020); a study of the reception of modernism in contemporary Irish literature; and a study of the digital archive of Osip Mandelstam.

Anna Fyta received her doctorate in June 2015 from the Departments of Comparative Literature and Classics at the University of Ioannina. Her dissertation *H.D.'s Poetics and Euripidean Drama* investigates the impact of Euripidean dramaturgy on H.D.'s oeuvre. She has presented at the conferences 'H.D. and Feminist Poetics' and the European Association of American Studies, and she presented at Princeton University's Modernist Fragmentation and After in 2016. She currently teaches at H.A.E.F. Psychico/Athens College in Athens, Greece.

Eileen Gregory is Professor of English at the University of Dallas. Author of *H.D. and Hellenism: Classic Lines* (Cambridge University Press, 1997), she has published extensively on H.D. (e.g. 'Rose Cut in Rock', *Signets*, 1990; 'Virginity and Erotic Liminality', *Contemporary Literature*, 1990), as well as work on Carolyn Forché, Margaret Atwood, Kathleen Fraser and William Faulkner. Her chapter on H.D. and translation appears in the *Cambridge Companion to H.D.* (2011). Current research addresses the status of lyric in contemporary culture.

Anett K. Jessop is Assistant Professor of English at The University of Texas at Tyler, where she teaches twentieth- and twenty-first-century American literature, with an emphasis on the experimental vanguard, feminist theory and creative writing. She received her doctorate from the University of California, Davis, in 2013. Recent publications include 'The Classical Past and "the history of ourselves": Laura Riding's Trojan Woman' (*Brill's Companion to Classical Receptions: International Modernism and the Avant-Garde*, 2017), 'Geopoetics and Historical Modernism: Gertrude Stein, Laura Riding and Robert Graves in Mallorca, 1912–1936' (*Mediterranean Modernism; Intercultural Exchange and Aesthetic Development, 1880–1945*, Palgrave-MacMillan, 2016) and 'Modernisms, Pure English and Poetry: Laura (Riding) Jackson's "Linguistic Ultimate"' (*Inventive Linguistics*, Presses Universitaires de la Méditerranée, 2010). Forthcoming is 'Modernist Revisionist Mythmaking: Laura Riding's Lilithian Poetics,' (*Women Poets and Myth in the 20th and 21st Centuries*, Cambridge Scholars, 2019). Additionally, she has published essays on Persian Modernist poets. Her book in progress analyses revisionist historiographies, hagiographies and mythography in the work of twentieth-century experimental American women writers.

J. Alison Rosenblitt trained as an ancient historian at Oxford University and publishes in both the fields of Roman history and classical reception. She is currently Director of Studies for Classics at Regent's Park College, Oxford. As an historian, she works with ancient historiography (especially Sallust), late republican political history and Roman oratory. In classical reception, she focuses on early modernism and its relationship to the classics: articles in this area include 'a twilight smelling of Vergil: E.E. Cummings, Classics, and the Great War' in *Greece & Rome* (2014) and 'Pretentious Scansion, Fascist Aesthetics, and a Father-complex for Joyce: E.E. Cummings on Sapphics and Ezra Pound' in the *Cambridge Classical Journal* (2013). She is the author of *E.E. Cummings' Modernism and the Classics* (Oxford University Press, 2016); her *Rome after Sulla* will appear with Bloomsbury Academic (2019). Her book of creative non-fiction on E.E. Cummings is forthcoming through W.W. Norton.

Matthias Somers holds degrees in English and Ancient Greek and received his PhD from the University of Leuven (Belgium) in 2015 with a dissertation on Anglo-American modernism and the rhetorical tradition. Currently a postdoctoral fellow at the University of Leuven, he is a member there of the MDRN research lab, which investigates the multiple modalities of literary change in Europe in the period 1900–1950 (www.mdrn. be). He has co-authored MDRN's *Modern Times, Literary Change* (2013), and published work in *Arcadia* and *Affirmations*. Recent work includes 'Modernism at the University: New Elocution, New Criticism, and New Poetry', *Orbis Litterarum* (2017) and 'The "New Negro", the Sermon, and the Postwar Modernism of Baldwin and Ellison' in the 2016 *Revue Belge de Philologie et d'Histoire – Belgisch Tijdschrift voor Filologie en Geschiedenis*.

Catherine Theis is a poet. She holds an MFA in poetry from the Iowa Writers' Workshop, and is pursuing a PhD in literature and creative writing at the University of Southern California. Her first book of poems is *The Fraud of Good Sleep* (Salt Modern Poets, 2011), followed by her chapbook *The June Cuckold: A Tragedy in Verse* (Convulsive, 2012). She has received various fellowships and awards, most notably from the Illinois Arts Council and the Del Amo Foundation. Her play *MEDEA* (Plays Inverse Press, 2017) is an adaptation of the Euripides story set in the mountains of Montana. Her scholarly interests focus on the intersections among translation, poetics and performance studies.

Demetres Tryphonopoulos is Dean of Arts, Brandon University, Manitoba, where he also teaches courses in modernist American poetry. He continues to supervise graduate work at the University of New Brunswick, where he taught for several decades. He has published extensively on Pound, H.D. and other modernists. He is author, editor, or co-editor of fourteen books, including *The Celestial Tradition: A Study of Pound's Cantos* (Wilfrid Laurier University Press, 1992) and two editions of H.D.'s prose work: *Majic Ring* (Florida University Press, 2009) and *Hirslanden Notebooks* (ELS, 2015). Current projects include a book on Pound's late *Cantos*; translations of Andreas Embeirikos, Odysseas Elytis and Iakovos Kambanellis; and a book on Pound's and H.D.'s Hellenistic prosodies. He is a member of the editorial collective for the journal *Paideuma: Modern and Contemporary Poetry and Poetics*.

Elizabeth Vandiver is Clement Biddle Penrose Professor of Latin and Classics at Whitman College in Washington State. She is the author of the book *Stand in the Trench, Achilles: Classical Receptions in British Poetry of the Great War* (2010, re-issued in paperback in 2013); her book in progress is entitled *'Gold Words of a Greek Long Dead': Richard Aldington's Reception of Classics*. She has published extensively on classical reception, with articles and book chapters on Herodotus, the figure of the hero, translation and Catullus;

recently her work has focused on the reception of the classics during World War I, with emphasis on figures such as Richard Aldington. She has contributed to companion volumes on classical reception from Brill, Oxford and Blackwell.

George Varsos is Assistant Professor of literary translation at the University of Athens and teaches in the History of European Literature at the Hellenic Open University. He was Visiting Research Fellow at Princeton University in 2011. He holds degrees in Comparative Literature from the Université de Montréal and the University of Geneva (PhD, 2002). His published research emphasizes relations between literature, philology and history, with a particular interest in Walter Benjamin. He is co-editor of a special issue on 'Disappearance' for the journal *Intermédialités* and author of the first volume of the *History of European Literature* (Hellenic Open University). He has also translated a variety of texts into Greek: literature (Vladimir Nabokov, Ezra Pound, Walter Pater) and theory (Fredric Jameson, Paul de Man).

Jeffrey Westover is Associate Professor of English at Boise State University, Idaho; he has also taught at Howard University and the University of Nevada, Reno. Publications include *The Colonial Moment: Discoveries and Settlements in Modern American Poetry* (Northern Illinois University Press, 2004) and recent articles on William Carlos Williams, Langston Hughes, Lorine Niedecker and Wallace Stevens. His chapter 'Voicing Political Justice and Personal Dignity in African American Sonnets' appears in the *Blackwell Companion to Poetic Genre* (Blackwell, 2012), and work on James Merrill ('Eros and Psyche: The View "From the Cupola"') appears in *Classical and Modern Literature* (1998) and *Critical Essays on James Merrill* (G.K. Hall, 1996).

Nancy Worman is Ann Whitney Olin Professor of Classics at Columbia University (Barnard College). Her work focuses on Greek drama and oratory, performance and the body and modernist reception. Her publications include *Landscape and the Spaces of Metaphor in Ancient Literary Theory and Criticism* (Cambridge University Press, 2015), *Place, Space and Landscape in Ancient Greek Literature and Culture* (co-edited with K. Gilhuly, Cambridge University Press, 2014) and *Abusive Mouths in Classical Athens* (Cambridge University Press, 2008). Current projects address embodiment in Greek tragedy and Virginia Woolf's gendering of Greek tragic style.

Steven Yao is Edmund A. Lefevre Professor of Literature at Hamilton College. He has authored two books, *Translation and the Languages of Modernism* (Palgrave/St. Martins, 2002), and *Foreign Accents: Chinese American Verse from Exclusion to Postethnicity* (Oxford, 2010), which was selected by the Association for Asian American Studies for its Book Award in Literary Studies. He is co-editor of *Sinographies: Writing China* (Minnesola 2008), *Pacific Rim Modernisms* (Toronto 2009), and *Erza Pound and Education* (National Poetry Foundation 2012). He has earned fellowships from the American Council on Education; the American Council of Learned Societies and the Stanford Humanities Center.

FOREWORD
THE CLASSICS, MODERNISM AND TRANSLATION: A CONFLICTED HISTORY

In the essay 'How to Read', Ezra Pound famously declared that 'English literature lives on translation, it is fed by translation; every new exuberance, every new heave is stimulated by translation, every allegedly great age is a great age of translations'. Nor was Pound alone among modernist writers in the United Kingdom and the United States in seeing the practice of translation as essential to cultural renewal and innovation. In fact, as the essays contained herein richly demonstrate, writers such as Richard Aldington, H.D., T.S. Eliot, Ezra Pound and W.B. Yeats, to name only the most famous, all produced numerous and diverse translations, including most especially renderings of classical authors – ranging from Homer and other Greek poets to the tragedians Euripides and Sophocles to the Latin love elegist Sextus Propertius – as part of their collective effort to transform society by freeing art from the comfortable decorum of Victorian morality and aesthetic conventions.

In their translations of Greek and Latin classics, the modernists rejected the norms and values given authoritative expression by that most eminent of Victorians, Matthew Arnold. Scholars, thought Arnold, ought to take precedence in judging translations, of Homer for example, 'for the scholar alone has the means of knowing what Homer is to be reproduced'. In direct contrast, the modernists strove to renew the classical tradition by passing its luminous rays through the prism of their own respective individual literary talents, often without serious regard to formal language training. By doing so, they sought through their efforts at translation to wrest control over of the classics, to liberate their cultural prestige from what they considered to be the death-grip of existing institutions and to redeploy that prestige in support of their own revolutionary purposes. Seeking most of all to rescue the classics from what they saw to be an intellectually moribund educational system, modernist writers openly challenged established scholarly protocols and rejected academic standards and regimes of value. Thus, Richard Aldington declared in the Introduction to the Poets' Translation Series from 1915:

> The object of editors of this series is to present a number of translations of Greek and Latin poetry and prose, especially of those authors who are less frequently given in English. . . . This literature has too long been the property of pedagogues, philologists, and professors. Its human qualities have been obscured by the wranglings of grammarians, who love it principally because to them it is so safe and so dead.

Not surprisingly, the 'professors' of the academic establishment did not take well to such challenges to their authority. In the most famous instance, William Gardener Hale, the esteemed classicist at the University of Chicago, responded with great indignation to Pound's treatment of Sextus Propertius in *Homage to Sextus Propertius*. He not only chastised the poet in the very public pages of *Poetry* magazine for numerous grammatical 'howlers', but did so in a particularly condescending manner that only deepened the divide between the two camps. 'If Mr. Pound were a Professor of Latin', Professor Hale archly lamented, 'there would be nothing left but suicide. I do not counsel this. But I beg him to lay aside the mask of erudition.' This incident did not merely touch off a personal feud at the time between the poet Pound and Professor Hale. Unfortunately, the feud itself has spread beyond these individuals, resulting in a persistent misunderstanding and mutual suspicion between scholars of modernism and classicists ever since. Modernist translations of classical authors have continued to be viewed with suspicion, never quite achieving the same broad popularity or academic recognition (i.e. legitimacy) as that enjoyed by the luminaries of the Victorian literary establishment.

Yet with every estrangement comes an opportunity for reconciliation. And now, as this volume of varied and impressive essays shows in no uncertain terms, that initially traumatic breach has at last begun to heal.

The modernists were ultimately successful in their campaign to replace their Victorian predecessors as the dominant aesthetic order; and so modernism has come in its turn to face repeated challenges to its authority. Over this same period, the classics themselves have gone from an intellectual staple, part of what every educated person learns, beginning as early as grade school and continuing on through to the post-secondary level, to more and more of a niche field, with a steadily receding horizon of exposure and influence across the educational spectrum.

As it turns out, then, whatever their initial and even ongoing differences, scholars of literary modernism and academic classicists have more in common than what separates them, now more than ever. Essentially both agree on the fundamental importance of classical Greek and Latin authors as part of our cultural heritage and upon the importance of translation as a means to sustain and even renew that legacy. On this, I think we can all agree.

Steven Yao

ACKNOWLEDGEMENTS

We are grateful to the many people who have contributed to the inception of this emergent community of 'classical modernisms'. Our thanks go first to Liz Pender, who organized the excellent conference at the University of Leeds in 2014, 'The Classics and WWI', which initially inspired the project, and who has supported the work along the way with sage counsel. Thanks go also to Katherine Horgan, whose work as a research assistant during the early stages of the project was handled with fortitude, presence of mind and enlivening wit over many months. We thank CADRE, the Centre for Ancient Drama and Its Reception at the University of Nottingham and Lynn Fotheringham, who organized the stimulating colloquium 'Iphigenia through the Ages', which helped to focus the work. Among those whose pathfinding work formed the project in important ways, we would like to extend gratitude especially to Helene Foley, Eileen Gregory, Lorna Hardwick, Alison Rosenblitt, David Scourfield, Christopher Stray, Nancy Worman and Steven Yao. The artistry and rich intelligence of Myrna Wyatt Selkirk and Shanti Gonzales brought H.D.'s *Iphigenia in Aulis* to performance for the first time. We are thankful to Lisa Banks, Leah Werner, Viola Chen and James Dunnigan for their professionalism and fine eye for detail. To Alice Wright of Bloomsbury we owe immense thanks for support and exciting discussions – thanks also to Emma Payne and Clara Herberg for their constant help. We are fortunate to have engaged the work of those participating in the conversation along the way – Jane Benacquista, Dean Casale, Theresa Choate, Sophie Corser, Andrea Eis, Karen Lee Hart and Isobel Hurst. Our greatest thanks go to the contributors to this volume not already mentioned, for their excellent work, live-minded ideas and gracious willingness to 'cross . . . sand-hills' with us – Gregory Baker, Marsha Bryant, Massimo Cè, Michael Coyle, Sara Dunton, Mary Ann Eaverly, Leah Flack, Anna Fyta, Anett Jessop, Matthias Somers, Demetres Tryphonopoulos, Elizabeth Vandiver, George Varsos and Jeff Westover.

INTRODUCTION
Miranda Hickman

Placed at the intersection of classics and anglophone modernist studies, this volume emerges from awareness that within the growing field of classical reception studies,[1] the early twentieth century, and the work of experimental anglophone 'modernists' in particular, remain comparatively underrepresented.[2] This gap is keenly surprising in light of how crucial classical reception was to the making of modernism: the pioneering cultural work of modernist literature was pivotally shaped by translations of, responses to and reinventions of literary and cultural material from classical antiquity. For many major modernists – such as Ezra Pound, H.D., E.E. Cummings, T.S. Eliot and W.B. Yeats – encounters with classical texts provided resources crucial to the development of their innovative ideas, art, and, as Steven Yao notes in *Translation and the Languages of Modernism* (2002b), even their broader commitments to 'cultural renewal' (6). Thus we aim to contribute newly to a still comparatively uncultivated area of classical reception studies – by reviving work in what remains a vital, if recently dormant, area of Modernist Studies.

Considering Ezra Pound's engagement with Ancient Greek, Hugh Kenner asks '[W]hat was he responding to when he read Greek? To rhythms and diction, nutriment for his purposes' (1968: 226). Our project accents such sources of vital 'nutriment' for modernist work, once taken for granted, then with the twentieth-century recession of the classics in many anglophone educational contexts,[3] later marginalized within Modernist Studies.

Drawing on a rich variety of classical resources – languages, genres, poetic models, topoi, mythemes and narratives – these early twentieth-century experimental writers pursued their signature double commitment to old and new: they often innovated by building upon what they read as vitalizing sources of inspiration from the classical past. As classicist J.W. Mackail noted in a 1916 review of the Poets' Translation Series focused on the classics, overseen by modernists H.D. and Richard Aldington, 'The "dead languages" are proving themselves, not for the first time, alive and life-giving' (1916: 210). For many modernists, the classics were also integral to both the critique and regeneration of contemporary culture they construed as waste land: they reached to 'dead languages' to bring lilacs and life out of a 'dead land'.

Rationale

Addressing a range of modernist writers and varieties of reception, this project thus seeks to redress a relative dearth of work on the early twentieth century in classical reception. Moreover, the volume aims to re-enliven study of an important area within Modernist Studies, notably less active in recent years, meriting new attention. We seek to define and bring to wider awareness a developing, intersectional area of study in its own right, which we call 'classical modernisms'.

This volume appears amid a recent wave of interest in 'classical modernisms' by both newer and more experienced scholars, emergent in roughly the last half decade. Yet this group is working in an area both relatively disregarded in classical reception and scarcely represented in Modernist Studies. For instance, of approximately 430 papers and roundtables at the 2015 annual Modernist Studies Association conference, only one addressed in any sustained and direct way modernist writers' engagement with the classics. Of a comparable number in 2016 and 2017, none addressed classical texts. This may be in part because of the comparative rarity these days of training in classics among scholars in Modernist Studies – and this partly because methodologies involving Ancient Greek and Latin literature are often, albeit problematically, construed in contemporary contexts as backward-looking and conservative.[4] By our reckoning, the last sustained study to appear on Anglo-American modernist literature and Hellenism of the kind this volume addresses was *H.D. and Hellenism* (1997) by Eileen Gregory, who contributes to this volume. Diana Collecott's comparable *H.D. and Sapphic Modernism* appeared in 1999.[5]

Whatever the factors, they often prevent today's modernist scholars from addressing how the moderns drew foundationally from classical texts for their innovations, conceptual and aesthetic. Our contributors spotlight the modernists' frequent engagement with such figures as Homer, Euripides, Aristophanes and Sophocles. We look forward to future projects treating modernist work with Sappho and the poets of the Greek Anthology, Theocritus and Aeschylus; and those approaching the nexus from a Latinist perspective, emphasizing modernist engagement with, for instance, Ovid, Horace, Catullus and Propertius.[6]

The moment also seems right for this volume, given recent reappraisals of the nature and importance of modernist engagements with the classics. In decades past, modernists' work with the classics was often read as so non-traditional as not to merit serious treatment: by scholars of his time, Pound was often charged with irresponsible translations of the classical poets on which much of his poetic vision relied, though his departures from strict, literal translation were usually principled and intentionally irreverent.[7] H.D.'s translations were praised for poetic brilliance but often went unrecognized as purposeful re-fabrications of classical materials.[8] While Cummings was trained in classics at Harvard, and noted by peers as 'steeped in the classical tradition' (Rosenblitt 2016: 4), mid-twentieth century criticism tended to exclaim so much at his mannered style as to bypass the seriousness of his engagement with classical material; if he was credited with erudition at all, acknowledged sources tended to be Romantic and Elizabethan.[9] Moreover, his pervasive association with the category of the 'Romantic' likely hindered perceptions of his work as classical, given the assumed early twentieth-century opposition between 'Romantic' and 'Classic' epitomized by T.E. Hulme,[10] together with the influential Eliotic notion of 'Classicist' (indebted to Hulme's), suggesting cultural posture rather than specific cultural traditions. Yet recent work has begun to turn such views around: the modernists are increasingly credited (to adapt Carne-Ross's formulation) as progressive poet-translators who deliberately transformed the classical work they engaged and pursued translation as both a critical and creative mode. As Vandiver observes here, modernist work with classical materials was often based in critique of what the moderns saw as pedantry; our volume stresses that what were once perceived as modernist failings born of ignorance or irresponsibility are now often seen as deliberate departures from traditional scholarly methods, aimed to 'make it new'.

Accordingly, this volume seeks to approach modernist engagements with the classics with what Adrienne Rich calls 'fresh eyes'.[11] Very recently, work at the intersection of classics and modernism has begun enjoying renewed attention through such commentators in this volume as Leah Flack (*Modernism and Homer*, 2015), J. Alison Rosenblitt (*E.E. Cummings' Modernism and the Classics*, 2016), Elizabeth Vandiver (*Stand in the Trench, Achilles*, 2010) and Marsha Bryant and Mary Ann Eaverly, from English and classical archaeology respectively, who publish and exhibit collaboratively on modernist responses to the Ancient world. We also note Jean Mills's *Virginia Woolf, Jane Ellen Harrison, and the Spirit of Modernist Classicism* (2014) and Yopie Prins's *Ladies' Greek* (2017), the latter of which, focused on Victorian Hellenism, closes with commentary on H.D. This volume also dovetails with work in preparation in the area of 'Classical Modernisms' from the Classical Reception series (Bloomsbury Academic) and Classical Presences series (Oxford University Press).

Modernist translations

The moderns often engaged the classics by way of their favoured strategy of 'translation'. This, as Yao argues, was integral to modernist work, both in the stricter sense of translating specific classical texts and the broader sense of carrying across ancient materials toward contemporary cultural revitalization.[12] As Yao notes, 'feats of translation not only accompanied and helped to give rise to, but sometimes ... themselves constituted, some of the most significant Modernist literary achievements in English' (2002b: 3).[13] Yao illuminates how exploratory work with translating texts from other languages and cultures not only significantly informed the modernists' formation, but also proved crucial to the development of their 'original' literary texts and their cultural work more broadly: for the moderns, translation was an importantly generative 'mode of literary production' (12). They often pursued what Gillespie calls 'creative translation' (2011: 28; cf. Sullivan 1964). As Venuti situates this, with Benjamin, the modernists followed a nineteenth-century view of translation as less derivative and more 'as a creative force in which specific translation strategies might serve a variety of cultural and social functions' – such as enriching languages and literatures, and for the modernists, even 'revitalizing culture' of their time (2000: 11).

Accordingly, we take 'translation' as our central organizing concept; using it in the elastic modernist sense to encompass various forms of reception, including free translation, appropriation, adaptation, hybrid, intervention and re-figuration. In this, we look to Lorna Hardwick's capacious definition of translation in *Translating Words, Translating Cultures* (2000) and her lexicon in *Reception Studies* (2003).

One of our primary objectives is to present 'translation' as intentionally reinvented through the work of various modernist writers: modernist approaches to translation often moved far beyond standard definitions of translation and translation practices of their time. They reimagined translation by their lights and for their moment, gravitating towards new translation strategies that, as Vandiver notes here, had not yet been theorized, and of which they themselves were not always fully and clearly aware. What emerged was what Yao calls a modernist 'revolution' in translation as a 'means of textual production' (2002b: 15). This often involved shedding concerns with traditional 'fidelity' to carry access across something other than literal meanings of a source text – and moving deliberately toward novelty. Typically distrustful of traditional scholarship, they often saw 'scholarly command' of the language of the texts they translated as not only unnecessary but in fact a 'barrier to authentic translation' (Yao 2002b: 12). If Benjamin reflected from the midst of the modernist period on the 'task of the translator', many anglophone modernist writers not only sought to redefine that 'task' for a new twentieth century, but also experimented with the temporality of the translation, deliberately exploring non-traditional approaches to translation, so as to reimagine and reinvigorate ancient texts for a new era. George Steiner observed of Pound's approach to translation that it 'altered the definition and ideals of verse translation in the twentieth century' (1966: 33). Gillespie notes that many other modernists followed suit, approaching translation with a signature sense of 'irreverence' (16).

In this spirit, they often developed markedly creative translations which, in the lexicon of contemporary reception, would be called 'appropriations' or 'adaptations' of ancient texts, even what Hardwick terms 'interventions' (2003). Strikingly, however, the modernists often nonetheless insisted upon calling their projects 'translations', thus bending the term and concept in new directions.[14] This volume probes why, and how, the moderns so often turned to classical texts in particular for this cultural work of translation – for resources (linguistic, aesthetic, generic and conceptual) with which to respond to the needs, questions, and conflicts of the early twentieth century.

In part, they sought to reach for new aesthetic effects in English radically different from those of older English translations. H.D. and Pound, for instance, after exploring the host of previous English translations in the 1885 H.T. Wharton edition of Sappho, responded to Sappho's fragments with markedly austere Imagist language: this suggests a defiant and exploratory turn from the more lavish renderings of poets such as Tennyson and Swinburne, as inspired by an aesthetic they associated with Ancient Greek. Through engaging classical texts, they also sought to enrich the resources of English. As Eliot articulated in his cutting response to the translations of early twentieth-century classicist Gilbert Murray, ideally, translations from the Greek would have a 'vitalizing effect upon English poetry' (28), and Eliot credited H.D.'s translation work with Euripides with such impact.

The modernists also often shaped their translations towards 'making new' the older texts they translated – fostering what Benjamin calls the 'afterlife' of such texts, carrying them across to audiences of a new age. Moreover, they developed through translation their own lines of criticism, both of the texts they engaged and of topics these texts addressed. Thus the modernists called upon the classical heritage during an early twentieth century whose 'culture trouble' they sought to both critique and redress by way of classical resources.

Structure of the volume

Of the modernist work represented here, Ezra Pound's and H.D's engagement with classical texts is most sustained and integral to their poetics: the volume's essays spotlight Pound's responses to Homer and H.D.'s to Euripides. Essays also address T.S. Eliot, James Joyce, Laura Riding and W.B. Yeats. Focused chiefly on modernist attention to the literature of Ancient Greece – reflective of the Hellenism animating many modernist writers' work, which guided writers featured here more frequently towards Greece than Rome – these essays also represent work with classical resources for a gamut of cultural-political projects. Some of these are more trained on literature and the arts, others more attuned to public crises, leaning towards what Venuti calls 'functionalism' – a 'yoking of translation projects to cultural and political agendas' (2000: 13). As Matthias Somers notes, T.S. Eliot calls upon the 'Aristophanic' to theorize modern comedy, and Anna Fyta suggests that H.D. engages Euripides to renew the genre of the palinode. As essays by George Varsos, Massimo Cè, and Demetres Tryphonopoulos and Sara Dunton suggest, Pound draws upon Homeric epic to respond to a modern world fractured by war and cultural decline. For Leah Flack, Eliot and Joyce turn to the 'siren songs' of Homer to respond to global violence; as Gregory Baker illuminates, Yeats reaches to Sophocles to reckon with Irish nationalism. Essays by Anna Fyta, Jeff Westover and Miranda Hickman and Lynn Kozak trace H.D.'s turn to Euripides to develop the feminist thought of her early career.

The volume opens with Elizabeth Vandiver's essay on the Poets' Translation Series. This series emerged from the years just before and during World War I, edited by Richard Aldington and H.D., exemplifying both the modernist commitment to translation and the often maverick spirit in which their experiments with translation, here focused on classical texts, were pursued. The following essays are then clustered not only according to writer, but also by emphases associated with different writers: three essays on Ezra Pound (Varsos, Cè, Tryphonopoulos and Dunton) accent how Pound's work with the classics often foregrounds 'translation' per se; the next four essays on H.D. (Fyta, Westover, Theis, Hickman and Kozak) address resources of genre, form and lexicon to which H.D. sought access through translating the classics. Four further essays, on Laura Riding, Joyce, Eliot, and Yeats (Jessop, Flack, Somers, Baker), feature more 'functionalist' translations overtly responsive to cultural problematics of their moment. These chapters close with an essay by a collaborative pair of scholars from English and classical archaeology (Bryant and Eaverly) on how their work with modernist classical reception has entered the museum and the classroom.

In the spirit of dialogue between classics and modernist studies the project aims to foster, these contributions are framed by brief essays from respondents from the fields of classics and classical reception (Michael Coyle, Eileen Gregory and Nancy Worman). The volume closes with an afterword by J. Alison Rosenblitt, tracing how modernist mediations of classical materials have informed later literature, especially contemporary poetry.

Except where noted, all translations are the authors' own.

CHAPTER 1
'SEEKING ... BURIED BEAUTY': THE POETS' TRANSLATION SERIES
Elizabeth Vandiver

The principle of the 'literal-literary' translation will be kept to as before, the idea being not to produce a work of 'scholarship' but to give the ordinary man (like ourselves) an opportunity of reading some of the lesser-known but yet exquisite classics in simple English prose. The translators make no claim to philological scholarship; the title of the series implies that we are interested in these authors for their poetry and for nothing else.

[Aldington] 1919b: [2][1]

seeking ... buried beauty

Pound, Canto 7

Thus the Poets' Translation Series (PTS) announced its forthcoming 'second set' in July 1919, after a hiatus of three years. Begun in 1915 by Richard Aldington and H.D., the PTS had been surprisingly successful; the first set's six pamphlets sold over 3,000 copies and made a modest profit. As Zilboorg (1991a) has shown, the PTS was crucially interwoven into H.D.'s and Aldington's development as poets and into their personal relationship.[2] From its beginnings, the PTS reflected these two writers' ideas and ideals concerning poetry and the importance of the classical (especially Hellenic) world. They saw the series as more than merely a set of translations; it was, in addition, a poetic manifesto. But the exact nature of this manifesto is complicated by the apparent tension between the PTS's stated goals and methods and its actual achievements. In this series, Aldington and H.D. pioneered modernist translation as a process of remaking and refashioning texts; yet their stated aims for the series espoused traditional goals of lexical and semantic fidelity to the original, while simultaneously discounting formal scholarship. This essay explores some aspects of this tension between actual practice and stated goals. Modernist translation would become 'not a staged literary museum, but an act of cultural renewal' (Brinkman and Brinkman 2016: 45), but when they inaugurated the PTS, H.D. and Aldington were in fact enacting a translational practice that neither they nor anyone else had yet theorized. Thus, the PTS is a Janus-figure, looking back to traditional assumptions about translation and forward into modernism's unmooring of translation from formal knowledge of the source language.

The Series' original 1915 announcement had laid out its goals in some detail:

The object of the editors of this series is to present a number of translations of Greek and Latin poetry and prose, especially of those authors who are less frequently given in English.

This literature has too long been the property of pedagogues, philologists and professors. Its human qualities have been obscured by the wranglings of grammarians, who love it principally because to them it is so safe and so dead.

But to many of us it is not dead. It is more alive, more essential, more human than anything we can find in contemporary English literature. The publication of such classics, in the way we propose, may help to create a higher standard for poetry than that which prevails, and a higher standard of appreciation of the writers of antiquity, who have suffered too long at the hands of clumsy metrists. We do not deny that there are many good translations in English of classical writers—Lang's 'Homer' and 'Theokritos,' Mackail's 'Anthology' or Adlington's 'Apuleius,' for instance; but too often such works are lonely and austerely expensive.

The Poets' Translation Series will appear first in 'The Egoist' (starting September 1st) and will then be reprinted and issued as small pamphlets, simple and inexpensive, so that none will buy except to read. The translations will be by poets whose interest in their authors will be neither conventional nor frigid. The translators will take no concern with glosses, notes, or any of the apparatus with which learning smothers beauty. They will endeavour to give the words of these Greek and Latin authors as simply and as clearly as may be. Where the text is confused, they will use the most characteristic version; where obscure, they will interpret.

The first six pamphlets, when bound together, will form a small collection of unhackneyed poetry, too long buried under the dust of pedantic scholarship. They range over a period of two thousand years of literature—a proof of the amazing vitality of the Hellenic tradition.

If this venture has the success its promoters look for, other similar and possibly larger pamphlets will be issued.

[Aldington] 1915a

The 1915 claim to 'give the words ... as simply and as clearly as may be' and the 1919 avowal of the 'literal-literary principle' conceal several unstated but crucial assumptions, presented as self-evident truths but in fact highly contestable. Among these are that 'scholarship' and 'poetry' are somehow incompatible; that poetry always and everywhere consists in 'simple' words, never in elaborate artificiality; that lexical and semantic accuracy (the 'clear words' of the original) are necessary to translation, and are easily achievable without formal philological training; and that form, including meter, is incidental to poetry, not essential to it. Aldington made similar assertions in his review of Bryher's 'Lament for Adonis,' published some months before the 1919 prospectus:

It is a pleasure to note that the principles of translating laid down in ... the Poets' Translation Series are being followed by other translators. That this 'literary-literal' method has a distinct advantage over all others is proved by a very sensitive version of Bion's *Lament for Adonis*, recently published by Miss Winifred Bryher. The ideal of such translations comes, of course, from France ... And whether Miss Bryher evolved independently her ideas of translation, or derived them from the French and the Poets' Translation Series, is not important. The great thing is that she is on the right track; and with all the discouraging mass of the Loeb classics, the 'copious' pedantry of almost every extant version of Hellenic poetry, it is really a delightful surprise to find some one who cares more for literature than for philology, who has the swift spirit to kindle at the poetry rather than the dull brain to plod after it.

Aldington 1919a: 10–11[3]

Aldington is being disingenuous here; in September 1918, in his first letter to Bryher, he had encouraged her to translate for the PTS and had described its translational method.[4] Furthermore, Bryher had introduced H.D. to the publisher Clement Shorter, whom Aldington hoped to enlist as the publisher of the renewed PTS (Gates 1992: 46; Zilboorg 2003: 152).[5] More to the point here, Aldington's review reiterates the underlying assumptions that a translator who is a scholar inevitably misses the poetry, and conversely that someone with a 'swift spirit' does not need exact training in philology in order to capture and convey the crucial essence of a poem written in another language.

Selection of translators

In their original conception of the PTS, Aldington and H.D. envisaged the series as a chance 'to forge principles of translation . . . as the act of bringing the past into the present, the Hellenic into modernist poetry' (Zilboorg 1991a: 74). In addition, they hoped that the serious work of translation would increase the Imagists' name recognition and gain wider acceptance for Imagism and its standards. Aldington wrote to Amy Lowell in 1919 that the PTS 'seems to me a useful bit of propaganda for us all' (Gates 1992: 46), and he wrote to Bryher that he wanted the renewed series 'to establish a canon of taste, *our* taste, against a mob of clergymen & schoolmasters & professional critics; that will give us a point d'appui for our own work. Then I want it also for almost educational motives, to rescue exquisite personalities from oblivion or the pedants' (Zilboorg 1991a: 82). For all these reasons, H.D. and Aldington recruited translators from their circle of literary acquaintances, and evaluated them first for their adherence to Imagist principles and only secondly for their skill in Latin and Greek.[6] Indeed, Aldington and H.D. themselves were not fully adept in the ancient languages.[7] They began translating Greek poetry together almost as soon as they met, concentrating on the Greek Anthology and (perhaps) Sappho, and Aldington published his first translations almost immediately. These early translations contain many errors on the level of vocabulary and syntax, often suggesting that Aldington mistook similar words and forms for one another. In *Bid Me to Live*, H.D. implies that they recognized the limitations of their skill, and found Pindar too difficult: 'They . . . barricaded themselves with yellow-backed French novels, Pindar in the original which they could not read (she picked out a word here, there, with a dictionary, he manipulated a telling phrase now and again), the Greek Anthology' (H.D. 1960: 11).[8]

For the PTS, Aldington had no hesitation about recruiting translators whose acquaintance with the source languages was less than thorough. In December 1918, he described to Bryher what she would need to translate for the series:

> You will need Jacobs' Anthologia . . . and the latest edition of Liddle [sic] & Scott's Lexicon (containing all the special anthology words) and a good Greek grammar. The Latin translation in Jacobs' [sic] will help you to be sure you have the precise literal sense, & for the rest I am secure in your own taste.
>
> *Zilboorg 2003: 152, n. 2*[9]

He seems to assume that, armed with a grammar, a lexicon and a Latin 'crib', anyone can make sense of Greek poetry. James Whitall, who translated Leonidas for the PTS, frankly admits in his memoir *English Years* that he was nervous about his lack of qualifications to translate Greek:

> [I] listened with suspended breath to some vague plans for a translation project in which I might conceivably participate . . . I began to turn the pages of the Greek Anthology, whose existence I had only just discovered, and to wonder whether my forced acquaintance with the language in school and college could ever be brightened up enough to make me a translator of Greek as well as French . . . [I] trembled a little at the memory of my collegiate struggles with Homer.
>
> *1936: 58–9*

Nevertheless, when Aldington asked him to translate Leonidas, Whitall jumped at the chance:

> Richard's confidence in my ability to produce a printable version of the ninety-odd poems of Leonidas of Tarentum was very flattering, and I tried to justify it in advance by assuring him of my intention . . . to renew what I also assured him was an adequate acquaintance with the Greek language for the purpose. My confidence in this acquaintance or in my ability to renew it did not begin to justify the line I took with Richard.
>
> *1936: 126, 128*

Aldington allowed Whitall only three weeks to produce his translation. Despite a full-time job, Whitall 'set to work' with a Teubner text of Leonidas, 'wondering whether I would be able to penetrate even as far as the meaning of the words'. Once he had found the words in his lexicon, 'it was only after a week of frantic struggling to recapture my flimsy knowledge of Greek declensions and conjugations that I could identify the cases and tenses which met my distracted eye'. Still, he had preliminary versions done in two weeks, and then spent two days 'polishing with what I hoped was the right mixture of regard for the Greek text and care for the smoothness and simplicity of the English phrases' (1936: 137). He was uneasy about his competency and frequently turned to his mentors with questions about Greek grammar and syntax.[10] Whitall's account provides a fascinating glimpse of H.D.'s and Aldington's underlying assumptions about how successful translation worked. No translator equipped only with Whitall's slight acquaintance with Greek could possibly detect or appreciate nuances of wording in the original text. Whitall's lexicon could tell him a word's basic sense (though he made some errors even on this level), but the word's wider contextual meaning and any subtlety of the poet's usage would be far beyond his skill.[11] The choice of Whitall as a translator, then, implies that the PTS editors thought the 'unhackneyed poetry' they so prized was accessible through simple dictionary definitions and did not depend on rich knowledge of a word's semantic range or field.

The translations

The first set of the PTS (1915–16) contained six pamphlets: Aldington's translation of the complete poems of Anyte; Edward Storer's Sappho; H.D.'s selected choruses from Euripides' *Iphigeneia at Aulis*; Aldington's selected Renaissance Latin poets; Whitall's Leonidas of Tarentum; and F.S. Flint's *Mosella*, by Ausonius (Aldington [1915]b; Storer [1915]; H.D. [1915]; Aldington [1915]c; Whitall [1916]; Flint [1916]).

The plan was to continue the series immediately after the first set appeared; an announcement in the January 1916 *Egoist* said that additional pamphlets would appear on the first of each month, starting in March 1916. These were to include Asklepiades' *Windflowers* and Poseidippos's poems, translated anonymously; H.D.'s translation of choruses from Euripides' *Ion*; Aldington's translation of Meleager; Aelian's *Rustic Letters*, by Storer; Columella's *On the Care of Gardens*, by Alec Randall; and Musaeus's *Hero and Leander*, by Whitall ([Aldington]1916). In fact, the growing pressures caused by Aldington's imminent enlistment and his subsequent service from June 1916 to February 1919 meant that the announced second set was put on hold (Zilboorg 1991a: 81).

In late 1918, while waiting for demobilization, Aldington conceived the idea of reviving the PTS on an enlarged scale, to include modern languages (French, German, Italian, Russian, Spanish and modern Hebrew) as well as Latin and Greek, with himself as editor in chief and sub-editors for various languages, including H.D. for Greek. H.D. was an unacknowledged co-editor of the first set (Zilboorg 1991a), but her involvement on the eventual second set was much more tangential. In the winter of 1918–19 the relationship between H.D. and Aldington was extremely delicate and difficult; their marriage was breaking down, H.D. was pregnant with Cecil Gray's child, and Aldington was involved with Dorothy ('Arabella') Yorke. Nevertheless, Aldington clearly hoped that he and H.D. could once again work together intensely and companionably. He writes to her on December 1: 'I am planning to restore the P.T.S. Are you willing to collaborate?' After mentioning that the scale would be 'larger than before' and that he would pay individual royalties, he says, 'Let me know if this agrees with you & what choruses you would care to do' (Zilboorg 2003: 138).[12] H.D.'s side of the correspondence does not survive, but she must have answered positively, for Aldington's letters soon enlist her help for finding a publisher and for recruiting translators. His letters indicate an almost hectic excitement about the project.[13] On 13 December 1918, he sent H.D. a 'Scheme for Poets' Translation Series', describing an extremely elaborate plan for an ongoing series, to continue indefinitely, with the intention that 'when complete the Poets' Translation Series will form a choice collection of Belles Lettres' (Zilboorg 2003: 142).

However, influenced in part by Amy Lowell's lukewarm response to the idea of incorporating modern languages, Aldington quickly scaled back his expectations (see Gates 1992: 467). Nevertheless, he planned a more extensive set than actually appeared. The July 1919 prospectus ([Aldington] 1919b) announces five pamphlets that were printed in due course: Aldington's translation of the *Anacreontea*; a reissue of his Anyte printed with Storer's Sappho; a reissue of H.D.'s *Choruses from the Iphigeneia in Aulis* with the addition of choruses from *Hippolytus*; an enlarged edition of Aldington's Renaissance Latin poets; and a translation of Asklepiades and Poseidippos by Storer (Aldington 1919c; Aldington and Storer 1919; H.D. 1919; Aldington 1919d; Storer 1920). In addition, the prospectus announces five more pamphlets 'in preparation'. These include the phantom pamphlets announced in 1916: a reprint of Flint's *Mosella*, augmented by his translation of Columella's *On Gardens*; Claudian's *Carrying Off of Persephone*, to be translated by A. W. Randall; Aldington's Meleager; Storer's translation of Aelian's *Country Letters*;[14] and Musaeus's *Hero and Leander*. Of these five works 'in preparation', only Aldington's Meleager ever appeared (Aldington 1920a).[15] Thus, the second set as printed featured primarily Aldington's own work.

Source texts

The PTS translators worked from standard texts, using whatever commentaries and previous translations were available to them. Close correspondences of wording and interpretation in Aldington's Meleager and Louÿs's French translation (1893) indicate that Aldington relied heavily on Louÿs's text; similarly, Flint almost certainly worked from de Mirmont's French translation (1889) of Ausonius, given the numerous turns of phrase in Flint's English that reflect wording in the French.[16] Paton's Loeb of the Greek Anthology was not yet available for the translators of the first set, but the translations in Mackail's *Selections from the Greek Anthology* (1890) gave help in some instances.[17] Whitall's introduction to Leonidas says that he 'has accepted the attributions of Geffcken, though his text has not always been used' (Whitall [1916]: 1; Geffcken 1896). A collation of Whitall's translation with Mackail's selections from Leonidas shows that, when Mackail and Geffcken differ, Whitall invariably follows Mackail's reading. Storer cites Wharton's Sappho, which includes a 'literal' English translation ([1915]: 1; Wharton 1887). In one instance, Storer seems to have borrowed from Aldington; his phrase 'the sterile Atthis' almost certainly comes from Aldington's 'To Atthis', which also uses the idiosyncratic 'sterile' (rather than 'gentle') to translate ἀγόνας (*agonas*) (Storer [1915]: 3; Aldington 1913: 114).[18]

Form and content

The PTS volumes did not use formal, regular meter, despite the fact that the Greek originals were written in a variety of highly structured meters. Thus, the PTS implicitly claims that 'poetry' is a quality detachable from form, so that a prose translation can preserve the essence of a metrical original; and indeed, with the exception of H.D.'s free verse renderings of Euripides' choral lyrics and Storer's rather odd long-line Sappho, the translations in the PTS are all done in prose.

The effect is to impose a uniformity of style both within the works of individual poets and across the range of authors. No one would know, from these translations, that both Leonidas and Sappho wrote poems in a variety of meters, as different from one another as a sonnet is from a Spenserian stanza; equally, no one could tell that Anyte used elegiac couplets or that Ausonius's *Mosella* was in dactylic hexameter. The series thus strongly privileges content over form, even though it never states this stance explicitly (beyond the comment on 'clumsy metrists' in the 1915 announcement).

The final sentence of Aldington's 'Foreword' to his translation of Meleager reads: 'Those who know French and wish to see how a Greek poet ought to be translated, should read M. Pierre Louÿs's translation of a hundred poems of Meleager' (1920a: [4]). Louÿs's prose translation nods to its original's form by marking the beginning of each Greek line with an asterisk; Aldington dispenses even with that trace of the verse structure and prints all his PTS translations as paragraphed prose.[19] Flint and Whitall also use plain paragraphed prose for their translations. Storer's Sappho seems uneasily balanced between free verse and prose. It is printed in lines that are much longer than those in Storer's own *vers libre* poems, and are not noticeably rhythmical. Notably, Storer turned to prose for his translations of Asklepiades and Poseidippos.[20]

The PTS's overall avoidance of verse, even free verse, as a means of representing ancient poetry is all the more noteworthy, given the Imagists' perplexing insistence that ancient poetry – lyric and choral – *was* free verse (which of course it was not).[21] If Aldington genuinely believed, as he claimed, that Sappho and other lyric poets had written free verse, the decision to translate into prose is marked out all the more clearly as theoretically driven. Indeed, by the time the pamphlet advertising the second set was published in July 1919, prose had become an explicit desideratum; the series was to consist of 'some of the lesser-known but yet exquisite classics in simple English prose' ([Aldington] 1919b: [2]).[22] The apparent implication is that the clarity of diction involved in simple, straightforward prose outweighs any value to be found in indicating, by the translation's form, that the original was written in highly regular meter. 'We are interested in these authors for their poetry and for nothing else' (ibid.); even though he believed that Greek lyric poetry was a form of free verse, Aldington apparently thought that any English verse form would somehow dilute the purity of the original's poetic essence.

H.D. continued to translate into free verse, but her doing so was now in opposition to the series' stated goals. Nor was this the only way in which H.D. was an outlier in the series. Most of the other texts in the PTS were, by deliberate choice, rare or non-existent in English translation. But H.D. translated Euripides, who had been the focus of extremely well-received and famous translations by Gilbert Murray. Murray's metrical, rhymed translations were widely praised by critics and actors alike for their power, their success as living theatre, and their overall fidelity to the Greek.[23] H.D.'s choice to translate Euripides, and especially to translate choruses from *Hippolytus*, put her in direct contrast with the most celebrated scholar-translator of the day, and the form she chose in effect offered a challenge to Murray's method.[24] And she alone among the PTS translators explicitly addressed the question of meter in her introduction to the 'Choruses':

> A literal, word-for-word version of so well-known an author as Euripides would be useless and supererogatory; a rhymed, languidly Swinburnian verse form is an insult and a barbarism. It seemed, therefore, that the rhymeless hard rhythms used in the present version would be most likely to keep the sharp edges and irregular cadences of the original.
>
> *[1915]: 1*[25]

In all these ways, H.D. seems almost to have been working on a different project, or at the very least from a different set of assumptions, than were the other translators for the series.[26]

Reviewers' reactions

The most enthusiastic reviews of the PTS came from writers who admitted they could not read the originals and thus could judge the translations only as English poetry (or prose).[27] Reviewers who could compare the PTS versions with the originals were less favourable. The Classics scholar J. W. Mackail anonymously reviewed the PTS for the *TLS* in 1916; he found much to like in the translations, especially H.D.'s, but much to criticize as well. Mackail appreciated the translations' 'novelty', but he also made it very clear that he considered the translators' grasp of the ancient languages deficient:

> With defects of scholarship, with some wanton mistakes and apparently deliberate distortions, and with occasional lapses into unseasonable or erroneous pedantry (is 'Alkander' meant to be Greek, and what is a 'death-paeon'?) the renderings are nevertheless vivid, arresting, stimulating, even for scholars, and still more for those who, whether scholars or not, have a feeling for the common spirit, the essential kinship, of all poetry.
>
> *[Mackail] 1916: 210*

While this is not negative, it does not vindicate the skills *as translators* of the poets who made these 'wanton mistakes'. Turning in more detail to H.D.'s choruses, Mackail says that 'the writer, who veils his [sic] identity under the initials H.D.', shows 'an interpretative genius which is both provocative and singularly illuminating'. So far, so very favourable. But then he notes the assertion that 'the sense of the Greek has been strictly kept' (H.D. [1915]: 1):

> This is not the case. Whether from perversity or from some defect of scholarship, he sometimes quite misinterprets his original, or reads into it something quite

illegitimate. By no stretch of imagination can ἐπὶ κρηναίαισι δρόσοις (*epi krēnaiaisi drosois*, 'in the dews of the springs' upon Ida) be tortured into meaning 'among the fresh-shallows of the strait'.

1916: 210

However, Mackail thinks that H.D.'s choruses 'repay study, and that none the less *if our judgment should not approve them without reserve*' (ibid.; emphasis added). In the end, Mackail is ambivalent. He unquestionably admires the power of H.D.'s lyrics as English poetry, but he cannot unqualifiedly approve of these lyrics as translations. In part, Mackail's difficulty arises from the fact that he takes H.D. at her (apparent) word when she says that 'the sense of the Greek has been strictly kept'. As would almost any reader in 1916, Mackail takes this statement as an assurance of straightforward lexical and semantic fidelity. Thus, when H.D. renders a Greek word that means 'dew' as 'shallows', and one that means 'springs' as 'straits', Mackail notes that the sense is incorrect and assumes error, not interpretation; the form of modernist translation that H.D. is pioneering is, at this point, so unfamiliar that Mackail is left unable either to fully approve or disapprove.

Despite Mackail's reservations, the translators and their friends hailed his review as an unambiguous triumph. Aldington called it to Amy Lowell's attention, and Lowell remembered the review four years later.[28] Writing to Florence Ayscough, Lowell said that the PTS had been 'a complete success, so complete that Professor Mackail wrote an article in the *Times* commending H.D.'s "Choruses from Iphigenia [sic] in Aulis" for their beauty *and accuracy*. Believe the poets, Florence, and let the pedants go hang' (MacNair 1945: 107–8; emphasis added). James Whitall recalled that Mackail 'declared his enthusiastic approval' and praised 'the six translators *for the skill with which they had accomplished their part in it*' (1936: 137–8; emphasis added). It is understandable that Lowell and Whitall did not remember Mackail's exact words years afterwards, but it is remarkable how fully both transform his reservations about the translations' accuracy into praise.[29]

Mackail also reviewed the second set of the PTS in November 1919. Here, his admiration for H.D.'s method has increased, as has his scorn for blunders in construal, particularly in Aldington's Anacreon. Concerning H.D.'s Euripides translations, Mackail writes that they exhibit 'a new method of translation corresponding to a new appreciation of the Greek spirit' ([Mackail] 1919: 666). Trying to define this 'new method' more closely, he says, 'What the modern spirit seems to be searching after . . . is the language of some new Impressionism; something crisp, acute, discontinuous' and this, he thinks, H.D. has approached (ibid.).

But if Mackail's 1919 review gestures towards recognizing the new parameters of modernist translation in its praise of H.D., it is nothing short of savage towards Aldington's inaccuracies of vocabulary, grammar and syntax. Aldington worked on his Anacreon translation while in the Army, and admitted that its accuracy suffered in consequence:

A small and imperfect dictionary was the only one light enough to carry on active service; the translator is aware that this fact, added to a lack of practice in Greek during the past years and the general effect of unpleasant surroundings, rendered the translation less accurate and spirited than is desirable. But it is hoped that a reader, familiar with modern writing, will find this humble prose version less repellant than that of . . . the contemporary translators whose object seems to be to prove that the Greeks wrote doggerel.

Aldington 1919c: [3][30]

Mackail shows no mercy towards Aldington's frequent misconstruals of the Greek, saying that in this translation 'the unscholarliness which more or less permeates the whole series reaches a height which is almost incredible' ([Mackail] 1919: 666). Noting that the Greek is extremely simple, he remarks, 'But no Greek, however easy, can be translated without some elementary acquaintance with Greek accidence and syntax' and surmises that Aldington proceeded

on the bold and cheerful working hypothesis that any word in the dictionary which began with the same, or nearly the same, letters as the word sought was in fact that word, and that no nice distinctions need be drawn between a noun and a verb, or between two proper names which bore some resemblance to one another.

Ibid.

Mackail wonders, even 'with all allowances made' for the circumstances under which Aldington worked, why he felt compelled to publish at all. The best Mackail can say of Aldington's work is that it shows that 'there is in the seething . . . new world an intense if ignorant thirst for the classics' (ibid.). It is worth noting that when Aldington republished his collected PTS translations a decade later, he had silently corrected their errors in vocabulary and syntax (Aldington 1930).[31]

Conclusion

Standing as it does at the very cusp of modernism, the PTS prefigures many directions that modernist translation will take, but simultaneously asserts – at least nominally – a conservative and traditional allegiance to the ideal of lexical and semantic precision as crucial to 'faithful' translation. Yao has identified 'the extent to which formal knowledge of the source language no longer constituted a requirement' for translation as 'the most dramatic indication of the change that took place during the Modernist period in the dimensions of translation as a literary mode' (2002b: 10–11). But while the PTS challenges the hegemony of formally trained scholars over translation of classical texts, it adheres to the idea that translators should 'give the words' of the texts they render 'as simply and as clearly as may be' ([Aldington] 1915a). The obvious question, of how a translator who lacks deep knowledge of the source language is to determine the 'simple and clear' meaning of the original, is never addressed.

Yao reads H.D.'s introduction to the *Iphigeneia* choruses as seeking 'to extend the boundaries of the practice of translation … beyond the limits of merely semantic equivalence' (2002a: 99). While there is no doubt that this is what H.D. in fact achieved, Yao's comment glosses over too easily her introduction's direct claim that 'the sense of the Greek has been strictly kept' ([1915]: 1). The translators of the PTS did not, like later modernists, directly query, or intentionally destabilize, assumptions that 'accuracy' requires close adherence to the original's meaning; instead, they insisted that the translator's task is to 'give the words' of the source text. While they privileged simplicity and clarity, they still claimed to be reproducing the original's semantic meaning. Zilboorg is surely correct that Aldington believed 'there was an audience to whom one was linguistically and morally responsible' (1991a: 90).[32] Indeed, in later years Aldington criticized Pound's 'Homage to Sextus Propertius' specifically for lexical inaccuracy, writing that 'Ezra was apt to get into ludicrous difficulties with his languages' and citing the 'schoolboy howler "night dogs"' (Aldington 1941: 137).[33] The PTS's insistence that their translations met traditional standards of lexical accuracy and semantic fidelity made it impossible to respond to criticism as Pound did, by claiming that the intent had never been straightforward translation at all.[34] Instead, the PTS translators reacted to criticism of their accuracy by either ignoring or misunderstanding it.

Yet at the same time that the PTS insists on its own semantic accuracy, the announcements of 1915 and 1919 also assert that the series will recover some essence of 'true poetry' that cannot be found through scholarship. More, they imply that scholarly proficiency somehow *precludes* poetic understanding. Later, H.D. returned to this mystical view of the true nature of 'Poetry' in her 'Notes on Euripides':

> I know that we need scholars to decipher and interpret the Greek, but we also need: poets and mystics and children to re-discover this Hellenic world, to see *through* the words; the word being but the outline, the architectural structure of that door or window, through which we are all free, scholar and unlettered alike, to pass.
>
> *H.D., [1927] 2003: 278*

H.D. here reiterates the divide between 'scholars' and 'poets', and again assumes that a scholar cannot also be a poet or vice-versa. And she specifically allies poets with 'mystics', who are able to intuit shades of meaning that 'mere' scholarship cannot. While Aldington did not use the terminology of mysticism, this is not far distant from his description of the ideal translator as one 'who has the swift spirit to kindle at the poetry rather than the dull brain to plod after it' (1919a: 10–11). (Neither Aldington nor H.D. ever explain why a 'swift spirit' cannot also be a skilled philologist.) This mystic – and essentially Romantic – view of poetry helps explain H.D.'s and Aldington's relative lack of concern about their translators' actual proficiency in the source languages and their insistence that their translations in fact *were* accurate; when H.D. claims to have kept strictly to 'the sense of the Greek', she is in effect claiming this special, esoteric poetic knowledge – of the poetry, rather than the Greek.

Thus, as editors of the PTS, H.D. and Aldington were balancing uneasily on a line that they themselves probably had not fully conceptualized. Certain as they were that, as poets themselves, they had a privileged and innate ability to recognize 'true poetry' across eras and languages and to reproduce it 'simply and clearly', at the same time their reverence for their imagined Hellas was such that they considered each word of the original almost as though it were a talisman; the famous passage in which H.D. describes 'brooding' over each word to 'hatch' it is central here (1960: 162–3). They were, in fact, inaugurating a new approach to translation, in which thorough knowledge of the source language was no longer necessary; but they presented themselves as protectors and renewers of a deeply traditional body of poetry, one that had been 'buried under the dust of pedantic scholarship' and that their privileged understanding could rescue. Far from claiming, in the PTS, to be distancing translation from the original texts, they claimed to be bringing the originals back to life, 'hatching' them, 'rescuing' them. As influential as the form of translation embodied in the PTS would be for modernist practice, its two begetters claimed not to be forging a new practice but rather to be returning to the wellspring, the source, of poetry.

PART I
EZRA POUND ON TRANSLATION

CHAPTER 2
OUT OF HOMER: GREEK IN POUND'S *CANTOS*
George Varsos[1]

Pound's Canto I opens with the translation of extended fragments from Homer's *Odyssey*, making for a peculiar reading experience. Its language feels charged with time, yet somewhat suspended: while carrying a perspective of historical depth, it also seems to confuse past and present; words sound imposing, but remain puzzling. Such is the enigma of Pound's poetic work with Ancient Greek poetry, especially in the *Cantos*.

Greek words, phrases, or larger fragments are integrated into Pound's poetic text in various ways, from repetition in Greek to interpretative paraphrase – with translation occurring anywhere in between. Discussing selected passages of the *Cantos*,[2] I aim to investigate the significance of Pound's words to translators of Greek: 'more sense and less syntax [...] might be a relief' (1954a: 273).[3] What exactly does 'more sense' when combined with 'less syntax' amount to, especially with regard to the semantic and stylistic value of the poetic word in Pound's modernist poetics?

My discussion includes methodological and theoretical considerations of how Pound, in both essays and poetry, describes and evaluates his own poetry and translations. Pound's statements are often marked by unresolved uncertainties or tensions. And his poetic translations, at least in the case of Greek in the *Cantos*,[4] even if only fragmentary, retain their exceptional significance precisely because they can be read against the grain of his explicitly stated theoretical views and expose the complications suggested thereby. This divergence becomes evident where Pound's translation practice informs his modernist poetic writing, but also where translated passages can be read as commenting – explicitly or allegorically – on this practice. To further illuminate Pound's paradigm from a comparative perspective, I will trace connections to Walter Benjamin's theory of literature and translation, largely contemporaneous with Pound's early *Cantos* but linked to ideological views manifestly divergent from Pound's, especially with regard to the crucial question of how literature relates to history.[5]

To begin, we should note that the apparent simplicity of Pound's famous modernist dictum 'make it new!' (Pound 1935b) does little justice to the intricacies of the issues it raises. Literary classics were also regarded by Pound as always already new and consequently in no need of renewal: 'A classic is classic [...] because of a certain eternal and irrepressible freshness' ([1934] 1951: 13–14). This situates Pound's queries on 'a poem including history' (his succint definition of epic poetry) within the broader tendency of his time to rethink relations between aesthetics and history ([1934] 1951: 46). Benjamin echoes analogous concerns when, in 'The Task of the Translator', he claims that 'Translatability is an essential quality of certain works' ([1923] 1968a: 71). Translatability is inherent, that is, to the 'life and afterlife' of the work itself that has a capacity to generate its own history in ways quite foreign to both materialist and spiritualist commonplaces regarding 'such tenuous factors as sensation and soul' ([1923] 1968a: 71).

I will first probe a number of formulations from Pound's essays and letters regarding the function of the literary word and of its translation, especially its semantic and stylistic potential. I then turn to examples from the *Cantos* and their implications with respect to questions raised by Pound's views. Finally, I will discuss how this compares with fundamental commitments of Benjamin's theory that could help to better situate Pound's poetic translation – including its significance with respect to methodological concepts of translation studies, in particular to notions of foreignization and domestication.

Expressions such as 'eternal and irrepressible freshness', or 'life and afterlife', should not be misread as instances of conventionally hyperbolic rhetoric, since they raise the crucial question of what exactly it is that, in literature, cuts through different times and cultures. Kenner's paradoxical question concerning Pound's relation to Sappho is germane, though his answer sounds overly conclusive: 'what was [Pound] responding to when he read Greek? To rhythm and dictions, nutriment for his purposes' (1971: 69). Perhaps, as Pound wrote in a 1935 letter to Rouse, translator of Homer, 'The deep is so deep, like clear fathoms down' ([1950] 1971: 274). Pound's admixture of depth and clarity merits closer inspection.

In 'How to Read' (1929), Pound defines literature as 'the art of "charging" language with meaning' (1954a: 29). He likewise refers to qualities such as clarity, exactness, vigour and solidity that allow literary language to be 'saying *the thing* once for all and perfectly' (1954b: 10, emphasis added). Different languages, Pound notes, respond to this common challenge in quasi-agonistic terms: 'No one language is complete. A master may be continually expanding his own tongue, rendering it fit to bear some charge hitherto borne only by some other alien tongue, but the process does not stop with any one man' (Pound 1954a: 36). Literary meaning is connected to the heavy imprint of a particularly effective mode of expression. Yet what if this unique charge of meaningfulness risks blurring or even breaking semantic contours? Kenner suggests as much when he reformulates Pound's 'Don't bother about the WORDS, translate the MEANING' into the much more ambiguous advice 'to convey the energized pattern and let go the words' (Kenner 1971: 150). When Pound states that 'one does not need to learn a whole language in order to understand some one or some dozen poems' and that it suffices 'to understand thoroughly the poem, and every one of the few dozen or few hundred words that compose it' (1954a: 37), he implies that literature makes sense in ways that have little to do with the kind of meaning that is at work in current communication practices.

There is, however, considerable vagueness as to the nature of what Kenner calls the 'energized pattern', or, in Pound's terms, the 'thing' in question at the heart of translation. In *Guide to Kulchur*, Pound notes 'ideas which are intended to "go into action"' (Pound [1938] 1952: 34), but elsewhere he explicitly repudiates the term 'idea'.[6] In *Guide* he also proposes the more problematic Greek term of '*nous*, [that is] mind apart from any man's individual mind, of the sea crystalline and enduring, of the bright as it were molten glass that envelops us, full of light' (44). This indicates Neoplatonic traditions and may involve 'presentations of eternal truths' or even an 'embodiment of the transcendental, the divine or permanent world' (Liebregts 2004: 102–3). But although Neoplatonic or related intellectual traditions often illuminate Pound's views, one should also probe how his writing, whether essayist or poetic, in turn reconfigures such images: the crystal or glass to which Pound often refers is occasionally marked by a haziness or even obscurity, however luminous the overall impression. In his essay on Cavalcanti, Pound stresses the value of the '"medieval clean line" as distinct from the medieval niggle' (Pound 1935a: 150), while also using the equivocal imagery of 'glass under water, the form that seems a form seen in a mirror' in a 'world of moving energies, "*mezzo oscuro rade*," "*risplende in sè perpetuale effecto*," magnetisms that take form, that are seen or that border the visible' (1954a: 154). The use of Italian, here, reinforces a paradoxical, and typically Poundian, sense of obscure accuracy.

An analogous tension arises in Pound's essays (especially around the time of the 1930 publication of the *Draft of XXX Cantos*), where Neoplatonic ideas are combined with the 'late modernist tendency toward geometric arrangements' (Hickman 2005: 12). Such arrangements necessarily imply ideals of formal clarity and conceptual solidity. At the same time, however, in Pound's lexicon they also carry connotations of fluidity and even formlessness, suggested by the correlative figure of the vortex.[7]

These and similar complications prevent us from taking what Pound calls 'more sense' for granted, especially when it is coupled, as so often in Pound, with loosened syntactic structure and, even more pervasively, minimized syntagmatic cohesion. Pound's favoured discursive heterogeneity hinders reference to specific socio-cultural backgrounds required by hermeneutic approaches. Pound's essay on Cavalcanti offers a complex argument along these lines, not entirely consistent with the commonplace notion of 'interpretative translation' with which the essay closes (1935a: 200). As Venuti remarks, Pound seeks 'a poetic discourse linked to a specific historical moment that is neither Pound's nor Cavalcanti's nor Rossetti's' (1995: 197). Indeed, while Pound frequently revisits questions of vocabulary and rhythm, and often in erudite terms, he refrains from grasping 'oldness' in terms of antiquarian cultural tones – of any specific cultural tone, for that matter. Instead he seeks an intriguing 'fervour of the original' for which 'there is no ready-made verbal pigment' – another way of indexing the enigma of Pound's literary 'thing' to be translated (Pound 1954a: 200).

Pound's quest often seems to be pointing to a realm 'to which the poet can only have furtive access in the mystic trance of privileged communication with genius' (Aji 2003: 12). However, in his conception Pound may be closer, even if only intuitively so, to basic facts also pinpointed by philological research and, more specifically, by the paradigm of the Homeric Question. As Kenner notes when commenting on Pound's Homer, 'we've not even settled on what the Homeric poems *are*' (1985: 2). Such indecision is certainly justified by the long and varied history of the formation of Homeric poetry, which not only problematizes the principles of stable textuality and identifiable authorship, but also undermines the hypothesis that languages and literary works are substantially attached to clearly delineated cultural conditions. Uncertainties inevitably arise concerning the linguistic value of many Homeric words or structures, as well as about the grounds on which related questions could be addressed: there is a radical indeterminacy of linguistic value.

We can better appreciate the distinctiveness of Pound's approach to Homer by juxtaposing his translation in Canto I with the long tradition of English translations of Homer.[8] Of course there is considerable variety among the latter; on the whole, however, they opt to dispel the enigmas of Homeric texts according to linguistic and literary norms of their times, such that the vagueness or obscurity of their original is echoed only locally, if at all. At risk of oversimplification, we can say that Homeric translations tend to exemplify Venuti's analysis of domesticating transparency that governs modern practices of translation (1995).[9] In the case of early and mid-twentieth-century translations, this combines with a resistance to modernist breakthroughs in poetry and prose.[10] Pound's approach to translation is distinctive in that it resolutely addresses the indeterminacy carried by the ancient text, turning it into a pivot that emphatically marks his own poetic language in English. This unsettles the usual antinomy between domestication and foreignization, as the foreignness of the text translated sets the very conditions and limits of its domestication. I will return to this complication. At this point suffice it to underscore that by radically informing his poetry, Pound's translation strategies link the reading of ancient texts to modernist poetics – and transpose the challenges of ancient foreign languages into the literary dynamics of the modernist premises.

The fragments of the *Odyssey* translated in Canto I are from Book XI, also known as the *Nekuia* (the 'calling of the dead'). Pound closely follows the initial narration of the voyage to the land of the dead and the encounter with Elpenor (*Od.* XI.1–83), retaining disparate phrases from Tiresias's foretelling of Odysseus's return to Ithaca and from the emergence of Anticlea's soul. He closes with a rather hermetic reference to Andreas Divus's Renaissance Latin translation of the *Odyssey*, one of Pound's main sources,[11] and with lines alluding to the second *Homeric Hymn to Aphrodite*.

Kenner sees the first part of the Canto as 'a triumph of the literal' in which 'English words map Divus's words which map Homer's words and the whole goes to "Seafarer" cadences' (1985: 5). The figure of the map is telling, but one should also bear in mind Pound's guiding concept of a 'periplum, not as land looks on a map/ but as sea bord seen by men sailing' (1986: 324). Indeed, lands one approaches bear little, if any, schematic resemblance to the maps that have led to their shores.

The main characteristic of Canto I is a pronounced heterogeneity of prosodic, lexical and syntactical registers – Modern English, Ancient Greek, Latin, Old English. No one register predominates as the main frame of reference or serves as the 'ready-made verbal pigment' against which Pound warns. Within the ensuing sense of disorder, distinct words or phrases, along with their rhythmic values, come to be highlighted in a kind of suspended state: as intermittent historical frames cut through one another, there is an acute sense of elusiveness with respect to images and cadences, which invite but also resist hermeneutic illumination. The *Cantos* open this way:

And then went down to the ship,
Set keel to breakers, forth on the godly sea, and

We set up mast and sail on that swart ship,
Bore sheep aboard her, and our bodies also
Heavy with weeping…

Pound 1986: 3

Andreas Divus had rendered the passage in Latin almost literally:

At postquam ad navem descendimus, et mare,
Navem quidem primum deduximus in mare divum.
Et malum posuimus et vela in navi nigra:
Intrò autem oves accipientes ire fecimus, intrò et ipsi
Ivimus dolentes, huberes lachrymas fundentes:

Pound 1954a: 259–60

Meanwhile, there was also Chapman.[12] His distances from the original can be seen as domesticating Homer, yet quite uneasily so, since his English, both malleable and textured, is significantly affected by his process of translation. This makes his version sound closer to Pound than other modern translations:

Arriv'd now at our ship, we lancht, and set
Our Mast up, put forth saile, and in did get
Our late-got Cattell. Up our sailes, we went,
My wayward fellowes mourning now th'event

Homer 1967a: 187

Older English resounds within Pound's alliterative vocabulary, while Divus's Latin may be present in his choice of 'godly sea' for the Homeric εἰς ἅλα δῖαν (with *dîan* denoting Zeus's splendour).[13] Chapman too echoes in the wording and syntax of the Canto, including the ellipsis of the subject – which is also reminiscent of Greek or Latin syntactic structures. The breaking of the pentameter is coupled with unmistakable allusions to the four-beat line of the 'Seafarer'; but we may also discern non-iambic pentameters or even broken hexameters with metrical feet of unequal length and wavering accent – a partial undoing, that is, of Chapman's pentameter, itself marred by its repeated enjambments.[14]

As Canto I continues, the image of a strong push towards utter physical darkness is stressed to a degree found neither in Divus nor in previous English translations. In this, however, the Canto is quite faithful to the overall opacity of the original image. Most characteristic is the case of Homer's αὐτοὶ δ' αὖτε παρὰ ῥόον Ὠκεανοῖο / ἤομεν, ὄφρ' ἐς χῶρον ἀφικόμεθ' (*Od.* 11.21–2). The phrase can be understood as in Chapman's 'And walkt the shore till we attain the view / Of that sad region' (Homer 1967a: 188).[15] Pound, however, by turning Homer's παρὰ (*parà*) into a paradox, points to how, as noted by scholiasts since antiquity, our sense of geographical coordinates is thwarted: 'The ocean flowing backward, came we then' (1986: 3). If there is mediation from Divus, here it consists in Pound's possible misreading of the expression *rursus apud* in *ipsi autem rursus apud fluxum Oceani / Ivimus* (Pound 1954a: 260).

Pound also upsets the image of the emergent dead, thereby emphasizing the old riddle of the Homeric notion of the dead soul. He does not exclude 'soul' or 'spirit' as possible versions of the Homeric ψυχή (*psukhḗ*). But he also exposes the pathetic connotations that can be felt in the repeated Homeric expression ἀμενηνὰ κάρηνα (*amenēnà kárēna*, lines 29 and 49), which he renders as 'sickly death's-heads' (1986: 3) and as the paradox of 'impetuous, impotent dead' (1986: 4). This is much more emphatic than Divus's *mortuorum infirma capita* or *impotentia capita* (Pound 1954a: 260, 261). Divus is more clearly present in Pound's 'cadaverous dead' that combines imagistic expressivity with semantic discomfort (1986: 4). The phrase repeats Divus's unusual *cadaverum mortuorum* (Pound 1954a: 260) but also renders Homer's formulaic yet paradoxical νεκύων κατατεθνηώτων (*Od.* 11.37), which could be literally read as 'deceased that have utterly died'.[16]

In short, Pound tends to undo the geographical coordinates and figural contours that other translations seek to capture. In his version, the whole of Odysseus's journey is, in fact, ultimately cut to an elliptical minimum: 'Odysseus / Shalt return through spiteful Neptune, over dark seas, / Lose all companions' (1986: 4–5).

If Canto I is read as allegorizing Pound's poetic quest for literary tradition, then his translation can be seen as a hazardous endeavour to address remains of literary formations persisting in an outlandish state of effacement and disarray. Accordingly, the reference to Divus's translation, which includes its year of publication, can be read as echoing Odysseus's consoling promise to the soul of his comrade Elpenor.[17] This makes Pound's exhortation sound more ironic than reassuring: 'Lie quiet Divus. I mean, that is Andreas Divus, / In officina Wecheli, 1538, out of Homer' (1986: 5). 'Out of Homer' is equivocal, of course. It implies that the only way to derive from Homeric poetry is to keep sailing outward in the seas of its afterlives. In the subsequent line of Canto I, 'outward and away' is, in fact, where Odysseus is said to sail as he keeps returning.

The end of Canto I, with its highly eclectic links to the two *Homeric Hymns* to Aphrodite, presents a paradigm of poetic language informed by translation in ways that blurs conventional historical borderlines between languages and cultures:

> Venerandam,
> In the Cretan's phrase, with the golden crown, Aphrodite,
> Cypri munimenta sortita est, mirthful, orichalchi, with golden
> Girdles and breast bands, thou with dark eyelids
> Bearing the golden bough of Argicida. So that:

Pound 1986: 5

This passage opens with an explicit reference to the Latin translation of the *Hymns* by Georgius Dartona ('the Cretan'), appended to Divus's *Homeri Odyssea*. This is followed by a grid of Greek, Latin and English lexical forms echoing the uncertainties attendant upon their linguistic transpositions in time. 'Orichalchi' approximates the Homeric ὀρειχάλκου (*oreikhálkou*, *Hom. Hymn Aphr.* 6.9, designating a metal of uncertain substance) while reiterating Dartona's dubiously spelled 'orichalchi' and also echoing the English *orichalc(h)*. The morphologically ambiguous 'Argicida' suggests both its Greek and Latin sources but also carries the enigma of Ἀργειφόντης (*Argeiphóntēs*, *Hymn Aphr.* 5.177 and *Hom.* 121), an epithet of Hermes, god of exchange and interpretation seen as the slayer of Argos (guardian of Ios, Hera's priestess) or of the Argeian Greeks – or perhaps simply as a swift emergence (Cunliffe 1963: 53).[18]

Canto XXIII also involves a series of translation gestures that read as implicit comments on translation, especially on the quest for semantic equivalence. The Canto combines references to Greek mythology and lyric poetry, episodes of personal history and fragments of troubadour stories. It begins with a reference to an idea of intellectual multiplicity linked to the Neoplatonic tradition: '"Et omniformis," Psellos, "omnis / Intellectus est." God's fire' (Pound 1986: 107).[19] Multiple-formness also runs through the riddles that follow:

> With the sun in a golden cup
>   and going toward the low fords of ocean
> Ἄλιος δ' Ὑπεριονίδας δέπας ἐσκατέβαινε χρύσεον
> Ὄφρα δι' ὠκεανοῖο περάσας
>   ima vada noctis obscurae
> Seeking doubtless the sex in bread-moulds
> ἥλιος, ἅλιος, ἅλιος = μάταιος
> ("Derivation uncertain." The idiot
> Odysseus furrowed the sand.)
> alixantos, aliotrephès, eiskatebaine, down into,
> descended, to the end that, beyond ocean,
> pass through, traverse

Pound 1986: 107

The first two lines translate the quoted Stesichorus fragment describing the setting of the sun through the Ocean in a golden cup.[20] The sun is referred to as Ἄλιος Ὑπεριονίδας (*Hàlios Hyperionídas*): both words occur in Homer, the first designating the sun, the second being an adjective of uncertain meaning (son of Hyperion or of heights or a combination of the two). There follows a series of words or phrases that explore but also undo the proposed translation. More precisely, we observe the following: a Latin version of the quoted Greek lines;[21] a hypothesis about erotic intentions ironically intoned; three phonetically similar Greek words, the first being the Homeric word for 'sun' (*hèlios*), the other two being adjectives that are morphologically identical (*hàlios*) but semantically unrelated, one designating relations to the sea, the other remaining unclear ('fruitless, unprofitable, vain, idle', according to Liddell and Scott); a possible meaning for the latter a lexical comment in parenthesis, followed by a remark on Odysseus, perhaps as an example of feigned folly; two Greek transliterated words that come before and after the lemma ἅλιος (*hàlios*) in Liddell and Scott, each denoting sea-related qualities; a transliteration of the main verb in the quoted passage implying, if vaguely, downward and inward movement (ἐσκατέβαινε, previously rendered as 'going toward the low fords'); and, finally, six English words or expressions relating to this verb, forming a semantic field of descent and crossing while also suggesting images of sunlight on seawater. This last group of words configures not only the problematic task of reading the quoted Greek passage but also, more generally, the Poundian translation practice, especially of ancient Greek texts: an intellectual journey involving multiple forms in successive tentative transpositions, sliding and missteps, recurrently intercepted and redirected.

In several cases, the phonetic component of a word takes on a significance that overrides its semantic value. In the third line of Canto IV, for example, the reader is surprised by the invocation of a rare compound adjective from Pindar's second Olympian Ode, noting that the hymns reign over the musical instrument of their performance: 'ANAXIFORMINGES! Aurunculeia! / Hear me' (Pound 1986: 13). The exact significance of the Greek adjective (typed in capitals) as well as that of the Latin bridal name of Aurunculeia (alluding to Catullus) may ultimately not matter. Both words impose their peculiarly combinable phonetic values, each from its own language. Apropos of this, in a 1916 letter, Pound referred to Pindar's Ode as a 'big rhetorical drum, [. . .] which one should get carefully fixed in the mind' after noting that 'I prize the Greek more for the movement of the words, rhythm, perhaps than for anything else' (1950 [1971]: 91). One should refrain from reading Pound's use of terms such as 'movement' or 'rhythm' as denoting clearly discernible patterns. Drums may involve compelling cadences but not necessarily clarity of musical lines. In the case of Canto IV, an accentual reading of the Greek and Latin words can bring out metrical ambiguity between dactyl and iamb.

An important form of movement Pound's poetry brings into play is often one of multiple transpositions of meaning fluctuating from and into various languages or modes of expression. In many instances, the *Cantos* propose various forms of given semantic cores, ranging from literal renderings in different languages to interpretative comments. In Canto LXXX, for example, we encounter multiple versions of the notion of 'all' within the context of lines referring to Baroque painting and Chinese philosophy, first in Greek, then transliterated, and finally translated in non-grammatical English: 'τὸ πᾶν/ [*toh pan*, the all]' (1986: 511). Such repetitions amplify but also diffuse and even blur the meaning of a word that otherwise reads as relatively simple. Similarly, the Odyssean 'no one' (οὔ τις) which Odysseus gives as his name to the Cyclops, is persistently repeated in Cantos LXXIV and LXXX. It recurs in multiple forms (including Greek) that add up to a cloud of semantic switches: 'Odysseus / the name of my family, / the wind also is of the process', '"I am noman, my name is noman"', 'a man on whom the sun has gone down', 'now there are no more days/ οὔ τις/ ἄχρονος' (Pound 1986: 425, 426, 430, 499). A Chinese ideogram is also presented as part of the same semantic field (430). Thus the *Cantos* often highlight the very contours of the Greek alphabet, suggesting functions of iconic significance similar to those attributed to Chinese ideograms. Such is the case in Canto LXXXV where wisdom or intelligence are associated with the Greek word Σοφία and with related Chinese forms, reproduced graphically and phonetically, along with Italian and French equivalents. It all concludes with an ironic reminder:

The sun under it all:
Justice, d'urbanité, de prudence
wei heou, Σοφία
the sheltered grass hopes, chueh, cohere.
(No, that is *not* philological)

1986: 544

Such clusters of lexical variations passing from language to language are crucially significant for Pound's approach to poetic translation. As at the end of Canto I, they present written words in a state wherein meaning constantly leaks from shapes: shapes that make sense only as contours pumping diffuse flows of sound and sense, persistently suggestive yet impossible to contain. We are no longer in quest of semantic or stylistic equivalences; rather, Poundian translation seeks to evoke patterns of drastic intellectual uncertainty.

The above brings to mind how Benjamin, in his essay on the mimetic faculty of language, considers 'nonsensuous similarity': 'if words meaning the same thing in different languages are arranged about that thing as their center, we have to inquire how they all—while often possessing not the slightest similarity to one another—are similar to what they signify at their center' (Benjamin 1986: 335). Such threads of Benjamin's theory can illuminate crucial aspects of Pound's translation practice.

For both Pound and Benjamin, translation is as much about the display of cultural alterity as about the persistence of a kind of sameness. The main transposition with which literary translation must cope is neither temporal nor inter-cultural; instead it is the leap from cultural concerns to ontological alertness. As Kenner notes, the conflicting ways in which Pound strives to define the importance of poetry have 'metaphysical implications' pertaining to the longstanding philosophical issue of a 'doctrine of substantial form' (1951: 87). In other words, the literary 'thing' to which Pound refers when addressing translation (what is to be translated) touches upon the question of quiddity, that is, of the very nature of literary thingness. Benjamin's more developed ontological reflections shed informative light on the issue.

Translatability, for Benjamin, as an essential attribute of the literary work, enacts the capacity of the work to live historically, a capacity emanating from the very nature of the linguistic sign. Human languages include along with their semiotic character a non-semiotic dimension of 'pure language' (1968a: 74), something close to an ideational infrastructure linked but also irreducible to the functions of language as a historically situated communicational code. This element of pure language also accounts for how 'Languages are not strangers to one another but are, a priori and apart from all historical relationships, interrelated in what they want to express' (Benjamin 1968a: 72). Works of language can thus acquire literary potential, including literary translatability, to the degree that they effectively activate the double nature of language, which allows them to express but also to transcend their epoch – a theoretical proposition implied, in a way, not only by the clouds of linguistic shifts in the *Cantos*, but also by Pound's idea of agonistic inter-linguistic relations.

This does not presuppose the permanence of already formed or otherwise given ideas or the constancy of entities remaining similar to their given selves. If there is similarity, it is, according to Benjamin, 'non-sensuous'. The original indicates, in a historically compelling fashion, something that can only exist as a field of multiple series of unsteady reconfigurations running through times and cultures – and this could be close to Pound's understanding of the 'thing' that literary language ventures to seize, which Kenner reads as 'patterned energy'.

The comparison to Benjamin also illuminates Pound's translation method, especially with regard to sense and syntax. Benjamin favours 'a literal rendering of the syntax which proves words rather than sentences to be the primary element of the translator' (Benjamin 1968a: 79). This, however, is quite far from an approach that aims at bending the language of the translation according to the grammar of the original. The main task of Benjamin's translator is to detach the literary work from the socio-cultural conditions of its receptions *and* from those of its original formation: 'A real translation is transparent' in the sense that it 'allows the pure language, as though reinforced by its own medium, to shine upon the original all the more fully' (ibid.). Technically, this can be achieved by way of syntactical rearrangements (including but not limited to imitations of the original syntax) that allow us to face the challenge of the foreign language while transgressing the sentence as a communicational syntagmatic unit: 'For if the sentence is the wall before the language of the original, literalness is the arcade' (ibid.). The words brought to the fore as 'the primary element of the translator' are knots or fragments that have little to do with links of clearly identifiable structures of positive semantic value. In fact, translation, says Benjamin, should touch meaning rather fleetingly: as a manifold robe envelops a body or as tangent touches periphery or, finally, as wind touches Aeolian harps (Benjamin 1968a: 75, 80, 81).[22]

All of the above concur with how Pound breaks syntactical coherence – often echoing, however eclectically, the syntax of the original – and highlights specific words or phrases, foregrounding the precariousness of their written contours, together with the indeterminacy of their meaning. There is, indeed, 'less syntax': loose syntagmatic ends rather than syntactical cohesion. As for 'sense', there is certainly 'more', as an overflow of uncontained meaning runs though textual schemas that it constantly tends to break.[23]

In broader methodological terms, this underscores the inconsistent, even rickety, character of poetic translation. Poetic translations can and even must be confusing even if informed by philological research, arbitrary even though connected to systematic study and supported by reliable argument, inconsistent however disciplined by methodical concerns.

We are thus lead beyond binary frames and polarities that often structure debates about translation strategies: such as the outworn distinction between freedom and fidelity but also the more telling one between foreignization and domestication. Venuti himself, in his insightful analysis of the Poundian translation paradigm, hints at how foreignization can stem from a concern for the overthrow of domestic values and practices rather than from an adherence to foreign ones: 'Pound's translations signified the foreignness of the foreign text, not because they were faithful or accurate [...] but because they deviated from domestic canons in English' (1995: 200). Pound often performs appropriations so intensely literary that their effects of estrangement are stronger than those of usual techniques of foreignization.[24]

Benjamin and Pound both show that the language of literary translation is estranging not because it echoes specific patterns of cultural foreignness but mainly because it foregrounds how all language is somewhat foreign to its socio-cultural usages and, as such, akin to all other languages. This is even more the case with ancient languages, to the degree that they are 'dead' – i.e. detached from topical usages and current communication concerns.

A remaining question is how history can be 'included' (as Pound puts it) in poetry that strives to connect to historically distant traditions while also coping with the way language at once links us to and detaches us from socio-cultural settings. This breach between language and culture does not imply that historical dynamics no longer matter; rather, it changes our sense of the 'historical' as it transposes us to a field where historical temporality condenses in ways that allow crucially engaging historical occurrences to cut through established patterns. The very antinomy between historicism and aestheticism is thus suspended: aesthetic works are historical to the degree that they compel us to rethink history beyond the confines of socio-cultural laws and taxonomies.

Such suspensions unleash forces that do not allow us to separate poetics from metaphysics or politics, while preventing us from reducing any one of these domains to any other. We might bear this in mind when struggling with what we read in Benjamin, and especially Pound, as points of contradiction, even 'betrayal' of one line of conviction by another (the concept of *traddutore* as *traditore* grazes the idea). The connection between metaphysical problematics and Marxist engagements in Benjamin has long puzzled critics, both theoretically and politically. Meanwhile, Pound's scandalous political activism has been a source of aporetic distress for poets, translators and literary critics alike. As Hickman phrases it, 'one of Pound's severest betrayals' is that 'of his own anti-abstractionist epistemological wisdom' (2005: 131). Such treason threads through Pound's critical writings and political practice but also his poetry. His poetic forms, especially when involving translation, signal radical epistemological distrust of abstract cultural or ideological wholes; yet these stand in constant tension with a persistent pursuit of coherent wholeness that resounds throughout both the *Cantos* and Pound's essays.[25] Modernism faced such tensions consistently and intensely – and might even be seen as made out of the dynamics generated thereby.

This reconfirms that literature can be an open field of indeterminate occurrences and transformations, especially when the historical persistence of the classics is at issue. Where poetry 'Scratches the eye; so violent it can be seen / Across three thousand years' (Logue 2001: 207), nothing follows either naturally or culturally, yet historically everything remains possible. From Walcott's *Omeros* (1990) to Logue's *War Music* (2001), to Oswald's *Memorial* (2011), poetry has ventured to rework our notions of epic and history, reminding us that Pound's legacy can lead to uncharted waters, both old and new – out of Homer.

CHAPTER 3

TRANSLATING THE *ODYSSEY*: ANDREAS DIVUS, OLD ENGLISH AND EZRA POUND'S CANTO I

Massimo Cè

At the incipit of *The Cantos*, Pound translates the opening of the Homeric *Nekuia* (*Odyssey* 11). Ending this partial translation, Pound makes explicit that his version is not based on Homer directly, but rather adapts the Renaissance Latin translation of the *Odyssey* by Andreas Divus:

> Lie quiet Divus. I mean, that is Andreas Divus,
> In officina Wecheli, 1538, out of Homer.

Cantos I.68–9

Pound's partial quotation of the title page of that translation (*in officina Wecheli, 1538*) pinpoints the particular edition he used. As Pound says in 'Translators of Greek', in the section entitled 'Early Translators of Homer',[1] in 1906–10 he came across 'a Latin version of the *Odyssey* by Andreas Divus Justinopolitanus':[2] the extant *Homeri Odyssea ad verbum translata*, printed in Paris in 1538 by Chrétien Wechel (Christianus Wechelus).[3] This early printed edition of Divus's *Odyssea Latina* also contains a Latin translation by Aldo Manuzio (Aldus Manutius) of the *Batrachomyomachia* as well as Georgius Dartona's Latin rendering of the *Homeric Hymns*. Two of these *Hymns*, the greater and lesser hymns to Aphrodite (*Hom. Hymn* 5 and 6), feature as 'fragmentary'[4] snippets in the last five lines of Canto I (72–6).[5] Pound's focus, however, falls on *Odyssey* 11, lines 1–153, which he renders more or less freely. These lines include Odysseus's first departure from Circe's island, his arrival in the land of the Cimmerians, and his subsequent encounter with the shades of Elpenor and Tiresias, and finally, his deceased mother:[6]

And then Anticlea came.	*Cantos I.67*
mater | venit ('mother came')	*Divus 11.151–2*
μήτηρ | ἤλυθεν (*métēr éluthen* 'mother came')	Od. *11.152–3*

This essay examines Canto I's poetic technique, focusing on Pound's translation of the *Odyssey*, which, in its definitive 1925 version,[7] makes up more than 90 per cent of the poem.[8] As I will demonstrate, Pound's translation overwhelmingly draws on Divus's Renaissance Latin rendering over Homer's Greek, and this preference has important consequences for the language and style of Canto I. While Divus's conceptual import for Pound's poetic agenda has been well recognized,[9] this will be the first systematic study of Divus's equally fundamental linguistic and stylistic presence in Canto I.[10] I will also discuss the 'Saxonist' texture of the poem, and the ways in which Pound aligns the Renaissance aesthetic of Divus with that of eighth-century Old English poetry.[11]

As Pound observes in 'Early Translators of Homer', Divus's version is essentially a 'crib' to assist a reader with Homer's Greek:[12] Divus's rendering translates word for word and tries to convey, as far as the Latin language allows,[13] the meaning and syntactical function of each Greek word. As a result, Divus's version does not aspire to be read independently of Homer's Greek and does not claim for itself any patent literary merits. Unsurprisingly, the Latin that results neither attempts to replicate Homer's hexameter nor abides by the rules of Latin prose style.

Comparing the first two lines of *Odyssey* 11 with Divus's rendering exemplifies his translation technique. I add a verbatim English translation to capture Divus's method:

αὐτὰρ	ἐπεί ῥ'	ἐπὶ νῆα	κατήλθομεν	ἠδὲ θάλασσαν,
at	postquam	ad navem	descendimus,	et mare,
but	*after*	*to the ship*	*we went down*	*and the sea*

νῆα	μὲν ἄρ	πάμπρωτον	ἐρύσσαμεν	εἰς ἅλα δῖαν
navem	quidem	primum	deduximus	in mare divum
the ship	*for one*	*first*	*we drew down*	*into the divine sea*

Although Divus's text was printed without the Greek, his version amounts to a run of interlinear glosses.[14] A phrase's word order, as in *ad navem descendimus et mare*, only gives the impression of Latin prose: the main verb separating the two accusatives (*navem, mare*), without repeating the preposition *ad*, would be inconceivable in classical Latin prose.[15] Likewise the collocation *mare divum* has no parallel in extant Latin but only makes sense against the Greek.[16] Divus translates nearly every word, including particles like μέν (*mén ~ quidem*) and δέ (*dé ~ et* or *autem*),[17] and replicates such artificial features as tmesis[18] and nominative present participles.[19] Both are found at *Odyssey* 11.4–5:

ἐν δὲ	καὶ αὐτοὶ	|	βαίνομεν	ἀχνύμενοι	(Od. 11.4–5)
intro	et ipsi	|	ivimus	dolentes	(*Divus* 11.4–5)
in	*ourselves too*	|	*we went*	*grieving*	

Translating literally, Divus's *versio* contravenes both the practice of ancient Roman translators of Homer – Livius Andronicus, Catullus, Vergil, Horace and Baebius Italicus – and many more consciously literary Homeric translations in the Latin Renaissance –

such as Angelo Poliziano's verse translation of *Iliad* books 2–5 (1470), Lorenzo Valla's prose *Iliad* (1474) and Raffaello Maffei's prose translation of the *Odyssey*, with select passages in meter (1523).[20] Divus's faithfulness to the *Odyssey*'s language has led many Pound scholars to assume that we can treat both equally as source texts, with Divus acting as a window onto Homer.[21] I argue instead that Divus's rendering fundamentally informs Pound's translation of the *Nekuia* episode and both anticipates and motivates countless lexical, syntactic and metrical features of Canto I, while systematically evading,[22] with a few minor exceptions, the Homeric Greek *Odyssey*.[23]

Divus's *Odyssey* translation regularly uses a simplified Latin vocabulary in rendering Homer's often unusual and diverse word choices. In the passage translated by Pound (*Od.* 11.1–153), Homer uses two different words to refer to Odysseus's sword, ἄορ (*áor*, at 11.24) and ξίφος (*xíphos*, at 11.48):

ἔσχον· ἐγὼ δ' <u>ἄορ</u> ὀξὺ ἐρυσσάμενος παρὰ μηροῦ	(Od. 11.24)
αὐτὸς δὲ <u>ξίφος</u> ὀξὺ ἐρυσσάμενος παρὰ μηροῦ	(Od. 11.48)

The parallel narrative context and the repeated adjective ὀξύ (*oxú*, 'sharp') strongly suggest ἄορ and ξίφος as synonyms.[24] Divus translates both words with the Latin *ensem*.[25]

faciebant: ego autem <u>ensem</u> acutum trahens a foemore	(*Divus* 11.24)
at ego <u>ensem</u> acutum trahens a foemore	(*Divus* 11.48)

Comparing Canto I's rendering of the two instances (*sword* at both 20 and 39) shows that Pound follows the simplified vocabulary of Divus, not the lexical variety of the Greek.

And drawing <u>sword</u> from my hip	(*Cantos* I.20)
Unsheathed the narrow <u>sword</u>	(*Cantos* I.39)

Given that English has several synonyms for 'sword', including 'dagger' and 'blade', which Pound could have used to convey the *Odyssey*'s lexical diversity, it might be either that Pound, working directly and exclusively from Divus's text, never encountered Homer's two different renderings of 'sword', or – and perhaps more interestingly – that he, although familiar with Homer's Greek, chose to follow Divus.[26]

Where two instances of an identical word or phrase in Divus lie far apart in the text, such as with *ensem*, Pound regularly opts to similarly translate both instances. When the two occurrences fall closer together, however, such as in consecutive lines of Divus's text, Pound's technique changes. Finding the repeated mention of the same word at close quarters undesirable, Pound in such cases generally omits one of the two instances, like in Pound's rendering of the first two lines of *Odyssey* 11, already quoted above.

αὐτὰρ ἐπεί ῥ' ἐπὶ νῆα κατήλθομεν ἠδὲ <u>θάλασσαν</u>,	
νῆα μὲν ἄρ πάμπρωτον ἐρύσσαμεν εἰς <u>ἅλα</u> δῖαν	(Od. 11.1–2)

at postquam ad navem descendimus, et <u>mare</u>,
navem quidem primum deduximus in <u>mare</u> divum   (*Divus* 11.1–2)
And then went down to the ship, [and the <u>sea</u>]
Set keel to breakers, forth on the godly <u>sea</u>, and   (*Cantos* I.1–2)

Here Pound omits the first reference to the sea (Divus 11.1 *et mare*), while translating the second (Divus 11.2 *in mare divum* ~ *Cantos* I.2 *forth on the godly sea*). Pound appears to choose Divus's precedent over Homer's Greek. The verbal repetition (*mare ... mare*), which motivates Pound's omitting the first term, does not exist in Homer, where the first line's θάλασσαν/*thálassan* changes with the second line's ἅλα/*hála*. Had Divus duplicated the Greek's lexical variety, translating the second phrase as *salem, altum*, etc.,[27] Pound might have translated the first instance as 'sea' and the second as 'salt flood', 'deep', etc.[28] Divus creates verbal redundancy where Homer has *variatio*; and Pound takes his cue, here and elsewhere,[29] from Divus's lexical choice in providing his twentieth-century reader with a minimalist version of the *Odyssey*.[30]

Many commentators have failed to explicitly note Pound's largely exclusivist intertextual relationship with Divus. Even Jean Robaey's exhaustive comparison of Canto I with its Latin and Greek sources shies away from making global claims about the textual connection between Pound, Divus, and the *Odyssey*.[31] Although Robaey occasionally concedes that Pound bases his translation on Divus's Latin alone, such cautious claims always concern specific passages.[32] With the exception of the orthography of proper names, where Pound in two isolated instances follows the Greek,[33] Canto I consistently excludes the Homeric Greek, except what Homeric features Divus's version transmits.[34] Pound, then, deploys Divus not so much as a window onto the Homeric text as a means to render it invisible, thus thwarting the *Odyssea Latina*'s professed function as a crib. Simplification, rife in Divus's own technique, combined with Pound's programmatic selectiveness and condensation – transposing a single section (lines 1–153) of a single book (11) within a single work (the *Odyssey*) in accordance with a single translator's version (Divus) – represents one of the instruments by which Canto I both conjures and, simultaneously, suppresses its Homeric poetic model.

Divus's influence on Pound's wording of Canto I appears not only in these structural ways, where Divus 'positively' influences Pound to translate what he finds in Divus, or 'negatively' influences Pound to omit Divus's choices: Divus's Latin itself often plays a role. Pound frequently employs English cognates of particular Latin words, infusing his text with a prominent 'Latinate' veneer. Considering that English possesses a mixed lexicon, made up of both Latin and Germanic roots ('beef' vs 'cow', etc.), the language lends itself particularly well to the kind of appropriation of these two major European linguistic and literary traditions.[35]

There are clear instances where Pound exploits English's malleable Germanic–Latinate composition specifically to amplify its Latinate stratum. The following line (*Cantos* I.12) demonstrates Pound's very recognizable translation – approximating a transcription – of Divus 11.14.

To the Kimmerian lands, and peopled cities   (*Cantos I.12*)

Illic autem Cimmeriorum virorum populusque civitasque   (*Divus* 11.14)

Pound's translation is both loose and literal. Pound subtly undercuts the syntactic role and morphology of virtually every word in Divus's Latin. The original's static description becomes an end-point of movement in Pound; Pound substitutes *lands* for 'men' (*virorum*), and makes explicit the hendiadys of *populusque civitasque* ('the people and the city') by joining the two nouns into the single adjective–noun phrase *peopled cities* and innovating the plural. Only the adjective *Kimmerian* preserves the exact meaning and grammatical function of its corresponding word (*Cimmeriorum*) in the *Odyssey*. Yet Pound's translation is also literal, closely replicating its source in visual and phonetic terms. Two function words (*illic autem ~ to the*) precede a prominent demonym, and the line closes with a *p- c-* sequence. Pound's translation achieves such close similarity to the original – the Latin, not the Greek – because the words he uses, *people* and *city*, are etymologically cognate with *populus* and *civitas*.[36]

Pound appropriates Divus's Latin again in his rendering *regionem* as *region* (*Cantos* I.61) from Homer's χῶρον (*Od*.11.94, *khôron* 'land'), *cadaverum mortuorum* as *cadaverous dead* (29) from νεκύων κατατεθνηώτων (*Od*. 11.37, *nekúōn katatethnēótōn* 'corpses having died'), and *virgines tenerae* as *girls tender* (31) from παρθενικαὶ ἀταλαί (*Od*. 11.39, *parthenikaì atalaí* 'tender maidens'), this last example also preserving word order. Further examples demonstrate that these occurrences of Latinate forms in Pound, far from being the inevitable result of writing in the Romanized idiom of English, emerge from poetic choice. A stylistic marker regularly gains prominence by being repeated at close quarters: for instance, Tiresias's opening address to Odysseus contains two Latinate forms in quick succession.

'Stand from the <u>fosse</u>, leave me my bloody <u>bever</u>
'For soothsay'.   Cantos *I.62–3*

Sed recede a <u>fossa</u>, remove autem ensem acutum,
Sanguinem ut <u>bibam</u>, et tibi vera dicam.   *Divus 11.95–6*

Here Pound closely adapts Divus's clause-final words *fossa* (94) and *bibam* (95). More than being Latinate synonyms of the Germanic 'pit'[37] and 'drink', these particular lexemes stand out because they are uncommon in twentieth-century English. The *Oxford English Dictionary* labels *fosse* (n.) in the required sense (*s.v.* 3a 'a hole, a pit') as '*rare* and *poetic* or *historical* in later use', while *bever* (n.) is '*obsolete*' with no secure attestations bearing the meaning 'drink' or 'drinking' (*s.v.* 1 and 2) later than the early 1600s.

These cases show that Pound's translation, in its strong Latinate coloring, results from a systematic poetic strategy to highlight his source text's Latin. Pound's emphasis on Divus may be motivated, as David Ricks has suggested, by a desire to 'escape the idiom of Victorian and Edwardian Hellenism' and to do so by engaging a 'voice less distinguished than

Homer's own' (1989: 143). Pound was also confronting eighteenth-century Augustan classicism's role in translating ancient poetry, and although his rejection of Pope's Homeric translations was not as extreme as Keats's and the Romantics', he, like them, reached back further in time to the Renaissance for an adequate poetic model.[38] I would argue generally that in co-opting and promoting Divus's secondariness vis-à-vis Homer, Pound articulates and embraces the secondariness of his own project. Showing that products like Divus's crib possess value gradually removes the pressure to return to the tradition's foundation, Homer. So Homeric translation changes from an agonistic gesture, whereby the translator strives, but ultimately fails, to equal or even surpass Homer, to a collaborative act, whereby translators, from backgrounds as linguistically and historically distinct as Pound's and Divus's, work together towards fashioning a new poetic idiom. The continuities in the practice and experience of poetic secondariness come to outweigh the question of sameness and difference – success and failure – with regard to the tradition's source text.

Steven Yao has similarly argued that in *Cathay*, Pound champions translation as 'a collaborative mode of textual production' (2002b: 31) through explicitly acknowledging his intermediary sources, specifically the American art historian Ernest Fenollosa and the Japanese scholars Mori and Ariga, in the collection's subtitle.[39] We have seen that within Canto I, Pound also explicitly references his chief collaborator, Divus, through his full name and his publisher's name (*Cantos* I.68–9). After Divus, Pound's most important filter for engaging the *Odyssey* is Old English poetry – however Pound's only comments on this source emerge outside of Canto I.

In a 1916 letter Pound remarks, 'I have tried an adaptation [of *Odyssey* 11] in the 'Seafarer' metre, or something like it',[40] referring to his translation of the Anglo-Saxon poem *The Seafarer*, first published in *New Age* in 1911 and then again in *Ripostes* in 1912. In this translation, also entitled 'The Seafarer',[41] Pound fashions a new idiom based on the rhythmical and stylistic features of his source. Pound's 'Seafarer' exemplifies so-called 'Saxonist' poetry, that is poetry 'written in direct imitation of Old English', as Chris Jones defines it (2006: 15).[42] Following Jones's (2006: 31–7) excellent survey of Pound's Saxonist poetics on the basis of 'The Seafarer', I want to bring those insights to bear on my reading of Canto I. I argue (with Jones 2006: 45) that, even as Pound transitions from the often-jarring use of Old English elements in 'The Seafarer' to a more nuanced Saxonist poetics, a Saxonist strand persists in Canto I. Considering Jones's five Saxonist poetic features – alliteration, falling rhythm, lexical archaisms, compound phrases and departures from standard English syntax – in turn will demonstrate this.

Pound uses alliteration more sparingly in Canto I than in his 'Seafarer', virtually confining it to stress-bearing syllables as it was in Old English.[43] Even the opening of the poem's comparatively frequent alliteration is never as insistent as in 'The Seafarer' or Old English verse, with the exception of line 5, where four syllables participate in an alliterative *w* sequence.

And then went down to the ship,
Set keel to breakers, forth on the godly sea, and

We set up mast and sail on that swart ship,
Bore sheep aboard her, and our bodies also
Heavy with weeping, and winds from sternward
Bore us out onward with bellying canvas,
Circe's this craft, the trim-coifed goddess.

Cantos I.1–7

Alliteration in this opening sentence sets the tone for Canto I, flagging the poem's engagement with and continuation of the Old English poetic tradition. One major deviation from that tradition, shared with Pound's 'Seafarer', consists in the frequent carry-over lettering, whereby 'syllables alliterate across adjacent line divisions':[44] *s* connects lines 2 and 3, *sh* continues from line 3 into 4, *w* is prominent in lines 5 and 6, and *c* (variously realized as /k/ or /s/) straddles lines 6 and 7. In addition to accelerating the poem through phonetic enjambment, this stylistic departure from Anglo-Saxon practice, by extending alliteration's reach, paradoxically, magnifies the poem's Germanic layer. Jones observes of Pound's use of alliteration in Canto I: 'Although not a metrical principle, the phonetic texture of the poem is made tighter, denser and more audible through this Saxonesque lettering.'[45]

Part of Pound's more subtle deployment of alliteration in Canto I consists in extending Germanic lettering to otherwise Latinate phrases.

Stand <u>from the fosse</u>, leave me my <u>bloody bever</u>   Cantos I.62

The Latinate lexemes *fosse* and *bever*, discussed above, are here, in each case, contained within an alliterative phrase. That the words that alliterate with *fosse* and *bever*, that is, *from* and *bloody*, are themselves Germanic underscores the alliteration's Saxonist effect.[46]

Pound develops a Saxonist poetic rhythm for 'The Seafarer' that comprises a mixture of metrical flexibility (a variable number of stresses to each line) with a predominantly falling movement (a line dominated by dactyls and trochees; e.g. v. 3 features both: 'Hárdship endúred oft').[47] Of Canto I's first twenty lines, thirteen (65 per cent) begin with a stressed syllable characteristic of the falling scheme;[48] of the remaining seven lines, which start out with a rising rhythm, only three also end that way (1: *to the shíp*; 17: *to the pláce*; 20: *from my híp*), while the others conclude with a falling rhythm. In sum, seventeen out of twenty lines (85 per cent) are either falling throughout (13) or at line-end (4).[49] Thus Canto I avoids iambic metrical patterns and prefers trochees, much like 'The Seafarer'. Pound explicitly advocates for this style at *Cantos* LXXXI.518, where he parenthetically states that '(to break the pentameter, that was the first heave)', and in his essay 'A Few Don'ts by an Imagiste', first published in the March 1913 volume of *Poetry*.[50]

Canto I's opening boasts some interesting metrical features, with its first two lines completely composed in the rising rhythm, made up of iambs and anapests:

And thén went dówn to the shíp,
Set kéel to bréakers, fórth on the gódly séa, ‖ and

Cantos I.1–2

These first lines lack alliteration and they also resist much of the rest of the poem's Saxonist cadences. Only the poem's second *and* (the last word of line 2), missing in Ur-Canto III and seemingly added as an afterthought here, breaks with the iambic movement and leads into the next few lines' uninterrupted run of falling cadences. Pound's revisions in the following two lines further underscore this rhythmical shift: rewriting *swárthy shíp* as *swárt shíp* in line 3 (already in *The Future* edition) and inverting *Sheep bóre we* as *Bóre sheep* in line 4 both substitute a rising iambic with a falling trochaic scheme.[51]

While a number of lexical archaisms, such as *fosse* and *bever*, form part of Canto I's Latinate layer, most of the poem's archaisms derive from Anglo-Saxon, including *swart* (v. 3, instead of 'black'; also *swartest* at 16), *amidships* (v. 8), *aforesaid* (v. 18), *pitkin* (v. 21, diminutive of 'pit', apparently Pound's invention),[52] *dreory* (v. 33, *OED s.v.* dreary 'gory, bloody'),[53] *mid* (v. 57, for 'amongst', 'amid'),[54] and *soothsay* (v. 63, as a noun 'rare' according to *OED s.v.* 2b).

Morphological archaisms form a distinct category in Saxonist writing, which comprises Canto I's several compound phrases. The category includes two main types, compound nouns, like 'sea-bord' (*Cantos* I.55),[55] and compound genitives, like *death's-heads* (24),[56] both of which are ubiquitous in 'The Seafarer'.[57] A third group, consists in compound adjectives: Canto I has *trim-coifed* (7), *close-webbed* (13) and *ell-square* (21). These most closely resemble Homeric epithets such as 'rosy-fingered' (ῥοδο-δάκτυλος; *rhodo-dáktulos*).[58] However, only the first example actually corresponds to a compound in Homer and Divus (*Od.* 11.8 ἐϋπλόκαμος *eüplókamos* ~ *benecomata* 'fair-haired'). The other two condense Divus's longer phrases *caligine et nebula* (11.15) and *quantum cubiti mensura hinc et inde* (11.25). While Pound likely conceived of *close-webbed* and *ell-square* as Saxonist rather than Homeric or Latinate features, *trim-coifed*, like the alliterative phrases *from the fosse* and *bloody bever*, suggests an unresolved ambiguity between the two idioms and neatly epitomizes Pound's general conflation of the Germanic and Latinate traditions.[59]

Canto I also demonstrates Jones's fifth and last category of Saxonist characteristics – syntactical peculiarities arising from inverted word order and omission of articles and verbs – in inversions of both subject–verb and adjective–noun. Subject–verb inversion occurs throughout the first third of Canto I,[60] often close to the beginning of a line, giving it a falling rhythm, as in line 11 with *Cáme we thén*. Adjective–noun inversion, with *girls tender* (31) and *men many* (32), occurs twice in immediate succession. Similarly, the phrase *toils urged other* places 'other' after 'toils' (45). Although adjective–noun inversion features in Saxonist poetry – 'The Seafarer' has *mirth most magnified* (86) and *delights undurable* (88) – and so participates in the Germanic strand of the poem, two of the three cases in Canto I additionally draw on Divus's Latin inversions (*virginesque tenerae*, 11.39; *labor alius*, 11.54) – again contributing to a mixed Germanic–Latinate idiom.[61]

To more precisely formulate how the relationship of the Latinate and Germanic layers in Canto I shapes Pound's poetics, I now consider several poetological passages in the poem. Canto I's set of metatextual markers, both following (*Cantos* I.68–69) and preceding (Ur-Canto III.70, 72) the Poundian *Nekuia*, which refer to Divus, Homer and the process of literary composition, flag the *Nekuia*'s status as a poetic journey and conjuring the dead as a poet's engagement with the literary past.[62] The Poundian *Nekuia* itself contains numerous phrases that hint at literary practice. *Circe's . . . craft* (*Cantos* I.7), as Flack shows, leaves behind the straightforwardness of Divus's *navis* ('ship') and instead plays on 'the multiple associations' of 'craft' (2015: 39–40): Circe's vessel, her cunning, and the role the goddess plays in crafting Odysseus's story, which functions as an analogue to Pound's own poetic craft. Pound also metapoetically departs from Divus's Latin when he has Elpenor ask Odysseus for a written epitaph (*Cantos* I.55: *be tomb by sea-bord, and inscribed*). Flack shows that this detail enacts a significant anachronistic shift from the preliterate world of Homer to the hyperliterate world of Pound, typographically marked by the italics of the tomb inscription, which Canto I symbolically preserves for the reader, guaranteeing Elpenor's immortality in print (ibid.).

In another passage, Pound's otherwise literal translation of *Odyssey* 11.36–7 pointedly suppresses one of two main verbs, streamlining the phrasing and creating verbal parallelism between the actions of the Odyssean protagonist and Canto I's narrator:

Dark blood flowed in the fosse,
Souls out of Erebus, cadaverous dead . . .

Cantos I.28–9

In fossam fluebat autem sanguis niger, <u>congregataeque sunt</u>
Animae ex Erebo cadaverum mortuorum

Divus 11.36–7

Omitting *congregataeque sunt* ('and were gathered') effects poeticization through condensation, replacing the image's gradual construction across line break in Homer and Divus ('gathering' . . . 'souls' . . . 'out of Erebus') with the stark, pared-down epiphany *souls out of Erebus*.[63] Here Pound prompts the reader to resupply the verb of the preceding clause (*flowed*). The result evokes a symmetrical exchange, whereby blood flows into the underworld and souls flow out of it, highlighting the reciprocal nature of Odysseus's blood-offering. The more compact, even iconic, phrase *souls out of Erebus*, moreover, constitutes a close match for *out of Homer* (69), suggesting a parallel between the underworld (*Erebus*) and the literary tradition (*Homer*) that emphasizes the poetological dimension of Pound's *Nekuia*.

The phrase *out of Homer* repays further scrutiny, both for its importance to the present argument and its inherent semantic multivalence. Even while the phrase's literal meaning pinpoints Divus's translation source, the preposition 'out of' perhaps also calques the Greek phrase ἐξ Ὁμήρου (*ex Homérou*; *ex Homero* in Latin): Plato uses the phrase three times in the *Ion*'s discussion of poetic inspiration, while Porphyry also uses it to state the general hermeneutical principle of 'explaining Homer out of Homer'.[64] Beyond activating Homer's traditional association with the 'origin of all things' through the identification with Ocean,[65] we might read the choice of 'out of' as polemical: the phrase may evoke separation, placing the Poundian project 'outside' the Homeric source; there may also be a subtle suggestion that the narrator (and Divus before him) has, through the act of translation, exhausted – 'run out of' – Homer.[66] Canto I's polemical edge to its rewriting can also be found in the very instrument the Poundian narrator uses to fend off Homeric ghosts, *the narrow sword* (*Cantos* I.39) – transforming Divus's *acutum* 'sharp' (11.48) – refiguring the poet's pen as a combative weapon.[67] Finally, Canto I's translation focus on Odysseus's narration rather than that of the Homeric narrator may further underscore Pound's qualified opposition to the master discourse of ancient Greek epic. While the *Odyssey* signals the functional parallelism between Odysseus and its narrator – at 11.368 Alcinous compares Odysseus's story-telling to that of a 'poet' (ἀοιδός, *aoidós*) – their rhetorical agendas are sufficiently distinct to provide Pound with a productive tension.[68]

Whatever the full import of Pound's literary re-fashioning of Homer's authorial presence, Canto I forcefully foregrounds and combines two literary layers, one Latinate, the other Saxonist, that evade Homeric language. Pound effects further distancing from the Homeric text by accessing both these layers through translation, in the case of Renaissance Latin, through the translation idiom of Divus, in the case of the Anglo-Saxon *Seafarer*, through his own previous translation. Beyond the larger cultural associations of both Anglo-Saxon poetry and Renaissance Latin, which motivated Pound to forge a unique blend of the two, Pound identifies in their respective anticipation of free verse a common principle and for his synthesis of the two layers specifically exploits their potential, within the sphere of the English language, to be brought into direct dialogue with each other.

As to rhythm, Pound's critical writings show that he saw both Old English poetry's metrical flexibility and Divus's literal line-by-line prose rendering of the *Odyssey* as precursors to twentieth-century modernism's free verse. In an unpublished paper, Pound says that Anglo-Saxon poetry's alliterative meter 'is possibly radical in [i.e. at the root of] all proper *vers libre* in our language'.[69] Divus provides a complementary, if markedly different, model for Canto I's free verse. The *Odyssea Latina*'s accidental free verse evidently captivated Pound, and Hugh Kenner rightly remarks that when Pound describes Divus's *Odyssea* as 'even singable',[70] this 'amount[s] to asserting that Divus by simple fidelity has achieved Renaissance *vers libre*'.[71] Pound re-enacts his reception of Divus as poetic prose when Canto I enters the register of expository prose, or a colloquial version thereof (*I mean, that is,* etc.) in lines 68–9, without substantially disrupting its verse's flow. So while both Old English verse and Renaissance Latin 'interlinear' prose subvert the canonized rhythmical patterns of ancient epic (the dactylic hexameter) and classicizing English poetry (the iambic pentameter), Pound conceptually assimilates the two metrical schemes, suggesting a shared extra-Homeric principle of versification underlying the two traditions.

Pound carefully stages the dynamic relationship between the Germanic and the Latinate idioms and traditions from the beginning of Canto I. Thus, when six lines into the poem *canvas* appears as the first word of non-Germanic, that is, Latinate origin in the poem (from Latin *cannabis* 'hemp'),[72] the first proper name in the poem, *Circe*, immediately follows it, which in turn explicitly places the setting of Canto I in the Graeco-Roman world, specifically within the context of the *Odyssey*. This combination glimpses rather than reveals – but only a few lines later, with references to the ocean (10) and the cities of the Cimmerians (12), the Latinate stratum emerges more systematically.

As Canto I progresses, the two layers gradually achieve a balance, forging a collaborative relationship. Consider the following passage, where the Poundian narrator, after performing the blood-sacrifice, wards off the onslaught of ghosts in order to question the seer Tiresias:

> Unsheathed the narrow sword,
> I sat to keep off the impetuous impotent dead,
> Till I should hear Tiresias.

Cantos I. 39–41

Two adjectives characterize the dead here – *impetuous impotent* – in an alliterative patterning with Saxonist associations, while its individual lexemes participate in the Latinate layer (from Latin *impetuosus* 'violent' and *impotens* 'powerless', respectively). Pound likely takes the second adjective from Divus (11.49 *mortuorum impotentia capita*), while he builds the first, with no equivalent in Divus, to mirror it, albeit with a diametrically oppositional meaning. When the same Greek phrase Divus translates here occurs twenty lines earlier,[73] Divus chooses a different Latin synonym for 'powerless', *infirmus* (11.29; *mortuorum infirma capita*). Pound also varies his phrasing in adapting the earlier passage, opting there for the pointedly Germanic *sickly death's-heads* (*Cantos* I.24), where the genitive in Divus's Latin (*mortuorum*) anticipates the Saxonist genitive-compound. In sum, the literary shades Pound alternately conjures (*Then prayed I many a prayer*, 24) and restrains (*I sat to keep off*, 40) artfully combine Germanic and Latinate elements, in keeping with Pound's overall poetic agenda for this poem and *The Cantos* as a whole.[74]

CHAPTER 4

TO TRANSLATE OR NOT TO TRANSLATE? POUND'S PROSODIC PROVOCATIONS IN *HUGH SELWYN MAUBERLEY*

Demetres Tryphonopoulos and Sara Dunton

Encountering the ninth line of the opening poem of the *Hugh Selwyn Mauberley* sequence – ἴδμεν γάρ τοι πάνθ᾽ ὅσ᾽ ἐνὶ Τροίῃ / For we know all the toils that are in wide Troy[1] – today's reader will certainly turn to scholarly annotation for enlightenment. But to what degree can translation or gloss reveal the depth of allusion held within this single line of a poem written nearly a century ago? Surely, Pound expects the reader to recognize how this line works rather than expecting them to translate it. After all, the Sirens are telling Odysseus here something of which they have heard but through which he himself has lived. Of course, twenty-first-century readers and editors are far removed from what Peter Nicholls identifies as 'the cultural matrix Pound clearly felt he shared with his readers, a matrix grown by accumulation from centuries of reading and commenting on the Bible and the Classics' (2010: 11) – and, thus, they miss the point. Pound performs a version of Homer's line not only to align Mauberley with Odysseus but also to draw attention to the act of translation. In so doing, Pound intends to negotiate a new understanding of Homer with his reader: the point is not to simply seek an accurate translation but rather to translate desire for readerly attention into a narrative which is, in this instance, being emptied of its original meaning and reinvented for the twentieth century.

The fact that Pound's original audience had knowledge of the classics and classical prosody was important, but this did not prevent Pound from complicating his readers' task by obliging them to navigate the poem's copious references; as they proceed to read while recognizing (or missing) nuances and ironies, Pound effectively introduces himself into the quoted text. He further provokes his audience into a relationship with the classics by integrating modified passages from classical poets into his modern lament, wielding what Nicholls calls Pound's particularly 'allusive habit of mind' (2010: 11). *Mauberley* is the kind of text that nurtures in readers this requisite habit of mind, helping them to discover, appreciate and comprehend certain behaviours of language that Pound revives and modernizes at the same time. It is worth remembering that Pound began deliberate experimentation with classical prosody considerably before composing *Mauberley*. Most notably in his 1912 poem 'Apparuit', Pound uses the constrained quantitative meter of Sapphic stanzas,[2] a meter that Stephen Adams classifies as 'wholly artificial' (1997: 66) to English readers and their perceptions of sound and rhythm.[3] In *Mauberley*, Pound alludes to his own process of experimentation, to the disjunction between the classical verse he reveres and the free verse that, as a modernist prosodist, he is championing: in the third section of part I, the poet laments: 'The pianola 'replaces' / Sappho's barbitos' (I.3.35–6), and Pound then presents a sequence of allusions to classical writers and works concealed within the prosodic structure of the poem. He fully exploits this significant strategy throughout *The Cantos*, beginning with Canto I, wielding allusions to Homeric and Sapphic texts through layered translations and appropriation of prosodic fragments.

There is ample evidence of Pound's tactics – his subtle deployment of prosody as a hermeneutic tool – in three distinct instances found in Part I of *Mauberley*. This discussion examines these three passages, and aims to explicate how Pound uses original classical passages which, if they are only translated literally, lose their function and readerly power in modern contexts. Pound himself draws attention to these limitations at the outset of *Mauberley* by announcing the failure of his poet-speaker to 'resuscitate the dead art / Of poetry; to maintain "the sublime" / In the old sense. Wrong from the start –' (I.1.2–4). This essay invites today's readers not only to follow Pound's lead in 'resuscitat[ing] the dead art' by explaining allusions in this manner, but also to re-evaluate how (and why) Pound himself provoked his own audience to do the same.

Most importantly, the three chosen passages demonstrate Pound's dexterity: his motions of tactical omission, lexicographical play and syntactical grafting all constitute the 'prosodic allusions'[4] under study here. The first example, already introduced, is the Homeric line that appears in the poem's third stanza, where Pound does far more than evoke a learned text by 'borrowing' a line from *The Odyssey*. Closer comparison of *Mauberley*'s line with its appearance in Homer's text reveals that Pound omits the final word of Homer's line, εὐρείη, a feminine epithet translated as 'wide'. Most editors, however, miss Pound's act of omission, and include εὐρείη in their annotations of his poem without explanation, or perhaps by simply copying the original line without recognizing that this is proof, in Pound's eyes, of the gaps in their poetic (and prosodic) *paideia*. In the second instance, from the final quatrain of section 3, Pound again tests his reader's knowledge of classical Greek literature not only by integrating words from Pindar's Second Olympian Ode but also by playing a lexical game with the sequence of Pindar's line. And so, 'O bright Apollo, / τιν' ἄνδρα, τιν' ἥρωα, τίνα θεόν / What god, man, or hero / Shall I place a tin wreath upon!' (I.3.57–60) appears as an abridged, inverted version of the original line followed by a direct translation of Pound's version. Lastly, in the third example, Pound adapts a passage from Bion's *Lament for Adonis* (81–5): 'Some quick to arm, / some for adventure, some for fear of weakness, / some for fear of censure' (I.4.63–6) and deftly 'translates' not Bion's words but rather his syntactical patterns and characteristic use of figures of speech.

By presenting these three examples with exegeses and prosodic explications of Pound's complex and ironic praxis, this discussion of Pound's provocative tactics is intended not only to educate today's readers but also to urge them to compare themselves with Pound's audience as they read his poetry. Despite having been trained in classical works and languages, Pound's readers then (as now) need to investigate beyond straight translation of a foreign word or phrase inserted into verse. Leon Surette emphatically identifies this requirement in an interview from 2005, when he discusses the challenges of reading difficult modern texts. When asked what initially drew him to studying Pound – *The Cantos* in particular – in the 1960s, Surette replied that the appeal lay in the 'opacity of the poem' (as quoted in Tryphonopoulos 2005: 281) and in the 'necessity to do a great deal of basic spade work' (2005: 279) without relying on compendia. Surette's approach to Pound's poetics enforces the value of readers nurturing the allusive habit of mind needed to help them discover, appreciate and comprehend certain behaviours of language or semantic gestures – what Pound calls *logopoeia*, 'the dance of the intellect among words' (Pound [1934] 1954: 25). At the same time, it is also crucial for today's readers to dig into Pound's critical prose to uncover his attitudes towards the classical tradition as well as its relevance to the literary movement he was instigating. As Eileen Gregory astutely observes, Pound 'was preoccupied from the beginning of his critical writing with complex details of textual transmission, with the cultural reception of ancient texts through the medium of specific scholars, editors, translators and commentators' (1997: 44).[5] It might well be argued that, in parallel fashion, Pound integrates half-concealed prosodic allusions to classical works as 'textual transmissions' – transmissions meant to be received by his discerning and well-educated audience through the medium and traditions of prosody.

The first instance under consideration in this essay exemplifies the deftness of Pound's tactics of allusion: it is the subtle yet consequential omission of one word from the line Pound 'borrows/translates' from *The Odyssey*. Here Pound does far more than evoke a learned text: his gesture constitutes what Gregory Machacek refers to as a 'phraseological adaptation' (2007: 526). This differs from a referential allusion, Machacek explains, because it 'treats preexisting phraseology almost as a sort of physical raw material that can be cut, reworked and incorporated into a new setting' and so 'words omitted from the adopted phrase can come to be seen as significant' (2007: 527). Pound's adaptation subverts the prosody of Homer's text and undermines the narratives of Odysseus and Homer to situate his modern Mauberley in their midst. Pound deploys prosody itself as a hermeneutic tool to layer meanings meant to be unearthed by industrious readers; but he also effectively uses the implied and required act of translation as a narrative tactic, as a language of its own for the new modern age. Notably, in his discussion of Pound's 'cultural matrix', Nicholls chooses *Hugh Selwyn Mauberley* rather than *The Cantos* as his text because it 'testifies to [Pound's] anxiety that such a tradition was profoundly threatened by the violent embrace of modernity whose 'accelerated grimace' signalled the rise of consumerism and social uniformity' (2010: 2). In *Mauberley* Pound laments, then, the passing of an age and the arrival of another one that increasingly rejoices in things made of 'plaster, / ... with no loss of time' while, at the same time, it undervalues things made of 'alabaster', which constitutes a failure of appreciation for 'the 'sculpture' of rhyme' with its semantic and phonic nuances.[6] Arguably, this is not so much a case of readers' inability to identify specific references since, with a bit of help, one can make sense of the majority of a poem's copious allusions; but though the resources are available for helping a reader identify the names and even comprehend the use of the rhetorical figure in a line like 'His true Penelope was Flaubert', how is one to explain the allusive habit of mind that finds it attractive to couple Penelope and Flaubert together in this particular way? How does the poet train a reader to look beyond regular rhythm and rhyme, to recognize that such oxymorons turn out to be powerful figures of speech? Or how is one to promote the requisite allusive habit of mind given that it is something acquired and developed over time and at considerable effort? In other words, explaining who Penelope is and who Flaubert is and identifying the rhetorical figure of antonomasia is one thing; appreciating the intricacies of this coupling (and other couplings it initiates) is quite another matter altogether.

Factored into this as well is the consideration of Pound's poetic strategies before and at the time he wrote *Mauberley*. From the 1910s into the 1920s, his plaiting of Homer through citation/quotation/allusion relied heavily upon what Leah Culligan Flack identifies as his 'extractions ... from the *Odyssey* [of] fragments, images, echoes and verbal rhythms for his poetry' (2015: 110). Layered upon (or perhaps beneath) these extractions, moreover, is Pound's reliance upon prosodic manipulation of Homer's work to re-direct attention to 'the 'sculpture' of rhyme'. For Pound, these layering tactics were essential to his mission to toughen modern verse. In 'A Retrospect', he decrees that poetry must be 'as much like granite as it can be ... At least for myself, I want it so, austere, direct, free from emotional slither' (Pound [1918] 1954: 12). His choice of granite, the medium of sculpture, at once reinforces his decree and reiterates his penchant, at the time, for the modern sculptors – Gaudier-Brzeska and Epstein – he extolled in his critical writings. It also supports his formulations about interconnectivity within the creative processes of writing poetry, sculpting forms and painting canvases. Attributing materiality to verse, as he does at the outset of *Mauberley*, echoes the progressive tenets of Imagism and Vorticism – 'direct treatment of the thing' – that he wanted to uphold but already felt slipping away by the late 1910s. Reflecting on that situation in 1917, Pound positions himself alongside T.S. Eliot:

> At a particular date in a particular room two authors, neither engaged in picking the other's pockets, decided the dilutation of vers libre ... general floppiness had gone too far and that some countercurrent must be set going.... Remedy prescribed ... Rhyme and regular strophes. Result: Poems in Mr. Eliot's second volume ... also 'H.S. Mauberley'.
>
> *Pound 1932: n.p.*

Like his plea for austerity, Pound's remedy of 'rhyme and regular strophes' recalls a certain asceticism inherent in classical poetics. In *Mauberley*, the stratification of layers of textual references and allusions reflect the complexity of Pound's own discomfort in his own age; but they also demonstrate his purposefulness in incorporating fragments of ancient texts that draw attention to prosody. And so, in line 9 of *Mauberley*'s opening section, readers encounter Homer's line: ἴδμεν γάρ τοι πάνθ᾽, ὅσ᾽ ἐνὶ Τροίῃ. In his study of the poem, John Espey provides a sophisticated gloss:

> The basic theme is the portrait of the poet as Odysseus, who has heard the Sirens' song (ἴδμεν γάρ τοι πάνθ᾽, ὅσ᾽ ἐνὶ Τροίῃ εὐρείῃ: 'For we know all the things that are in Troy', *Od.* 12.189), who has fished by the 'obstinate isles' of his voyage ...

whose 'true Penelope was Flaubert' not only in his search for exact expression but also in his effort to expose the stupidity of accepted ideas, and who prefers to admire and actively love beauty for itself however dangerous ('Circe's hair') rather that applaud the banalities inscribed on sundials or the clichés of public action summarized by 'the march of events'.

1955: 85

Espey's exegesis exhibits skilled erudition. And yet, much of the 'spade work' remains to be done and, moreover, our understanding of what Pound means by his quotation/allusion remains unsaid. What Pound might mean in quoting it in the original language straight from the *Odyssey* rather than, as he does in Canto I, through a translation of a translation into an Anglo-Saxon sounding, alliterative modern English? A translation of the line is made readily available by editors: 'For we know all the toils that are in wide Troy' – which for many readers will be sufficient. And, thus, a reader familiar with Homer's epic in translation may think immediately of the seductive female Sirens, sitting in their meadow with a huge pile of bones around them, charming Odysseus with their clear-sounding song of all that happened in wide Troy or of Odysseus *polytropos* – 'the man of many twists and turns' – who is enjoying the song without risk to his wellbeing or that of his companions who have been prevented from experiencing this thrill by having their ears smeared with 'honey-sweet wax' (*Od.* 12.39–54).

Closer attention to Pound's quotation of this line read alongside Homer's text yields two surprising facts: first, many of the familiar scholarly editions get the Greek wrong; and second, most editors and readers miss the fact that in transcribing the line Pound has omitted the final word of the original line, εὐρείη (wide), which is included nonetheless in most annotations without explanation. Adding to the confusion, Espey provides the Homeric line intact, but his translation ignores its final word. Editors who translate the word without pointing to its absence in Pound's text are possibly unaware of this fact – and, more significantly, they fail to identify the fragmentary or at least incomplete nature of Pound's quotation, despite Pound's deictic gesture in omitting the line's final word. (So much for Pound's later attempt in Canto 105 to persuade readers to learn a 'little Greek' along with him if we wish to understand his poetry and the tradition he is resuscitating in it!)[7] Presumably, in omitting this epithet, Pound is testing the reader's knowledge of classical literary tradition. More specifically, the omission of εὐρείη tests the reader's rhythmic sense, since it deprives the heroic dactylic hexameter Homeric line[8] of its concluding three syllables, something Pound cunningly insinuates with his macaronic rhyme (Τροίη [Troīēi]/lee-way). In other words, Pound withholds the pleasure of the Homeric line (besides withholding the sense of syntactical arrival), substituting the internal rhyme (Τροίη [Troīēi]/εὐρείη [eureiēi]) with that of the easy satisfaction of macaronic rhyming. And all of this in a line that presumably celebrates wisdom, historical knowledge as well as the mystery, power and danger of *melos* and of *melopoeia*, the Sirens' and the text's tempting song. Indeed, Pound tampers with the Homeric line's *melos*: the disyllabic gap he introduces undermines the Sirens' narrative and the power of their temptation while setting up a mocking, macaronic, 'cheap' temptation with the disyllabic 'lee-way' – indeed, here 'The pianola "replaces" / Sappho's barbitos' (I.3.35–6). But is anyone paying attention, or, rather – given the distance from the 'cultural matrix' identified by Nicholls – is anyone trained today to pay attention?

Second, for a poet so intent on using personae or masks, it is important to think about who the speaker of this line might be: (i) 'E.P.', the poem's speaker, is quoting a line in a poem by Ezra Pound who is (ii) quoting from an epic poem in which (iii) 'Homer' is quoting (iv) Odysseus telling his story (Books 9–12) to the Phaeacians while he is (v) remembering Circe's warnings and instructions earlier in Book 11 and (vi) quoting the Sirens who are (vii) quoting a story that turns out to be (viii) the first and last singing in the *Odyssey* of the story of 'Homer's' *Iliad* ('Homer' quoting himself), which is referring to Odysseus's own heroic deeds in 'wide Troy'. This layering or paratactic narrative regarding the line's transmission (especially given the emphasis on Peisistratus's role in ensuring the establishment of the Homeric texts)[9] is surely a matter of great significance, especially in a poem concerned with the role of the Athenian tyrant in ensuring the canonical formulation, survival and transmission of the Homeric epics. The poem is concerned with the preservation and transmission of the tradition of *melos*, which Peisistratus made possible.

Still, there is another kind of layering that is taking place here: the line Pound transmits by including it in his poem alludes to the dangers of the epic *periplous*/journeying – physical, intellectual and perhaps spiritual. Pound also suggests, by staging this omission himself, that there are dangers in mis-transmission or inadvertent omissions. Though the line reports on what Odysseus later says he heard the Sirens sing, it also evokes at least three other instances where the incident has been foretold and its dangers explained: (i) In *Od.* 12.39–54, Circe has outlined how the Sirens charm all men who approach in ignorance, advising Odysseus on what to do in order to avoid the danger while still enjoying the experience of listening to the bardic song; (ii) in 12.158–64, Odysseus passes the message on to his crew, turning Circe's teasing suggestion into a compelling proposition; and (iii) in 12.178–83 Odysseus describes how his companions tied him to the mast just as the Sirens, aware of the ship's approach, were beginning their 'clear-sounding song'.

The Sirens sing and Odysseus listens: they sing of his famed heroism in the Trojan War, as recounted in the *Iliad*, reproducing the diction and rhetoric of that epic and claiming the power to bestow knowledge and pleasure:

Come hither on your way, renowned Odysseus, great glory of the Achaeans / stop your ship that you may listen to the voices of us two. / For never has any man rowed past the island in this black ship/ until he has heard the sweet voice from our lips; / instead, he has joy of it, and goes his way a wiser man. / For we know all the toils that in wide Troy / the Argives and Trojans endured through the will of the gods, / and we know all things that come to pass upon the fruitful earth.

12.184–91

The *Odyssey*'s listeners sail past the meadow of the Sirens without stress or restraint, knowing only that they have not really heard the Sirens' song. It is this song's clear and piercing melody, issuing paradoxically from the beguiling Sirens' song, that enchants Odysseus, while the audience's ears remain forever protected by temporal distance, just as the crew's are by the filter of sweet wax. Ultimately, Odysseus, the only one to hear the Sirens' song, is also the only one left to be heard, and to be heard about; he alone survives in song. In this exegesis or digression without end, the Sirens' song/*melos* contains – and this is the height of irony – no new information for Odysseus, who has 'lived' through the very toils they claim can make him 'a wiser man'. Such is the power of allusion and quotation in the hands of Pound! The narrative of experience cannot surpass the experience itself; it can only insert itself into the present with no certainty as to how it will be understood.

In addition, the very inclusion of this single quotation – not just in *Mauberley* but in any modernist poem by a writer like Pound – is a purposeful act. The presence of the fragment of the fractured Homeric line breaks the diegesis with a reminder of the present text's intertextuality and materiality. Coming to terms with these characteristics may be a precondition to discovering the key to the poem's form and/or meaning, and so, effectively, Pound wields intertextuality – as he does prosodic allusion – as a hermeneutic tool. To paraphrase Jacques Derrida, 'A [modernist] text is not a [modernist] text unless it hides from the first comer (*le premier venu*), from the first glance (*le premier regard*), the law of its composition and the rules of its game' (1981: 63). It is also helpful to think of Pound's allusion in *Mauberley* in the context of T.S. Eliot's explanation for identifying Dante's *Inferno* (lines 55–7) as his source in his notes to line 63 ('I had not thought death had undone so many') of *The Waste Land*: 'I gave the reference in my notes, in order to make the reader who recognized the allusion, know that I meant him to recognize it, and know that he would have missed the point if he did not recognize it' (1965: 128). Ultimately, Pound's ironic reading of a Homeric line suggests myriad connections and echoes; allusion to a classical text is by means of translating not the words but the rhetorical and prosodic qualities of the original – something that begins in *Mauberley*, and then in *The Cantos* becomes – as Stephen Adams has demonstrated – a Poundian signature: 'Where Pound begins with classical metres', Adams asserts, 'he makes them new' (1997: 107).[10]

Assiduous readers will search for evidence of this signature in Pound's poetry and would be well advised to dig into his critical prose to discover his preferences for the metrics and rhetoric of specific classical writers. Pound makes it clear (in many of his essays written before *Mauberley*) that his mission is not to revive their words through traditional translation but rather to determine which of their words were so enlivened that they should remain relevant in modern times. In 'A Retrospect', Pound writes: 'If a certain thing was said once for all in Atlantis or Arcadia, in 450 Before Christ or in 1290 thereafter, it is not for us moderns to go saying it over and over, or to obscuring the memory of the dead by saying the same thing with less skill and less conviction' ([1918] 1935: 11).[11] Here Pound implies that writers must demonstrate more skill and conviction to make these words new; but he is also indirectly instructing his readers to do the same. In the *ABC of Reading*, Pound offers his audience another such directive with his 'must read' list of classical writers. 'YOU WILL NEVER KNOW why I chose them, or why they were worth choosing', he asserts, 'or why you approve or disapprove of my choice, until you go to the TEXTS, the originals' (1934: 45). When it comes to his preferred ancient language, Pound affirms that 'the maximum of *melopoeia* is reached in Greek' (1934: 42), and he places Homer at the top of his 'must-read' list: 'I have never read half a page of Homer without finding melodic invention', Pound writes, 'I mean melodic invention that I didn't already know' (1934: 43). He also includes Sappho – 'the great name' – 'because of antiquity and because there is really so little left that one may as well read it as omit it' (1934: 47) and cites Bion as an important writer of melody, similar to the Provençal troubadours he admired, as one who should be held 'in contrast' to Homer and Sappho. However, on his list Pound notably does not include Pindar, the ancient poet whose 'peculiar excellence seems to have lain in the composition of victory odes' (Lattimore 1947: viii) – and he is on record as disliking Pindar's excessive style. Pound complains loudly that Pindar – 'the prize wind-bag of all ages' – bangs too loudly on a 'big rhetorical drum' (Espey 1955: 87).[12] Nevertheless, Pound's distaste for Pindar does not prevent him from adapting Pindaric phraseology: the second instance of Pound's prosodic play in *Mauberley* – somewhat surprisingly – is appropriated from the 'wind-bag'. Pound does so, perhaps, in a negative spirit, but it is not meant to undermine the significance of his act of appropriation.

And so, in the final quatrain in section 3 of Part I, Pound alludes to Pindar, tests his reader's knowledge of classical Greek literature and rewards the one who has bothered 'to learn a little greek':[13] 'O bright Apollo, / τίν' ἄνδρα, τίν' ἥρωα, τίνα θεόν / What god, man, or hero / Shall I place a tin wreath upon!' (I.3.57–60) Pound's ideal reader recognizes the context of the quotation in Pindar's Second Olympian Ode and shares in the ironic playfulness of the lexicographical game:

Ἀναξιφόρμιγγες ὕμνοι,
τίνα θεόν, τίν' ἥρωα, τίνα δ' ἄνδρα κελαδήσομεν;
ἤτοι Πίσα μὲν Διός·Ὀλυμπιάδα δ' ἔστασεν Ἡρακλέης
ἀκρόθινα πολέμου·

Pind. O. 2.1–4

A less seasoned reader may run to her Liddell and Scott's *Greek–English Lexicon* and, with some effort, make out the Greek line: 'What man, what hero, what god'; having made the considerable effort to do this and having subsequently located the original, she will be irritated to find out that Pindar's line is rendered into English in the very next line – but not quite, since Pound has inverted the original's three phrases and, additionally, has mixed up the order in his rendering and omitted the final word, the key verb, κελαδήσομεν (*keladésomen*): (i) τίνα θεόν, τίν' ἥρωα, τίνα δ' ἄνδρα κελαδήσομεν (original); (ii) τιν' ἄνδρα, τίν' ἥρωα, τίνα θεόν, (Pound's transcription, inverting the order and omitting the conjunctive particle and verb); and (iii) What god, man, or hero (Pound's translation, mixing up the order of the three items so that the rising or falling arc is no longer apparent). And as one tries to comprehend this lexicographical game and its relevance in a poem addressing Pound's 'denunciation, his contrasting [of] modern degeneracy with the classic ideal' (Espey 1955: 86), one appreciates, perhaps, the poet's ingenious questioning of modern values via a lexical game of juxtaposition, mistranscription and appropriation. And yet, the lexical game is not over since Pound picks up an elided form of the accusative interrogative masculine pronoun for 'what' (τίν') and, in the next line, transliterates it so that the line can be read sardonically as 'Shall I place a tin wreath upon' but also 'Shall I place a τίν' (= what) wreath upon?' – a pun that punctuates the poet's satirical sense of cultural degeneration.

Pound's allusions to Pindar's ode certainly demonstrate his dexterity with prosodic and syntactical play, but they also allude to his own relationship with the Greek language he extricates from ancient texts. Poundian scholarship has long weighed in – with differing viewpoints – on his limited knowledge of the language, and his ironic self-deprecation in that regard. Like his readers, the poet himself relied upon Liddell and Scott, as well as bilingual, translated editions of the Greek works, especially the Loeb Classical Library (Liebregts 2010: 172). But there is some evidence of conflicting assessments of Pound's proficiency, as Peter Liebregts reports:

> Michael Reck, one of Pound's close friends in his later years, observed that the poet's Greek was not large, and was mainly read with the help of the Loeb Classical Library translations. However, James Laughlin, Pound's American publisher, claims that Pound did have a fair knowledge of Greek, but that only the accents posed a problem . . .
>
> *2010: 172*

Liebregts notes the paradoxical probability of truth in both these accounts from Pound's friends; but he then goes on to make an interesting evaluation of his own, namely that, 'the occurrence of Greek in Pound's writings sometimes demonstrates a meticulous precision' (2010: 172). Liebregts's statement is a cautious endorsement of the poet's skill, and it certainly (though not intentionally) pinpoints the meticulous aspect of Pound's play with prosody in the sophisticated appropriations of Homer and Pindar under discussion here. It is worth noting, however, that Liebregts is concerned with Pound's ability to convey the meaning of the Greek language as he *translates* words, not as he *transmits* them through the less transparent and more nuanced form of prosody. This distinction enforces the key characteristics of Pound's early poetic practice that are manifested in *Hugh Selwyn Mauberley*: the displacement of traditional form by the modern poet and the accompanying destabilization of language. If Pound himself lacked confidence in his linguistic skills, he certainly did not doubt his own mastery of prosody, nor, for that matter, have critics then (or since) disagreed with his prosodic insights. In *Mauberley*, then, Pound turns to the ancients to draw attention to his own plight and his strategy – 'to translate, or not to translate' – to engage with the inherent organic nature of language as a medium that is both concrete and malleable, and to play with the complex structure of prosody to transform it into a pliant medium for his age.

Mauberley is the quintessential 'quoting poem',[14] oscillating as it does between citation, quotation and allusion, and exhibiting several instances of prosodic allusion. Perhaps the most spectacular of these is found in the last instance under consideration: it is encountered in the celebrated passage from section 4 of Part I, in which Pound's speaker mourns the betrayed young soldiers of World War I. Pound is on record for pointing to a Greek text surviving in fragment, Bion's *Lament for Adonis*, as his source.[15] But even Pound's identification does not prepare us for the grafting of the Greek poem's rhetorical flair into Pound's English, a brilliant adaptation of lines of a passage from Bion's bucolic pastoral which deals with the Loves' ritual preparation of Adonis's body for burial:

χὥ μὲν ὀστώς,
ὃς δ᾿ἐβαλλεν, ὃ δε πτερόν, ὃς δὲ φαέτραν·
χὥ μὲν ἔλυσε πέδιλον Ἀδόνιδος, οἵ δὲ λέβητι
χρυσείῳ φορέουσιν ὕδωρ, ὃ δὲ μηρία λούει,
ὃς δ᾿ὄπιθεν πτερύγεσσιν ἀναψύχει τὸν Ἄδωνιν.

81–5

This flung upon him arrows, that a bow, this a feather, that a quiver. One hath done off Adonis' shoe, others fetch water in a golden basin, another washes the thighs of him, and again another stands behind and fans him with his wings.

Trans. Edmonds 1977: 387

Pound 'translates' not Bion's words but rather his syntactical patterns and characteristic use of figures of speech. And so, when the lineation of Bion's text is rearranged, and set beside Pound's, the patterns emerge visually:

χὥ μὲν ὀστώς,
ὃς δ᾿ἐβαλλεν,
ὃ δε πτερόν,
ὃς δὲ φαέτραν·
χὥ μὲν ἔλυσε πέδιλον Ἀδόνιδος,
οἵ δὲ λέβητι χρυσείῳ φορέουσιν ὕδωρ,
ὃ δὲ μηρία λούει,
ὃς δ᾿ὄπιθεν πτερύγεσσιν ἀναψύχει τὸν Ἄδωνιν.

These fought in any case,
and some believing,
        Pro domo, in any case . . .
Some quick to arm,
some for adventure,
some for fear of weakness,
some for fear of censure,
some for love of slaughter, in imagination,

learning later ...
some in fear, learning love of slaughter; ...

I.4.61–70

Even those who do not read Greek should be able to appreciate the syntactical (and typographical) repetition that is at the very heart of Bion's rhetorical thrust. Of all the rhetorical devices Bion employs in his poem's highly patterned form, two stand out: isocolon (the repetition of phrases of equal length and usually corresponding structure; in this instance, a string of lines that repeat the exact syntactical progression [pronoun/ preposition/adverb/noun/[adjective]/verb]) and epanaphora. Otherwise, Bion's rhythmic structure employs regular meter (a refined, mostly dactylic, hexameter,[16] with a caesura after the third foot); normal syntax (uninverted and uninterrupted); and a controlled graphic layout (unrhymed hexameters, and standard punctuation and orthography). The text's structural discipline offers an orderly, symmetrical form used here to control and ritualize the Loves' lament for Adonis.

Since in comparison to Bion's highly inflected and syntactically flexible Greek the English available to Pound is uninflected and syntactically restrictive, Pound approximates the original's syntax (pronoun/preposition/noun/preposition/noun) and maintains Bion's use of the epanaphora. But his passionate invective against those who caused and profited from World War I is inscribed in a rhetorical explosion that draws on a number of additional figures of amplification and repetition, including (in addition to epanaphora and isocolon) epistrophe, anadiplosis, aposiopesis, anastrophe and anacoluthon – all figures that one can trace to Bion. Nevertheless, while the rhetorical devices of parallelism and order may seem to contain and control Pound's invective, it turns out that their accumulation (amplification) overwhelms the text's informational impact with an emotive and climactic force that, once unleashed, cannot be contained or qualified. In other words, syntactic expectation and visual parsing may suggest a kind of ritualizing of the experience or reaction to the experience – but the various figures of parallelism, repetition and syntactic inversion converge to question the text's regularity, further accentuating the differences between syntactical neatness and emotive raging.

The exegesis of the first example demonstrates Pound's ironic reading of a Homeric line and suggests myriad connections and echoes; in the second example, the bombastic language of a Pindaric victory ode is a superficial allusion to the ancient poet, while the clever lexical shuffling of his phrases illuminates the modern poet's purpose; in the third example, the allusion to a classical Bucolic pastoral is by means of translating not the words but the rhetorical and prosodic qualities of the original – a tactic which emerges in *Mauberley* and evolves into the complex and often obscured Poundian signature that imprints *The Cantos*.[17]

The questions raised in this discussion include the following: If we were to recognize the allusion with the poet's or editor's help, what are we likely to lose or miss, and what are we to gain? Is it possible to appreciate Poundian allusion and its meaning(s) if it has to be explained to us? Is Poundian allusion something that must depend entirely on the reader's diligence and her identification, independently of compendia and editors' annotations? Does the text withhold (by design) its subtle pleasure (τέρψη) when its provenance is not recognized by the reader themself? Does Poundian allusion gain anything from exegesis or does the Sirens' sweet song (μελίγηρυν μέλος) make sense to the few (Pound's ideal readers) only since the rest of us are not equipped to, or are prevented by our inadequate preparation from hearing it? Habits and processes have always determined scholarly practices, just as they have poetic practices; perhaps it is time now in the early twenty-first century to revive Mauberley's century-old lead: to 'resuscitate the dead art' of disciplined reading of difficult texts explicating the allusions to prosody that Pound transmitted to us through his texts, and expected us to excavate.

RESPONDENT ESSAY 1
RINGING TRUE: POUNDIAN TRANSLATION AND POETIC MUSIC
Michael Coyle

> A Great age of literature is perhaps always a great age of translations; or follows it.
>
> Pound, 'Notes on Elizabethan Classicists'[1]

> All ages are contemporaneous.
>
> Pound, *Spirit of Romance*

Over the course of his turbulent career, Ezra Pound offered numerous explanations of what *The Cantos* is about – be it 'the tale of the tribe', or 'the repeat through history', or 'a poem including history'. Scholars have discussed all of them, often brilliantly, but nearly half a century after Pound's death just about the only certainty is that there will never be certainty or consensus on the question. By contrast, there has long been a generally tacit agreement about the significance of Pound's title, 'Cantos'. When I was a graduate student exploring Pound for the first time, the late Dan Albright told us that the title was merely provisional. In this understanding he was on sanctioned ground: Hugh Kenner thought so, too. Nevertheless, it has always struck me as odd, unlikely even, that so restless a poet as Pound would have clung to a mere stop-gap of a title for the better part of a long lifetime. What if he meant it? What difference would it make to our reading of *The Cantos* if we were to take this title seriously? To a certain extent, this critical consensus that the title doesn't matter reflects an unease caused by the very mission of academic criticism. We are here to explain the *meaning* of complex and difficult things. Except for the handful of scholars with philological training who find their way into modernist studies – among which small number we are here fortunate to find Massimo Cè, Demetres Tryphonopolous and George Varsos – most of us who write about modernist literature are hermeneuts, schooled in one form or another of interpretation. We tend to be more comfortable explicating *Hugh Selwyn Mauberley* or Canto IV than we are, say, something apparently simple, like the red wheelbarrow poem in William Carlos Williams's *Spring and All*. So, again, what if 'Cantos' is exactly the title that Pound wanted? It has been my growing conviction for some time now that the principles distinguishing one canto from another are less about sense than they are about sound. Despite the rhythms and cadences that link cantos into groups, no two cantos *sound* alike.

For serious translators, sound – the material *feel* of a poem – often pulls against attempts to render the meaning of a poem. As Varsos suggests, there is often a tension between 'formal clarity and conceptual solidity'. Is it, for instance, more important to preserve Dante's *terza rima*, or render precisely his theological, philosophical, or political meanings? Should a translator preserve the oral formulae of the Homeric poems so important to Bronze Age audiences (and 'audience' in the literal sense is the important factor here – poetry to be heard) or minimize them so as not to weary modern *readers*. Pound himself, as Varsos notes, was very much alive to this conundrum, to the tension between 'meaningfulness' and 'semantic contours'. Advising Michael Reck over the latter's work with Japanese poetry, Pound enjoined him 'Don't bother about the WORDS, translate the MEANING' (Kenner 1971: 150). But, famously, as the poems of *Cathay* or 'Homage to Sextus Propertius' make clear, Pound was much less interested in 'meaning' in its hermeneutical sense than he was in the cultural 'impact' of great work.

Ronnie Apter, in her too seldom noticed study of translation after Pound (1984: 9), explored this commitment in the context of Matthew Arnold and F.W. Newman's debate over translation. Arnold laid out both positions in his essay 'On Translating Homer' (1860):

> It is disputed, what aim a translator should propose to himself in dealing with his original. Even this preliminary is not yet settled. On one side it is said, that the translation ought to be such 'that the reader should, if possible, forget that it is a translation at all, and be lulled into the illusion that he is reading an original work; something original', (if the translation be in English), 'from an English hand'. The real original is in this case, it is said, 'taken as a basis on which to rear a poem that shall affect our countrymen as the original may be conceived to have affected its natural hearers'. On the other hand, Mr. Newman, who states the foregoing doctrine only to condemn it, declares that he 'aims at precisely the opposite: to retain every peculiarity of the original, so far as he is able, with the greater care the more foreign it may happen to be'; so that it may 'never be forgotten that he is imitating, and imitating in a different material'. The translator's 'first duty', says Mr. Newman, 'is a historical one; to be faithful.' Probably both sides would agree that the translator's 'first duty is to be faithful'; but the question at issue between them is, in what faithfulness consists.

Today neither Arnold nor Newman are much respected as translators, but like Pound before us we are still debating the question. What is it that the translator endeavours to carry over? Apter argues that 'at heart, Pound was a convinced follower of Newman, imbued with a sense of the wondrous otherness of the past' (1984: 21) and, for all the differences in language and form that distinguish Pound's translations from those of the Victorian, she makes an important point. Pound's translations work to make readers experience again the impact of the original. This effort to 'make it new' involves a deeply aestheticized sense of history as well as an intensely historicized sense of aesthetic power. What worked for Sextus Propertius can't work for moderns precisely because they already know, or think they know, Propertius. As translator, Pound works to foreground our distance from the original even as he carries it over to us. For the affirmation that 'all ages are contemporaneous' to carry any force, readers must first sense cultural otherness in historical distance ([1910] 2005: 8).

Introducing the New Directions volume of Pound's translations, Kenner proposed that 'translating does not, for [Pound], differ in essence from any other poetic job; as the poet begins by seeing, so the translator by reading; but his reading must be a kind of seeing' (Pound 1970: 10). For all that Pound celebrates the vision of the masters before him, he is finally more interested in the material traces they have left – not 'behind' but forward. Massimo Cè's focus on that Poundian meme 'out of', as in 'out of Erebus' or 'out of Homer', proves here especially fortunate, especially because he links it to Porphyry's principle of 'explaining Homer out of Homer'. All three of these essays observe that principle. But, as a motif in *The Cantos*, 'out of' leads to the question of historical mediation. Twenty years ago, now, as Dunton and Tryphonopoulos note, Eileen Gregory observed that Pound 'was preoccupied from the beginning of his critical writing with complex details of textual transmission, with the cultural reception of ancient texts through the medium of specific scholars, editors, translators, and commentators' (1997: 44). In other words, his interest was less in origins than in the process of movement through time, and in the formal and material changes that accompany such movement. But Cè rightly pauses over the 'semantic multivalence' of the phrase (and thanking both the editors and Varsos for instigating his further reflections), Cè notes that

> the phrase may evoke separation, placing the Poundian project 'outside' the Homeric source; there may also be a subtle suggestion that the narrator (and Divus before him) has, through translating itself, exhausted – 'run out of' – Homer.

Cè's immediate concern is Pound's self-conscious relationship with Homer, but his argument offers to be read more broadly as a way of framing Pound's activities as a translator. In Pound's hands translation is less about reverence than it is revision; it leaves behind the original text in a journey necessary for a return, of sorts. For Pound, the past is never really gone. The classics survive as something infinitely more alive than artefacts of a vanished culture. Instead, the classics represent the possibility of recovering the materiality of an otherwise vanished past. As literary translation thus offers a way materially to re-present the past it simultaneously provides a way for literature really to be 'news that stays news' ([1934] 2010: 29).

Poetic material history differs from the kinds collected in museums – that other site where Victorians pursued their obsession with history and their own place in it, hoping to find guidance for their empire building. Translating ancient languages differs from the transporting of ancient artefacts because the materiality of poetry is something that can be felt and experienced but not exactly touched: patterns of sound – poetic 'music', the unfamiliar sounds of a foreign tongue. Where museums typically present fragments or ruins, plunder from a global empire, translations endeavour to deliver an artwork whole: not as a relic but as something still living, or something to which the poet-translator has brought new life. Translation was for Pound a form of criticism, and Pound resolutely maintained that the strongest form of criticism is always the creation of a genuinely new work of art. Pound's translations effectually solve the problem of nineteenth-century historicism; where historicists like Leopold von Ranke or even Sir Walter Scott saw the past as irreducibly strange, Pound's translations simultaneously celebrate 'the wondrous otherness' of the past while affirming that 'all ages are contemporaneous' ([1910] 2005: 8). A great translation requires both sides of this tension to remain in place. Without the experience of alterity the affirmation of contemporaneity could not but be trivial. In Pound's translations, this balance is managed on the level of language itself, a language invariably alive to its own material properties. Language, Pound wrote in 1915, 'is made out of concrete things' ([1950] 1981: 91).

The arguments of Varsos, Cè, Dunton and Tryphonopolous all, in their distinct ways, proceed from this recognition. All recognize the materiality of poetry as crucial to Pound's praxis. But these three essays get there in different ways and do different things with their insight. Varsos frames his discussion of Pound by turning to another modernist – one whose ideological commitments would have put him at odds with Pound but who nevertheless was no less preoccupied with modernity's relation to history: Walter Benjamin. Varsos deploys, of course, Benjamin's essays 'On Translation' (1923) and 'On the Mimetic Faculty' (1933), taking especial interest in Benjamin's sense that 'translatability is an essential attribute of certain works'. Needless to say, in noting that 'certain' works invite translation Benjamin suggests an inevitable corollary: other works resist it. The nature of that resistance is not Dunton and Tryphonopolous's focus, but they nonetheless comment that

> Pound turns to the ancients to draw attention to his own plight and his strategy – 'to translate, or not to translate' – to engage with the inherent organic nature of language as a medium that is both concrete and malleable, and to play with the complex structure of prosody to transform it into a pliant medium for his age.

It is in this condition of being 'both concrete and malleable' that something made out of air – out of breath – finds its peculiar condition. The concreteness of language is sensible, but it is also subject to change across time and space alike. Dunton and Tryphonopolous focus on 'Mauberley', but their argument pertains much more broadly. For instance, in 'Mauberley' I.4, 'Pound 'translates' not Bion's words but rather his syntactical patterns and characteristic use of figures of speech'; he translates, insofar as differences between the two languages allow, the feel of Bion's language – what he imagines as the impact of his poetry. This is good, but Dunton and Tryphonopolous carry their point an important step further, observing that Pound's attribution of 'materiality to verse, echoes the progressive tenets of Imagism and Vorticism – 'direct treatment of the thing': in the case of translation the 'thing' becomes the original poem. The translation thus attempts to represent not the original vision of another poem but that poem itself.

To be fair, my interest here is in something that Dunton and Tryphonopolous, as well as Cè and Varsos, observe in the course of making their sometimes rather different points. And yet all three essays observe the materiality of language – and that they do so is by no means a given. These three essays together might be a sign of still-forming twenty-first-century attitudes about translation. In any case, this attitude shapes arguments that are not overtly about linguistic materiality. When, for instance, Dunton and Tryphonopolous question whether poetic allusions can still do their work if readers rely on editors or scholars to notice them, the question seems to be about meaning and significance, but soon enough implicitly acknowledges the music of the original phrases:

> Does Poundian allusion gain anything from exegesis or does the Sirens' sweet song (μελίγηρυν μέλος) make sense to the few (Pound's ideal readers) only since the rest of us are not equipped to, or are prevented by our inadequate preparation from hearing it?

My suggestion would be that this music, siren or otherwise, does not depend on a recognition of source, and even if an English-language reader does not know how to pronounce the Greek the sheer alterity of the Greek tells them that they are not in Kansas anymore. As T.S. Eliot wrote in his 1929 essay 'Dante', 'genuine poetry can communicate before it is understood' (2015: 701). Pound himself was the inheritor of what was even then already a century-old tradition, going back to Hegel, of thinking that music is the art of arts precisely because it bypasses the rational mind and works directly on the soul; Pound was no great reader of Hegel, but he was intimate with Yeats, who pushed the argument even harder than his German forebear. 'All art', Yeats wrote in 'Speaking to the Psaltery' is 'a monotony in external things for the sake of an internal variety, a sacrifice of gross effects to subtle effects, an asceticism of the imagination' ([1902] 1961: 25). Poetic music needed to be subtle and must work against the bullying of reason and a demand for simplicity and for sense. Poetic music may acquire meaning, but its principal function is beyond, or at least other than, meaning. It is the crucial feature by which a poem will always be something more than any account of it. For something to ring true it first has to *ring*.

I am grateful for the ways in which Varsos follows and extends Venuti's (1995) analysis of the domesticating transparency that governs modern practices of translation. This kind of domestication typically takes the form of making modern translations sound as close as possible to something emerging from our own time. Varsos sustains a productive focus on Pound's word to translators of Greek: 'more sense and less syntax', and carries us a good way towards understanding that injunction more fully. But I note, too, his raising 'the question of quiddity, that is, of the very nature of literary thingness'. Varsos's emphasis is generally more hermeneutic than mine here, but this question of 'quiddity' pulls in a different, and rich, direction. Not surprisingly, because Cè is clearly familiar with Varsos's work, it also informs Cè's explanation of how Pound's translation can be both loose and literal. In fact, Cè's demonstration of Pound's deliberate strategy to highlight the Latinity of his source text, Andreas Divus's *Odyssea Latina*, is here invaluable. Of course Pound was interested in 'the repeat through history' – in the formal changes he discerned while watching a particular vision change form through history – but he was also struck by what he heard in Divus's Latin music. I could do no better than to quote Cè's conclusion:

> In sum, the literary shades Pound alternately conjures (24 *Then prayed I many a prayer*) and restrains (40 *I sat to keep off*) are an artful composite of Germanic and

Latinate elements, in keeping with Pound's overall poetic agenda for this poem and *The Cantos* as a whole.

Among the many other things we can understand them to be, the *Cantos* are a compendium of music across both time and space, and translation appears beginning and late as one of Pound's most important means of incorporating other musics into his poem including history.

I am reading these three essays in what is certainly a pointed way: my reflections are prompted by the cumulative effect of having read them together. Curiously, it proves that attending to Pound's work as a translator offers to afford insight into the very heart of his poetic practice. Translation is thus not marginal to Pound's work but central. It seems to me that, over the course of his career and depending on his subject material, Pound's objectives in translation were subject to change. His approach was always that of a poet; it was never mechanical – never one formula to be applied in all cases. But he continued to practise the art of translation from his very earliest work until the last years of his life: *Love Poems of Ancient Egypt*, on which he worked with Noel Stock, was published in 1961 – one of the last things he lived to complete – and Richard Sieburth's edition of *Poems and Translations* (2003) concludes with uncollected translations that Pound completed between 1905–71 – from before the publication of his first book of poetry until just months before his death. These essays, then, suggest that translation for Pound represented perhaps his ultimate form of engagement with language itself.

PART II
H.D.'S TRANSLATIONS OF EURIPIDES: GENRE, FORM, LEXICON

CHAPTER 5
TRANSLATION AS MYTHOPOESIS: H.D.'S
HELEN IN EGYPT AS META-PALINODE
Anna Fyta

In his unpublished paper on the motif of wealth in Aeschylus's *Persae* and Herodotus's *Historiae,* Ioannis Perysinakis makes a most poignant observation: 'The tragedians turn History into tragic myth or "mythicized history"' (2016: 1). A similar, anthropologically tinted view arguing that myths become embodied in a community's sphere of truths has also been noted by Gregory Nagy in his foreword to Richard P. Martin's 1989 study *The Language of Heroes: Speech and Performance in the Iliad.* Nagy's understanding conveys the shortcomings of modernity for which 'myth has become the opposite of fact, the antithesis of truth' (1989: xi). In a letter to Bryher (Winifred Ellerman) dated 2 September 1953, H.D. expresses parallel concerns over an author's quest for validation of the mythic construct. In seeking authentication through dramatic agency, she observes that the encounter between Achilles and Helen, the pivotal incident that marks the reconnaissance of the two heroes, is 'authentic, Euripides refers to it' (Hollenberg 1997: n. 62, 171). H.D.'s enigmatic caption at the beginning of the 'Pallinode', the first segment of her tripartite long poem *Helen in Egypt,* her own translation of Euripides' play and Stesichorus's poem on Helen of Troy, announces with stark matter-of-factness that '[Helen] is both phantom and reality' (1974: 3). Like Herodotus, who alludes to Aeschylus's dramatic rendition of the Persian expedition to Greece to create a textual springboard for his *Historiae,* H.D. resorts, once again, to Euripides the dramatist, and Stesichorus, begetter of the term 'palinode', to validate and historicize her own 'Pallinode', the translation and re-writing of Helen of Troy in *Helen in Egypt* (1974: 1).[1] Her apprenticeship in Euripidean dramaturgy takes a different turn in this poem as its 'anti-mythic' subjectivity, Helen, is filtered and translated through the form of the palinode.[2] The focus of this essay is Euripides' rendition of *Helen* as instrumental text in the making of *Helen in Egypt.* I challenge the directives of this form and deploy its capacity to be malleable or unsettled in relation to its origins. H.D. reaches beyond the restorative, corrective aims of Euripides' or Stesichorus's works and transforms her long poem into what I call a 'meta-palinode'. The prefix 'meta-' evokes a narrative of *nostos,* a return, or a regressive attempt to retrieve the originary text while the term 'palimpsest', with its circuitous dynamics pointing toward the beginnings, further enhances the notion of *nostos,* the Odyssean-like desire for a figural return homeward.[3]

As meta-palinode, *Helen in Egypt* first negotiates with, and muses on, the nature and boundaries of the palinode and, second, the temporal and spatial fluidity of Egypt enables H.D.'s translation to assume its allegorical status in the realm between philosophy and poetry.[4] Embedded in *Helen in Egypt* are three seminal, meta-palinodic practices to furnish the poetic and tropological body H.D. deploys when she translates *Helen* 'after' Euripides' play. The first is generic; the poem never drops its theatricality or, in H.D.'s phrasing, its dramatic *accoutrements* such as the stage, the stage set and the chorus; the second practice involves H.D.'s application of arcane prosodic practices she borrows from epic and lyric poetry; and the third practice posits the philosophical alongside the poetic.[5]

Theorizations on the nature and generic peculiarities of the palinode have a long history. Chamaeleon, a peripatetic scholar and philosopher of the fourth century BC, asserts that the palinode is a transgressive poetic form rebelling against Homeric authority; according to him, Euripides has followed Stesichorus in devising the genealogical line and portrayal of many of his original characters.[6] Based on this assumption, the palinode has frequently been classified as a protean poetic form voicing from the start its insubordination to the originary sources to which it owes its textual 'being'.[7] Not coincidentally, critical assessment of H.D.'s long palimpsestic poem has articulated similar concerns over its generic instability and ideological framing: 'H.D. opens *Helen in Egypt* with a clear statement of this revisionary nature, signaling that it will in many ways de-familiarize familiar ideas about Helen and her story' (Bibb 2010: 110).

In 1918, during her post-Imagist engagement with classical Greece, H.D. still pursues her translation projects with Euripidean choral odes and the Greek Anthology. In a feature article in the *Dial*, the poet Richard Aldington, H.D.'s former husband and co-editor of the short-lived Poets' Translation Series, offers three installments titled 'Letters to an Unknown Woman'. His views on the unknown women who strive to break away from the shadows introduce the fine semantic line that divides palimpsest from palinode:

> Helen the queen and Sappho the poet are 'unknown' to us because their legends have been altered and overlaid by so many men of different personalities that we have difficulty in deciphering the true character from the additions. Like all very great people they have become what we wished them to be, and those who seek the truth about them must search for it among a thousand lies.
>
> *226*

Aldington's choice of the names of Helen and Sappho as instances of male misconception or phantasmal outgrowth translates them into paradigms for the definition of the palimpsest. His interpretive example sheds light upon a part of the groundwork for H.D.'s *Helen in Egypt* which, as a palinode, sets out to correct the 'thousand lies' that have been told in her name and about her name.[8]

In its first stages the Helen project includes two preliminary works in progress: H.D.'s 'uncorrected', sporadically annotated essay 'Helen in Egypt' from *Notes on Euripides, Pausanias and Greek Lyric Poets* (1920) and the poem 'Helen' (originally written in 1923 and published in H.D.'s 1924 collection *Heliodora*).[9] The latter poem presages H.D.'s epic with its embedded irony and its 'use of Greece as a synecdochal representation of the western world . . . [and as] a culture that loves to hate the war and loves to compose songs for beautiful scapegoats' (Fyta 2015: 269). H.D. begins working on *Helen in Egypt* in the summer of 1952 at Lugano. She first divides the written poem, totalling twenty books, into three sections, 'Pallinode', 'Leuké' and 'Eidolon'. Helen's reconstructive journey takes her to Egypt, the island of Leuké, locus of Achilles' afterlife, Troy, Mount Ida, Sparta and back in Egypt.

Helen in Egypt recognizes its own textual ancestry through its complex structure, multiple referentiality, temporal dislocation, targeted multiculturalism, presumed generative indebtedness, and ongoing exchange with Ezra Pound's *Cantos*.[10] H.D.'s long poem becomes the direct descendant of two authors who break away from the norm of the Helen myth: 'Stesichoros was the first to treat Helen, an established figure of the Homeric saga, at variance with the epic tradition [. . .] [In tragedy] the heroine is [also] seriously re-evaluated, especially in the works of Euripides' (Constantinidou 2008: 166). The dialogue between Euripides and Stesichorus and their intention to work 'at variance' with the canonized tradition of the epic does not escape H.D. when she purposely breaks from the norm of the Helen myth and becomes involved in the re-evaluative process.

In her praxis, H.D. pays homage to both Greek authors and then orients her palimpsestic poem in alignment with Euripides' dramatic text: 'Stesichorus of Sicily was the first one to tell us. Some centuries later, Euripides repeats the story [. . .] the later little understood. *Helen in Egypt* is a Pallinode, a defense, explanation or apology' (1974: 1). H.D. returns the palinode back, 'again', to poetry, its generic source, but chooses to furnish the body of her poem with stage instructions and prose meditational pieces, or, to use Susan Barbour's cinematographic term, 'prose captions'.[11]

H.D.'s second choice in the construction of the meta-palinode occurs within the poetic writing process; it signals an advancement in her conjoint treatment of the lyric mode and choral voice. In its assimilation of other Euripidean textual precedents, *Helen in Egypt* revisits previous Euripidean plays, summoning transgressive figures like Iphigenia, Clytemnestra and Electra, women from the House of Atreus. H.D.'s mythic genealogical gesture alludes to earlier stages of her Euripidean apprenticeship when she was translating choral and lyric parts from *Iphigenia in Aulis* or fragments from *Electra*. Her third practice, involving the trope of the eidolon, Helen's spectral subjectivity, in the philosophical discourse H.D. receives from Euripides, Stesichorus and their predecessors, serves as one of the cornerstones in the ideological structure of H.D.'s epic poem.

Caroline Whitbeck eloquently outlines the difference between palinode and palimpsest, counterpoising these two frequently used central notions in H.D. discourse:

> whereas palinode and palimpsest alike are multiply-written or phantasmic texts, palinode splits from palimpsest, as it does from notions of dialogism, in the irruptions it stages of mixed media (such as textuality with orality, textuality with visuality, and so forth) that 'repeats' the palinode's tradition of lyric poetry ventriloquizing and revising epic, the phantom replacing the 'real'.
>
> *2013: 3*

The theoretical premises Whitbeck postulates in this distinction between palimpsest and palinode disclose the interconnectedness of the latter to other genres and tropological variables. The imitational, 'ventriloquistic' aspect of the palinode enables its simultaneous departure from and co-existence with the epic, progenitor of all 'real' texts.

In attempting to delineate briefly the sources that inspired Euripides to write his own *Helen* Palinode, a heretic play and a recantation for the unfavourable portrayal of Helen in his previous works, facts, and conjecture blend.[12] What is generally accepted is the fact that the Homeric Helen and Stesichorus's reinstated, corrected version of Helen emerge as mythic paradigms that Euripides explores in *Helen*.[13] The palinodic plot in Euripides' *Helen* relates the years she spent in Egypt under the protection of King Proteus while her phantom, her *eidolon*, was in Troy (44–6).[14] Following Euripides, the reference to the palinode as an intricate form of song is found in Plato's *Phaedrus*; Stesichorus's poem on Helen is referred to as 'a hymn that interweaves a complex narrative fabric that celebrates Eros in mythical and poetic language [...] But the form in which the palinode is cast should not mislead. Its serious purpose guarantees as far as Socrates is concerned that it is a **true** story' (Pl. *Phdr.* 257a3–4n). But similar concerns with narratological veracity have already been expressed in the Euripidean *Helen*. In her opening monologue, Helen of Troy questions the truth of her conception and birth: εἰ σαφὴς οὗτος λόγος, 'if this story is true' (Eur. *Hel.* 21). The rhetorical hypothesis gives her a starting point to explain that her story is the 'true' one unlike the spurious version of herself, the illusion, the *eidolon* that went to Troy.

Froma Zeitlin's interpretation of the Euripidean Helen myth in 'The Lady Vanishes' adds the ontological parameter of its female protagonist into the equation; the palinode exists because of the eidolon: 'the palinode is, [...] itself a doublet in verse, functioning as one side of a diptych, or better still, it is like a mirror effect that returns a reversed image of the first' (2010: 265). The refractive angle Zeitlin poses as a necessary link in her definition presupposes an exclusive polarity in the relation between mirror and eidolon and yet in the case of *Helen in Egypt* the palinode reads more like a shattered mirror whose shards refract multiple spectral facets of the original image, or, in H.D.'s words, 'she whom you cursed/ was but the phantom and shadow/ thrown from a reflection' (1974: 5). The inconclusiveness of Helen's persona, both real and spectral, does not escape H.D.'s attention since the co-existence of 'phantom' and 'shadow from a reflection' multiply indefinitely the textual variables on Helen and underscore the difficulty in distinguishing between real and spectral.

As a song of recantation, and a poetic mosaic of many faces and forms, *Helen in Egypt* is palinode *and* palimpsest, the result of several, tenuously related works in progress, including H.D.'s sound recordings of the text before its final published 1961 version. The audio tapes, now at the Beinecke Library at Yale University, present H.D. in the roles of nuanced reader, performer and the phantasmal presence of the poem's voice-over: 'between the poem's prose and verse sections H.D.'s voice changes in tone and pitch. This changing intonation not only signals H.D.'s performance of the characters in the poem, it also suggests her identification with the shifting identities of Helen' (Connor 2004: 84).[15] The personae the author consigns to speak in her text and the polymorphic authorship that lends its echoes to H.D.'s *Helen* at once re-invoke the past and seek to revive Helen's ancient enchantment.

The opening prose segment in *Helen in Egypt* retraces its textual ancestry and replaces Helen's apertural monologue in the Euripidean play with what comes across as cinematic voice-over:[16]

We all know the story of Helen of Troy but few of us have followed her to Egypt. How did she get there? Stesichorus of Sicily in his Palinode was the first to tell us. Some centuries later, Euripides repeats the story [. . .] Helen of Troy was a phantom, substituted for the real Helen, by jealous deities. The Greeks and the Trojans alike fought for an illusion.

1974: 1

Helen carries the weight of a complex mythic past. Intermingling her memories of war scenes at the ramparts of Troy with the present time, she establishes a subtle sense of performativity.

Helen makes her opening appearance as if walking on a theatrical stage facing a live audience: 'the scene is empty and I am alone / yet in this Amen-temple, / I hear their voices, / there is no veil between us, / only space and leisure' (1974: 1–2). Deploying the language of the stage, H.D., whom Horace Gregory sees as wearing 'the mask of Stesichorus' (H.D. 1974: viii), instructs that her Helen be positioned on holy grounds much as Euripides' Helen is standing at Proteus's tomb. In an act of δεῖξις (*deixis*), a gesture of showing, she points to the audience the location of 'this Amen-temple', while the voice-over of the prose heading informs us that the woman we witness standing on holy grounds has sustained her Euripidean '*accoutrements*'.

Helen, a theatrically-apparelled personage on H.D.'s stage outside Amen's temple, recalls the Greek heroine as a cultic, semi-divine figure drawn from some pre-Spartan ritual as well as a performer or, as Aristophanes portrays her in *Lysistrata,* ἁγνὰ χοραγὸς εὐπρεπής, 'a pure, modestly clad chorus-leader' (1315).[17]

In Leuké, the second part of *Helen in Egypt*, the goddess Thetis appears on the stage as well; H.D. reminds us that 'she of the many forms / had manifested as Choragus, / Thetis, lure of the sea' (1974: 117). The lines resonate with allusions to the *Iliad*'s Thetis, where she acts as goddess-*choragus* (the chorus-leader) in lamenting her son's death and afterlife. H.D.'s lines evoke the man-of-many-forms Proteus and signpost the generic malleability and multi-formity of palinodic writing. Egypt, the land of H.D.'s 'phantasia', to use Robert Duncan's term, stages the same old play and the same polymorphous cast comprised of Proteus, Thetis, Helen, Amen and Isis:

This is Formalaut's temple,
not far from Athens,
not far from Eleusis,

Yet Egypt; not far
from Theseus, your god-father,
not far from Amen, your father

But dedicated to Isis,
or if you will, Thetis;
not far from the blessèd isles

1974: 212[18]

The rhythmic, ritualistic, choral beat of the repetition 'not far' echoes as constant reminder of the proximity of mythological worlds that the poem has set out to map and the oneness of both the human and divine personages that inhabit them.[19] The holy grounds of Athens, Eleusis, the Amen temple and the Hesiodic 'Blessèd Isles' become a geographical nexus hosting a syncretic cluster of divine or glorified humans whose subjectivities are aligned.

The veil of Cytherea, a surviving thread from Helen's mythic and epic past and an ambiguous trope in *Helen in Egypt*, may additionally be viewed as a key dramatic prop.[20] H.D. wonders whether it is 'a symbol' complementing the elusiveness of Helen of Troy; but the veil also functions as the torn, or 'rent' stage curtain, sheathing Helen while its tatters draw attention to her the moment she flees the ramparts of the sieged Troy. The veil demarcates theatrical space yet it also blurs spatial and temporal boundaries. When the curtain falls, one act of the play is over; the next is about to begin, or perhaps the previous one is about to re-commence. H.D. writes, 'Now Helen's garment or "veil" is

Figure 5.1 'Immerso nell'acqua frangosa': a painting from the exhibition *Sabir* by Elena Papadimitriou, Gallery Skoufa, Athens (18 January–10 February 2018). © Elena Papadimitriou.

"rent." Is the garment of the apparition synonymous with the "veil" of Helen? Is "the torn garment" [...] a symbol? Paris has seen and must accept "a tattered garment" or an incomplete or partial manifestation of the vision' (1974: 145).

As an uncertain, fleeting vision, Helen must a priori hold the myth up 'to view' while, according to Simon Goldhill, 'a recognition of its use is forced into the light, and its value and manipulation as a paradigm is laid open to question' (1986: 257). In 'Pallinode' the choral voice speaks to supersede the age-old scenario of Helen as a boundary crosser of her sex: 'Alas, my brothers, / Helen did not walk / upon the ramparts' (1974: 5). The preceding prose caption corroborates Helen's 'concern with the past, with the anathema or curse' (5). H.D.'s chorus introduces a highly experimental dialogical bond between a negation related to what the 'others' thought was true and to that of an affirmative action – that is, Helen's palinodic, redemptive gesture to restore the damage and to expunge herself from the anathema for the 'holocaust of the Greeks' (5).

H.D.'s amalgam of poetry and prose has engendered a new form of choral ode assimilating Helen's monodies and collective choral odes from Euripides' *Helen*. The Euripidean chorus in H.D. seems to resound with the choral song of the foreign women in Euripides' *Iphigenia among the Taurians* (another play H.D. had extensively studied and intended to translate along with *Helen*). Helen invites the chorus of captive Greek women to come carrying with them Λίβυν / λωτὸν ἢ σύριγγας ἢ / φόρμιγγας, 'a Libyan flute or syrinx or forminx' (Eur. *Hel.* 170–2), and to sing with her in music her mournful song for the dead. Mythic references to Persephone 'in her halls of night' (ὑπὸ μέλαθρα νύχια, Eur. *Hel.* 175) inspire the song of the Euripidean *parodos*. In the second *stasimon* (Eur. *Hel.* 1301–68), the chorus recaptures its mythic repertoire on chthonic deities by singing the hymn to the great mother Demeter in the so-called '*Magna Mater*' ode, representing a 'syncretism between Cybele, the Phrygian nature-goddess, and the Greek worship of Demeter and Aphrodite with its mention of exotic musical instruments, rattling cymbals and Dionysiac revels' (Wright 2005: 180).

Helen in Egypt as meta-palinode ranges between a choral 'we', the 'out of time' and 'out of this world' experience H.D. sets out to recount, and, according to Jeanne Heuving, Helen as an eidolonic 'post-human subjectivity' (2016: 102). H.D. rids her of both the masculinist portrayal of a dominant, self-assured *femme fatale* and the guilt-torn image of the suppliant woman in Euripides' play kneeling at the tomb of King Proteus. She exploits the blurred duality of the setting (Egypt both as physical and psychic realm) and the intentional incongruity in Helen's subjectivity to create what feels like a cinematographic montage: she demarcates for Helen an autonomous, inner choral voice composed of her various selves, 'echoes' from the works written over time. Then, as if aware of its performative role and its connectedness to the world outside, the voice skips into its external choral dimension, listening, overhearing, reciting/remembering lines from the collective of echoes, ghosts of the past, splinters from the Homeric epics or fragments of post-epic poems. The cinematographic, cut up-like scenes in Book Two of 'Leuké' offer a glimpse of the final battle at the buttresses of Troy as Helen disappears while soldiers meet their death. Their voices in the clamour of the battle sound like fragments of a Trojan chorus at the siege of Troy:

'how do you know?'
'– she flashed as a star,

Then vanished into the air'
'– it's only a winding stair,
a spiral, like a snail-shell';

'– a trap – let the others go –'
'– into the heart of the earth,
Into the bowels of death – stand back –'

'– it's only the fumes
From the camp fires without –'
'– they have fired the turrets from below',

We are ringed with fire;
Follow the others or go back?'
'– go back, go back, go back –'

1974: 127–8

The stitched, polyphonic narrative fragments, frantic punctuation signalling the disjointed positioning of the chorus, the paratactic arrangement of the lines and Helen's eidolon disappearing in the fumes of the battle trigger a fissure between real and unreal. The synesthetic effect of the alliterative lines 'stair, / a spiral, like snail-shell' disrupts the singularity of the space – the tower in which the battle is fought – into a more esoteric, labyrinthine structure. In this way, 'the rhythmic texture of prosodic sound effects [break] the law of the sign' (Wenthe 1995: 114) and allow for the release of other associations.[21] The transition from and into a world of warfare happens once again, in indeterminate spatial and temporal coordinates.

H.D. lines up a series of prosodic associations within the phantasmagoric, auditory frame of Troy on fire in a series of haunting verses, while the dashes, visual signs of the split between memory and recollection, bring to the surface the scenes of devastation described by the chorus in the *Trojan Women* mourning the siege of Troy:

> I was dancing about the temple,
> when a murderous cry throughout the city
> possessed the dwelling places of Pergamum.
> Beloved young children threw frightened arms
> about their mothers' skirts.
> The war god was emerging from his ambush,
> . . .
> The slaughtering of Phrygians about the altars
> And, in our beds, desolation wrought by the headman's blade

Eur. Tr. 555–63, trans. Kovacs

Goldhill argues that Euripides' plays, expounding on the crisis of self-representation in culture, threaten to break the tragic masking convention. Thus, they become a sound confirmation of the Nietzschean oracle and its ominous disclosure that Euripides is the instigator of the genre's demise. The tragic mask, Goldhill continues, is a malleable, multivalent form of representation that is limited, nonetheless, in its capacity to represent the truth. As a result, this crisis is transferred from characters onto the generic form itself (1986: 259). Conversely, *Helen in Egypt* does not merely address generalized crises of culture or genre. In intentionally exploiting the meta-palinode, the hybrid that serves and undermines the shadowy self upon which it is constructed, H.D. sings again, repeats, revokes and reconstructs the mythic body. Helen assumes the authority to license herself to be simultaneously 'the writing', a ghostly erasure, a correction, the trans-cultural subjectivity of mythic and cultic hieroglyph, and the multifarious yet elusive body of Eros.

If the palinode suggests a repetition or translation of some 'original', H.D. brings πάλιν, 'again', or, as this Greek word suggests, on another level, returns, in seemingly random patterning, to the full mosaic of the Euripidean plays she had translated in previous decades, whether in the form of choral poems, or in choral translations or in texts 'after' Euripides. In a resurgence of an array of Euripidean plays, a palimpsestic parade of mythic personae linked to Helen comes to the fore. Apart from Helen's eidolon, H.D. employs the spectral reincarnations of earlier Euripidean personae. Re-surfacing from both poets' treatment in *Iphigenia in Aulis*, *Electra* and *Orestes*, Clytemnestra, introduced as Helen's 'shadow' sister (1961: 68), the mystic rhododendron, and the sister not 'signally favored' (1974: 74), appears in Book Five of the 'Pallinode'.[22] Iphigenia, Hermione, and then Electra and Orestes, along with a cohort of shadows from the house of Priam, namely Cassandra, Hecuba and their genealogical linkage to their divine mothers – Nemesis, Nepenthe, Hecate, the Erinyes and Ate – are methodically excavated, their mythic threads identified and their power reinstated.[23]

Iphigenia's sacrifice is re-enacted in 'Leuké' whilst H.D.'s montage assembles once again the actual moment. The scene is compressed into a single image, as Clytemnestra recalls,

the glint at the throat

of her child at the altar;
Artemis snatched away
the proffered sacrifice

1974: 72

The iambic pattern of the verse with anapaestic substitutions in lines one and two also contains edited fragments from the Herald's speech at the end of *Iphigenia at Aulis* when he recounts the scene of the sacrifice, Iphigenia's salvaging through divine intervention and her etheric 'translation' to another realm (Eur. *Bacch.* 1565–89).

At the closure of 'Pallinode', Helen confirms that she and her sister are born from the Swan: 'we are children of Zeus' (1974: 77). Helen delivers an epode as supplication, pleading with her divine twin brothers, the Dioskouroi, to 'grant Clytemnestra peace' (86) and redeem her from the stigma of murder. Near the end of 'Leuké', the voice-over of H.D.'s bard wearing the mask of Theseus announces that 'Helen must be re-born, that is, her soul must return wholly to her body' (162) if she is to stop being a 'psyche with half-dried wings' (165), thus providing another allusive token of the restorative potential of the new palinode, a song that will counter the lies of the past and correct the faulty narratives.

At this point I would add one final juncture to the poetics of H.D. and Euripides, which has received little critical attention. H.D.'s meta-palinode captures Euripides' philosophical treatment of the trope of the eidolon in his play during the exchange between the prophetess Theonoe and Helen who converse on the notion of the divine.[24] The real Helen is placed in folds of ether and then carried from Mount Olympus, seat of the gods, to Egypt.[25] The sky or *aether* in Euripides is a crucial philosophical locus that connects Helen to her divine ancestry and marks her miraculous transition as an etheric body from Greece to Egypt; however, the heavenly plane is not just a privileged site reserved for divinities since, in the case of Theonoe, Euripides creates a half human and half divine *nous*, a mind that belongs to both the spiritual and physical planes. Theonoe, as *mantis*, knower of the gods' design (as her name suggests) and as a priestess that has devoted herself to a life of cultic service, holds a lifelong allegiance to truth.[26]

Theonoe's association with Helen lies in the figure of *aether* since both mythic figures possess shared experiences with the etheric, divine sphere. In Euripides' oeuvre, *aether* is a word whose semantics conflate with sky or heaven or 'a repository of consciousness after death and a true and lasting object of reverence' (Burian 2011: 250). Theonoe is not part of the cast of characters in *Helen in Egypt*; her mantic, prophetic qualities become, nevertheless, integral to Helen's half-human, half-divine identity. Since Helen is both eidolon and real, she is a part of the celestial or etheric as much as she is part of the real, physical world. Her palimpsestic vision, the gradual, often simultaneous unravelling and concealment of her different facets expose an otherness that reaches beyond the concreteness of the physical realm.

H.D. inlays the character of Theonoe in *Helen in Egypt* during a heart-rending address to some invisible audience. Helen captures the notion of divinity in the manner of Theonoe's contact with the notion of God. The quest for the divine crosses cultures, time periods and names of different deities that converge into one whose essence is reserved for the initiate:

what few may acknowledge and live
what many acknowledge and die?
He is One, yet the many

manifest separately; He may manifest
as a jackal and hound you to death?
or is He changeable like air,

and like air, invisible?
god is beyond the manifest?
He is ether and limitless space?

you may ask forever, you may penetrate
every shrine, an initiate,
and remain unenlightened at last.

1974: 78–9

The final exhortation alludes to the aspiring initiate of the Eleusinian Mysteries; no promise is made that one's desire to be enlightened will ever be fulfilled if deemed unworthy of it. In the Euripidean *Helen*, Theonoe was born with an inner 'great temple to justice' (ἔνεστι δ᾽ ἱερὸν τῆς δίκης ἐμοὶ μέγα/ ἐν τῇ φύσει, 1002–3). To her, death signals a transmigration of the soul into an ethereal plane from which they 'have eternal sensation once it has been hurled into the eternal upper air' (Eur. *Hel.* 1015–16). Theonoe is then not unrelated to Helen, since Helen's eidolon is εἴδωλον ἔμπνουν οὐρανοῦ, 'imbued with sky' (Eur. *Hel.* 34). Helen as *eidolon* is attached to some etheric, celestial dimension with which Theonoe is also aligned. Ruth Padel correctly identifies an important Euripidean thread also underlying H.D.'s reception of Euripides as visionary poet and philosopher: 'Air and sky are important in the language of this play' (1974: 239–40 n. 6). The *Helen*'s rhetoric focuses on the divine and the ethereal, including Euripides' processing of Egypt as a country that 'first proclaimed the immortality of the human soul and suggests that Euripides sought to "Hellenize and modernize" the old belief' (Conacher 1967: 296 n. 12). H.D.'s investigations into the occult at that time may also concur with Euripides' explorations into the findings of Herodotus about Egypt and the current philosophical trends related to Anaxagoras's views.[27]

As a writer of palinodes, H.D.'s Helen reassures us near the end of 'Eidolon' that the palinode in its mythopoetic dimension is a dynamic act of translation of the 'Eternal Moment'. As palinodist, Helen sings the song of the 'eternal moment' while 'we stare again and again over the smoldering embers' (1974: 269) of the lost Troy. As meta-palinodist, H.D. draws from Euripides' visionary plays translating this eternal, out-of-time moment of unification happening in the crucible of poetry and philosophy.

CHAPTER 6
REPRESSION, RENEWAL AND 'THE RACE OF WOMEN' IN H.D.'S *ION*
Jeff Westover[1]

Steven Yao has called H.D.'s *Ion* her 'most ambitious feat of translation' (2002a: 83). Two contexts are relevant for thinking about H.D.'s work on this project. One is psychoanalysis, and the other is the scholarship which interprets myth as a narrative reflection of ritual practice. Both contexts are significantly tied to H.D.'s personal life and writing career. Matte Robinson even claims that one of the major characters in the play, Kreousa, 'becomes an extension of H.D.' (2013: 270). This claim may be overstated, but Kreousa's quest for recognition from Apollo does resemble H.D.'s effort to supply her daughter, Perdita, with a patronym in order to secure the girl's legal standing. Richard Aldington refused to allow H.D. to register him as Perdita's father, though she did so anyway (Robinson 1982: 179–80; Guest 1984: 111). Aldington did not publicly contest H.D.'s action, even when he sought a divorce from H.D. in 1937, the year she published her translation of the *Ion* (Zilboorg 2003: 239–40). However, H.D. told Ezra Pound that he did threaten 'to use Perdita to divorce me and to have me locked up if I registered her as legitimate' (Friedman 2002: 466). This threat was the source of anxiety for H.D. and it kept her and her daughter in a precarious legal position until Bryher and Kenneth Macpherson legally adopted Perdita in 1928 (Friedman 2002: 467).

While the play is obviously not an allegory about H.D.'s personal life, her translation evidently led her to consider features of its plot in relation to her experience as a single mother. On 25 August 1935, H.D. reported to Bryher that she had completed her version of the *Ion*, recalling that 'this was work I was doing after the first confinement and during my pregnancy with old Pups [Perdita]' (Friedman 2002: 203). H.D.'s translation emphasizes Kreousa's quest for Apollo's acknowledgement, since the god impregnated her without publicly admitting he did so. H.D. sought the kind of legitimation for her daughter that Apollo confers on Ion when Athena confirms that Ion is the god's son. Although the seven years between Perdita's adoption and H.D.'s publication of the *Ion* should lead one to be wary about oversimplifying the relationship between the play and H.D.'s experience, H.D. often returned to earlier moments in her life, and such retrospective ruminations frequently inform her work. At the same time, the *way* in which she treats this material reflects a feminist theory of translation as a mode of transformation. As Barbara Godard explains, 'Feminist discourse works upon language, upon dominant discourse, in a radical interrogation of meaning'. According to this view, 'translation [...] is production, not reproduction' (1990: 90). In both her verse renderings and her prose interpolations, H.D. 'works upon the language' of Euripides' play, producing something new in an English text that reflects her concerns as a twentieth-century woman.

As Susan Stanford Friedman explains, 'it was the completion of Euripides' *Ion* in August of 1935 that represented the immediate capstone of H.D.'s Vienna Experience' when she was psychoanalysed by Freud for the last time (2002: 51). Nonetheless, while H.D. pays homage to Freud in her memoir about their sessions together (in *Tribute to Freud*), she also registers her disagreement with him (H.D. [1956] 1974: 110, 119). According to Eileen Gregory, H.D.'s translation of the *Ion* reflects her personal reshaping of her own sense of identity, particularly in terms of a shift from crystalline imagism (embodied by Ion) to a more assertive poetics based on the figure of the woman-mother-as-poet (1997: 213).[2] Robert Duncan views the *Ion* as 'the pivot' in her career (2011: 210), and Patricia Moyer concludes that H.D.'s prose characterization of Kreousa 'signals an expansion of H.D.'s long fascination with female figures in relation to her own life in the wider context of the twentieth century' (1997: 111). Moreover, by publishing her version of Euripides' play, H.D. publicly associated herself with a mythic text that could complement, if not quite rival, Freud's Oedipus myth.

For these reasons, instead of interpreting H.D.'s translation in primarily biographical terms, I focus more broadly on the cathartic effect of the mutual recognition scene in *Ion* as well as the role of the Arrephoria as a feminine rite of passage encoded in the play. (Kreousa's story echoes that of the Arrephoroi, three sisters entrusted with a basket bearing an infant.) In particular, I show that enclosed baskets and the cave where Apollo rapes Kreousa and where Kreousa gives birth to Ion resemble symbols of metamorphosis (in the form of boxes enclosing cocoons) that H.D. reprises and develops in such texts as *Trilogy* and *Tribute to Freud*. I also examine the parallel between the burnt but blooming olive tree in one of the late prose comments of H.D.'s *Ion* and the image of the flowering rod in *Trilogy*. In each case, H.D. artfully synthesizes the materials of Greek mythology, literature and religion to achieve a sense of personal triumph that is also a cultural triumph. Kreousa's attempt to bring her experience into words while seeking redress for her mistreatment represents the experience of many women, not just her own. H.D. calls attention to this fact by using the phrase 'the race of women' twice in her translation. While the Greek phrase γένος γυναικῶν (*génos gunaikōn*), does not appear in the original text of Euripides' play, it does play a significant role in Hesiod's *Theogony* and the concept is important throughout ancient Greek culture. Moreover, in the original text of the *Ion* Kreousa generalizes her complaint at 252f. (ὦ τλήμονες γυναῖκες/ὦ τολμήματα/ θεῶν [*ō tlēmones gunaikes/ ō tolmēmata theōn*]), before speaking specifically against Apollo and about herself at 384ff., where H.D. mentions the 'race of women' a second time.[3]

Speech and repression

H.D. closely follows Euripides by emphasizing the centrality of speech and secrets throughout *Ion* (Zeitlin 1996: 306–7).[4] Secrets are also fundamental to the plots of the *Hippolytus* and *Iphigenia in Aulis*, two other plays by Euripides which H.D. adapted or partially translated. For example, in *Hippolytus* the Chorus mentions that Phaedra suffers from κρυπτῷ πένθει (Eur. *Hipp.* 139), which H.D. translates as 'secret hurt' (1983: 86). In *Iphigenia*, Agamemnon arranges to have Clytemnestra bring their daughter to Aulis to be sacrificed under the pretext that she is to be married to Achilles. Whereas the central conflict of *Ion* is resolved and harmony ultimately achieved, the disclosure of secrets in *Hippolytus* and *Iphigenia* do not result in reconciliation. Instead, revelations intensify conflicts. When principal characters such as Agamemnon, Menelaus and Theseus speak in *Iphigenia in Aulis* and *Hippolytus*, they frequently do so to promote political designs or convey their own personal concerns, even to the detriment of social or kinship ties. Although there is an important rapprochement between Artemis and Hippolytus in the last act of *Hippolytus Temporizes*, Hippolytus and Phaedra both die after their secret tryst (H.D. 2003: 98–9).

In *Ion*, speaking is often performative (as when Hermes ritually identifies Ion at the end of the Prologue, or when Apollo designates Xouthos as Ion's father). In contrast to H.D.'s treatments of situations in the other two plays by Euripides, speaking is also the means by which the burden of the main character's secret past is lifted. The conflict between speech and repression parallels the conflict between Kreousa's quest for justice and Apollo's assertion of divine authority. The first conflict resolves when Kreousa and Ion recognize their true relation to one another through Apollo's indirect intervention. H.D. characterizes this event as a form of renewal by connecting it to the imagery of the budding olive tree in a key prose passage she includes in her translation. The image of a burnt but budding tree is important to the play and to its classical historical context, after Athens is besieged by Persian conquerors, but it also appears in *Trilogy*, her epic poem of World War II. She turns the image into a palimpsest, a symbol of hope that unites various moments in time. This palimpsest may be regarded as H.D.'s version of the 'mythic method' T.S. Eliot describes in his discussion of James Joyce's *Ulysses* (1975: 177).

A mythic context also contributes to the theme of secrecy. At one point in the play, the Choros refers to a dance of 'three sisters' on 'the rock of Makra', associated with the god Pan (H.D. 2003: 189). Peter Burian explains that this passage refers to the daughters of Kekrops and Aglauros (Kreousa's ancestors), and he mentions the festival that commemorates their experience, sometimes called the Arrephoria (Euripides 1996: 90). The name of this festival refers to the bearing of secret or 'unnamed' items by participants (Harrison [1908] 1975: 122). The first part of the word may come from τὰ ἄρρητα (*ta arrēta*), literally meaning 'unspoken things', connoting things 'secret' or 'shameful to be spoken'. In the context of mystery rites, Walter Burkert argues that the term should be translated as 'unsayable' ([1962] 1972: 461). The festival of the Arrephoria is linked to the violation of a taboo: the daughters of Aglauros look in a basket entrusted to them, in which they discover the infant Erichthonios and are punished for their disobedience (H.D. refers to Erichthonios as Erechtheus throughout her translation, conflating two of Kreousa's ancestors). Since this passage refers to an event that occurs in the same place where Apollo had sex with Kreousa and where Kreousa abandoned her baby (H.D. 2003: 215–16), secrets become linked with repression, ritual and speech in a powerful but contradictory way that puts Kreousa's anger about the god's injustice in the context of her family's history and the natural cycle of seasons (Goff 1995: 363). H.D.'s translation calls attention to the psychoanalytic links between repression, symptom, speech and healing. Her phrasal repetitions correspond at the level of style to Kreousa's angry outbursts against Apollo at the level of plot.

The play's repetitions of the story of Apollo's rape and abandonment of Kreousa provide an opportunity for expressing her sense of injustice and confronting its traumatic effects so as to overcome them. This pattern of development echoes Freud's ideas about trauma, repression and repetition ([1914] 1950: 145–57).[5] However, since the father of Ion is a god, Kreousa must capitulate to the god's solution and learn to live with it. As H.D. puts it in a different context, 'It is terrible to be a virgin because a Virgin has a baby with God' (1998: 115). Although H.D. emphasizes Athena as the epitome of rationality overcoming the destructive effects of passion, Kreousa's eventual acceptance of Apollo's treatment of her seems to exemplify her pragmatic accommodation to 'the reality principle' as much as her recovery from the trauma that produces her symptoms of despair and rage (Freud [1920] 1960: 7). While this may strike modern readers as contradictory, it is nonetheless true that Euripides devotes much of his plot to the psychological process by which Kreousa comes to understand herself, her son and Apollo's treatment of her. In her adaptation, H.D. focuses on this process and retains the pattern of Euripides' plot, which binds Kreousa and Ion by dramatizing their parallel quests for knowledge and recognition. Ion's maturation is profoundly connected to his need for his mother,[6] while Kreousa's need to be acknowledged by Apollo is just as firmly tied to her discovery that Ion is her son. H.D. emphasizes the mutuality of their quests by calling attention to corresponding episodes of speech and silence throughout her translation.

To give one example, H.D. uses chiasmus to emphasize the separation of mother and child as well as their reunion. In the prologue, Hermes announces that

> Phoibos loved Kreousa:
> daughter of Erechtheus, on the Acropolis:
> masters of Atthis call the place Makra:
> that Athenian cliff, great-rocks:
> the god kept her father ignorant:
> she bore her secret, month by month:
> in secret, she brought forth:

> *H.D. [1927] 2003: 151–2*

H.D. underscores the secrecy of Kreousa's pregnancy and delivery through the chiasmus in the last two lines. This syntactic pattern is her own; it does not echo the original Greek. The pattern also plays on the meaning of 'bear' as enduring a burden or hardship and as giving birth. The secret is her pregnancy, which she both endures and successfully brings to term. In syntax and wordplay, H.D.'s style reflects a feminist practice of translation as 'production' rather than mere 'reproduction' (Godard 1990: 90). In this passage and in a key speech by Kreousa ([1927] 2003: 209), H.D.'s chiasmus amounts to a verbal form of weaving that parallels the plaiting of Ion's baby basket and that of Kreousa's ancestor,

Erichthonios/Erechtheus.[7] As Haun Saussy observes, 'chiasmus selects and binds (*chiasmos* is also the Greek term for a kind of butterfly bandage)' (235).

H.D. emphasizes the theme of secrecy by repeating it in parallel but mirror-reversed terms. In the first part of the phrasal pair ('she bore her secret'), she presents secrecy as a burden, but in the second phrase ('In secret she brought forth'), she puns on 'bore' as 'give birth', which makes the relation between the phrases more than parallel, since the second phrase marks a change or culmination – the transition from gestation and the pain of one form of secrecy to the birth of Ion and the pain of Kreousa's public shame for being an unwed mother. However, the birth is also a completion, as we learn later in the play, when Kreousa recognizes and reunites with her son and thereby extends her lineage. In the stylistic texture of H.D.'s translation, as in the plot of the text, the cradle becomes an abiding sign of reunion and renewal.

Moreover, because the basket used as Ion's cradle plays such a critical role in the recognition plot, the play may be regarded as a contest over control of the womb. Explicit references to the cradle as a woven basket, or 'hollow' (κύτος [*kútos*]), make the basket a double for the womb, for the verb κύω [*kúō*] can mean 'conceive' (Loraux 1993: 204). Without Apollo's intervention, mother and son cannot be reunited because only Apollo, Hermes and the audience know that Ion is Kreousa's son at the outset of the play. To guarantee the legitimacy of the royal Athenian line, Apollo must admit his paternity to Ion, not just to Kreousa. In the cultural logic of the play, Kreousa's role as bearer is subordinate to the god's status as impregnator. This contest for control is also reflected in the myth of the Arrephoroi, since the girls who look for the baby inside the basket are punished for doing so.

Scholars have noted the similarities between the *Ion* and *Oedipus Tyrannus*, both of which are about foundlings. According to Charles Segal,

> The *Ion* re-envisages the action of the *Oedipus* through the eyes of Jocasta and in so doing fully develops the affective bond between mother and child that is barely hinted at in the *Oedipus* [...] The perspective of the *Ion* is [...] almost the reverse of that of the *Oedipus*, for there the relation between fathers and sons is particularly prominent, whereas the *Ion* scants the father-son relation in favor of that between mother and son.
>
> *1999: 101*

Segal's insight that the *Ion* rewrites *Oedipus* can serve as a basis for assessing H.D.'s accomplishment in rendering the play into English, for her emphasis on the mother–child dyad is not only true to the original but a means of challenging the normativity of patriarchal models of selfhood and social arrangements. In the *Ion* Euripides reveals that the father is a legal fiction when he portrays Apollo as giving his son Ion to Xouthos as his heir. H.D. emphasizes the secondary status of Xouthos with respect to Kreousa in the prose interlude of section V of her translation, which acknowledges his importance but portrays Kreousa as spiritually superior. In H.D.'s account of their marriage, Kreousa 'has lived only half a life with him' (2003: 182). In passages such as this, H.D. makes the world of the play her own, offering more than a slavish recapitulation of Euripides.

Moreover, by focusing on a play that recasts the storyline of Oedipus, H.D.'s rendering of the *Ion* may be regarded as a significant reply, if not quite a rejoinder, to Freud. While Euripides' *Ion* may not be as famous or influential as Sophocles' *Oedipus Tyrannus*, as a work of classical drama it has a degree of cultural prestige. In addition, while H.D.'s tribute to Freud is genuine, it is not monolithic. As Duncan observes, 'The Oedipus complex itself does not preoccupy H.D.' (2011: 376). Instead, she concentrates on the pathos of the mother–child dyad and the jubilant reunion of Ion and Kreousa after years of separation and mutual attempts at violence. This dynamic seems to correspond with Freud's claim during analysis that H.D. was seeking union with her mother, as she reports in *Tribute to Freud*. According to Thomas Jenkins, H.D. intensifies the dramatic exchanges between Kreousa and Ion while decreasing the impact of the father–son dialogue between Xouthos and Ion (2007: 137). H.D. sent Freud a copy of her translation, and in his letter thanking her for the gift he suggests that he and H.D. were in agreement about the need for conscious reason to reckon with and control the unconscious in a healthy way (H.D. [1956] 1974: 194). In the *Ion*, the symbol for rationality is Athena, the deus ex machina who resolves Ion's lingering questions about the identity of his father, and H.D. explicitly hails her as the goddess of reason in one of her prose interpolations, a gesture that parallels her description in *Tribute to Freud* of an Athena figure that Freud owned (H.D. [1956] 1974: 124).

Kreousa's need to be recognized as the bearer of a child fathered by Apollo drives the plot of the play. The site of both Apollo's rape and Kreousa's abandonment of Ion is a cave, which is not only a symbol of the chthonic origins of the House of Kekrops but also of feminine fertility. Kreousa is the birth mother of Ion, but Apollo must arrange for the reunion of mother and son, and his authority in designating Xouthos as Ion's adoptive father provides the guarantee of a paternal name, a guarantee necessary for Ion's legitimate participation in Athenian society. According to Nancy Sorkin Rabinowitz, 'The myth of autochthony [at the heart of the play and of Athenian culture] excludes the human female from the ideal of reproduction yet retains the earth, a privileged metaphor for a female body' (1993: 193).

As Apollo's representative, Hermes is authorized to open the cradle containing the infant Ion so that the Pythian will find him and raise him in the temple. In the prologue, he refers to his brother Apollo with an epithet that may mean 'slanting' or 'oblique', declaring,

> I obeyed my brother, Loxias:
> I found the reed-basket:
> I left the child there, on these steps:
> I opened the basket, revealed the contents:

> *H.D. [1927] 2003: 152*

H.D. conveys the god's authority through balanced and forceful anaphora, a pattern of lineation that is distinct from that of the Greek original at lines 36–40. By contrast with

Hermes, the daughters of Kekrops and Aglauros are prohibited by Athena from looking in the basket containing Erichthonios and die after they violate the taboo. For her part, Kreousa feels constrained by her shame to put her secret into the basket, to hide the baby there. Her action is the opposite of Hermes's and conforms with cultural codes that reinforce men's power over procreation. In the passage above, H.D. renders the Greek phrase πλεκτὸν κύτος (*plektòn kútos*) as 'reed-basket' (*plektòn* means 'woven').

Moreover, H.D. parallels the basket that contains Ion's birth-tokens in the box-and-butterfly symbolism of such later publications as *Tribute to Freud* and *Trilogy*, thereby echoing and building upon the pattern of death and resurrection in the recognition plot of *Ion*. The basket was buried with Ion yet it is also the sign and means of his rebirth, since the tokens enclosed in the basket provide the basis for Kreousa's recognition of her son. H.D. provides striking parallels to the cradle-basket symbolism of *Ion* in the 'little boxes conditioned // to hatch butterflies' she describes in *Trilogy* (1998: 53) and in the cocoons that she remembers putting in a box as a child in *Tribute to Freud* (1974: 126–8).

When she broaches the subject with Ion regarding the prophecy she seeks from Apollo, Kreousa hedges and invents the story of a friend who was raped by the god. In the process of explaining this, both characters suppress their speech. Kreousa does so through inhibition, while Ion does so through prohibition:

> Kreousa: – I dare not speak –
> Ion: – speak and tell me –
> Kreousa: – she was Phoibos' –
> Ion: – do not say that –

> *H.D. [1927] 2003: 177*

Ion repeats his prohibition in forthright terms a little later, reasserting his authority when he admonishes Kreousa to refrain from offending Apollo, saying, 'provoke not / unwilling utterance' (H.D. [1927] 2003: 180). These two forms of verbal suppression are informed by the gender codes of the period. As Adele Scafuro points out, Kreousa's shame is shared by 'other tragic heroines before they embark on narratives of sexual exploitation at the hands of gods' (1990: 140). Kreousa curbs her feelings and her articulation of them in order to comply with Ion's demand that she respect the god by keeping quiet. In effect, Kreousa's passive silence undergirds Ion's commanding masculinity. H.D.'s rendering of their stichomythia calls attention to this dependency through the brevity of her lines and the repetition of *speak* and *say*.

Kreousa tells her story again but in more forthright terms to an old family servant. As I have mentioned, his progressive expression of her story is like Freud's process of working through memories of traumatic events in order to avoid reliving them. Kreousa's second account reflects the conflict between her desire to tell her story and her shame about making it known, but this time she is more assertive about articulating it because now she believes she has lost all hope of recovering her son or of having another child (she has just learned that Apollo has given Ion to Xouthos as his son).

Soul,
soul,
speak,
nay, soul, O, my soul,
be silent, how can you name an act
of shame,
an illicit act?
soul,
soul,
be silent,
nay, nay, O, my soul,
speak;
what can stop you,
what can prevent?

H.D. [1927] 2003: 209

Echoing the syntactic pattern of the passage from Hermes' prologue I quoted earlier, H.D. uses chiasmus as a counterpoint to Kreousa's repetitions in this speech (soul, / speak / . . . soul, / be silent: soul, / / be silent / . . . soul, / speak). The contrasts of the chiasmus reflect Kreousa's turmoil, but the repetitions reflect the urgency of what she has to say and her need to tell it. While the lines have the syntactic form of chiasmus, meaning repeats in the first and last lines as well as the second and third lines, so that they function as a form of parallelism. Within the parallel, however, is the basic conflict between remaining silent and speaking out. That antithesis is fundamental to Kreousa's character, so H.D.'s use of chiasmus is not merely a piece of ceremonious formalism but an organic expression of her protagonist's turmoil, especially in relation to others – the old servant, in this scene, but Ion in others. Kreousa's capacity to tell her story is a turning point in the play, but it is not an easy or unequivocal success. In her speech Kreousa finally expresses her feelings about what has happened to her in an overt and assertive way. Her anger about Apollo's injustice against her takes the form of the plot to kill Ion, but the god ultimately foils that attempt in order to effect the mutual recognition of mother and son.

When Kreousa and Ion finally recognize each other, the play enacts a ritualized rebirth of Ion. The sentence patterns that H.D. devises to signal this ritual may be regarded as the figurative or linguistic equivalent to the plaited strands of wicker comprising Ion's cradle: Euripides characterizes it not only as *plékton* but also as ἑλικτόν (*heliktón*), a semantically similar word meaning 'rolled, twisted, or weaved'. With the mutual recognition of mother and son, what was formerly secret finally comes to light. This results in psychological healing for both. Like the chiasmus in Hermes' speech about Kreousa's secret pregnancy and delivery, Kreousa's chiasmic expression of her inner conflict when she finally tells her story openly forms a kind of syntactical weave that rounds out the contours of the play. As a result, H.D.'s translation imitates the shape of Ion's cradle.

If the Arrephoria is a rite of passage where girls prepare for married life and motherhood, then the play echoes the rite by telling the story of Kreousa's abandonment and her subsequent recognition of Ion (Burkert 2001: 47). Kreousa's reunion with Ion makes her willing to forgive Apollo. It also ensures the continuance of the political lineage of Athens. Regarding the Arrephoria, Barbara Goff argues that

> This rite provides for the correct development of female identity by enactment of the ἔργα γυναίκων [*erga gunaíkōn*], the 'works of women'. During the Arrhephoria, selected girls in the service of Athena act out the tasks of motherhood and weaving, the ἔργα γυναίκων, knowledge of which ensures that a young girl may successfully take her place in the community as an adult woman. Kreousa's story [...] has been read to draw on elements of this ritual. Kreousa's story is simultaneously a perversion of the Arrhephoria, because she unwittingly tries to kill her child. But if we allow that the ritual is legible within her actions, it can be seen to offer itself as a model for the successful integration of the female into the community.
>
> *1995: 363*

H.D. seems to favour Goff's optimistic view of the rite as a model for 'successful integration', especially in the later prose interpolations of her translation.

One example of H.D.'s optimism may be found in the recognition scene. When Ion asks Kreousa whether there is anything else in his cradle returned to him by the priestess who raised him, Kreousa answers,

>   yes,
>   there's one thing more;
>   O, olive
>   of Athens,
> O, crown of wild-olives,
> I plucked
> from the very holy rock;
> it is sacred;
> the very branch,
> the goddess herself
> brought;
> it never loses its silver
> immortal
> leaf;
> it is there;
>
> *H.D. [1927] 2003: 247–8*

As in other passages of H.D.'s translation, a parallelism not evident in the Greek is quite prominent here, providing another example of the way she makes the play her own instead of reproducing Euripides' manner of expression. The olive crown is not only the final token that confirms Ion's recognition of his mother, but it is also a sign of his chthonic heritage as Kreousa's progeny. Since the tree is to the earth as Ion is to Kreousa, this token reaffirms the mythic association of the earth with female reproductive power.

In addition, the olive-tree fantasy in a prose commentary near the end of H.D.'s translation corresponds to the flowering rod imagery of *Trilogy* as well as to the box which is both a coffin and a cradle for the dead and reborn Ion (line 1441), whom Kreousa characterizes as an avatar of Erechtheus: the youth of their ancestor is restored by Ion (ἀνηβᾷ [*anēbai*], 1465). In her ecstatic elaboration on a short passage from Herodotus (8.55), H.D. describes an Athenian fleeing foreign conquerors who returns with hope to seek the sacred olive tree of his city. The Athenian

> *reached out his hand toward the charred stump of the once sacred olive tree, to find –*
>
> *Close to the root of the blackened, ancient stump, a frail silver shoot was clearly discernible, chiselled* [sic] *as it were, against that blackened wood; incredibly frail, incredibly silver, it reached toward the light. Pallas Athene, then, was not dead. Her spirit spoke quietly, a very simple message.*
>
> H.D. [1927] 2003: 257

This excerpt reflects the remembered context of the Great War, when H.D. began her translation. Given H.D.'s experience during that period of her life, her completion and publication of the translation also reflect her concerns about militarism and the threat of another world war. She had in mind the looming threat of Germany, which she worried about when she witnessed the signs of violence in Vienna while working with Freud. In that respect, H.D.'s translation of the *Ion* looks ahead to her composition of *Trilogy*. As for the classical context, Erika Simon views the Arrephoria as a ritual connected to the economy of olive production in Athens. If Ion's cradle corresponds to the basket carried by initiates in the Arrephoria, then the olive-tree imagery in H.D.'s prose interpolation should be regarded as central to the play instead of merely a flight of fancy (Simon 1983: 45).

In *Tribute to the Angels*, the second book of *Trilogy*, H.D. fuses Judeo-Christian tradition with various pagan religious sources, including that of Aphrodite. In a powerful epiphany, she testifies to a divine indwelling, insisting that

> it was not a dream
> yet it was a vision,
> it was a sign,
> . . . .
> a half-burnt-out apple-tree
> blossoming
>
> H.D. 1998: 87

Here and in other passages from *Tribute to the Angels*, H.D. borrows the classical tale from *Ion* and rejuvenates it in the trying circumstances of World War II. She offers a clear 'sign' of hope and renewal, demonstrating that the play is a milestone in her personal development and a palimpsest that modernizes an ancient mythic image. The parallel between the tree-images in *Trilogy* and *Ion* reflects an aesthetic view H.D. articulates through her character Raymonde Ransom in *Palimpsest*: 'Art wasn't seen any more in one plane, in one perspective, in one dimension. One didn't any more see things like that. Impressions were reflected now [. . .] – they were overlaid like old photographic negatives one on top of another' ([1926] 1968: 154).

H.D.'s feminist cultural critique

I have shown how H.D. situates her version of the play in relation to her own experience and in relation to the mythic method. Now I will focus more on the way H.D. portrays Kreousa as a cultural icon in order to critique misogynist concepts, just as she does in such lyric poems as 'Helen', 'Eurydice' and 'Callypso', and in such long poems as *Trilogy* and *Helen in Egypt*. As Yao has argued, 'H.D. expressly employed translation as a means to pursue her belief in the classics as both a precedent and a source of inspiration for a feminine literary conception distinct from the sentimental modes of her immediate female predecessors' (2002a: 102).

H.D.'s *Ion* pits the idea of a separate race of women (*genos gunaíkōn*) against the role and tasks of women (*erga gunaíkōn*) integrated into a patriarchal society. In doing so, she calls attention to the contradiction between the social and biological necessity of women on the one hand and, on the other, the patriarchal fantasy that women are superfluous or inferior. In keeping with a view of translation as the 'radical interrogation of meaning' (Godard 1990: 90), H.D. deploys 'the race of women', a phrase from a different Greek text, in her translation of the *Ion* in order to question the cultural assumptions of classical Greek literature (H.D. [1927] 2003: 172, 181). According to Nicole Loraux, the *genos gunaíkōn* in Hesiod's *Theogony* functions as a *locus classicus* of ancient Greek beliefs about the differences between men and women and the inferiority of women (1993: 87). In H.D.'s usage, the phrase expresses the beleaguered, second-class status of women in a man's world.

By using the phrase twice in her translation, H.D. situates Kreousa's plight in terms of women as a whole, in the present as well as the past. As Mary-Kay Gamel observes, 'The play sets Creousa's situation in a larger context of women deceived, disregarded, manipulated, exploited, [and] violated' (2001: 162). H.D. not only accentuates Kreousa's representative status, but she also evokes Hesiod's account of the origin of women in the *Theogony* in order to criticize and revise it, much as she hails alternative accounts of Helen by Stesichorus and Euripides in her long poem, *Helen in Egypt*. Hesiod portrays the first woman as a punishment for men, because of the theft of fire. And just as Athena is a female produced from the male god Zeus, so is the first mortal woman created by him (Loraux 1993: 80). The ancient Greek view of femininity is summed up in the following couplet from the *Theogony*:

ἐκ τῆς γὰρ γένος ἐστὶ γυναικῶν θηλυτεράων

τῆς γὰρ ὀλώιόν ἐστι γένος καὶ φῦλα γυναικῶν

ek tēs gàr génos estì gunaikōn thēluteráōn

tēs gàr olóión esti génos kaì phûla gunaikōn

Hes. Th. *590–1*

Loraux renders these lines as 'The race of women and all femininity come from her (the first woman) / From her comes that cursed race, the tribes of women' (1993: 73). Like Hesiod, Semonides of Amorgos composed a diatribe that also portrays women as created 'separately' (χωρὶς) from men (Lloyd-Jones 1975: 63). The opening sentence of the poem reads, χωρὶς γυναικὸς θεὸς ἐποίησεν νόον / τὰ πρῶτα (*chōrìs gunaikòs theòs epoiēsen nóon / tà prōta*), which Diane Arnson Svarlien renders as 'From the start, the gods made women different' (1995).

H.D. adapts Hesiod's phrase in her English translation of the *Ion*. But as Loraux points out, the same line of reasoning about women pervaded classical Greek culture. For example, in the *Hippolytus*, another play that inspired H.D., Euripides articulates the same idea in lines 616–17. Loraux translates the lines as 'Women, the fraudulent curse! Why, Zeus, did you put them in the world, in the light of the sun? If you wanted to multiply the race of mortals, the source of it should not have been women' (1993: 72). While H.D. does not include this passage in *Hippolytus Temporizes*, she would have encountered it in the process of composing her variation on Euripides. Translations of other speeches from the *Hippolytus* appear in her *Collected Poems* (1983: 85–93).

By referring to the race of women in her *Ion*, H.D. indicates her familiarity with this ancient Greek idea. In doing so, she puts the phrase to work against misogynistic notions of femininity. By attributing the phrase to Kreousa, moreover, H.D. makes her a representative woman, not just a tragic individual. She adapts Euripides' story by emphasizing his sympathetic portrait of Kreousa, but she also underscores the social injustice at the very heart of the plot. In order for her conflict to be resolved, Kreousa must accept her subordinate status. In coming to terms with what Freud called the reality principle, H.D.'s Kreousa reveals the social construction of this particular reality. This message comes across clearly in H.D.'s modern rendering, but knowing the literary provenance of the phrase *the race of women* enriches one's sense of H.D.'s acuity and accomplishment as a cultural critic and translator.

Moreover, in a speech that H.D. leaves out of her version of the *Ion*, the chorus explicitly indicts male sexual misbehaviour. The part of the speech in question occurs at lines 1090–98. Anne Pippin Burnett points out that this speech is similar in tone and meaning to one in *Medea* at lines 410–30, where the chorus inveighs against men's injustice against women, zeroing in on the power of poetry to shape widespread beliefs (Euripides 1970: 97).

Whatever reasons H.D. may have had for cutting the final antistrophe of the Chorus in her translation of the *Ion*, she clearly summarizes its sentiments in the following passage:

And the choros of witch-women, now taking tone from their queen, the leader of their moods and emotions, reviles the sun-god. Who is he anyway? No such things, we can imagine them thinking, ever happens in our holy city. There, intellect, justice, integrity rule, and gods and men step forth to prescribed formula. This sun-god had mixed the vibrations, has committed that most dire of spiritual sins, he has played fast and loose with the dimension of time and space. He appeared for a whim, to a girl, and that girl, their queen; and for a whim, deserted her. A god should know his place, all values have been reversed.

H.D. [1927] 2003: 222

Like the other prose interludes in H.D.'s *Ion*, this one is marked by linguistic verve and a distinctive perspective on Euripides' plot. Like the characteristic parallelism in her verse sections, the interludes exemplify Godard's claim that the 'feminist translator [...] flaunts the signs of her manipulation of the text' in order to critique it (1990: 94).

H.D.'s reference to reversal in the prose interlude may echo the antistrophe of lines 1096–98 (beginning παλίμφαμος ἀοιδὰ (*palímphamos aoidà*). David Kovacs renders the passage as 'Let song *reverse* its course, / and the muse of blame / assail men for their amours' (Euripides 1999: 451; italics added). Liddell and Scott identify Euripides' phrase with the palinode. Citing the line in question, they define the phrase as 'a song of recantation, reproaching the male sex instead of the female'. The palinode is of course central to H.D.'s *Helen in Egypt*, where she defines the genre as 'a defence, explanation or apology' (1961: 1). As she points out in that poem, the palinode in question was composed by Stesichorus, to counteract the hostile characterizations of Helen pervasive in classical Greek culture.

The fragments of Stesichorus's work that remain do not tell the story of the phantom Helen, but other ancient sources do. Plato reports the story in *Phaedrus* 243a, and Isocrates provides an account of it (Campbell 1991: 92–7). Norman Austin explains that

when Stesichorus was proposing that Helen herself was only an eidolon, Xenophanes was arguing that even the gods are no more than idols, self-projections of humans, who venerate them as gods. Projection and representation were emerging as key concepts in philosophical discourse. Debates arose, among both poets and philosophers, as to the correct reading of the traditional myths.

1994: 111

In this context, H.D.'s reference to Stesichorus exemplifies her effort to redress misogynist representations of women. Indeed, H.D.'s entire career is often characterized as a persistent feminist rewriting of classical myth, a series of rebuttals of traditions that damn women. Her translation of the *Ion* should be regarded as an integral part of this project.

While it may seem surprising that H.D. excised the last antistrophe, the balance of her translation calls attention to the asymmetrical relations between men and women.[8] Although H.D. never explicitly identifies Apollo's treatment of Kreousa as rape, she certainly calls attention to his injustice against Kreousa. By Englishing Hesiod's phrase in two of Kreousa's polemics against Apollo, H.D. deploys her deep familiarity with ancient Greek culture to help improve the footing of women in the war between the sexes. As she wrote to Bryher in 1935, 'My work is creative and reconstructive, [...] if I can get across the Greek spirit at its highest I am helping the world, and the future' (Friedman 2002: 530).

CHAPTER 7
BRAVING THE ELEMENTS: H.D. AND JEFFERS
Catherine Theis

Mixing poetic genres is the first step on the road to anarchy or revolution.

Jonathan Culler, *Theory of the Lyric*

At the end of Terrence Malick's 1973 film *Badlands*, Kit stops his Cadillac, shoots a bullet in the front tyre, then hops on the car's hood scanning for police cars in the distance. He quickly jumps down and begins collecting rocks. Police sirens wail. The script reads: *He makes a stack of the rocks to mark the site of his capture for posterity, finishing just as the police car skids to a stop.* Before he is handcuffed, Kit nods to a stack of rocks near the blasted Cadillac – his sense of the monumental great. He commemorates his capture with a rock sculpture. *X* marks the spot. In this way, Kit writes upon the earth his signature into exile. Maurice Blanchot notes, 'whoever writes is exiled from writing, which is the country – his own – where he is not a prophet' (1980: 63). Kit's modest stack of stones, his inscription upon the badlands, resounds as a talismanic tracing in the language of voiced rock. Throughout the film, we see Kit breaking stones, throwing stones, making love on the rocks near the riverbed, carrying souvenir rocks and otherwise scoring terrain with his repeated refrain – *I was here, I was here . . .*

In *A Thousand Plateaus: Capitalism and Schizophrenia*, Deleuze and Guattari define the refrain, or *ritornelle*, as 'territorial, a territorial assemblage'. They name the Artist as the 'first person to set out a boundary stone, or to make a mark' (1987: 312). Kit's deeply intuitive sense of how a landscape's natural materials work in tandem with an American mysticism – its animating fusion between spirit and matter – encourages his renegade practice of outlaw rituals. Deleuze and Guattari would have us believe that Kit marks his boundaries because he *possesses only distances*. When Kit's misguided sense of right and wrong finally catches up to him, we do not really know if a larger rock in the mountains would have saved him, but we do know that his ready-made cut from the badlands announces a lyric entrance. Kit enters into arrest on his own terms. He *stages* the entire production, landing in a fissure of rock broken into new expressive vocabularies. His rock sculpture creates a melodic line out of the landscape. It echoes back as reclaimed land.

Malick's filmic inhumanism, his sense of divinity in the natural world, and of a geological time operating beyond human understanding, speaks to a competing mysticism found in the work of Hilda Doolittle (H.D.) and to the sacredness found in the work of her contemporary, Robinson Jeffers. All three artists seek to brave the elemental forces in prophetic ways. This essay braves a way in considering how H.D. and Jeffers weave melodies from Euripides' plays into their own counter-modern work, an autonomous pilgrimage into bacchic territories of songscape.

Voice as strategic resistance

Northern California's stark beauty shares much in common with Homer's Ithaca, Jeffers famously wrote (2000: 392). H.D. and her friend Annie Winifred Ellerman (Bryher) seemed to have felt the same way. The two women pasted nude photographs of themselves taken on the beach near Carmel, California during the fall of 1920 alongside images of temple ruins they photographed in Greece a year earlier. They pose like Greek choral figures – columns of living rock – at the water's edge. Their palimpsestic cataloguing flashes as stylized tableau scenes. Is it too strange to think that H.D. drops a note among the rocks that Jeffers found, initiating a literary exchange to include a poetics of rocks?

No historical evidence exists of a meeting between H.D. and Jeffers. Writing on opposite ends of the high modernist continuum, these native Pennsylvanians born within four months of one another in closely knit Christian households, each undergo a life-changing visionary experience in 1919 that forever changes their writing lives. These spiritual epiphanies place H.D. and Jeffers in an American lineage of Transcendentalism. H.D. documents her first visionary experience in 1919 in *Notes on Thought and Vision*, an artistic manifesto pinpointing how the experience of consciousness intersects with a bodily intelligence to create the artist's over-consciousness. Because H.D.'s definition of an artist's 'over-mind', what she likens to 'a cap of consciousness over my head' (1982: 18), shares much in common with Ralph Waldo Emerson's concept of the Oversoul and Jeffers' acute sensitivities to the 'grave and earnest energy packed within stone' (Karman 1995: 48), it is not implausible to read their work in such a light.[1] Both writers subscribe to the phenomenon of finding 'books in the running brooks, sermons in stones'.[2]

In the autumn of 1920, while H.D. works on 'Notes on Euripides, Pausanius, and Greek Lyric Poets' in Carmel, a few miles away Jeffers begins building his writing studio, Hawk Tower. A year earlier, Jeffers experiences his own vision while building Tor House. His wife Una Jeffers describes the event in a letter to friend: 'As he helped the masons shift and place the wind and wind-worn granite I think he realized some kinship with it and became aware of strengths in himself unknown before . . . there came to him a kind of awakening such as adolescents and religious converts are said to experience' (2011: 310). This intimacy with stone, hauling boulders, stacking rocks, turns into an intuitive operation. Hauling million-year-old granite boulders from the Big Sur coastline, Jeffers contemplates what James Karman calls a 'phenomenology of stone' (2001: 25) alongside his ever-deepening pantheism. Rock reappears in Jeffers' work representing a divine geological time, a talismanic earth.

In her highly idiosyncratic *aftering* of Euripides' *Ion*, H.D. writes: 'A woman is about to step out of stone, in the manner of a later Rodin' (1986: 30). The past must come into the present, bodies bearing weight in ancient gold. H.D.'s statue stepping out from marble folds speaks to the stone's ability to communicate across time. For H.D., ancient Greek provides not just an imaginative portal into the past, but a conduit to her physical body. H.D.'s translation tactics disclose a phenomenon more invested in an exploration of the generative quality of her own work as a modernist visionary and post-

World War II poet than in Euripides' originals. Euripides provides the Hellenistic landscape for H.D. to inhabit with her imaginative, re-vivifying voice. By approaching H.D.'s translations of the choral odes in *Bacchae*, I read her alongside Jeffers' own choral adaptation, called 'A Humanist's Tragedy'. Through such a reading, I conjecture as to why and how both writers felt compelled to reimagine the choral odes in Euripides' *Bacchae*.

Why did this origin story of the myth of Dionysus, with seemingly no performance history in the early modern period or eighteenth century, seduce both H.D. and Jeffers to translate and adapt its choral odes into free-standing poems? Perhaps the clue lies in the publication of Gilbert Murray's Euripides translation (1902–13) before the war, which sparked something of a classical renaissance of translation, and H.D.'s dissatisfaction with her Imagiste label. As Eileen Gregory notes, in *Euripides and His Age*, Murray 'speaks of the function of the chorus as expressing an emotion "that tends quickly to get beyond words: religious emotions of all kinds"' (1997: 124). She further stresses how Euripides' choral odes, easily detached from their dramatic contexts in comparison to other dramatists, exemplify the spare language and short line promoted in modernist poetry (ibid., 140). T.S. Eliot preferred H.D.'s Greek translations to those of Murray's. 'The choruses from Euripides by H.D. are, allowing for errors and even occasional omissions of difficult passages, much nearer to both Greek and English than Mr. Murray's' (1920: 77). But H.D. does not simply omit lines she cannot translate. Gregory writes that H.D.'s translations selectively edit 'because she is crafting a single lyric piece with its own interpretative emphases' (1997: 184), affirming the way certain intensities resonate within the translated choral odes. While Gregory argues for a 'single lyric piece', it seems that H.D and Jeffers use lyric in a more complicated sense.

Because H.D. and Jeffers remain fascinated by a living pastness, they comb the ruins of an ancient Greek theatre to collect the artefacts necessary in their writing lives – stones as words, stones as monuments hiding singing bodies, and a Greek architecture that is the 'high-water mark of human achievement' (H.D. 1986: 113). H.D. and Jeffers cultivate a poetics of rocks to include varied representations of women who 'voice' psychic experiences through mediation between physical objects such as stones and monuments, and the bodily but ecstatic realization of a psychic life. H.D. writes, '[w]here a Greek voice speaks there are rocks'.[3] For H.D., equating the sound of a Greek voice to an elemental substance illustrates the way a rock can function materially both as an obstacle preventing meaning and as a tool that can create new meaning. H.D. often saturates her writing with a hypnotic sonic quality ('Rose, harsh rose, / marred and with stint of petals' [1983: 5]), but the translation of choral odes allows her to cultivate many voices and the opportunity to play with amplification of voice. Both H.D. and Jeffers collect the rocks fallen from a Greek voice to build original works of literature.

In Euripides, they find a narrative architecture from which to quarry. This adaptation technique resembles *spolia*, the ancient practice of repurposing stone from built structures onto new monuments. Canvassing antiquities sharpens both H.D. and Jeffers' creative sensibilities in the sense that they search for alabaster portals everywhere. This technique ties their work to spatial metaphors. The wall's opening creates the free fall of imagination into language. The ancient theatre tradition provides both writers a complementary way of thinking through contradictory temporal states, which requires falling into mythic time, a requirement that was also expected of the original Greek audience. Theatre festivals were held in open-air theatres, where actors and spectators braved the natural elements. The spirit of Greek theatre relied on this circularity of space and weather.

While H.D. constructs materially rich superstructures, Jeffers re-engages dramas against the American West coastline's natural stage. Describing the Western Coast as a kind of natural theatre set in 'Thurso's Landing', Jeffers writes, 'the platform is like a rough plank theater-stage / Built on the prow of the promontory' (1989: 174). Jeffers accesses the high ritual of Greek tragedy quite easily. His adaptation of Euripides' *Bacchae* (1928) points to a cast of mind accustomed to the unstable boundaries of form that tragedy often brings.[4] Just as in his translation of *Medea* (1946), Jeffers works within an Ovidian tradition, incorporating female characters from myth alongside elements of violence, exile and elegiac eroticism, to create a Dionysian fiction.

Strangenesses: acts of cognition as revelation

As kindred spirits working in similar island waters, H.D. and Jeffers use dramatic conventions to challenge their sense of the poem, where translating and adapting include elemental forces (wind, stone, fire, water) corresponding to the physic forces (visions/ sparks/radiances) that weather the very bedrock of the inner landscapes of their creative beings. H.D. and Jeffers' engagement with complex narratives across their oeuvres suggests the shortcomings they felt of the lyric form and why they felt it necessary to adapt and transform lyric practice. In their respective ways, each poet develops an outlaw poetics to complicate traditional understandings of the lyric. This lyric complication involves the displacement of the tragic chorus thorough radical translation.

In some ways, the lyric narrows the listening field when it speaks out of itself, often with no contending interlocutors. The lyric form lacks the acoustical space to capture the complexities of life. Most often, it sings the song of a single consciousness. Complex narratives, comprising elements of the lyric, epic and dramatic form, promote multiple voices before an audience of many. The complex narrative structures found in H.D.'s and Jeffers' work promote such larger fields where various speakers and auditors can assemble. Specifically, their dialogic use of Euripidean choral odes showcases a polyvocality, a many-voicedness common in modernist works, acting in concert with the lip-synching of a translator in mediation with an unstable theatrical text. The lyric intensities of a Euripidean choral ode work not only to complicate a stable dramatic frame, thus compounding the composition, but, in this case, also exist as translation, adding another layer of complexity. Both writers assemble the elemental refrains of their choruses (composed of untranslatable Greek word-rocks) into new texts.

Instead of calling H.D. a revisionary mythmaker, I prefer calling her a counter-modernist.[5] Her work functions as part of a grander investigation of how to inhabit and organize modernist literary landscapes, often rewriting the landscape when 'the rock breaks or falls into ruins', flooding the cracks with cataracts of new language (H.D. 2012: 107). In poems such as 'A Dead Priestess Speaks', 'Cassandra' and 'Eurydice', H.D. showcases female characters acting as Hermes-like boundary makers, *speaking* a new language into being with those around her. As such, her work prefers the rhythm of a dramatic narrator who converses with the tragic voice – a collective voice upholding the rituals of a prescribed tragedy while also improving upon them. H.D.'s tragic voice, like Kit's inscription upon the badlands, repurposes raw material – i.e. Euripides' choruses – refining them through repetition, subtraction and alchemical transduction.

H.D. carries out these creative transductions, moving elemental matter (both material and mystical) across territories and time. Jeffers accomplishes a similar feat – artist as boundary maker, fugitive, cartographer and protectorate of sacred lands. As boundary makers, H.D. and Jeffers excise expressive vocabularies from classical literary landscapes. Both poets seek an opening in the rock through which their appointed choruses can pass. This sacred passage into the rock includes a territory and a refrain that marks the passage in song. But a territory, in the Deleuzian and Guattarian sense, is not simply a place. A territory can only be claimed through the organization of the individuals who inhabit it, which includes their customs, habits, gestures and language. H.D. and Jeffers explore this idea of the territory through the chorus's collective identity. Both poets claim a mythic language to imagine eternal dramas against the backdrop of their current time. While their individual projects prove different, both revolutionary writers seek openings out of Euripides' portals.

Dramatic work proves attractive to both writers because it provides landscapes for characters to inhabit. For H.D., the sound in the rock, the fascination with the aural – this being a rewrite of Alain Badiou's 'fascination with the visual' – allows her to weave the inter-milieu melodies of the refrain, or *ritornelle*. The refrain is the responsibility of the chorus; it must carry its song within the poem's lines, or make arrangements for it to reside elsewhere. If all theatre is political, as Badiou claims, H.D. helps to make his case by asserting the importance of a collective spectatorship, a chorus, collaborating with(in) a literary text.[6] From the extensive use of the 'we' pronoun in many of H.D.'s poems, especially in 'Choros Translations', to her claim that wisdom resides in communities, her sense of the political resides in the shared experience of the theatre's auditorium.

Critical emphasis often falls on the imagistic import of H.D.'s poetry, but her relationship to the aural also proves a rich avenue of study. In *Ladies' Greek*, Yopie Prins articulates a 'rhythmic body' at work in H.D.'s poetry, especially around the chorus, where 'coordinating movements of the body with verse that can be chanted "as they moved" exemplifies a kinesthetic experience of rhythm' integral to moving beyond the self and into true collective experience (2017: 203, 205). Prins' understanding of how H.D.'s poetic feet integrate poetry, music and dance into a phenomenological appreciation of 'dancing Greek letters' illuminates how H.D. performs a free-verse approach when negotiating the difficult prosody of classical choral odes. H.D. translates against the backdrop of tragedy, a form ideally suited for pursuing how the speaking voice's rhythm performs its drama upon the listening, landscaped world, 'visualizing these broken sentences and unfinished rhythms as rocks' (H.D. [c. 1920] 1982: 58). H.D.'s careful, albeit non-scholarly, study of

Sappho's poems helps fine-tune her ear, for it is the ancient poet's *broken sentences* that H.D. sees in the rocky distance of her own imagination. The scientific pursuits of both H.D.'s father and grandfather influence her poetics, superimposing a geological cast of mind to later literary pursuits. Adalaide Morris writes that H.D. 'aspired to recalibrate science and poetry by becoming what one of her characters calls a "scientific lyrist"' (2003: 153). Jeffers, too, incorporates scientific ideas into his poems using a 'public prose' speaking style, something Helen Vendler describes as a Greek oratorical style (1995: 58). H.D. and Jeffers' sense of a geological time makes them receptive to the rhythms in the natural world – the sound of the waves lapping, raindrops falling, or even the drumming of the human heart.

Classical tragedy appeals to H.D. and Jeffers because of the poetic shapes it cuts. From his desk in Hawk Tower, Jeffers witnesses the rugged California coast's violence, the injustices naturally occurring between land, animals and humans. Jeffers develops a way of thinking he terms *inhumanism*, which primarily focuses on the natural world rather than on humankind. Jeffers cultivates an imaginative listening that hears the cries of a tragedy before it is seen. H.D.'s first collection, *Sea Garden* (1916) alludes to the generative relationship between rock and storytelling, between the natural elements and its landscape, set within the scalloped edge of reverberating shell: 'It is a strange life, / patterned in fire and letters … If I glance up / it is written on the walls', the speaker in 'Prisoners' announces, recalibrating a poetics of rocks also found in 'Hermes of the Ways' that 'piles little ridges' only to have the 'great waves / break over it' (1983: 34, 37). H.D.'s preoccupations with speaking stones, breaking waves and singing fires points to her own sense of inhumanism at work, especially relevant in her bacchic translations.

Beyond tragedy's tower: Jeffers' panoramic auditorium

Jeffers equates his physical acts of stone masonry with poem-making. Tor House and Hawk Tower represent a statement of poetics. Jeffers brings into being physical artefacts that exist as handiwork of poetic procedure. More practically, Hawk Tower provides Jeffers a literal space for writing. In a Heideggerian sense, he builds his place of dwelling. He writes in 'To the Stone Cutters', clearly an *ars poetica*: 'The poet as well builds his monument mockingly; for man will be blotted out'. (1988: 5). Jeffers' intense physical labour, required to build his home, matches the California coastline's brutality. Building poems becomes akin to building stone houses – both processes include the experiential and mystical. The diction in Jeffers' work cuts itself out of the landscape. His characters' temperaments are often described using the qualities of stone, and his birds fly according to shape and character of rock. In his poem 'To The House', the speaker explains in the last line, '[t]he sea and the secret earth gave bonds to affirm you' (1988: 5). One cannot but think of H.D.'s sea poppies in her *Sea Garden*'s secret earth.

Like H.D., Jeffers demonstrates an affinity for women speakers such as Cassandra and Medea, who carry potent speech of ancient wisdom in their bodies. An early poem, 'The Songs of the Dead Men to the Three Dancers', reflects Jeffers' interest in combining song, music and dance in dramatic verse. It begins with a querying voice reminiscent of H.D.'s: '(*Here a dancer enters and dances*.) / Who is she that is fragrant and desirable, / Clothed but enough to wake wantonness' ([1917] 2000: 223). Jeffers' lyric narratives often include what Karman calls a feminine energy, but perhaps the chorus in the *Bacchae* exemplify qualities too inflammatory, too radical even for Jeffers.

By changing the title of the poem from 'Women on Cythaeron' (first published in *Poetry Magazine* in 1928) to 'The Humanist's Tragedy', Jeffers repositions the poem's point of view. Instead of celebrating a chorus of women, the poem memorializes the downfall of one king. But other than punctuation changes, the title change remains the only major revision. Although Jeffers chooses to mute the play's choral odes, its music ominously persists in counterpoint to a fixed dialogue between King Pentheus and his Messenger. The chorus's song remains audible but muffled, an undermelody built into mountainscape. In a sense, this only heightens its urgency. The chorus proceeds through a voided intensity, a crack in the mountainside singing this refrain: 'Oh sisters, we have found an opening' ([1928] 1988: 381).

Jeffers' poem reads as didactic parable between the human and divine. He uses long prosaic lines to fence in the drama, much of which focuses solely on Pentheus's discomfort of Dionysus's arrival in town. H.D.'s treatment, which we will examine later, highlights the democratic transmission of a roving choral voice in a free-verse blast of staccato lines. In contrast, Jeffers' long, declarative and narrative lines between Pentheus and his Messenger expose deliberateness; there are no ecstatic revelations in the king's court. Instead, intensities register themselves in the dramatic import of actions reported. We slow down to reconstruct scenes given in extended dialogues. Formal in its tone, Pentheus's restraint and the Messenger's subservience signal a rhythm of stateliness and a temporal distance from the events recounted. Repetition appears as epithets ('mindful of all his dignity as a human being, a king and a Greek') like those of epic. A sonorous quality fills the poem's expanse. We hover above described scenes but the chorus does not request an introduction to the king, almost knowing their wild bestiality prevents such a meeting with the humanist. Cordoned off, they remain hidden in the slit of mountain.

If H.D.'s poem-translation of the *Bacchae* displays a lyric ongoingness from its chorus, Jeffers' imperialistic recasting closes it down, driving it inward: 'A wild strait gate-way; / Slit eyes in the mask, sisters, / Entered the mountain' ([1928] 1988: 381). His chorus processes blindly into theatre's mask of deception. Oblivious to their king, the maenads sing: '[w]e are fire and have found an opening'. This refrain marks the entrance and exit of the chorus's territory. Little does Pentheus realize they 'have hewn in the stone and mortar' an entrance into the mountain's mask ([1928] 1988: 381). The chorus carries their refrain inward into the poem's molten core. But their entrance into the sacred rock does not tempt Pentheus. He ruminates outside the maenads' spell, missing his entrance in.

Jeffers' deliberate excision of Mount Cithaeron in his revolutionary revision of title absents a hallowed ground. Euripides' description of Cithaeron's glittering sublimity, along with E.R. Dodds' reminder of its permanently snowy summit, anoints the mountain as a liminal space, a site conducive to earth-shaking transformations. In a defiant act of *spolia*, Jeffers carries off mountain rock. His quarrying leaves only more questions. Jeffers demolishes the mountain in the title, moving its material – the refrain-cascade of falling rocks – outside the poem's landscape. Instead, we are meant to feel the cool austerity of the king's palace.

The rationalist humanist remains outside animated conversation, unmoved by the stolen fires of sacred wisdom. He will not notice the trap waiting for him: the drunken bacchants waiting to dismember him and throw him into the void. Agave holds the severed head of her son, his wet beard running blood down her forearms. This bloody scene reinforces Dionysus's earlier warning that 'human collectedness' will not save us, nor increase our power ([1928] 1988: 382). In fact, solidarity might even be more destructive than we think. But the true fire thief, Arthur Rimbaud tells us, is the poet herself.

Soundness, a salutary attitude of the depths

What does it mean to brave fire? What does it mean to rewrite one's landscape in a ritual of refinement? H.D.'s poem 'Eurydice' functions proleptically for H.D. since it foreshadows the styles and themes that will occupy her later poetics. Using fire to reclaim land in an interrogative refrain of agency, resistance and defiance, Eurydice floods her hymn in a sonic overload, using repetition and this interrogative mode to register presence. H.D. seems more interested in orchestrating a somatic vocality than in purifying language or making it referential. H.D.'s experiments with a participatory and repetitive orality disclose a difficulty for her readers. As Morris explains, even an aurally alert and sophisticated reader cannot generate a total visionary transformation. Ultimately, H.D. asks us to be better listeners. Her work challenges how characters (and readers) come to understand the world through phenomenological cues – that is, through voiced, vibrational language.

H.D.'s poetry suffers with critics who cite the tediousness of her static images, varied forms and paradoxical philosophies of art and literature. Pound famously brands H.D. an *Imagiste*, pushing her into an artistic corner. Perhaps feeling the heat of literary claustrophobia, H.D. responds by writing in various genres (diary, essay, memoir, autobiography, film, translation) that do not easily fit into the generic conventions of high modernism. Jeffers did not fit into the club either. Like Euripides, a playwright often described as prophetic, modern and not truly *classical*, H.D. and Jeffers destabilize notions of the accepted literary practice in their use of complex forms. They embrace the organization of a material, acoustic space as a way to control the chaos of creation. Their efforts stem from a simultaneous desire to rupture and contain new pockets of chaos. In the harnessing of a refrain, speakers sound out the *terra*, transducing ancient lyric voices across narrative forms in a renegade ritual of poetics.

H.D.'s personal classicism uses an intuition of fire.[7] H.D. presents herself a translator of the classics to her literary community, but as Gregory notes, 'she saw her role in terms of a subversive, erotic and visionary endeavor fundamentally challenging the assumptions of classical transmission' (1997: 57). Breaking bodies, reading into fracture fires, H.D. seems intent on re-writing her reputation as *Imagiste*. Her role as a radical translator enables such a revision, while translating energizes the production of original counter-modern work. In poems like 'Eurydice' she writes dramatic lyrics using mythic characters who sing odes against a backdrop of a heroic narrative. H.D. pursues how bodies respond to sonic immersion, or what Stefan Helmreich calls *transduction*, a process that 'describes sound as meaningful and material, reaching across (while also exceeding) sensory, cognitive registers' (2015: 224). Whether material or semiotic, transduction (from the Latin, *transducere*, 'to lead across') refers to a process where a conversion of energy takes place. For poets, the energy measured and transferred is the 'private melody or undersong hummed during composition by the poet as a spell or charm' that produces a materiality (Hollander 1981: iv). (The placing of one's hands on a large speaker and feeling the vibrations as music plays perhaps demonstrates how transduction is receptive rather than productive.) The human eardrum lives as a natural transducer. Transduction is also how one setting (or context) models for another; how new settings are established out of existing ones, or even how to deliberate between two different orders, thereby creating a third way.

H.D.'s use of rhyme, rhythm and repetition points to a literary practice invested in participatory song and ritual – the actual vibration of the eardrum important to trance. Hers is a mystical body, igniting the process by which outside energies shape a poetic interiority. This interest in sound and its material effect on the listener/audience, points towards a healing poetry, what might be termed a *curative poetics*. H.D. uses transduction in her choral odes to orchestrate an oversound, a collaborative voice that catches a territory entire.

H.D.'s translation practice serves as a necessary antagonism, an occult process and a training ground for her poetic voice.[8] H.D. introduces an irritant, a grain of sand in the oyster shell, when she self-initiates into the boys' club, a 'whole tribe of academic Grecians' (H.D. 1983: 328). H.D.'s continuing use of the Wharton 1885 dual text edition of Sappho even after newly available fragments of Sappho's poems were published and translated further solidifies her translation operation as decisively non-scholarly and personal (Balmer 2013: 47). When H.D. moves away from mastery, she names herself as Outsider. Whether she hopes to untangle a writing cure, or a dreaming field, or a parental knot, H.D. relies on Euripides' bitterness for the right measure of modern matter.[9] Just as Euripides uses the tragic form to meditate on the Peloponnesian War's atrocities, H.D. adopts Euripides' voice as a way to introduce her own anti-war sentiments. Gregory writes that H.D. finds in Euripides 'a mirror for the visceral and bewildering experience of war' (1997: 25). Euripides de-glamorized her time's accepted myths and introduced new plots audiences hadn't seen before.[10] By translating Euripides, H.D. enters unlettered into a largely male-dominated, classical Greek scholarship.[11] H.D. does not use classicism to impress upon her readers the rigor of her literary projects. And whether her motives rely the pleasures of linguistic estrangement or the desire to engender translation, her fascination with the female chorus discloses a radicalness at the heart of her writing.

Dramatic poems and theatrical works challenge ideas about performativity, theatricality and the textual with their use of embodied language. In her adaptation of *Ion*, H.D. initiates a dialogic exchange that includes fields of interrupting prose sections inserted into the play's lineated lines. By working with Euripides' lesser-known plays,

H.D. invites us to consider a formula of subtraction, a highly stylized negation; a privately funded laboratory researching alchemical powers in the wild. H.D. ghosts around Euripides' stories but leaves her own stony mark. The prose sections function like sedimentary rock, layers which include statements of poetics, translation theories and individual lines of poetry.

H.D. builds onto the existing structure of Euripides' *Ion*, but the new tile does not match the old. She showcases the incongruities because they reveal a literary history. Her work opens up a fracturing in time, a palimpsestic condition where by the ancient past emerges into present view. H.D. replaces Euripides' various stylistic choices with her own sense of ornamentation: 'What time is it? Greek unity gives us freedom, it expands and contracts at will, it is time-in-time and time-out-of-time together, it predicts modern-time estimates' (2003: 185). Ancient Greek theatre relied on synthesizing various codes and practices, but playwrights freely worked within this structure, giving shape to wildly unbounded content. H.D.'s prose passages catalogue the admissions, revisions and omissions of a shared theatre tradition.

Chorus as inner mood curtain: they wore veils over their eyes

Fire and earthquakes plague the landscape of *Bacchae*. Festive drunkenness and sweet delirium shake loosened limbs. When Dionysus calls for the female earthquake spirits to strike, flames included, we weather the brute force of an elemental authority not through language per se, but through a spectacle of sensation.

H.D.'s translations of Euripides' *Bacchae* appear in a lyric sequence titled 'Choros Translations' in *Red Roses for Bronze*. By translating only the lyric meters, H.D. creates a primarily aural world, where the chorus sings, 'wisdom is best / and beauty / sheer holiness' but is not subservient to plot ([1931] 1983: 227). With the narrative frame removed, the chorus transforms into high lyric song. While sections of H.D.'s poem-translation are titled 'Strophe', 'Antistrophe' and 'Epode', no dramatic dialogue surrounds them. Translating selectively, she forcibly corrupts the drama's linear narrative. Using wildfire sprung from Semele's grave-smoke, H.D. harnesses the play's elemental forces of 'hill and mountain worship' into a new kind of lyric procession ([1931] 1983: 233).

H.D.'s chorus transmits and represents the intense *lyrical now*, an event in sound.[12] Fixed in form, the chorus inhabits the literary text but generally does not influence the dramatic plot's outcome. H.D. reinterprets the Euripidean chorus's role when she repositions them beyond the theatre space's artificiality and its attending illusions. By extracting the chorus from its original context and focusing on their song's aurality, H.D. generates enough momentum to 'bring on a movement of absolute deterritorialization: 'Goodbye, I'm leaving and I won't be back' (Deleuze and Guattari 1987: 327). H.D.'s chorus wishes a similar farewell, marching outside the mountainous terrain of Pentheus's kingdom and into her poem-translation, distinguishing between a marked territory (Euripides'), a previously unmarked one (the Poem) and an unknown territory (of Beyond). These lines speak to the revolution afoot: 'Bromios leads us, / bearing aloft the narthex, / himself / even as the pine-torch / himself the flame and torch-light ([1931] 1983: 225). This deterritorialization also mirrors what H.D herself is doing within modernism, solidifying her label as a counter-modernist.

The chorus's singing marks out territory, and is territory at the same time. Gesture then – the chorus's dancing bodies, their shaking procession – speaks in felt intensities. The chorus speaks of new potentials: the polyvocality of dancing feet, clapping hands and nonsense words. This chorus does not speak of Zeus's birth found in the second *stasimon* of Euripides' original; instead it leaps forward to the third *stasimon*'s divine vengeance. These women walk away in spirited defiance, restructuring a feeling not found in Euripides. H.D.'s chorus embodies a lyric procession sonically rich and kinetically aware of its entrances and exits onto the sweet hills, the 'distant hill-peak' and the 'steep ledge of hillock' because 'the hills belong' to them ([1931] 1983: 230).

The collective speaker in H.D.'s 'Choros Translations' opens with questions seeking to score or mark its territory, the first of many echoing refrains. 'Who is there, / who is there in the road? / who is there, / who is there in the street? / back, / back, each to his house, / let no one, / no one speak' ([1931] 1983: 223). This call-and-response exposes a gnarled texture, challenging notions of addresser and addressee, the power of language in naming and how melodic landscapes are strung into being. The chorus asserts its authority because it takes its identity wherever it goes, carrying the wild fennel wand, the thyrsus, which includes this spell of 'swift, / be swift, / invoke and draw him back / from the Phrygian mountain-peaks' ([1931] 1983: 223). The women voice psychic experiences through the thyrsus and mountainside they dance as sacred. Their singing refrain 'always carries earth with it; it has a land (sometimes a spiritual land) as its concomitant; it has an essential relation to a Natal, a Native' (Deleuze and Guattari 1987: 327). What follows is simultaneous entrance and exit. Whenever H.D.'s chorus goes, they take their revolutionary refrain with them.

Their revolution subscribes to a necessary evacuation, a key movement placing themselves beyond the-beyond-realm of the Deleuzian mythic. H.D.'s poetic revolution anticipates the construction of something I define as processional poetics: the espousal of lyric intensity (sonic, material, kinetic) that revolves outward away from a source text in a ceremonial fashion, perhaps beyond a single consciousness. This intensity triggers and sets in motion the phenomenological dislocation necessary for a reader to truly inhabit a poetic experience. Processional poetics involves multiple entrances and exits, where language, landscape and meaning are interconnected. Processional poetics enacts a revolution, a flight from inside the cross-hatched lines of language.

Writing from no place

As a counter-modernist, H.D. willingly writes a kind of minor literature; a tradition that works against the more visible and accessible kinds of literature.[13] A minor literature is no less interested in telling major stories, but its agency comes from participating outside recognized social, political, or linguistic systems of order.[14] Desire is procedure, then, the molten lava flown from a form. H.D.'s project involves writing and reading *out of form*, *off form*, perhaps even *in bad form*. Her transcreative translation practice coaxes out a rupture. A crack in the terracotta pot breaches a capture of words. H.D.'s main preoccupation focuses on this experience of escape – what the scenery is like beyond the conscriptions of a word – a procession always already *in extremis*. Within minor literature, these intensities are experienced as raw material, like sound without signification.

Translation of a dramatic script is never one of equivalence because it must allow for the potentialities of performance – the actor's error a necessary revision. H.D.'s 'Choros Translations' include fictional elements taken from Euripides' *Bacchae* but the ritual lyricism is its own brand. The women speak the poem-translation into being – a refrain across the badlands standing in as replacement for Dionysus's speech. Two separate bands of women inhabit Euripides' play: the bacchants who travelled from Asia to the story's setting of Greece, and the Theban women, recent converts of Dionysus. Both bands of women travel outside the bounds of a civilizing force. Both choruses thrive on states of elsewhere: drugs, disasters, miracles, milk, wine, honey, fire. Their choral wall breathes a rhythmic and traveling *enclosure*, staking out a deeply pleasured freedom of elsewhere. In the secondary growth of Mount Cithaeron's mountain pine we read their walking notes: *Ritual, reunion, communion, collaboration, labour forces.*

H.D.'s poem-translation survives as counter-epiphanic, counter-programmatical, for it does not depend upon ancient tragedy's rituals. H.D.'s bacchants re-enact a catharsis of refinement rather than purification.[15] Receptive to the experience of tragic possibility, this chorus relocates to new reality without male protagonists' aid, seamlessly and without internal strife. Transductively, the chorus transcends dualities of form and content. Their relentless questioning, repetition (their fallen footsteps), and vatic holes read not as a failure of imagination but as an insistence of a transformation. Critics who fault the 'Choros Translations' for not adequately applying Imagist poetics do not appreciate H.D.'s sonic disturbances. When H.D. repeats a word like 'on' or 'this', she asks her readers to suspend sense – to enter nonsense's grand trance of asignifying sound. '[T]his, / this, / this, / this; / escape / from the power of the hunting pack' ([1931] 1983: 227) the bacchants trace in blue skies. This refrain, repeated elsewhere in the poem, enchants the reader and invites the pleasures of nonsense. Only when language stops being representational does it generate potency. Her translation's halting quality – its honeyed, drawn-out *ritardando* – represents an active intensity. H.D.'s connection to the political strives for disequilibrium and dislocation, not poetic momentum.

The chorus's bodily vocality of 'on, / on, / on; / the fields drip /honey' marches them into the valley of transformation ([1931] 1983: 225). H.D. recasts the chorus's behaviour as something other than Dionysiac emotionalism or enthusiastic reverence: they are a talented troupe of actors rebuilding a new order. Here, there is no need for Cadmus. Only a portion of Agave's speech appears at the end of 'Choros Translations'. The gift of translation remains one of loss. H.D. disallows conversation between Pentheus and Dionysus. Their dialogue remains buried underneath mounds of Greek. H.D. translates the fourth ode's frenzy describing the hunt for Pentheus, but this transcription records a mere stylized ritual to drive out a godless man. It is not a true exorcism, only an imagined one the bacchants devise to keep their landscape free from desecration. As actors, they enact a scene of their freedom.

And this point proves crucial: H.D.'s bacchants only speak this murderous refrain from the original play – 'slash him across the throat' (1983: 230) – to remember past offences. Although the dismemberment of Pentheus proves inevitable, the ritual of performance or a ritualized reading will never make us whole. And sonic memorials – monuments where wisdom resides as vibrating language in our open mouths – can only offer temporary consolation.

Agave erects such a sonic memorial for her shared sisterhood of the theatre. And yet, the bacchants do not convince Agave to renew her contract with the show. She hands off her tragic language, a democratic property, to the band of women seizing the last stretches of a territory in translation. 'The thyrsus shall pass on / to other Dionysians'; Agave laments, adding, 'O let me never see / haunted, mad Cithaeron / nor Cithaeron / see me' ([1931] 1983: 231).

If myth functions as speech stolen but never restored to its proper place, H.D. employs a thrilling variation of *spolia*, whereby instead of adding onto Euripides' house as she did in *Ion*, she convinces the bacchants to leave the *Bacchae* altogether—but not before claiming the choral odes. The intentional repositioning of the chorus outside the lines of the play creates a new meta-textual space. This departure emancipates the chorus, since they are not bound to the confines of any single text. Their processional refrain across the poem-translation recasts them as a talented troupe of actors who collectively create a post-text of performance. H.D.'s radical genre mixing enables a textual revolution unperformed by anti-modern classicists or modern materialists to date: H.D. presents herself as a counter-modern transducer.

Exodos

H.D. and Jeffers rewrite themselves out of Euripidean landscapes, taking stone hearth with them. Lyric refrains wrapped in fire (a mode of announcing oneself) does not simply extend beyond the theatre stage, it flames upward, revising our sense of the Deleuzan territorial to something more like the celestial. Both writers subscribe to language's ability to renew, restore and keep alive one's spirit in the materials of history – materials stitched from the strands of myth. Both celebrate the Artist as boundary maker, re-animating refrains etched in stone, translating the unmapped territories and heavens within us – the badlands tinged in smoke.

CHAPTER 8

REINVENTING *EROS*: H.D.'S TRANSLATION OF EURIPIDES' *HIPPOLYTUS*

Miranda Hickman and Lynn Kozak

And gods (and men) call her (the virgin deer-shooter), huntress, a great title. Love, loosener of limbs, never draws near to her.

Sappho 44A=Alc. 304

With respect to shameful things, people are ashamed, whether speaking them or doing them or intending to do them, just as Sappho replied when Alkaios said: 'I want to speak, but shame holds me back . . .': 'but if you had desire for good and beautiful things, / and your tongue wasn't churning up something evil, /shame wouldn't ravage your eyes/ and you'd state your claim.'

Aristotle. *Rh.* 1367a

Out of the Hellenism that guided her work, early and late, modernist writer H.D. turned with notable frequency to Euripides. As Eileen Gregory notes, H.D.'s engagement with Euripides would be among the most formative and sustained of her career (Gregory 1997, 25–6). Between 1915 and 1919, during the period when she was publishing her first volume of poems, *Sea Garden* (1916), H.D. began translating a significant cluster of Euripides' plays.[1] Especially during the years around the Great War, H.D. looked to Euripides for resources – narrative, characters and lexis – to address questions brought to the fore in her mind by wartime, often about the cultural position of women. Her translations, notably liberal and creative, figured crucially in the development of what we read as her emergent queer feminist thought. In 1915, H.D. reached to Euripides' *Iphigenia in Aulis*, whose narrative involves the Trojan War, to meditate on the situation of women in wartime; at nearly the same moment, she also turned to Euripides' *Hippolytus* – which does not address war – for less evident reasons. In 1919, the two translations were published together, placing them as projects in dialogue. At this juncture, why did H.D. address the *Hippolytus*? As with all of her translations, what H.D. chooses to translate from the original Euripidean play (from which she excerpts radically), together with how she renders the Greek in English, indicate her paths of interest.

As Gregory notes, H.D.'s early work shows fascination with one figure in particular from Euripides: the virginal male, what H.D. calls the 'intellectualized, crystalline youth'.[2] H.D. often engages with such virginal figures, frequently from Euripides, to explore erotic liminality (Gregory 1990: 134) – and for this, initially H.D. turns more often to the young male, the *ephēbos*, than the unwed girl, *korē*, a preference to which we will return.

The 'crystalline' qualities H.D. associated with the *ephēbos* may also have resonated for her with the aesthetics of her own early verse. In the 1910s and 1920s, H.D. repeatedly addresses a nexus of issues she associates with the Hippolytus figure specifically: after publishing her *Choruses from the Hippolytus*, she continues consideration of Hippolytus with four poems published from the early to mid-1920s. Her play *Hippolytus Temporizes* (1927), a culmination of this line of work, extrapolates from an earlier poem of the same name, composed in 1920.[3] Building from Gregory, we maintain that H.D. engages with the Hippolytus figure, as mediated by Euripides, to develop commentary on the subject of *eros*, which becomes increasingly central to her thought. Through her translation of Euripides' *Hippolytus*, H.D. develops an ethically inflected critique of the reading of *eros* articulated in Euripides' play, toward developing an alternative.

Guiding H.D.'s engagement with the *Hippolytus* are three interrelated conceptual knots, for her all linked to the figure of Artemis, who strongly interests H.D. as feminist conceptual resource between 1915 and 1919: 1) the need to acknowledge the experience of *eros* in feminist thought; 2) the discourse of shame through which *eros* is often culturally understood; and 3) the need to reconsider the assumed opposition featured in Euripides' *Hippolytus* between the 'Artemisian' and the 'Aphroditic'. Both Euripides' *Iphigenia in Aulis* and *Hippolytus* feature Artemis (an important part of why H.D. engages with these plays): Artemis's demand for sacrifice catalyses the events of the *Iphigenia in Aulis*, and Hippolytus's dedication to Artemis, coupled with Phaedra's longing for Artemisian chastity as she seeks to surmount her illicit desire for her stepson Hippolytus, drives the destructive machinery of the *Hippolytus*.

While developing her early interest in Hippolytus, H.D. concomitantly often turned to Artemis as a potentially empowering figure for feminist thought. As a chaste huntress in open spaces, Artemis suggests ways out of what H.D.'s early work calls the 'sheltered garden' of Victorian domestic femininity. In part, H.D. turns to the Artemisian under the influence of Pater (Gregory 1997: 267–8), whose own interest in Hippolytus, 'ardent follower of Artemis, goddess of hunting and chastity',[4] guided H.D. to the chaste Artemisian mode.[5]

At this same moment, the Artemisian register also allows H.D. to imagine a lesbian *eros*, one which increasingly inflects her feminist thought during these years. As Laity explains, through the idea of 'sister love' (for H.D. a trope for a lesbian ethos, and for her importantly connected with the Artemisian), H.D. suggests theoretical forays on lesbian desire different from – even illegible to – theorizations of lesbianism from early twentieth-century sexologists such as Havelock Ellis, whose thought H.D. admired (Laity 1992: xxi–xxiv). H.D.'s autobiographical novel *HERmione*, composed 1926–7 but reflecting thought patterns of H.D.'s late teens and early twenties, indicates her investment in an Artemisian 'huntress' figure. When the novel's H.D.-linked protagonist Hermione tells Fayne of her desire for her, she remembers how Fayne looked playing Pygmalion on stage: 'You might have been a huntress ... I mean a boy standing on bare rocks and stooping to take a stone from his strapped sandal' (H.D. 1981: 163). The flickering here between 'huntress' and 'boy' suggests the Artemisian–Hippolytan node of H.D.'s thought: the two figures often form a nexus. Yet through her *Hippolytus*, H.D. will begin to distinguish between a Hippolytan mode of devotion to Artemis, predicated on misogyny and refusal of *eros*, and an alternative Artemisian mode of H.D.'s making, philogynous and affirming *eros* as a source of creation and vitality.

H.D. reaches an apex of such Artemisian conceptual work in another novel, *Paint It To-day*, composed 1921–2, but registering thought developed over the preceding half decade. As Friedman notes,

> Artemis is the ruling presence in *Paint It To-day,* the liminal spirit ... who governs its
> authorial, narrative, and symbolic structures .... By the time she wrote *Paint It To-day*,
> H.D. had already translated choruses from two Euripidean tragedies in which Artemis
> features centrally. She had also written the sequence of related Phaedra poems about
> Artemis and Aphrodite that served as the initial core for her verse drama, *Hippolytus
> Temporizes*, an adaptation of Euripides' *Hippolytus* that she began as early as 1923 and
> published in 1927 .... H.D.'s Artemis is a figure of female independence and rebellion
> against the desire of men. Her inviolate chastity represents a female desire for freedom,
> the escape from the sheltered garden of domesticated love for the wilderness of space
> without men. H.D.'s Artemis is a *presence* in her texts that crystallizes a lesbian refusal
> to accept an androcentric construction of desire.
>
> *Friedman 1990: 191*

Indeed, through her construction of Artemis, H.D. refuses one model of (androcentric) desire in favour of another – and, we argue, displaces one model of the Artemisian with another. Specifically, H.D.'s translation choices indicate an effort to imagine a version of Artemisian 'inviolate chastity' distinct from that suggested by Euripides. H.D.'s *Hippolytus* translation moves beyond both a Euripidean and Paterian understanding of the Artemisian – to an alternative theorization of the Artemisian mode, one including *eros* in ways empowering for feminist thought.

Read as commentary, H.D.'s *Choruses from the Hippolytus of Euripides* involves three major interventions, responding to the problems articulated above. By choosing a play featuring the commanding influence of *eros* and emphasizing excerpts foregrounding its supremacy, H.D. 1) obliquely emphasizes the importance of recognizing *eros* in feminist thought of this time; 2) exposes and critiques how desire in Euripides' text is understood through a discourse of shame;[6] and 3) interrogates how the Artemisian is understood vis-à-vis the Aphroditic in Euripides' play. These interventions move towards H.D.'s re-vision of the Artemisian, which in turn underwrites a major vector of her project – a reinvention of *eros*.

Defying *eros* 'in vain'

As Zeitlin notes, the dominant concept of Euripides' *Hippolytus* is the 'power of Aphrodite' (1996). H.D. crops and translates Euripides' text so as to underscore this power. The last word of her translation reads:

you alone, Kupris,
creator of all life,
reign absolute.

VII.19–21; cf. Eur. Hipp. *1280f.*

And elsewhere:

For neither lightning-shaft
nor yet stars shot
from a distant place
can equal the love-dart,
sped from your hands,
child of God, Eros.

In vain along Alpheos,
in vain (if we defy Eros)
are the Greek altars
bright with blood ...

IV.15–16; cf. Eur. Hipp. *525–42*

This last passage foregrounds the searing through-line of H.D.'s translation: 'we defy' – and in this reading, deny – the force of Eros 'in vain'.

Accenting this strand of the *Hippolytus* as her feminist thought is in formation, H.D. insists that any future-directed discussion for women of the early twentieth century must factor in the play of *eros*. Partly through Euripides, H.D. devotes work to thinking through stances of potential liberation for women – psychic strategies for 'New Womanhood' – that will allow women of her generation to supersede conceptions of Victorian womanhood,[7] toward perspectives more open to real elemental forces of the 'unsheltered' world.[8] H.D. suggests that as new cultural roles and spaces for women emerge, such strategies must take into account the dire force of Sappho's 'sweet-bitter' *eros*: γλυκύπικρον, alive in H.D.'s emotions during these years as more painful, ἀλγεινός, than sweet.

As H.D. developed her *Hippolytus*, she was also addressing the baneful power of *eros* in poems of 'The Dorset Trio': 'Amaranth', 'Envy' and above all, 'Eros' itself – all tracing the awesome power of desire to afflict those under its sway. H.D.'s work often recognizes the force of what Sappho calls *eros lusiméles* ('love, loosener of limbs') as part of a new range of wisdom for 'New Women' of her time:

Ἔρος δηὖτέ μ' ὁ λυσιμέλης δόνει,
γλυκύπικρον ἀμάχανον ὄρπετον

Now Love masters my limbs and shakes me,
fatal creature, bitter-sweet.[9]

Fragment 130

In 'Eros', H.D. uses the idea of 'shattering' to suggest her own reading of such *eros*:

> . . . to sing love
> Love must first shatter us.

H.D. 1983, 319[10]

Moving even beyond Sappho's *eros lusiméles*, H.D. expands viscerally on the ability of *eros* to wound, suggested in both *Hippolytus* and the *Greek Anthology* (cf. Eur. *Hipp.* 392; *GA* V.98, V.225). In H.D.'s 'Amaranth', contemporaneous with the *Hippolytus* translation, the fading of love spurs the speaker to approach the goddess of love as 'shattered' suppliant:

> . . . my flesh is scorched and rent,
> shattered, cut apart,
> and slashed open;
> . . .
> black, dark to purple

H.D. 1983, 311

Phaedra's position in the *Hippolytus* clearly resonates with that of this poetic speaker: while this speaker is 'scorched and rent' by thwarted desire, H.D.'s Phaedra is 'bruised', in 'bone and flesh' (III.2). 'Hurt' appears seven times in H.D.'s translation of the *Hippolytus*, as cued by a range of Greek words: clearly on the text's lexical mind, 'hurt' indicates damage going beyond love's metaphorical 'wounds'.[11] As in her *Iphigenia in Aulis*, H.D. emphasizes wounds of the flesh, in her thought figuring valorized ways of knowing: as Gregory notes, H.D. often features such wounds as part of initiatory process, towards both healing and new knowledge.[12] In 'Amaranth', H.D.'s signature violent idiom[13] suggests that commitment to the goddess of love facilitates a transformation and elevation, especially when involving a 'shattering' of the being. 'Shattered', a word pervasive in H.D.'s lexicon, marks H.D.'s sublime – a breaking open that brings greater knowledge – often achieved through the force of *eros*.[14] Thus for H.D.'s thought, such undoing is not always negatively valenced: in the name of evolution and healing, she often affirms that which 'shatters' cultural and ideological structures in need of supersession.[15] Accordingly, one way of moving beyond what H.D. calls 'our restricted minds' (H.D. 1986: 133) is to step to an enlarged conception of the shattering powers of *eros* – for H.D., it can undo and loosen in the name of new making.

Thus in part, H.D. emphasizes *eros* towards a widened feminist consciousness. In the early twentieth century, she implies, knowledge of such desire is important to women for reaching new positions of strength. With this emphasis, H.D. aligns with avant-garde feminists of this moment candidly acknowledging erotic experience for women, even elevating it as liberatory. Natalya Lusty describes this comparatively small group as 'libertarian advocates such as Stella Browne, Dora Marsden and Rebecca West', promoting what they called 'a new morality of free sexual unions', explicitly challenging the anti-sex stance of social purity feminists' (Lusty 2008: 253). Yet H.D.'s conception of *eros*, shaped by her engagement with Greek antiquity, differs importantly from such 'libertarian' conceptions. Her experiences in bohemian London (and its atmosphere of 'blithe arrangement' [H.D. 2011: 3]) left her burned by an attempted 'morality of free sexual unions'. As H.D. came to know, especially for women, such 'free unions' often meant not only 'hurt' but even 'danger' (H.D. 2011: 82). Her choice to articulate her vision of *eros* through Euripides' *Hippolytus* thus indicates a wish to register such danger, for both women (Phaedra) and men (Hippolytus, Theseus): as Zeitlin notes, Euripides' *Hippolytus* inscribes in scarring terms that '*eros* is the most dangerous of all relations' (Zeitlin 1996: 223).[16]

Yet H.D.'s *Hippolytus* nonetheless insists on the inclusion of *eros* as a mode of being and relationship – and if she distrusts the 'morality of free sexual unions', her work with *eros* is nonetheless significantly guided by ethical considerations. H.D.'s ethical force comes through in her efforts (registered in her translation choices) to free thought from conventions which, as she puts it, 'cripple … and dwarf the being'; and access the knowledge and creative vitality that *eros* can bring, while still remaining realistic about both its life-affirming and baneful effects. In 'Notes on Thought and Vision' (c. 1919), H.D. accents the affirmative dimension of erotic relationships:[17]

> All reasoning, normal, sane, and balanced men and women need and seek at certain times of their lives, certain definite physical relationships . . . . Not to desire and make every effort to develop along these natural physical lines, cripples and dwarfs the being.
>
> *H.D. 1982: 17*

H.D.'s *Hippolytus* thus supplements the blind spot of this perspective: it conveys the elements of 'danger' also bound up in *eros*, insisting that there is nothing 'sane', or 'balanced' about *eros* when one knows its power fully.

H.D.'s translation of *Hippolytus*, especially through its critique of the play's train of destruction, does something more: it gestures towards an Artemisian erotic mode offering an alternative to the play's utterly damaging vision of *eros*. If H.D. seeks acknowledgement of both *eros* and its potentially destructive valences to form part of an enlarged feminist awareness, as her translation registers, in Euripides' scenario the damage (both diegetical and ideological) reads to H.D. as destructive in the wrong ways, wrecking many things she holds dear. Such *eros* crushes individual mortals in its path, falling short of the Artemisian feminism she imagines as empowering, and lacking the mode of *eros* that she reads as catalyst for women's freedom and sublime knowledge. Thus a live question for H.D.'s nexus of work around the *Hippolytus* – not adequately addressed by her translation, requiring subsequent work – is how to revise and modulate understandings of *eros* so as to surpass such sheer (and mere) wreckage with valuable knowledge.

Clearly, Euripides' play articulates the devastating power of *eros* through both Phaedra's suffering and through Hippolytus himself, ultimately mangled and killed for his refusal to honour Aphrodite. Euripides' play distributes the responsibility for Hippolytus's death beyond the youth's own disdain for *eros*, to include Phaedra's deception and Theseus's curse. But H.D.'s cropped translation chiefly emphasizes the costs to Hippolytus of both his defiance of *eros* and the societal discourses that make of Phaedra's feeling for him something shameful. For H.D., these two are crucially related: cultural shame gives rise to Hippolytus's defiance, which in turn brings destruction. Shame discourse likewise stands behind Phaedra's condition of being 'bruised' in 'bone and flesh', bereft of redemptive knowledge. This leads to H.D.'s second intervention.

'Kupris/creator of all life'

H.D.'s dissatisfaction with the vision of *eros* articulated in Euripides' *Hippolytus* comes through in her translation's penultimate line, suggesting her last word: where 'Kupris' is 'creator of all life'. This phrase signals H.D.'s refusal of how Euripides' *Hippolytus* regards Kupris and Eros: there, they give rise only to death. This shift suggests H.D.'s critique not of the power of *eros* itself, but rather *eros* when framed (and reduced) by societal discourses of shame.

H.D. indicates her focus on such shame discourse through two main translation choices: the English word 'veils' and her adjacent use of 'scarlet'. Early in her translation, the Troezenian women note hearing about Phaedra's suffering where they do laundry. As they dip jars in the 'deep pool/below the rock shelf' and the 'friend' washes clothes, H.D.'s text notes that the friend 'steeped her veils' – and 'spread the scarlet stuff' across the rocks.

> At high-tide,
> the sea – they say –
> left a deep pool
> below the rock-shelf:
> in that clear place
> where the women dip
> their water-jars,
> **my friend steeped her veils**
> **and spread the scarlet stuff**
> across the hot ridge

In the Greek, there are 'cloths' (φάρεα), whose sense H.D. captures through 'stuff', but not veils per se. H.D. likewise insists on 'veils' in the following section, for φάρη, where other English translations use a range of different words.[18]

τειρομέναν νοσερᾷ κοίτᾳ δέμας ἐντὸς ἔχειν	She lies sick,
οἴκων, λεπτὰ δὲ **φά-**	faint on her couch
ρη ξανθὰν κεφαλὰν σκιάζειν·	within the palace;
τριτάταν δέ νιν κλύω	her thin **veils**
τάνδ᾽ ἀβρωσίᾳ	cast a shadow
στόματος ἁμέραν	across her bright locks.

H.D.'s emphasis on 'veils', somewhat beyond what the Greek encourages and other English translations provide, suggests H.D.'s interest in modesty and privacy culturally associated with women's veiling: customs whereby women are expected to remain 'veiled', both in the sense of remaining chaste in their desires and hiding their desires from view. H.D.'s use of 'veils' might also recall Euripides' first version of the *Hippolytus*, Ἱππόλυτος καλυπτόμενος, customarily referred to in English as Hippolytus Veiled, as H.D. likely knew from Pater. In this first version, 'veiled' suggests Hippolytus's efforts to shield himself from what he construes misogynistically as Phaedra's impure desire.[19] H.D.'s text surfaces and challenges the discourses and assumptions giving rise to a need for such veils.

H.D.'s related use of 'scarlet' to describe such cloth (πορφύρεα φάρεα) further suggests the discourse of shame pervading both Phaedra's mindscape and Hippolytus's ugly invective, requiring such 'veils'. This appears in H.D.'s choice to translate πορφύρεα (usually 'red', 'crimson', or 'purple') as 'scarlet', suggesting scarlet letters and scarlet women. H.D. likewise links 'scarlet' and 'shame' in her *Iphigenia in Aulis* (1916) through textual contiguity:

> Shame, scarlet, fresh-opened – a flower
> Strikes across my face.

> *II.4–5*

'Scarlet' in her *Hippolytus* similarly signals 'shame', which H.D. understands as why Phaedra's desire consumes her mind and body with 'hurt'.

Again, such 'shame' also breeds Hippolytus's defiance of *eros*. Yet as H.D. suggests here, as well as in other work on Hippolytus just afterwards, both this defiance and assumptions about the opposition of the Artemisian and Aphroditic on which it is predicated are mistaken: H.D.'s text suggests an alternative reading of *eros* and thus its relationship to the Artemisian.[20] H.D.'s interventions show her reading Phaedra and Hippolytus as hanged by the same discursive rope: with her ethical sense, reaching for a revised *eros*, H.D. seeks to undo the knots of that rope.[21] If H.D.'s ethical work begins by tracking the effects of a destructive *eros lusimélēs* ('love, loosener of limbs'), she continues it by seeking to 'loosen' the entangling strands of a discourse that brings death for both a Phaedra and a Hippolytus.

'how Kupris strikes' / . . . 'she incites all to evil'

H.D. also signals her critique of the conception of *eros* dominant in Euripides' *Hippolytus* through her conspicuous use of the word 'evil', invoked four times in her translation, often without an evident spur in the Greek. Of Aphrodite, at least as understood in this Euripidean thought-world, H.D.'s text suggests:

> she incites all to evil

> *IV.50*

This instance of 'evil' appears just one line after the translation gives, 'Ah evil wedlock! Ah fate!' (IV.49): the conspicuous reiteration emphasizes the word. 'Evil' also surfaces when the chorus laments Hippolytus's fate:

No more, O my spirit,
are we flawless,
we have seen evil undrempt

VI.1–3

While 'evil', redolent of Christian discourse, initially seems a surprising lexical choice for H.D., who often turned to the Ancient Greek for ways beyond Christian thought, here H.D. redirects Christian discourse, anticipating a central move of her long poem *Trilogy* – so as to frame an ethical problem driving her critique: in this scenario, where exactly does the 'evil' reside?

H.D.'s focus on 'evil' may have been spurred in part by the lexical choices of other English translations. For instance, H.D.'s line about Kupris, responsive to lines 555 ff. in the play, may be cued partly by a line from Hippolytus's rant against women from Murray's popular translation of this moment: 'For Cypris breeds most evil in the wise.' The 1910 translation by E.P. Coleridge also used 'evil' in Hippolytus's speech condemning women.[22] If so, H.D. seems to have been drawn to these because the problem of 'evil' was on her mind. She also uses 'evil' elsewhere in her work of this time. For instance, in an unpublished review of Yeats's *Responsibilities* (c. 1916), H.D. elevates Yeats's generation of the 1890s for their stand against 'the evil of ugliness' (H.D. 1987/8: 53). Such lexical emphases around 1916–17 show H.D. searching for what represents 'the evil' in a sense relevant to her own developing ethical feminist thought. Through her *Hippolytus*, she seeks the points at which both Phaedra's shamed *eros*, and then Hippolytus's refusal of Aphroditean desire, move into a zone of 'ugliness' and 'evil'. As her lexicon suggests, for H.D., 'evil' resides neither in the body or its desires, nor in women, but rather in ways these enter the social discourses of shame and misogyny.

Both the position condemning Phaedra and that shunning Aphrodite refuse to honour *eros* – 'the power of Aphrodite'. And such refusal, in turn, depends in this context on an assumed opposition between the Artemisian and Aphroditic, which H.D. seeks to undo and supersede. She does so in her translation by gesturing towards a form of 'chastity' alternative to that of the ephebe, figured by Hippolytus. Again, H.D. often elevates the chaste ephebe in her early work, through engagement with Pater and Euripides – even uses him as a figure for feminist thought. But in tandem with her reconceptualization of *eros*, her translation of *Hippolytus* begins to move beyond this Paterian conception towards another form of chastity, replacing the Paterian understanding of the Artemisian with a more philogynous version thereof. Her translation of the *Hippolytus* crucially paves the way for imagining a kind of chastity that, rather than deny *eros*, instead involves *eros*, itself reimagined in a non-Hippolytan (in H.D.'s thought, one might say post-Hippolytan) form.

Conclusion: 'that most passionate of passions, the innate chastity of the young'

H.D.'s last intervention moves past conceptualizing the Artemisian and Aphroditic in binary, mutually exclusive terms. If in the received vision of Artemis, *eros lusimélēs* never 'approaches' Artemis (see epigraph), H.D. imagines an Artemisian mode informed by an alternative model of *eros* allowing for life and creation.

Again, in her early work, the Artemisian figure that H.D. imagines as empowering for women is the chaste huntress, able to maintain detachment from deep uncontrollable desire, as chaste as young male ephebes in Euripides' corpus such as Hippolytus and Ion (H.D. also engages with Euripides' *Ion* during this time). H.D. foregrounds this figure in her novels *Paint it To-day* (1921), *Asphodel* (1921–2), *HERmione* (1926–7) and much of her early poetry (see Laity 1992); yet importantly, it evolves over time from an Artemisian as mediated by Pater to an alternative Artemisian mode.

Diverging from Pater in a series of steps, H.D. first indicates through the language of her *Hippolytus* that she is reaching for an Artemisian mode that allows women to escape from constructed roles for women (including the 'scarlet' woman) to enter an empowering register of the huntress. The huntress stands detached from desire, associated with ecosystems that H.D. uses to signify Hellenic freedom: open spaces, rocks, mountains, wild flowers, birds in flight. Such atmospherics emerge in H.D.'s reading of Hippolytus's first speech, rendered in language resonating with what H.D.'s *Sea Garden* (1916) uses to mark 'new beauty' associated with 'strength':

> flower set by flower and leaf
> broken by uncut grass,
> where neither scythe has dipped
> nor does the shepherd yet
> venture to lead his sheep;
> there it is white and fragrant

I.14–19

H.D. registers a similar environment of rough purity in her *Hippolytus*, in the Trozenian women's *parodos*:

> At high-tide
> the sea – they say –
> left a deep pool
> below the rock shelf
> in that clear place
> where women dip
> their water-jars

II.1–7

Phaedra's cries for release from the pain of her illicit desire likewise evoke this wild landscape:

> Take me to the mountains!
> O for woods, pine tracts,
> where hounds a thirst for death,
> leap on the bright stags

III.22–25

As 'bright stags' suggests, now Phaedra explicitly links this rugged, pure terrain with Artemis the huntress, as she invokes 'Artemis of the salt-beach' (III.36). The *Hippolytus* here thus provides H.D. with a hinge between such a language of landscape, integral to her early poetry of *Sea Garden*, and an Artemisian mode. In her novel *HERmione*, reflecting H.D.'s thought of 1905–10, H.D. shows her Artemisian mode through a line of desire from the protagonist, Hermione, likewise combining her ecosystem language (here, the windswept sea as code for freedom) with a 'hound' cue suggesting Artemis:

> She wanted the inner lining of an Atlantic breaker. There was one creature that could save her, a hound ... as she had often dreamt of, and ... a long sea-shelf

H.D. 1981: 9

H.D. uses such language to signal a form of chastity, liberatory for women.

In contrast, as H.D.'s translation indicates, the Artemisian mode that Hippolytus expresses in his dedication to Artemis entails only puritanism and radical misogyny – and for H.D., this is a wrong turn. Again, Hippolytus's misogynistic devotion to Artemis emerges in his bitter diatribe against women when he is made aware of Phaedra's desire. The alternative Artemisian H.D. suggests instead valorizes women, female–female desire, the erotic and a form of chastity not predicated on refusal of the erotic.

Shortly after the passage from *HERmione* cited above, for instance, H.D. freights an Artemisian mode with more explicitly lesbian significance through a language of 'sister love' – again, a concept through which H.D. often imagined lesbian desire. Here it is voiced through Spartan athleticism:

> A sister would run, would leap, would be concealed under the autumn sumac or lie shaken with hail and wind, lost on some Lacedaemonian foothill. A sister would have a companion hound, Hermione's the more lithe, her sister's heavier for whelping ....

H.D. [1926–7] 1981: 10

Euripides' Hippolytan version does not allow for such a vision; but in her *Hippolytus*, H.D. Houdinis her way out of such a Hippolytan Artemisian, rewriting Euripides and Pater with her own Artemisian. She does so in part by omitting from her translation the majority of Hippolytus's overt misogyny and puritanism. Then, crucially, she does so through her rendering of a choral passage asserting an attempted transcendent response to the confinements of Hippolytus's misogynistic diatribe.

> O for wings,
> swift, a bird,
> set of God
> among the bird-flocks!
> I would dart
> from some Adriatic precipice,
> across its wave-shallows and crests,
> to Eradanus' river-source;
> to the place
> where his daughters weep,
> thrice-hurt for Phaeton's sake,
> tears of amber and gold which dart
> their fire through the purple surface.
>
> *V.1–13*

The beauty and strength of this passage suggests the strength needed to counter the destructive logic from which it escapes. The language H.D. then develops for the Artemisian mode favoured towards the end of her translation similarly demonstrates an effort to fly by the nets of such Hippolytan discourse with an alternative Artemisian, involving a different form of chastity, one welcoming, even celebratory of, women and female desire.[23]

First, at the very end of H.D.'s translation, there is a rhyme between the call for 'wings, swift' like those of a 'bird', and the figure of bird-flight H.D. uses elsewhere in her work from the myth of Procne and Philomela. This is a myth she frequently engages with. She will later thread it through her novel *HERmione* (often as mediated by how Swinburne treats it in 'Itylus') to suggest the solidarity of 'sister love' between Hermione and Fayne, pitted against the 'world's division'. As Laity (1992) notes, for H.D. such bird-flight is linked to flight from worldly misunderstanding and androcentric conceptions of desire, as well as liberty achieved through lesbian desire. If Eros in the conventional iconography has 'wings', H.D.'s wings are those of sister-lovers united against ominous androcentric discourse.

H.D.'s translation of this choral passage also significantly twice features 'dart', another element of H.D.'s gestural language of lesbianism: as Friedman notes, H.D. uses 'Helga Dart' (derived from 'd'Art') as pseudonym for *Paint It To-day*, her novel foregrounding lesbian love. Even when not implying lesbian desire or identity per se, H.D.'s 'dart' suggests ways in which the female could, in an Artemisian mode, bypass the need for men by herself taking on 'male' attributes. As Friedman observes,

> Artemis is present in the authorial signature in *Paint It To-day*. Helga Dart is the *nom de plume* on the novel's typescript, a choice that . . . suggests the attributes of

power H.D. associated with Artemis . . . Dart suggests both a sharp, pointed object and a sudden, swift movement, the darting arrow of Artemis, the flash of her running feet . . . .

Friedman 1990: 195

Significantly, when Phaedra calls for relief, she calls for such an Artemisian 'dart':

> with my gold hair torn loose;
> I would shake the Thessalian dart,
> I would hurl the barbed arrow from my grasp.

III.27–9

Finally, in a last conceptual step, in this passage, the 'hurt' combines here with that specifically which 'darts' 'fire' and involves a rich 'purple' surface, and 'amber'. For H.D. these are colours suggesting the erotic and the Aphroditic.

> the place
> where his daughters weep,
> thrice-hurt for Phaeton's sake,
> tears of amber and gold which dart
> their fire through the purple surface.

V.9–13

As Gregory notes of *Hippolytus Temporizes*, which employs similar chromatics:

> [a] network of images in *Hippolytus Temporizes* reiterates the difference between the two goddesses. Artemis is associated with Greece, with wilderness, daylight, cold, white flower, with a silver head-band. Aphrodite is associated with Crete, with civilization, night, heat, citron, rose, myrrh and myrtle, with purple clothes and headband and with goldenness.

Gregory 1990: 145

In 'The Wise Sappho' (c. 1920), H.D. even forges a connection between such 'purple' and 'gold' and Sappho. These lexical cues thus suggest that she seeks in her *Hippolytus* not only to include the Aphroditic – *eros* – in her Artemisian vision, but also to revise an idea of the erotic away from the Aphroditic (as understood in Hippolytan terms) in the direction of the Sapphic – away from that which 'hurts' towards that which provides extraordinary 'light', 'heat' and 'warmth' (H.D. 1982: 57–8). In our reading, this is tantamount to H.D.'s queering both the Aphroditic and the Artemisian in the direction of a Sapphic mode.

Collecott likewise notes that H.D. fashions her preferred erotic through Hellenic sources, drawing upon the concept of *poikilia*, or subtlety, strongly associated with

117

Sappho, which 'connotes the play of light and texture, what is shimmering, artful, variegated' (Collecott 1999: 17), as well as that which is 'many-colored' or 'rainbow-hued'.[24] For H.D., that which is 'many-colored' and richly 'hued' in this way suggests a Sapphic *eros* she increasingly favours. In 'The Wise Sappho', just after the publication of her *Hippolytus*, H.D. even suggests a wish to invest 'scarlet' with a different significance, such that it connotes not shame but rather Sapphic desire. Here, H.D. imagines the 'words of Sappho' as 'scarlet':

> True there is a tint of rich colour ... violets, purple woof of cloth, scarlet garments, dyed fastening of a sandal ... I think of the words of Sappho as these colours, or states rather, transcending colour yet containing ... all colour .... And perhaps the most obvious is this rose colour, merging to richer shades of scarlet, purple, or Phoenician purple.
>
> *H.D. [c. 1920] 1982: 57–8*

H.D.'s 'Phoenician purple' thus rewrites πορφύρεα, as invoked in the *Hippolytus*. Cueing H.D. to unite such a Sapphic erotic with her Artemisian 'sister-love' may be the train of thought signalled by a Greek word describing Eros himself as *Hippolytus* closes: ὁ ποικιλόπτερος ('the many-hued winged one'). As H.D. translates this:

> and Eros helps you, O Kupris,
> with wings' swift
> interplay of light
>
> *VII.11–13*

In this context, ποικιλόπτερος reads as a kind of portmanteau, merging *poikilia* (the subtle variegation of the Sapphic erotic), *pteros* (wings for H.D. suggesting Artemisian sister-love and bird-flight) and even, through a pun, perhaps *eros* (ἔρος).

Moreover, given the nexus in H.D.'s rendering among 'wings', 'swift', 'waves' and 'dart' (all suggesting for H.D. the Artemisian) with 'amber and gold' and 'purple', H.D.'s language for the Sapphic (rather than the Hippolytan) modality of the Aphroditic, her language traces her imagined blending of the Artemisian and the Sapphic erotic, beyond and as counter to what the textual unconscious of the *Hippolytus* allows. Such blending forms H.D.'s healing answer to erotic 'hurt'.

Reinforcing this effect of intermixture of discourses (which the Hippolytan mind separates) is H.D.'s final passage: here Eros himself appears through this melded lexicon of H.D.'s reinvented erotic.

> Men you strike
> and the gods'
> dauntless spirits alike,
> and Eros helps you, O Kupris,
> with wings' swift

interplay of light:
now he flies above earth,
now above sea-crash
and whirl of salt:
. . .
he darts gold wings

VII.1–18, 19–20

H.D. clearly interweaves discourses of 'dart' (Artemisian), 'interplay of light' and 'gold' (the Sapphic erotic), and 'wings' (suggesting flight, sister love and ability to transcend pain associated with *eros*) – creating the ability to soar above 'hurt' through a newly imagined erotic, a philogynous *eros* combining the Artemisian and Sapphic–Aphroditic. This new vision of an erotic informs, and inflects the meaning of, the final ringing statement of H.D.'s translation:

you alone, Kupris,
creator of all life,
reign absolute.

VII.19–21

The reinvented erotic hinted at here will find voice most strongly in *Paint It To-day*, written *c.* 1921. Here H.D. unfolds a scene between lovers, female and lesbian, yet in this context loosed from their ordinary genders:

'I am alive', said Midget. . . .

Babies they were, girls or boys. . . . All the power of the wood seemed to circle between those two alert and vivid bodies. . . .

It needs two or more than two to make a living prayer of the passion of swift feet. . . and that most passionate of passions, the innate chastity of the young, the living spirits of the untouched, sacred virgins of Artemis.

H.D. [c. 1921] 1992, 83–4

Now a new *eros*, fully Artemisian, appears with a form of 'chastity' that is in itself 'passionate' ('that most passionate of passions'). The passage accents 'joy', 'swift feet' and 'living spirits'. If H.D.'s revised 'Kupris', 'creator of all life', in her *Hippoytus* gestures towards a revised *eros*, here, two years later, the protagonist of *Paint It To-day* cries, 'I am alive'.[25]

RESPONDENT ESSAY 2
H.D. AND EURIPIDES: GHOSTLY SUMMONING
Eileen Gregory

Thomas Jenkins, in his reflections on H.D.'s translation of Euripides' *Ion*, suggests the complexity of her notion of the 'ultra-modern', which in her notes she applies to Euripides' imagination. His ultra-modernity for H.D. lies in his exceeding the rationalism of his age, his 'knife-edge mind' seeing 'around the edge' (H.D. 1986: 14), just as in her own time scientists like Einstein or Freud propose ideas that apparently exceed rational conception, just as H.D. herself, in this translation, distorts and pushes beyond the original Greek text to enact its uncanniness, the way its characters shockingly step out of ancient time into the present, like Kreousa, stepping out of stone, 'in the manner of a late Rodin' (H.D. 1986: 30). Jenkins particularly emphasizes H.D.'s distinct sense of temporality. It is not simply the ordinary assertion of Greek timelessness, but something more: 'For H.D., two temporal planes, the ancient and the modern, run concurrently. Binary oppositions overlap or, better, collapse to a point' (2007: 127). He sees in H.D.'s commentary 'Einsteinian notions of a space/time continuum', that time constitutes a fourth dimension to spatial dimensions, and that conventional temporal distinctions of past, present and future are illusory. H.D., Jenkins proposes, deliberately evokes these 'radical notions of Time to achieve her poetic affect' (2007: 134).

H.D.'s evocation of 'radical notions of Time' in her commentary on the *Ion* seems congruent with the notion of 'Deep Classics' proposed by Shane Butler. He suggests that one see the intellectual engagement with 'antiquity' as an instance of 'Deep Time', found in sciences like geology, archaeology, or philology. In these disciplines, looking at the sequenced strata of events going back to pre-human or prehistoric eras leads to a kind of temporal disorientation. Considering comments of geologist Charles Playfair about the sedimentary strata in a Scottish cliffside, Butler remarks:

> Deep Time places us, on the one hand, face-to-face with almost unthinkable timespans … But in a second moment, Deep Time confronts us with the no less awe-inspiring presence of the distant past, right before Playfair's eyes and, indeed, just beneath his feet.

Butler claims this encounter with Deep Time for classicists as well; for, he says 'what is "antiquity" … if not precisely a word for the depth of time' (2016: 4–5).

I would agree with Jenkins that H.D. somehow grasps – even from the beginning, in the estranging daimonism of the classically inflected poems of *Sea Garden* – the alienating and sublime aspects of the encounter with antiquity. Her reflections on Kreousa in the notes to the *Ion* suggest this infinite, untimely otherness. She is as a stone that 'has always been standing there', carrying 'the inhumanity of a meteor sunk in the sea' (H.D. 1986: 29). But at the moment of the play, as the text is enacted, she steps out into terrible presence. She is at once like a statue come to life and like the evidence of violent cosmic disruption within fathomless space and time. And H.D. seems always to have carried an awareness of the 'stratigraphic' character of any access to a classical text.[1] As Butler points out, this sense of Deep Time informs not only the new sciences of geology and archaeology, but Freudian psychoanalysis as well, and the awe of depths informs the Burkean sublime. In light of H.D.'s affinities with these models, one can see why for her the encounter with antiquity carries uncanny resonances of temporal depth.

But this is not to say that H.D. is unaware of the 'surface' level of the event of classical reception, the historical/cultural contingency of the writer. As Charles Martindale famously proposed, 'Meaning . . . is always realized at the point of reception' (1993: 3). But such meanings cannot themselves be isolated in a single context, because our reception of the classics is mediated within 'a complex chain of receptions', with 'the effect that a work can operate across history obliquely in unexpected ways' (Martindale 2006: 4). Another way of framing the moment of classical reception retains something of the uncanny temporality that Butler describes. Davide Susanetti sees this encounter within the trope of summoning ghosts, as Odysseus famously offers blood to the ghosts in Hades so that he can ask questions and learn what he needs to know. Susanetti draws upon Walter Benjamin, who suggests in 'Theses on the Philosophy of History' that one knows the past only momentarily, in taking control of a memory or image as it 'flashes up a moment of danger' (1968b: 255). Susanetti comments:

> [C]lassic texts should be viewed as events that arise at the very moment they are called into action by questions that are clearly our own . . . The approach to these texts implies the explicit consciousness of a gaze that is never neutral; on the contrary, their value lies in their becoming part of a circuit of reproposal and interpretation.[2]
>
> *2016: 262*

H.D.'s writing reflects this complex sense of the reception of the classics – emphasis on the historical context of the reception; but awareness as well of a mediated reception, within a 'chain of receptions' over time; and, perhaps more deeply, the sense of felt urgency – the scene of summoning the ghosts to respond to life-or-death questioning. Add to these things her sense of the arbitrary and fragmentary transmission of classical texts – their preservation, compilation, translation, dissemination – within the violence of sequent historical catastrophes. These senses of classical reception are present from the earliest translations of lyric poems and Euripidean choruses until her late revisiting of the matter of Troy.

The feminist recovery of H.D., as well as subsequent exploration, has emphasized her engagement with classical texts as cultural critique, calling attention to the context of twentieth-century wars and of the status of a woman writer within the classical domain and within the masculinist poetics of modernism (e.g. DuPlessis 1986: 1–20). Critics have also acknowledged the way her reception of the classics comes by way of earlier receptions, within the classical world itself (e.g. Homer by way of Stesichorus and Euripides), from the immediate generations of Romantics and late Victorian writers, through her contemporaries, especially Pound and her husband Richard Aldington, and through classical scholars and archaeologists.[3] As for the urgency of her summoning of the ghosts, she turned to Euripides, and to the classical texts more generally, just as she turned to Freud, as a way of attempting to engage profound issues that were both personal and transpersonal (Gregory 1997: 179–82). This calling on ghosts has a religious dimension, carrying the hope of transformation, a dimension suggested in the ritualistic or performative nature of her lyric poetry and her work with Euripides.

More might be said about H.D.'s broad sense of the classical past and the historical dimension of classical receptions. At one level her conception of the ancient past seems to involve an idealization of the 'lost islands', a kind of Hellenic nostalgia. However, alongside this apparent romanticism, one also finds in H.D. the recurrent scene of a woman working at writing, in particular translating Greek, in the midst of a violent historical displacement – in early narratives such as *Palimpsest* and *Bid Me to Live*, and also in the translation of the *Ion* and in *Helen in Egypt*, both contextualized by the memory of old war and the fear of new war.[4]

'Hipparchia', more than any other of these scenes of writing, shows H.D.'s vivid sense of what it means to be actually within a network of classical transmission – that is to say, what it means to be translating precious manuscripts at a moment of outward peril and turbulence. She situates 'Hipparchia' in Rome of 75 BCE, when it was in the midst of a sequence of wars, having recently conquered Athens and Alexandria. Hipparchia, a Greek concubine of a Roman officer, has access to manuscripts and collects them, scrolls 'swarming from destroyed Carthage, from the numerous broken cities' (H.D. 1968: 69). Throughout the narrative she is translating Euripidean choruses and Greek lyric poets into the Latin of the conquerors (H.D. 1968: 77). The text makes clear the fragility of the survival of these manuscripts. They are being passed from hand to hand, borrowed and perhaps never returned, or passed on or sold (H.D. 1968: 34, 88 ff.). In Hipparchia's charge, as she moves from place to place, increasingly distraught and finally fevered, they are spread across the room, '[trailing] across the bench', or stored 'in the old box under the bed' and finally passed on to some wealthy patron who is collecting such things (H.D. 1968: 70, 68, 88). Beyond this local instability, the texts themselves that she is translating are linked to a sequence of violent historical destructions, the Persian and the Peloponnesian Wars, the Macedonian and the Roman conquests (see Gregory 1997: 59–60). Though aware of the 'depth' of the ancient, she sees that in human terms this depth means strata of destructions. She acknowledges extinction events within the deep time of classical receptions.

The increasing emphasis on classical reception within modernism that this volume of essays represents promises greater scope and depth in the study of H.D. While a preliminary ground for such a study exists in earlier commentary on H.D. from the 1980s and 1990s, this existing body of work invites more detailed and nuanced engagement with H.D.'s classical writing, but with an increased respect for her deliberateness and self-consciousness. Steven Yao's large argument concerning the centrality of translation within early modernism highlights H.D.'s translation efforts and places them firmly alongside those of other major modernists. Yao's discussion also suggests the further work to be done in focusing on acts of translation themselves, in relation to original texts and in comparison with other translations. Thus the participation of classicists like those represented among these essays gives depth and dimension to the study of modernist classical reception.

Taken together, the four essays here on H.D. represent a full range in H.D.'s reception of Euripidean texts throughout her career – from the early choruses of the *Hippolytus* (1919), to the choruses from the *Bacchae* (composed around 1920, published 1931), to the *Ion* (1935) and to *Helen in Egypt* (written 1952–5). In basic critical assumptions they fortunately have much in common. Each of them assumes from the outset the deliberateness of H.D.'s engagement with classical texts and the experimental, even radical, character of her treatment. In other words, they clearly represent a sophisticated third (or fourth) generation of H.D.'s readers, open to the surprises that H.D.'s poetic practices continue to yield. Moreover, they share the special emphases of classical reception that invite open engagement with a Greek text, as well as with the English translation. Further, these critics do not hesitate to draw not only from contemporary modernist criticism and from theory but also from classical scholarship, putting H.D.'s response to the classical texts beside scholarly ones – thus implying that H.D. is not arbitrary in her reading, but rather responsive to lexical patterns in the texts. Another implicit assumption here is that even when H.D. engages a portion of a play (the choruses of *Hippolytus* or of the *Bacchae*) – much less a full one (the *Ion* or the *Helen*) – she is responding as an intelligent reader to the whole of the play, with its implicit contexts, questions and thematic resonances.

How do these critics understand H.D.'s efforts as a translator? What is she doing, or attempting to do, in these Euripidean exchanges? The essays here follow established critical emphases, while at the same time they extend and deepen them in distinct ways. For assessing the adequacy of H.D.'s rendering of the Greek, a conventional approach to H.D.'s translations is clearly insufficient, because H.D. never imagines her translation in ordinary, conventional terms (Gregory 2012: 146). Nevertheless, she was self-conscious and deliberate in her translation practice, and her translations constitute acts of interpretation, showing awareness of lexical resonances, metricality and imagistic qualities.[5] Further, as Yao has pointed out, translation for H.D. was 'constitutive' of her poetics, co-existing with it from the beginning and shaping it (2002: 19, 85). So critics have consistently seen the way that translation offers H.D. a means of modernist stylistic experimentation – not only in the early spareness and directness of language, but also in the lyric implications of the 'choros-sequence', in the complexity of voice more generally, and formal and generic hybridity, particularly in the *Ion* and *Helen in Egypt*.[6] Finally, as feminist recovery of H.D. made clear, the translations are sites of cultural critique, of ethical engagement, a means for H.D. to reflect on, to contest and to revise distorting narratives and images, such as war and inherent forms of misogyny not only within the classical tradition but within her own literary generation.

Catherine Theis most forcefully engages the character of H.D.'s translations of Euripides as radical stylistic experimentation. Theis brings us close to an evocation of Deep Time such as Butler suggests, the way that ancient texts open both temporal and spatial distances and at the same time immediacy – a sense, in Theis's words, of the *living pastness*' experienced in performance. Focusing on H.D.'s and Robinson Jeffers' translation from the choral odes of the *Bacchae*, Theis emphasizes the choral voice as a soundscape and as an embodied voice that, in H.D., transgresses territorial boundaries of the play itself. The speaking voice, in H.D. the collective voice of the chorus, enacts a kind of *cosmopoesis*, a landscape which the voice brings bodily into being through sound. Thus the choral poems are performative, evoking the context of the theatre, yet standing outside of that territorial containment. Theis strikes me as herself experimental in her effort to create a metaphorically textured, evocative reflection on the poetic effects that H.D. achieves. Her essay also continues the fruitful practice of putting H.D.'s translations alongside those of her contemporaries, here Robinson Jeffers. This kind of comparative study, like those of Jenkins (2007) and of Jennifer Varney (2010a), more sharply clarifies the distinctiveness of H.D.'s poetic approach. Further, the emphasis Theis gives to sound is coming increasingly into focus among H.D. critics – such as Anna Fyta in this volume, as well as Susan Barbour. Perhaps most striking and convincing in Theis's treatment is her awareness of cosmogenesis in H.D.'s poems, the persistent way, throughout her career, that her poems evoke landscape, and especially the way that the Hellenic landscape is very frequently an elemental, archaic one.

Jeffery Westover presents H.D.'s translation work as an act of textual interpretation as well as personal and transpersonal enactment. He follows a line of critics who approach H.D.'s translation of the *Ion* in light of her Freudian psychoanalysis, which immediately preceded it. For Westover, Euripides' play itself, the plot surrounding Kroeusa, figures for H.D. a psychological transformation, and her translation serves to emphasize the psychological configuration of repression and secrecy, speech and healing implicit in the text. At the same time, he suggests that her work with this play constitutes an implicit critique of Freud's emphasis on the Oedipal pattern (violent paternal conflict), presenting instead a mother and son's mutual recognition and acceptance. While not giving extensive attention to H.D.'s translation in relation to Greek, his comments on H.D.'s echo of Hesiod in the translated phrase 'the race of women' suggest her broad knowledge of basic Greek texts. This essay highlights the complexity of the classical texts themselves which H.D. chose to engage, indicated in his extensive allusion to scholarly commentary on the play. His approach implies that H.D. acts here not only as an interpreter but as a scholar, cognizant of sometimes obscure mythical and ritual contexts. Thus, his essay implicitly raises a question in interpreting a poetic translation: how far can one go in claiming the translator's awareness of the lexical complexity of the text?

Anna Fyta's exploration of H.D.'s *Helen in Egypt* extends the already rich treatments of this poem concerning genre. She approaches the work as a 'meta-palinode' – 'meta' in that it shows H.D.'s self-consciousness in taking up this genre, 'cognizant of its textual ancestry' as a transgressive form. She acknowledges its mixed inheritance in both lyric and drama, Stesichorus and Euripides. Fyta also engages the complexity of voice in

H.D.'s text, not simply the choral voice of earlier translations, but a polyvocality within Helen herself, representing echoes of all of H.D.'s earlier choral voices, but, as well, the cinematic voice-over of the section headnotes. Fyta claims that H.D. carries over a Euripidean philosophical dimension implicit in the play in the figure of the priestess/prophet Theonoe. The question of genre that Fyta explores here is one of the most exciting areas of recent study, signalled in Leah Flack's and Barbour's explorations of *Helen in Egypt* in terms of mixed and layered genres. Further, Harriet Tarlo's exploration of H.D.'s early poetry in relation to the genre of pastoral is fresh and original, in taking account of this genre and placing H.D.'s poems in the American and contemporary context of landscape and ecological concerns.

Miranda Hickman and Lynn Kozak see H.D.'s *Choruses from the Hippolytus* as cultural work, both 'commentary' on and intervention in cultural configurations of erotic desire in the early decades of the century. H.D. finds in Euripides a 'conceptual resource' for addressing pressing and destructive cultural binds, and they attempt to read the 'lexical mind' of the translation, as it reveals a line of reflection or conceptual engagement. They highlight certain translation choices at the level of words and phrases of the Greek, in light of a larger, ambitious argument, that H.D. through these choices presents an 'ethically inflected critique' of *eros* is it appears in Euripides' play, in light of the erotic confusions implicit in the concept of the New Woman. H.D., they claim, attempts here to 'reinvent eros', to articulate a queer eroticism – a kind of chastity and an eroticism distinct from the misogyny of Hippolytus's abstinence or Phaedra's carnality. An argument of this kind is difficult, in that it goes beyond the rendering of line by line to suggest another level of intentionality within the translation-sequence as a whole. They show, in actual terms, how a translation practice reflects a theoretical or ethical problem with which the poet is contending. Linking together several early texts, they locate lexical patterns associated with kinds of desire to suggest a radical reinterpretation of erotic love. This detailed scrutiny of the original texts alongside the translation is one of the most promising critical avenues made possible within a consideration of H.D. and classical reception. Further, in its direct confrontation with the issue of erotic desire in H.D.'s writing, this essay is crucially important. For so central an issue, the erotic has received little deliberate attention until recently, with the groundbreaking studies by Hickman (2012) and by Jeanne Heuving (2016: 88–109).

Thus these essays suggest many ways that H.D.s classical writing can be further explored within new critical contexts: the close lexical study represented by Hickman and Kozak, the attention to the Greek plays themselves suggested by each of these writers, the further treatment of H.D.'s hybrid genres and her polyvocality, the ethical and philosophical dimension of H.D.'s explorations suggested by Hickman and Kozak and by Fyta, the cosmological or elemental dimension of H.D.'s classical writing that Theis evokes. Remarkably, all of these writers suggest ritual or performance as central to their argument: Westover highlighting the Athenian ritual of the Arrephoria alluded to in the *Ion*, which he relates to his psychological focus on Kreousa; Theis proposing a dynamic, kinesthetic aurality in H.D., developed in her work with Euripidean choruses; Fyta focusing on the complexity of voice in *Helen in Egypt* as it signals H.D.'s reconstitution of the palinode; Hickman and Kozak seeing H.D.'s translations as a way of working out her own ethical positions, but also, finally, of effecting political change by way of engaging readers in a complex presentation of eros. This aspect of H.D.'s poetry, indicated in the many valences it carries in these essays, certainly deserves more deliberate study.

Susanetti remarks, '[C]lassic texts should be viewed as events that arise at the very moment they are called into action by questions that are clearly our own' (2016: 262). It is exciting that study of H.D.'s classical work increasingly explores the character of those framing questions for her – not simply personal, but ethical and religious questions as well. And clearly in the context of modernism, these questions pertain as well to poetic experiment, allied with a fresh and radical sense of the activity of translation.

PART III
MODERNIST TRANSLATION AND POLITICAL ATTUNEMENTS

CHAPTER 9
'UNTRANSLATABLE' WOMEN: LAURA RIDING'S CLASSICAL MODERNIST FICTION
Anett K. Jessop

> I find myself regarding the officially historical history of ourselves as an alien record. Is not history supposed to be the history of ourselves – the past supposed to be our past? And how much of it can we read in the intimacy of self-recognition?
>
> Laura Riding, *A Trojan Ending*, 1937: xvi

History, accepted at the end of the nineteenth century as the chronicles of Great Men (Thomas Carlyle's description), became a contested category in the twentieth century. Feminist historians and literary scholars have examined the ways in which cultural power and social relations were shifting in the first decades of the new century. Critic Marianne DeKoven, for one, locates gender-role change as a 'key factor in the emergence of Modernism' (2011: 212). First-wave feminism secured equal suffrage for women in the United States (1920) and England (1928), and activists were likewise challenging equal access to education, among other issues. Indeed, access to the study of the classics became a battlefield in itself. While the United States offered more higher education opportunities for women during the nineteenth century and into the twentieth, neither Oxford nor Cambridge would confer degrees on British women until 1920 and 1947, respectively. According to Seth Schein:

> Unequal access to education was also an important means of maintaining the subordination of women [...] The education barriers to a classical, humanistic education both expressed and reinforced the lower status of girls and women and their inability to share in the prestige and power to which knowledge of the classics might lead.
>
> *2008: 80*

As such, Anglo-American women were institutionally denied cultural power and freedoms available to (white) men; likewise the authorized histories – from antiquity to the present – were biased to include narratives of principally male legacies and accomplishments. Even in avant-garde literary circles, despite manifestic proclamations for radical change, male writers predominated in publication and movement leadership – not to mention in the later historicizing and canonizing of modernism's 'Great Men' (Eliot, Pound, Joyce, et al.) by principally male literary critics.[1] Even so, the reverberations stemming from shifting gender roles were expressed by both male and female modernist writers. According to DeKoven (2011: 212–13):

The radical implications of the social-cultural changes feminism advocated produced in Modernist writing an unprecedented preoccupation with gender, both thematically and formally. Much of this preoccupation expressed a male Modernist fear of women's new power, and resulted in the combination of misogyny and triumphal masculinism that many critics see as central, defining features of Modernist work by men ... While [some of] the male Modernists feared the destructive power of the radical cultural change they desired – egalitarian change often embodied in various figurations of empowered femininity – the female Modernists general feared punishment for desiring that change.

Literary critics have noted the often-ambivalent gender relationships within and conclusions to late nineteenth and early twentieth-century works.[2] The anxiety and uncertainty – even the fear of punishment, as DeKoven claims – led some women writers to explore dramatic alternatives for female protagonists in settings safely removed from their contemporary times.

In 1997, Ruth Hoberman published a reception study, *Gendering Classicism: The Ancient World in Twentieth-Century Women's Historical Fiction*, in which she examines the ways women writers interpolate the classical materials and traditions differently from their male peers. Hoberman claims that her authors – Phyllis Bentley, Bryher (Annie Winifred Ellerman), Mary Butts, Naomi Mitchison, Mary Renault and Laura Riding – '*gender* classicism' in ways that 'expose apparently gender-neutral accounts of the past as stories of male experience' (1997: 3). She posits that the patriarchal hegemony of Western civilization insured that traditional historiography served to reinforce and legitimize androcentrism:

Traditional historical periodization ... is itself based on the exclusion of women's experience. ... Historians have divided up and categorized the past based on their understanding of men's lives alone. Those periods associated with 'progress' – Athenian democracy, the Industrial Revolution – tend to be periods in which women's lives are most restricted.

1997: 5[3]

Hoberman asserts that gender impacts reception and that an examination of the ways in which women writers create alternative historical narratives offers perspectives on the cultural changes of the writers' time as well as their critiques of the ideologies and values of the past and present. Indeed, Virginia Woolf, that most perceptive modernist cultural critic, quantified the problem: 'Imaginatively she is of the highest importance; practically she is completely insignificant. She pervades poetry from cover to cover; she is all but absent from history' (1929: 45). In that absence of accounts of historical women, women writers invent missing figures, as do Hoberman's twentieth-century writers and as does Woolf, in *A Room of One's Own*, when imagining the career of Shakespeare's 'wonderfully gifted sister' whom she names Judith, aptly evoking the heroic and avenging biblical figure (1929: 48). In her chapter 'Cressida's Complexity: Laura Riding Unwrites the White

Goddess', Hoberman makes a claim for Laura Riding's radical and empowered refigurations of historical and literary women. She reads Riding's historical novel *A Trojan Ending* (1937) as a counter – before the fact – to Robert Graves's *The White Goddess* (1948) or, more accurately, a refutation of the kind of 'oversimplified thinking about gender' Graves would present in the book (1997: 60).[4] Hoberman's revisionist project resurrected under-acknowledged twentieth-century women writers and made an important contribution to Riding studies as well as the growing field of classical reception.

Riding (1901–91) and Graves (1895–1985) were famously partnered from 1926 to 1940, during which time they co-authored *A Survey of Modernist Poetry* (1927), co-edited the journal *Epilogue: A Critical Summary* (1935, 1936, 1937), collaborated on multiple projects and founded Seizin Press, which published Gertrude Stein among others.[5] In *A Survey of Modernist Poetry*, one of the first critical and reflexive deliberations of literary modernism, Riding and Graves identify the preoccupation with history as a defining feature of what they term 'modernism' (1927: 68). The modernist project is not 'new' at all, they claim, merely obfuscated translations – 'rewritings' – of earlier masters in an attempt to 'civilize' literature, particularly through an 'abnormal cultivation of the classics, especially of the remote classics' (1927: 84). From 1929 through 1936, the pair worked from their island home in Mallorca, Spain, where they were steeped in the ruins of ancient Mediterranean cultures, to include Phoenician, Greek, Roman and Moorish. In succession, Graves published his popular historical novels refashioning Roman and Byzantine emperors with recognizably modern anxieties delivered in 'autobiographic' narratives: *I, Claudius* (1934), *Claudius the God* (1935) and *Count Belisarius* (1938); he would continue writing and publishing about classical goddess lore and mythology in *The White Goddess* and *The Greek Myths* (1955) to name just two publications.[6] During the 1930s, Riding also authored her revisions of the historical record through her recovery of the lives of classical women in *A Trojan Ending* and *Lives of Wives* (1939);[7] in addition she was pursuing an historical and linguistic study of women, published posthumously as *The Word 'Woman' and Other Related Writings*.

During the first decades of the twentieth century, Riding, Graves and many modernist writers – including Eliot, Joyce, Lawrence and Yeats – were heavily influenced by contemporaneous anthropological studies offering new theories and retellings of ancient mythology and religion, including James George Frazer's *The Golden Bough* (1890), Jane Harrison's *Themis: A Study of the Social Origins of Greek Religion* (1912, rev. 1927), Robert Briffault's *The Mothers: The Matriarchal Theory of Social Origins* (1927, 1931) and the translation of J.J. Bachofen's *Das Mutterrecht* (*Mother Right: An Investigation of the Religious and Juridical Character of Matriarchy in the Ancient World*, 1861). While there was great interest expressed in ancient matrilineal social systems, many thinkers, including Freud and Marx, saw the move from matriarchy to patriarchy as social progression. Both this attitude and the reification of goddess lore were problematic and digressive for some women writers (see Hoberman 1997: 59–60). While, as Hoberman claims, many male followers of comparative anthropology 'found fertility goddesses less threatening than women who achieved power in less traditionally "female" ways', many women objected to a definition of the feminine in simplistic binaries: female/male, earth/sky, body/mind, nature/culture (1997: 57, 59). Some, like Graves, conflated the goddess and the Muse to serve as inspiration-figuration for male writers and artists. Penny Murray, in 'Reclaiming the Muse', aligns Graves's version of the Muse to a history of objectification going back to the classical period: 'the male poet's invocation of the Muse is an act of appropriation or control: the poet objectifies his source of inspiration as a passive female figure, whilst simultaneously appropriating her creative powers and silencing her in the process' (2006: 341). In this example – an inversion of human birth – the male poet summons impregnation by the acceding female Muse, leading to the 'birth' of his artistic creation. While Graves might praise the matriarchal order, he retains the role of poet for males: 'woman is not a poet: she is either a Muse or she is nothing' ([1948] 1997: 437). The spell, however, is broken when the phantasm of the Muse converts to her flesh-and-blood relative, as Murray locates in this passage from *The White Goddess*:

> the woman whom he took to be a Muse, or who was a Muse, turns into a domestic woman and would have him turn similarly into a domesticated man. . . . The White Goddess is anti-domestic; she is the perpetual 'other woman', and her part is difficult indeed for a woman of sensibility to play for more than a few years, because the temptation to commit suicide in simple domesticity lurks in every maenad's and muse's heart.[8]

In *The Word 'Woman'*, Riding debunks the male writer's romance with the imagined Muse and she turns to interrogate the entire paradigm shift away from woman-generated creation and matriarchal origin stories (1993: 35):

> We know that earliest man tended to identify the productive process as female on the simple factual basis that women produced children. . . . The change from a production to a creation view of origin cannot have been due, in any instance, to a sudden change in natural process, necessitating a readjustment of ideas: the physical universe, and the fact 'man', and the fact 'woman', remained the same. The change must have been due to a gradual change in man's opinion of his own importance, a gradual intensification of will; . . . It is man's will which obscures the fact of production in the idea of creation, and not only makes production the accessory process but even obscures the female character of production in a comprehensive male notion of creation.

A premise of *The Word 'Woman'* – indeed of most of Riding's works – is that man needs to recognize and accept difference, in particular the difference between himself and woman, instead of trying to subsume her into his vision of himself and the world. Riding attests to an aspect to woman's nature that is an 'untranslatable residue' which man yet attempts to 'translate into himself' (1993: 27).[9] Graves's White Goddess is the reverse of the women Riding represents in her works of poetry and fiction: Riding's women are powerful, flawed, unapologetically political, or abstaining.

Reception studies contribute to our understanding of the ways in which modernist women writers interrogate history, and its narrative veracity, as well as their strategies for crafting parallel but alternative histories which constitute a claim to an inheritance of their own. Since Hoberman's study – which engaged a feminist psychoanalytic model of transference for tracing her authors' autobiographically based hero ideation (of predominantly male figures) to their writing of historical fiction – more recent reception scholarship working at the intersections of classical studies, modernist studies and feminist studies continues to deepen our understanding of past and present texts and cultural contexts as they relate to gender, power and change. In *Reception Studies*, Lorna Hardwick states that reception scholarship 'is and always has been a field for the practice and study of contest about values and their relationship to knowledge and power' (2003: 11). In particular, she underscores the ways in which reception studies offer insights into the 'cultural politics associated with change', especially as they affect the 'conceptual and theoretical frameworks that shape and define "knowledge"' (2003: 6). The first half of the twentieth century is rich for examinations of rapidly changing social, economic, political and aesthetic paradigms.[10] Classical reception studies have moved well beyond the traditional practice of classicism which interprets the legacy of antiquity as a 'linear progression of "influence"' as well as the chronicles of 'Great Men' toward a more nimble and comparative methodology that, according to Hardwick, assesses 'the interfaces between cultures ... [toward the] valuable effect of liberating the ancient texts for re-appropriation and reworking ("refiguration") by new generations of writers and artists' (2003: 2–3). Such latitude allows contemporary scholars to better determine the ways modernist women writers contest the canonical status of traditional classicism as practised by largely male historians in order to query the experiences of women, the colonized, slaves and other under-represented voices.[11] A particularly productive strategy for the modernist woman writer working in historical fiction is the vantage of 'critical distance' which would more safely allow her to comment on perceived disparities and inequities in her own time period. The advantage of overlaying the conflicts of the present onto an ancient setting would help to allay the fear of 'punishment' that DeKoven identifies. According to Hardwick, the idea of 'critical distance'

> is important both for envisaging the possibility of the individual or group enlarging horizons of expectation or even transforming them and for its potential when classical texts are used as critical devices for outwitting censors and enabling current social and political concerns to be addressed through the apparently neutral, 'distant' (and safe) medium of classical culture.
>
> *2003: 9*

Modernist women writers were well aware of the legitimacy that invoking the classics conferred upon them and that the separation through time might camouflage the more radical nature of their projects. By *gendering* the classics, women writers propose imaginative reconstructions of classical women's lives as alternative historiographies that evoke the past as a strategy for intervention, recovery and transformation. Further, through the reversion of the genre of story as history, women writers offer alternative accounts of the founding of the Western world and, by virtue of their narrative voice, an alternative reception of an historical period that might expose the fissures and silences in the record and open these for critique. As Riding 'translates' the lives of women of classical antiquity from scanty record into historical fiction, she proposes an alternative historiography in which women's power is exerted through dimensions of their lives 'untranslatable' for men seeking to understand women through their own frameworks and terms. In doing so, Riding counters stale archetypes like Graves's White Goddess.

Riding begins her reframing of the metanarrative of Western civilization with an origin story featuring Lilith, Adam's first wife – created before Eve – in the Apocrypha literature. Lilith rejects their coupling when Adam refuses to acknowledge their equality. Unlike Graves's White Goddess, Lilith is originating: the creator and destroyer. Riding's Lilith is an oracle, an interlocutor with God and the poet-orator.[12] (By the Middle Ages, Lilith is largely recast as demonic – a succubus, a hazard to pregnant women and a witch.) Often writing under the alias Lilith Outcome, Riding posits a mythopoeic new archaic through a feminist reading of the Adamic monogenetic tradition, which she develops in essays and short prose pieces: *Anarchism Is Not Enough* (1928), *Experts Are Puzzled* (1930), *Progress of Stories* (1935). The Lilithian prototype of rebellion and independence extends to the many portraits of women in Riding's corpus.[13] In *A Trojan Ending* and *Lives of Wives* she shapes a genealogy of female instrumentality and agency in early history, offering various formulas for female self-determination.

In her preface to *A Trojan Ending*, Riding reflects (1937: xvi): 'I find myself regarding the officially historical history of ourselves as an alien record. Is not history supposed to be the history of ourselves – the past supposed to be our past? And how much of it can we read in the intimacy of self-recognition?' Her foreword to the *Lives of Wives* pointedly states that she will write about the founders of the Persian, Greek and Roman impires 'as husbands rather than as heroes' (1939: 5). It is from these points of inquiry that Riding advances a philosophy of historicity that deliberates knowledge, memory and the human condition.[14] Something is missing from the established – an 'alien' – record, she claims, for she, as a woman, is barely represented. History, 'the history of ourselves', should be the human story, equitable and manifold, and her aim in her fiction is to redress the omissions. Riding asserts an aggregate experience of being alive that can imaginatively unite the living with figures from the past (1937: xiii–xiv):

> What is the mysterious difference between ourselves and those long dead – a difference that makes us feel as if we were defying a solemn law of propriety when we try to discern what people they were, how they once lived? ... Did they not walk the same earth, speak languages which are contained in ours? Why does our consciousness not contain their lives along with our own? When an age passes, is nothing left besides its story and its tombs?

Riding claims that her coming to knowledge about her classical subjects occurs as 'premonitions' (1937: xv), 'instinctive acts of memory' (1937: xxi) and 'an irresistible instinct of sympathy . . . a sense of long-distance understanding' (1937: xii). She finds 'the intimacy of self-recognition' in her female protagonists and in the everyday details of their lives. Affinities and familiarities incite her imagination – an affiliate reminiscence – to reconstitute lost and unfinished stories of lives. Her claim in the 'Afterword' to *Lives of Wives*, written in 1988, is that her stories are 'suppositious histories, but the foundations are factual. Fancy, in them, imitates knowledge, and delineation, truth'.[15] Riding's creative reception, 'refigurations' of the characters and events of the classical period, offers insights into what Hardwick terms the 'cultural politics associated with change' as well as the 'frameworks that shape and define "knowledge"' (2003: 6). Riding's retrospective call to history is both to question and answer the past according to her contemporary need for models of success and continuance: practically, to amplify and imagine stories of documented and legendary foremothers and to search for historical parallels, and lessons, from periods of intense social and political change and assault of the kind she was experiencing in the heightened state of emergency in Europe during the 1930s: by August 1936, she and Graves are forced off the island of Mallorca by Francisco Franco's invading Nationalist troops. The 'insistence' of the Trojan legend on her imagination is proof for Riding of its relevance for her stories and her time: 'I came to Troy – in search of a living past' (1937: xvii). For Riding, history is personal and accessible to the modern imagination and no less 'true' for its contemporary reframing. Indeed, both Hoberman and Sheila Murnaghan account for the ways Riding and other twentieth-century women writers, in Murnaghan's words, search for 'a connection to the ancient world that could circumvent traditional classicism and resonate with their own experience', particularly experiences from their girlhoods (2007: 125). That the private and personal are also political will shortly become a rallying point for second-wave feminists later in the century.

Developed by a creative writer, and not a scholar, Riding's philosophy of historical consciousness is also an *ars poetica* for creative recovery. In effect, the genre of historical fiction works for Riding as a form of translation of its historical sources. While, as Peter Christensen documents, Riding often remains 'close to the historical record, scanty as it may be' by paralleling events described by classical authors (1991b: 18), including Homer, Herodotus and Plutarch, as well as medieval and Renaissance receptions of the Troy cycles, she also imagines new characterizations, narrative points of view and dramatic outcomes. Academics, she states, are interested only in the chronology of 'what happened', which thereby 'abbreviat[es] the burdens of the historical consciousness' (1937: xxvii). For the writer, historiography becomes story, and the poetic imagination serves as a variation of human memory by which to contemplate and even shoulder those 'burdens'. She articulates why she chose the novelistic genre for her depictions of the classical world which, she admits, has its shortcomings as well as advantages. Riding upholds poetry as the highest linguistic vehicle for 'truth' and she writes that, had she been more certain about the historical events for her novel *A Trojan Ending*, she would have composed a poem depicting the Trojan conflict:

> That I have written only a novel, a tentative prose account of this first concentrated world-experience, should be taken as my apology of its faults of fact and truth. A

novel, whatever its faults, has a least the endearing virtue of homeliness. And it is the homelier aspects of the story of Troy that call for understanding.

1937: xii–xiii

Through the genre of fiction, prose and the prosaic, Riding finds herself 'at home' in history by envisioning the past through domestic details and common life experiences. Even her choice of language is cued to the familiar, as when she states that she will choose the Latin word form over the Greek, for its 'more accustomed ring' and English derivations over the original, as in 'Diomedes' over 'Diomede' – 'for its homelier, less poetical ring' (1937: xiii).

A Trojan Ending is an accounting of the final year of the legendary battle between Troy and Greece, culminating in the destruction of the ancient Trojan citadel. Riding's novel is less an epic and more a drama of the personalities, relationships and key decisions that impact events. She animates and, in some cases, reinstates Trojan and Greek women, and she amends their depictions as well as those of attendant classical men.[16] Riding's modernist retelling accentuates domestic spaces over battlegrounds, as sites for dramatic action: royal boudoirs, the Scaean viewing tower and camp tents are alternative locations of influence where women are present and relatively free to speak. Most pointedly, Riding engages the narratives surrounding two legendary women, Helen and Cressida, who are conventionally depicted as traitors to men. While the architecture of the elopement of Helen and Paris and the medieval and Renaissance Troilus and Cressida plots are maintained, she reworks the women's characters and motivations for their decisions. Riding offers Helen and Cressida as contrasting portraits of the traditional and the New Woman. Riding's Helen is virtuous yet resigned to the fate that her flight from her husband Menelaus brought. She wears a 'do-with-me-as-you-like look' (1937: 49), while Cressida is intellectual, ethical and decisive on her own behalf: she is 'almost in her time what woman may be in ours' (1937: 410). Cressida gently rejects Troilus as a romantic partner, for he is portrayed as unpredictable and moody (arguably stereotypical female temperaments). Instead, she chooses the brave and thoughtful Diomedes as a suitable match for her. Cressida is the hero of this tale, as her allegiance to Troy propels her first to volunteer to serve as a hostage during a truce with the Greeks – at which time she collegially confers with Achilles – and then to survive the destruction of Troy in order to preserve the memory of Trojan culture (which includes worship of the powerful mother goddess Cybele, who is contrasted with the Greek Apollo).

Cressida stands for Riding as a forceful personal progenitor, as she states in her preface (1937: xviii):

I have said that I came to Troy by no classical bias. It happened to me to begin thinking of Cressida – as I might have begun thinking of my girlhood, in the comfortable leisure of being older, if it had been a sharp and memorable one. At any rate, one's own girlhood cannot take one deep into memory.... The names of all women of the deep past have a legendary ring – but none seem so legendary as that of Cressida; even Homer, to whose imagination she must have been at least legendary-real, does not mention her.

As Hoberman (1997: 57) and Murnaghan (2007: 125) have argued, Riding's imaginative entry into history through memories of her girlhood is shared by other women writers of her time period. Riding likens the 'Great European War' and its innumerable 'miseries' as well as the 'monstrous war-preparations going on around us' to the classical conflict between the Trojans and Greeks (1937: xv), and she wonders about further parallels and how her world might withstand a similar decade-long conflict (1937: xiv). While she makes the point that a primary lesson of history is that the present never suffer the horrors of the past, Riding sees more at stake in resurrecting the Trojan story: a legacy that sparked a civilization. The Trojans, she proclaims, were responsible for 'inaugurating the intelligent world' while her historical moment must respond by 'arriving at the intelligent conclusions' (1937: xvi): 'History', she claims, 'governs history: but this is a rule that works backwards as well as forwards. We cannot do without our Trojan chronicle because we cannot do without an intelligent beginning of things' (1937: xxvii). Cressida, too, is an inauguration point – an 'intelligent beginning' for the restoration of classical women.

While Cressida is admittedly a literary construct, Riding faults Homer, whose own literary project, *The Iliad*, held a quasi-historical reputation.[17] She suggests that Homer willfully omits Cressida (more accurately, historical women like her) out of bias (1937: xxii): 'We must think of the *Iliad*, and other epic reports of the Trojan War on which subsequent "ancient authors" based their accounts, as the rare, dilatory newspapers of their time.' In the course of *A Trojan Ending*, Riding inserts plotlines that implicate the classical scribes Dares Phrygius and Dictys Cretensis in falsifying their chronicles, most prominently under pressure from an opportunistic Odysseus whose conduct during the war, she suggests, was unremarkable. Riding calls into question the legitimacy of historical recordkeeping as possibly influenced, incomplete, or even fictive. As such, she offers up her own literary version: might history not have happened in this way, too? Peter Christensen, in his article 'Historical Truth in Laura Riding's *A Trojan Ending*', claims that, '[u]nlike many twentieth-century reworkings of classical themes, *A Trojan Ending* is a serious investigation of the Trojan War, not just a fantasia on a theme by Homer' (1991a: 15). While acknowledging Riding's deviations from the *Iliad* – from the lack of supernatural interference, minimizing of the Trojan Horse ploy, elevation of Troy above Greece and demonizing of Odysseus – Christensen points to her novel's many alignments with Homer's epic, most notably events taken from Books 3 through 7 (battle depictions) and Books 22 and 23 (Hector's death and burial ceremonies). Christensen allows that Riding does not faithfully report accounts offered by Dares (the only scribe mentioned in the *Iliad*) and Dictys, still, he claims, she does repeat some of their biases, such as Dares's partiality for Troy and Dictys's antipathy toward Odysseus. Riding's inclusion of the two scribes in her narrative, Christensen concludes, cements 'knowledge of the Trojan War as an historical reality come to us through biases and distortions'; he concurs that '[t]here is a politics of power and censorship behind the received accounts'

(1991a: 5).[18] By chronicling the Trojan War from the woman's perspective – that is, constructing a more inclusive account in order to achieve a more faithful 'history of ourselves' – Riding sets the novel's narrative voice alongside the chroniclers of the past. In addition, she presages the postmodern novel in her refusal to terminate Cressida's story (1937: 432): 'What happened to Cressida after she left the island of Scyros with Diomedes no tale tells; nor dare we invent a tale to fill the gap ... we close the book and quiet our minds; this is as Cressida would have wished.' Cressida, as such, is not an ending but a beginning into a (post)modernist historiography that accommodates multiple perspectives and diverse lives.

Lives of Wives explicitly subordinates the exploits of classical men to the judgements and machinations of the women in their lives. Narrated by an omniscient (and sometimes editorializing first-person) chronicler, the novel dramatizes the destinies of the women associated with founders of the Persian, Greek and Roman empires: Amytis (Cyrus the Great); Olympias (Philip the Great); Pythias (Aristotle); Mariamne (Herod the Great); Cleopatra (Caesar and Mark Anthony). While Riding often parallels the classical sources, as Christensen again documents in 'Women as a Spiritual Force in Laura Riding's *Lives of Wives*', she refocuses the narrative to submit a gynocentric history of female ambition, both indirectly and overtly wielded, the dynamics of intimate and political power and examines the social station of 'wife' for its centrality to power afforded to the women of antiquity.[19] *Lives of Wives* can, in fact, be read as a history cum *speculum principum*, a Mirror for Princes(s) – of the genre famously penned by Machiavelli. Throughout her chronologies of intrigues and murders, Riding attests that women can be as ambitious, calculated and tenacious as men, as is here illustrated in a synopsis of the decline of the Persian Empire (1939: 78): 'It is a lurid period ... and its great men are of a sickly color. But the women whose names are associated with them make a more full-blooded show of life. Some of them achieve the reality of seeming monsters.' The roles of wife, mother, daughter and even consort when liaised to elite men are powerful positions. Strong women pilot men by virtue of their own force of intelligence and life experience, which might help counterbalance his weaknesses and inexperience, as does Riding's Greek hetaera Thaïs for Alexander the Great (1939: 153): 'Alexander did not love her; but, in his ignorance of the ways of the world, he had looked to her for instruction in the behavior becoming to a conqueror.' Wives' high expectations and ambitions can subtly pressure their husbands to complete important projects, as is illustrated by Amytis when Cyrus returns from military campaigning (1939: 38): 'Amytis would expect [Cyrus] to have the work done when he returned, so that he could live with her in peace until it seemed proper to wage some new war of conquest for the advancement of the Empire.' Riding provides numerous examples to confirm that kings did successfully and discreetly leave their kingdoms to the oversight of their wives and daughters while away on campaigns. In one example, Queen Nitocris successfully governs Babylon while her husband Nabonidus is in Arabia. In order to disguise her strength, she would often work through her son Belshazzar and send requests to neighbouring queens in lieu of their husbands (Riding 1939: 50). Such bonds of solidarity as well as cooperation among women are an important means to women's power, as reiterated by Nitocris in her message to Queen

Amytis (Riding 1939: 53): 'There should be a kindness among women above the events of men, and such love as perhaps, unknown to us, the gods have for one another.'

Riding's chronicler-narrator suggests that the darker side of a woman's personality results from the restrictions and injuries she endures, which then breed disillusionment and promote violence of character (as illustrated by Olympias and Cleopatra). As noted before, the disillusioned dreams of girlhood are a recurrent theme in Riding's novels and in *Lives of Wives* she suggests that these structure the more depraved actions of many of these women: for example, while Philip the Great deems his wife 'a wild-mannered, wild-minded woman, dangerous when her whims were not satisfied' (1939: 89), he does not understand 'what the grandiose dreams of her girlhood had meant to her, and what furious energies his disappointment of them had released in her' (1939: 97). In the novel, even the mythical world conspires to remind man of woman's power, as when Amytis describes the Sphinx (1939: 42–3):

> They say she appears sometimes to men in dreams and tells them the deep secrets of life. When they awake they forget what she has told them, and become frantic to remember, and kill themselves. It seems very cruel, but perhaps there is some justice in it. For men forget too easily what women tell them, and it is very annoying.

Such admonitions from a woman's perspective are comically at odds with canonical androcentric histories.

In 'Translation as Critique and Intervention', Hardwick submits that '[t]he ancient material provided [authors] a foil against which modern applications could be created and communicated' (2000a: 68).[20] In her novels Riding reworks, and thereby critiques, the classical sources to her contemporary ends, such that ancient chronicles prove foils for Riding's exposure of their biases of narrative perspective and the omissions of inclusion. In elaborate detailing, she performs a 'close reading' of lost lives, and her refashionings of historical and legendary women submit complex and nuanced portraits of female personality, perseverance and power – certainly not the gauzy stuff of goddess lore. She draws on the familiarities of domestic life and interpersonal relationships in order to advance her radical alternative historiography whereby the constraints of traditional roles and established legends are measured against more modern freedoms and attitudes for women. The novels' world-view is unabashedly woman-centred, and the perspective submits a female authorial voice to counter the canonical masculinist narrative. Riding takes advantage of what Hoberman and others have noted: that 'in writing historical fiction about Greece and Rome, [women writers] were working through the interrelationship of their gender, their desires, the possible roles with which reading history presented them, and the narrative power that the writing of history offered them' (1997: 2). Riding's modernist receptions of the classical record extend first-wave feminism's scope by modelling an alternative mode of cultural and social critique—as plied against the backdrop of history as well as by offering a creative feminist praxis.

CHAPTER 10
LOST AND FOUND IN TRANSLATION: THE GENESIS OF MODERNISM'S SIREN SONGS
Leah Flack

In the twelfth book of the *Odyssey*, Odysseus tells the story of his encounter with the Sirens to his Phaiakian audience. During this encounter, he was tied to the mast, revelling in the ecstatic torment of the beautiful song he heard. As Circe had warned him, the Sirens, sitting in a meadow littered with the bones of their victims, ensnare men with their sweet voices and foreclose their homecoming. Odysseus never sees the mass grave Circe described, and he discovers that the most seductive power of the Sirens' song rests not only in the beauty of their voices but also in their promise of an experience of comprehensive knowledge:

> Come this way, honored Odysseus, great glory of the Achaians,
> And stay your ship, so that you can listen here to our singing;
> For no one else has ever sailed past this place in his black ship
> Until he has listened to the honey-sweet voice that issues
> From our lips; then goes on, well pleased, knowing more than ever
> he did; for we know everything that the Argives and Trojans
> did and suffered in wide Troy through the gods' despite.
> Over all the generous earth we know everything that happens.
>
> *12.184–91*[1]

As Pucci (1987: 213 and 1998: 1–9) observes, the allure of Odysseus's past threatens his future as the Sirens tempt him to suspend his life listening to songs extolling his Trojan history. The Sirens claim a totalizing, all-encompassing knowledge of the past and present – they can, as Andrew Ford (1992: 85) suggests, 'offer the entire *Iliad* and more' – and they lure Odysseus with the promise of endowing him with this kind of full knowledge.[2] By dramatizing this experience of poetry as potentially fatal, this scene suggests that Odysseus – and Homer – understood the tantalizing danger of such promises. His homecoming in fact depended on his Phaiakian audience succumbing to the power of the story – after all, Odysseus's story seduced this audience into becoming active participants in it by delivering him to Ithaca, a move that would bring about their potential demise.

Nearly three millennia later, modernist writers James Joyce and T.S. Eliot reimagined the figure of the Sirens to consider the seductions and dangers of literature in an era of unprecedented global warfare. Literary history might suggest that Joyce and Eliot were themselves Sirens of a sort, promising professional literary scholars and bewildered students an experience of comprehensive knowledge and mastery as the reward for successfully navigating the climb up the textual Everests of *Ulysses* and *The Waste Land*. The consolidation of high modernism around values of formal and allusive complexity has had consequences for both modernism and the classics in the twentieth century – the writings of Joyce and Eliot would seem to imply that both the classics and modernism were intended for a coterie of specialist readers. Although linguistic and interpretive competence served as a signal of cultural cachet and class distinction in the early twentieth century (Stray 1998), in the twenty-first century, the values ascribed to modernism, particularly in its engagement with the classics, have made both vulnerable to charges of being elitist, Eurocentric and passé (Graziosi and Greenwood 2007: 14). This shared fate is perhaps one explanation for the recent emergence of studies of modernist classical receptions, more than a decade after the explosion of classical reception studies as an exciting new field of enquiry.[3] Modernist classical receptions could do little to reinvigorate classical studies when modernist literature and classics shared an uncertain future in the ongoing global crisis in the humanities and humanistic study.

Joyce's and Eliot's engagements with the Sirens in *Ulysses* and *The Waste Land* offer an alternative view of classical modernism, one that makes clear a gap between the ideals of authority and mastery that have so often been applied to modernist writing and the interrogation of these ideals inherent in their project of reimagining the classical tradition for the twentieth century. As figures of alluring, yet damaging claims to comprehensive knowledge, the Sirens were especially appealing for modernists responding to the war as an unprecedented human and cultural catastrophe. In different ways, Joyce and Eliot used the Sirens to question a range of cultural traditions implicated in nurturing the conditions for war in the modern imagination. In so doing, they justified and defended their formal experimentation as a revision of these traditions. As I will show, they engaged with the figure of the Sirens at key turning points in their composition of *Ulysses* and *The Waste Land*. Returning to these moments of composition helps us to rethink some of the prevailing views of modernist classical reception that arise from seeing works like *Ulysses* or *The Waste Land* as monuments. In the eleventh episode of *Ulysses* ('Sirens'), Joyce broke from the prevailing style of his novel (Groden 1977; Lawrence 1981). Prior to 'Sirens', he had mostly used interior monologue to depict the inner lives of Leopold Bloom and Stephen Dedalus on 16 June 1904. In 'Sirens', he plunged into the formal experiments for which his novel is known. In the fourth section of *The Waste Land* ('Death by Water'), Eliot, on the advice of Ezra Pound, scrapped 84 out of 94 lines of his drafts, which ultimately buried an extended Odyssean narrative, including a harrowing encounter with the Sirens. This editorial decision concealed what I take to be one of the key classical premises of Eliot's poem. At these pressure points of composition, both Joyce and Eliot translated the Sirens to work out their perspectives on the value of stylistic complexity and even of confusion as a productive mode of readerly engagement. Together, these modern Sirens foreground the ways in which intensive engagements with the classical tradition helped modernist writers define and defend their difficult art at a historical moment of global violence.

Eliot and the genesis of classical modernism

The publication history of *The Waste Land* sheds light on formation of a version of classical modernism that is grounded in the modernist text as a complex, harmonious masterpiece whose readers must possess an array of linguistic, historical and literary knowledge. Eliot first published *The Waste Land* in the *Criterion* (October 1922, England) and the *Dial* (November 1922, United States) without any footnotes. In December 1922, Horace Liveright released a book-length edition, complete with footnotes that have shaped the poem's reception. As Michael Edward Kaufmann (1992) observes, Eliot's notes – particularly his insistence that the poem's 'plan' was influenced by Jessie L. Weston's book on the Grail legend and his curious identification of Tiresias as the poem's 'most important personage ... uniting all the rest' – 'impose a pattern on the poem' and supports an ideal of the modernist text as 'organic, unified, and self-contained despite a fragmented and chaotic appearance' (78, 81). The number of classical references in the footnotes suggests a certain standard of classical knowledge is required to elucidate the poem's meaning. In the Eliotic version of modernism suggested by the readerly apparatus, knowledge of classical languages and literatures is taken to be part of the price of admission for correctly reading the poem. As Kaufmann (1992: 81) notes, the early influential readings of Eliot by critics such as I.A. Richards, F. R. Leavis and Cleanth Brooks all relied heavily on Eliot's notes, which affirmed this view of the classics at the consolidation of modernist studies.

The 1971 publication of *The Waste Land: A Facsimile and Draft of the Original Drafts* made visible aspects of the poem's complex textual genesis, including the extensive editorial work of Ezra Pound. It also undermined the sense affirmed by the notes of the poem's ritualistic and classical order. The drafts offer a fascinating, long buried history of modernism's uncertain, dynamic relationship to the classical tradition. And, the drafts for 'Death by Water' offer an echo of a silenced Siren song at the origins of the paradigmatic modernist poem. Eliot adapted the figure of the Sirens to conceptualize his poem's depiction of the horror of the modern mind confronting an overwhelming experience of modern history in the years following the Great War.

Although Eliot was relatively reticent about publicly responding to the Great War, in recent decades his poetry has been viewed as an important voice of Europe's post-war cultural despair (Fussell 1975; Sherry 2003). Eliot contextualized his poetry in terms of the war. In 1917, he dedicated his first book of poems, *Prufrock and Other Observations*, in the following way: 'Jean Verdenal, 1889–1915'. Eliot befriended the French medical student Verdenal in 1910 at the Sorbonne and paid general tribute to him with this 1917 dedication. Verdenal died at Gallipoli, but as John T. Mayer (1989: 201) observes, nothing in this dedication directly draws attention to Verdenal as a war victim. Eliot added the phrase 'mort aux Dardenelles' to the dedication in the 1925 volume *Poems: 1909–1925*, thereby suggesting that his grief for Verdenal serves as a 'buried theme' of his poetry in this era (Gilbert 1999: 194). To voice the confusion and grief opened by the war, Eliot turned to the classical tradition. As Paul Fussell (1975), Eileen Gregory (1997) and Elizabeth Vandiver (2010) observe, the proximity of Gallipoli and the Dardenelles to what was believed in the late nineteenth century to be Troy created the imaginative conditions for Eliot and other poets to view the Homeric epics (particularly the *Iliad*) as a framework for responding to the Great War.

As Jay Winter contends, the classical tradition enabled Eliot to construct a poetic language of grief and mourning that 'helped mediate bereavement' (1998: 223) through a 'complex traditional vocabulary of mourning' (Gilbert 1999: 183). The poem's first section, 'The Burial of the Dead', maps various traditions onto one another to depict the grief-stricken trauma of modern life, which it expresses via interwoven allusions to Baudelaire, Dante and Roman history. Eliot's speaker beholds post-war London as an 'unreal City' and reflects that he 'had not thought death had undone so many' (1971: 136). His traumatized apprehension of London as a modern inferno culminates in his seeming recognition of another war veteran: 'Stetson! / You who were with me in the ships at Mylae! / The corpse you planted last year in your garden, / has it begun to sprout?' (1971: 136). Eliot uses the First Punic War and the Trojan War to refract and express the trauma of the Great War and the anxieties it evokes in the speaker's obsession with the corpse, a figure that haunts the poem in various guises, most directly as Phlebas the Phoenician, the drowned sailor in 'Death by Water', the poem's fourth section.

During their collaborative editing process, Pound and Eliot cut most of this section in part, the drafts suggest, because Pound worried that Eliot's poem might appear to be derivative of *Ulysses*. They retained only the description of the drowned sailor, Phlebas the Phoenician, foretold at the beginning of the poem by the sham clairvoyant Madame Sosostris. Eliot's draft (1971) shows that he originally opened 'Death by Water' with an Odyssean sailor:

The sailor, attentive to the chart or to the sheets,
A concentrated will against the tempest and the tide,
Retains, even ashore, in public bars or streets
Something inhuman, clean and dignified.
Even the drunk ruffian who descends
Illicit backstreet stairs, to reappear,
For the derision of his sober friends
Staggering, or limping with comic gonorrhea,
From his trade with wind and sea and snow, as they
Are, he is, with 'much seen and much endured',
Foolish, impersonal, innocent or gay,
Liking to be shaved, combed, scented, manicured.

55

To introduce his land-roving sailor, Eliot here translates the Homeric phrase used to describe Odysseus's vast knowledge and experience in the invocation of the *Odyssey* (3–4); he signals his citation by putting the phrase in quotation marks. This citation locates this passage in a post-war context – Eliot's poem modernizes the Odyssean *nostos* narrative by situating it in a modern cityscape of 'public bars' and 'illicit backstreet stairs'.

It also generates a tension between the heroic and the anti-heroic, the mythic and the mundane consistent with the rest of *The Waste Land*. Eliot's sailor displays a dignity that coexists with his debasement, his 'comic gonorrhea' and his folly. Despite this conflicted characterization, Eliot's sailor lacks the gentle humour, humanity and prosaic heroism of Joyce's Leopold Bloom. Rather, this sailor is a crucial figure at the drafting stage that helps Eliot to forge a relationship between the literary past and what he called the 'anarchy' of contemporary history (1975: 177).

Eliot's drafts show that the Sirens were also instrumental in his poem's depiction of the modern mind's agonized confrontation with the unspeakable horrors of modern history. When Pound suggested that Eliot strike 83 out of 93 lines in 'Death by Water', Eliot was 'depressed by Pound's reaction to the main passage' and wrote to Pound, 'Perhaps better omit Phlebas also???' (1971: 129). Pound saw Phlebas as essential to the poem and urged Eliot to keep the section's ten final lines. This editorial decision buried the poem's Homeric subtext, which was critical to the poem's early development. The poem's conceptual framework becomes apparent in a draft for a sequence depicting a terrifying encounter with the Sirens, told from the perspective of Eliot's modern Odysseus:

> And when the lookout could no longer hear
> Above the roar of the waves upon the sea
> The sharper note of breakers on a reef,
> We knew we had passed the farthest northern islands
> So no one spoke again. We ate slept drank
> Hot coffee, and kept watch, and no one dared
> To look into anothers face, or speak
> In the horror of the illimitable scream
> Of a whole world about us. One night
> On Watch, I thought I saw in the fore cross-trees
> Three women with w leaning forward, with white hair
> Streaming behind, who sang above the wind
> A song that charmed my senses, while I was
> Frightened beyond fear, horrified past horror, calm,
> (Nothing was real) for, I thought, now, when
> I like, I can wake up and end the dream.

1971: 59

This passage is integral to the draft's use of the literary tradition to depict the modern condition as a shared experience of horror among the sailor and his anonymous crew: the sounds of the sea overwhelm the sailors into silence. The poem allegorizes the modern subject paralysed and silenced by an 'illimitable scream' as they confront 'a whole world', an alienating and alienated experience of history (such as Eliot develops not only in this poem but in several of his other poems as well, such as 'The Love Song of J. Alfred Prufrock', 'Gerontion', 'The Hollow Men' and others). Eliot's reference to three

Sirens rather than Homer's two suggests that he is adapting the figure from other mythic sources, but the juxtaposition of this reference with his explicitly Odyssean sailor associates these Sirens with Homer's. Eliot adapts the Sirens to convey the traumatized experience of modern existence.

Eliot's dialogical reading of the Sirens and Joseph Conrad's *Heart of Darkness* helped him conceptualize his poem's depiction of the modern mind. As the drafts show, the poem's epigraph came from the climax of Conrad's novel:

> Did he live his life again in every detail of desire, temptation, and surrender during that supreme moment of complete knowledge? He cried in a whisper at some image, some vision – he cried out twice, a cry that was no more than a breath – 'the horror! The horror!'
>
> *1971: 3*

This epigraph describes Marlow's contemplation of Kurtz's death and the potential significances of Kurtz's final words. Pound urged Eliot to change this epigraph, doubting that the modern novel was 'weighty enough to stand the citation' (Eliot 1971: 125). Eliot first defended his selection as both 'appropriate' and 'elucidative' for his vision of the poem before replacing it with an uncited, untranslated selection in Greek and Latin from Petronius's *Satyricon* (expressing the Cumaean Sybil's wish to die). This editorial decision concealed an important framework for *The Waste Land*, which seems to have emerged in part from the association the poem made between the Sirens and Kurtz (signalled by Eliot's repetition of the word 'horror' in the passage describing the Sirens cited above, e.g. 'horrified past horror'). It also recruited the weight of untranslated Greek and Latin in a way that separates readers according to their knowledge or ignorance of classical languages. As Rainey observes, this quotation is spoken by Trimalchio (who has just muddled the stories of Hercules and Ulysses before turning to the story of the Cumaean Sybil), possibly in a move to impress his guests by showing them that he can speak Greek (2006: 75). As much as Eliot's poem appears to use classical languages to set a kind of readerly standard, the epigraph also scrutinizes the logic for doing so.

Conrad's novel gestures towards a 'supreme moment of complete knowledge' while withholding from its readers (and from Marlow) the unambiguous substance of that knowledge. This ambiguity reproduces the insistent ambiguity of the Sirens' song, which is described by Homer and heard by Odysseus, but which remains outside of the frame of the *Odyssey*. Both texts ultimately interrogate the kinds of full knowledge claimed by the Sirens and Kurtz – the Sirens 'know everything' of the past and present, and Kurtz's life, Marlow surmises, seems to culminate in a moment of 'supreme knowledge'. Both texts mark this kind of knowledge as alluring, yet fatal not only for their characters but also for the cultures from which they emerged – Homer's Sirens expose the cultural relationship between war and knowledge, whereas Conrad's Kurtz dramatizes the ways that a desire for knowledge inevitably yields to the desire to master and destroy underlying Europe's imperial project. By withholding the Sirens' song and Kurtz's final vision, both narratives explore ambiguity and absence as alternatives to supreme, damaging knowledge.

The fact that this sequence culminates neither in homecoming nor in the valorization of the sailor's warrior virtues suggests that the Sirens helped Eliot's poem to dismantle the violent logic of the Western tradition in a way that clears a path for a new, more peaceful cosmopolitan tradition. The poem goes beyond merely omitting homecoming – it actually negates it in the line 'Not a chance. Home and mother' (1971: 61). Of course, Eliot and Pound struck this line and all lines already cited during their revision process. However, the remaining ten lines that found their way into the poem's final version have a similar effect in their presentation of the corpse of the drowned sailor, Phlebas the Phoenician. 'Death by Water' ends quietly with the simple line, 'Consider Phlebas, who was once handsome and tall as you' (143). Eliot's poem uses figures and language essential to Homer's heroic model ultimately to refuse it and envision the cultural conditions for peace and preservation.

At the end of *The Waste Land*, Eliot's speaker declares, 'These fragments I have shored against my ruins', thereby expressing the poem's ambition to use and thus preserve a culture left in ruins by war (146). In its original adaptation of Homer, 'Death by Water' imaginatively cleared a space for the poem's call for peace. To voice this call, the poem turns away from the languages and rationalist logic of the Western tradition towards the Sanskrit language of Hinduism. The poem ends with repetition of the Sanskrit language of prayer, 'shantih shantih shantih' (146), which Eliot translates in his notes as 'the peace which passeth understanding' (149). Reading this line in dialogue with its first epigraph and its buried Homeric sequence suggests that the poem promotes a counter-rational, metaphysical sensibility as an essential cultural precondition of peace. The comprehensive knowledge promised by the Sirens and experienced by Kurtz in his final moments leads to violence, ruination and death. In the end, Eliot's poem gestures towards a redemption grounded in its own vision of a cosmopolitan tradition that emerges from the fragments of East and West in dialogue.

Since the modernist era, Eliot's poem has played a central role in the institutionalization of modernism as a difficult and often elitist enterprise, meant for a specialized readership up to the task of managing its allusive complexity. The concealed drama running from Homer to Conrad in the poem's drafts suggests that the poem itself was sceptical about the kinds of claims of rationalist, full knowledge often projected onto it by its critics. In the aftermath of an unprecedented war, Eliot's poem used the literary tradition inaugurated by Homer to grieve the war dead and to try to write into being an imaginative foundation for peace.

Joyce's 'Sirens' and the nightmare of history

Most of the episodes that have earned *Ulysses* the reputation of a literary Everest occur in its second half ('Proteus', the third episode, is the most obvious exception). The novel's style departs from its prevailing logic and becomes more experimental in the Cubist collage of its tenth episode, 'Wandering Rocks'. As Michael Groden observes, in the eleventh episode, 'Sirens', Joyce distorts the novel's initial style 'practically beyond all recognition' (1977: 17). As Karen Lawrence notes, from the musical overture of the opening lines of 'Sirens', '*Ulysses* abandons even the pretense of being a traditional novel' (1981: 90). The musical, non-narrative opening of 'Sirens' signals the start of a new kind of novel, one defined by experimentation. As such, it might be taken as a textual transition between a more stable mode of classical translation in modernist writing and a more idiosyncratic, experimental mode that continually demands that readers recalibrate how they read.

'Sirens' might be taken as a kind of pressure point for both *Ulysses* and for modernism. Joyce wrote this episode in Zurich in late 1918 and early 1919, just as the terms of peace were being negotiated at the end of the Great War. Joyce had relatively little to say publicly in response to the war, but he understood his art as fundamentally opposed to it. During this time, he wrote that he was engaged in the 'eternal struggle' of the artist against the state, particularly 'those states . . . that have drowned the world in a bloodbath' (Fairhall 1990: 25). Even though *Ulysses* depicts the pre-war moment of Dublin on 16 June 1904, critics have long noted the ways that Joyce's novel indirectly responds to both the Great War and the subsequent struggle for Irish independence. Robert Spoo (1986) has noted the double temporality of Stephen's history lesson on Pyrrhus in 'Nestor' – taught to boys who will go on to fight and die in the war ten years later – which adapts the ancient war to generate echoes with the Great War. More generally, Fairhall points out, *Ulysses* 'analyse[s] and subvert[s] the ideology of nationalism, that all-powerful force which would lead to war not only on the continent but in Ireland' (1990: 35).

In 'Sirens', Joyce uses the Sirens to dramatize the damaging allure of sentimental nationalism in the twentieth-century Irish imagination. The classical tradition offers Joyce a template for his analysis of the problem of war in both ancient and modern history as a 'nightmare' from which Joyce's protagonist Stephen Dedalus is 'trying to awake' (34). Although Pound and Eliot – and generations of critics who have followed their lead – tended to view Joyce's reception of the *Odyssey* in mainly mythological, narrative and aesthetic terms, Joyce was long drawn to the *Odyssey* precisely because it so easily served his art's scrutiny of the subterranean ideologies that perpetuated twentieth-century wars. By revising the *Odyssey*, Joyce's *Ulysses* articulates a pacifist, life-affirming, anti-war agenda. Joyce admired Odysseus as the most 'well-rounded' man in literary history whose heroism was grounded in something other than his martial prowess: his intelligence and his will to survive and reach home so that his history 'did not come to an end when the Trojan war was over' (Budgen [1934] 1972: 220 and 18). As Joyce's 'Sirens' episode suggests, his modern translation of Odysseus into the cosmopolitan Irish-Catholic-Jewish-Hungarian-Greek everyman Leopold Bloom offers a modern hero for an Ireland that does not yet exist, one that looks to the future rather than to the past for its national identity. This episode uses Bloom to deconstruct damaging, nostalgic models of sentimental nationalism that it associates with the Sirens. In so doing, Joyce subtly extends and revises the Homeric epic's identification as that which must be overcome for the hero to return to his nation – in *Ulysses*, Bloom must reject a model of nationalism associated with the Sirens in order to make newly visible and viable an alternative model of the Irish nation for the twentieth century.

The novel's eleventh episode depicts Leopold Bloom at the bar at the Ormond Hotel at 4.00 p.m. It stylistically translates Homer's story via its musical, onomatopoetic language and its fugal structure. Its non-narrative overture, a condensed musical performance of the sounds featured in the rest of the episode, signals the novel's first major break from the predominant style of shifting interior monologues displayed in the first ten episodes, and it thus paves the way for the more daring stylistic experiments in the novel's final third. 'Sirens' illustrates the critical role music plays in shaping and entombing the Irish imagination via controlled sentimentality. There are multiple figures of the Sirens in the bar: initially and most prominently, the episode presents the flirtatious barmaids Miss Kennedy and Miss Douce who flatter the men and, as Bloom thinks, tempt 'poor simple males' (214). But, the episode quickly makes clear its more expansive use of this figure via the men in the bar who perform the various Siren songs of the Irish nationalist imagination.

'Sirens' dramatizes the various snares of an Irish history known all too well by modern Irish men and women. In its staunch refusal of the heroics of history, *Ulysses* analyses what Joyce called elsewhere the emotional and spiritual paralysis of modern Dubliners oppressed by their colonial history and the Roman Catholic Church (Joyce 1957: 83 and 88). In 'Sirens', the men at the Ormond bar perform a series of songs that increase in emotional pitch and intensity, starting with the performance of a series of sentimental songs of lost love. This unleashing of emotion culminates in the outpouring of nationalist sentiment via Ben Dollard's stirring rendition of 'The Croppy Boy', the episode's most dangerous Siren song.

'The Croppy Boy' replays a well-worn story in the Irish nationalist imagination: the betrayal and execution of the young romantic rebel fighting for Irish freedom (other similar songs, slogans and stories proliferate in the minds of other characters throughout the novel, showing the wide appeal of this narrative and the cultural work it performs). Set during the failed uprising of 1798, it depicts a young rebel (or croppy) on his way to fight who goes to confess first. The priest is actually a British soldier in disguise who arrests him and takes him to be executed. The men in the pub choose this song, which suggests the power these old wounds wield for them. When Ben Dollard goes to sing, Father Cowley suggests he sing '*Qui sdegno*', which is from Mozart's *The Magic Flute* and is a song about peace and the 'banishment of strife' (Bowen 1974: 194–5). The men refuse this suggestion and demand that he perform 'The Croppy Boy' (Joyce 1984: 232). Joyce's presentation of this choice suggests that the Irish choose to count their wounds and revel in their losses over peace. As 'Sirens' shows, an unceasing remembrance of a defeated history seduces and paralyses the men at the Ormond bar, who are 'all lost in pity for the croppy' (1984: 235).

In Homer's *Odyssey*, hearing the Siren song is a solitary adventure – Odysseus is tied to the mast, tormented by the enchanting song, while his crew's ears are stopped with wax. In Joyce's novel, hearing the Siren song is a collective, social experience, one that forms a cohering bond among the Irish men and women. Bloom's struggle is not only to maintain his sense of self, family and home in the presence of the Siren song but also to avoid being ensnared by the collective experience of mourning Irish defeat evoked by the song in the public space of the bar. The song demands a personal, emotional investment from the men who, outside of the context of the nationalist cause, have no direct involvement in the song's events. Bloom refuses this kind of investment by translating the distant nationalist past to his own personal experience, which can be seen when he recalls the nationalist anthem 'The Boys of Wexford' and thinks of his daughter Milly and his dead son Rudy:

> All gone. All fallen. At the siege of Ross his father, at Gorey all his brothers fell. To Wexford, we are the boys of Wexford, he would. Last of his name and race.
>
> I too, last of my race. Milly young student. Well, my fault perhaps. No son. Rudy. Too late now. Or if not? If not? If still?
>
> He bore no hate.
>
> Hate. Love. Those are names. Rudy.
>
> *1984: 234*

The call to the collective ('we are the boys of Wexford') passes through Bloom's mind before he directs his attention to his own family ('I too, last of my race') and his children. He mourns his son who died in infancy eleven years earlier before wondering, tentatively, whether it might be possible to have another son. By the end of this musing, he refuses abstractions altogether ('Hate. Love. Those are names') and grounds his thinking firmly in his own individual experience of loss and love ('Rudy'). Joyce translates Odysseus's heroism to twentieth-century Ireland by foregrounding Bloom's intellectual, emotional fortitude and control.

As the only character capable of overcoming the seductions of nationalist sentimentality, Bloom serves as an instrument in 'Sirens' that opens to scrutiny the logic of cultural nationalism. His detachment grants him an analytic perspective on both the song and its listeners. By refusing the song's seduction, Bloom recognizes that the other men 'know it all by heart' (234). He describes their emotion: 'Thrill now. Pity they feel. To wipe away a tear for martyrs that want to, dying to, die. For all things dying, for all things born' (ibid.). Bloom's thoughts identify the thrill and pity evoked by death as the engines of the Irish nationalist imagination. He refuses the imperative of a culture grounded in martyrs who 'want to, [are] dying to, die' and resolves to '[g]et out before the end' of the performance as the '[g]eneral chorus off for a swill to wash it down' (235). The episode ends with Bloom in the street seeing a 'gallant pictured hero in Lionel Marks's window', which makes him recall 'Robert Emmet's last words' (238). A nationalist martyr killed in a famously gruesome public execution in 1803, Emmet delivered his famous 'Speech from the Dock' the night before his death that contained the stirring, defiant words that rang in the minds of several of Joyce's characters a century later in *Ulysses*: 'When my country takes her place among the nations of the earth, then and not till then, let my epitaph be written. I have done' (238–9). Bloom unceremoniously farts as he recalls these words, transferring Emmet's message from a lofty, sentimental register to the insistently quotidian, bodily realm of *Ulysses*. This moment debunks the mythic sentimentality of Emmet and the heroic model he represents.

Both the *Odyssey* and *Ulysses* emerged in dialogical engagement with enticing heroic ideologies represented through masculine self-sacrifice. Odysseus's encounter with the Sirens reanimates the Iliadic interrogation of a model of *kleos* that depends on the hero's death, which helps to articulate the *Odyssey*'s grounding of heroic identity in the hero's endurance, intelligence and homecoming. Rejecting Irish models of the heroic based in sacrificial death, *Ulysses* bases its own vision of modern heroism in Bloom's pacifism, his endurance of the ordinary struggles of an average day and his unceasing desire to survive. 'Sirens' adapts the *Odyssey* to deconstruct a cultural system of martyrdom also familiar to Homer's audiences. In so doing, 'Sirens' plays a critical role in the ambition Joyce expressed for his writing early in his career: to author a 'moral history' aimed at achieving the 'spiritual liberation' of an oppressed Ireland (Joyce 1957: 88).

In 'Sirens', Joyce voiced his long-standing scepticism about static forms of knowledge and expression. It is no accident, then, that 'Sirens' is the first episode in *Ulysses* to embrace the kind of formal experimentation for which the novel is (sometimes infamously) known. The musicality of 'Sirens' anticipates the more radical stylistic experimentation of 'Circe' (a closet drama), 'Oxen of the Sun' (an embryonic performance of the English language from origins through the twentieth century) and 'Ithaca' (a mathematical catechism). When Joyce's first readers criticized 'Sirens' for veering too far stylistically from the preceding ten episodes, Joyce responded (1957: 462):

> I understand that you may begin to regard the various styles of the episodes with dismay and prefer the initial style much as the wanderer did who longed for the rock of Ithaca. But in the compass of one day to compress all these wanderings and clothe them in the form of this day is for me possible only by such variation which, I beg you to believe, is not capricious.

Joyce defended the programme of stylistic innovation announced in 'Sirens' as an essential part of his novel. 'Sirens' helps orient this defence. This musical episode suggests that, once it crystallizes in the human mind that longs for the familiar 'rock of Ithaca', any song can be a Siren song. The most radically experimental parts of *Ulysses*, then, did not emerge in opposition to a static reading of Homer's *Odyssey*. Rather, Joyce learned from Homer the seductive danger of the past, even one's own past and the value of sailing past the Sirens into an uncertain future.

Conclusion

Ulysses and *The Waste Land* have been a kind of Siren song for both the champions and critics of high modernism who have seen in these works a kind of endorsement of full knowledge that they often resist and overthrow. Academic industries have sprung up around modernism's allusive masterpieces, and the dozens of readers' guides available for *Ulysses* and *The Waste Land* convey to readers an at times overwhelming standard of erudition one must have to sufficiently navigate these high modernist texts. The classical tradition has subsequently served as a kind of gate-keeping instrument for this brand of high modernism – only a reader who knows her Homer, Ovid and Dante can claim even a partial understanding of *Ulysses* or *The Waste Land*.

As their inventive adaptations of the Sirens suggest, *Ulysses* and *The Waste Land* reject such a limited and limiting vision of classical literature. In very different ways, these works anticipate and unsettle this kind of reading practice and the assumptions that undergird it. The conclusion of Leopold Bloom's Odyssean journey through Dublin performs and denies the desires of high modernism's readers for full knowledge. As already noted, Joyce knew full well that his readers longed for the 'familiar rock of Ithaca' as they navigated the rocky waters of his novel's increasingly experimental final third. Joyce parodies the notion that mastery might be the goal of this textual journey, that if a reader can successfully overcome the novel's challenges in form and content, she will be richly rewarded with a transcendent moment of comprehensive understanding. His 'Ithaca' episode takes the form of a mathematical catechism, a series of questions and answers that parody the idea of full disclosure by cataloguing in humorously obsessive detail the contents of Bloom's kitchen, his expenditures for the day and his exact impressions of his day. These exhaustive details confront Joyce's readers with the vanity and futility of such desires for knowledge as a form of mastery.

The Sirens helped modernist writers to articulate a model of poetry attuned to history that allowed for gaps, blank spots and the absence of knowledge. The Sirens' song is, after all, one such gap in the *Odyssey* – we hear what the Sirens promise, but Homer never delivers on that promise. Homer's poetry thus distinguishes itself from the Sirens' song and invites its audiences to analyse the seductive power of poetry to evoke a desire for full knowledge. Instead of granting an experience of comprehensive knowledge via the Sirens, the *Odyssey* liberates its ancient and modern audiences alike from the dangers of such knowledge. In so doing, the *Odyssey* joins *Ulysses* and *The Waste Land* in exploring the potential power of ambiguity and that which cannot be known.

CHAPTER 11
'TRYING TO READ ARISTOPHANE': *SWEENEY AGONISTES*, RECEPTION AND RITUAL
Matthias Somers

'If only someone had said among all those critics, that the book is really damn *funny!*' is, if we are to believe Ezra Pound, the only 'mild complaint' James Joyce formulated about the reception of *Ulysses* (Pound 1967: 271). One of the most famous and successful acts of classical reception in the modernist canon was read too seriously and solemnly according to its author: *Ulysses* was, in Joyce's eyes, a comic novel – and Joyce entertained some serious ideas about comedy being 'the perfect manner in art' (1959: 144). Yet, the dominant critical view – from very early on, as Joyce knew from experience – of modernist literature as a profoundly serious enterprise has long prevented a sustained study of the status of comedy in modernism's literary legacy. From the perspective of classical reception, moreover, modernist receptions of the classics have frequently, and often with good reason, been read as 'also a response to the thought of the German-speaking world' (Jenkyns 2007: 278) – Nietzsche and Freud in particular. Given the prominence of the tragic plays in Nietzsche and Freud's thinking, the study of the reception of drama in the modernist period has strongly focused on tragedy. Much like continental avant-gardists such as Guillaume Apollinaire and Karl Kraus, however, anglophone modernist writers showed great interest in ancient comedy, and in Aristophanes in particular: W.B. Yeats, Ezra Pound, H.D., T.S. Eliot, D.H. Lawrence, Wyndham Lewis, Virginia Woolf and James Joyce all mentioned the Greek comic playwright in their poems, essays, or letters and read his plays in Greek or in English.

'A man of high seriousness'

This essay focuses on T.S. Eliot's *Sweeney Agonistes* as a particular instance of the modernist reception of Aristophanic comedy. The play's subtitle, 'Fragments of an Aristophanic Melodrama', has puzzled readers from the start. In a contemporary review, Geoffrey Bridson offered the following remarks about *Sweeney Agonistes*:

> We do not readily think of Mr. Eliot as the modern Aristophanes. Aristophanic his moods may be, but Aristophanic they have certainly never appeared. The belly-shaking laughter of many passages in *Ulysses* are as Aristophanic as we choose to call them. But an Aristophanic melodrama by Mr. Eliot. . .! Sooner a parody of the

Sermon on the Mount by St. Thomas Aquinas! And when a man of high seriousness (such we esteem Mr. Eliot) turns himself (as Mr. Eliot has done) to satiric melodrama or farce on the broad scale, we can hazard a guess at the result. We can remember Flaubert's dreary 'Candidate.' And we can remember also the tremendous 'Apes of God' which Mr. Lewis gave us in a spell of disgusted mirth. How well will Mr. Eliot's humour compare with Mr. Lewis's? We know very well (say, we suspect) that it won't compare at all.

Grant 1982: 286–7[1]

It was no doubt true at the time, and it is still true today, that we do not think of T.S. Eliot as the modern Aristophanes. Eliot simply cannot be funny. His art is of the sort that is called 'high' or 'serious', and such art has nothing to do with humour or laughter. Bridson's review is a perfect illustration of what David Chinitz has described as 'the strain placed upon the sensitive critic faced with the discrepancy between what Eliot has actually written and what he is supposed to have been capable of thinking' (2003: 7). By jumping to the conclusion ('we can hazard a guess', 'we know very well') that Eliot's humour 'won't compare at all' solely on the basis of Eliot's reputation as a 'serious' poet, Bridson reinforces 'an image of Eliot as the hero or antihero of a losing battle to defend a pristine and sacralized high art from the threatening pollution of 'lower levels' of culture' (Chinitz 2003: 5).

Chinitz and others have done much to redress this image, mainly by uncovering Eliot's enthusiasm for various forms of popular culture. However, this has not necessarily led to an understanding of Eliot as a *comic* writer. In that sense, Bridson was not at all wrong: Eliot's humour, his comedy, cannot simply be placed in one box with writers like Lewis or Joyce, who are in many ways better candidates for the title of 'modern Aristophanes'. Bridson quite sensibly associates Aristophanes with biting satire and with farce and obscene jokes. Topical humour and satire are important elements in plays such as *Wasps* and *Clouds*, which feature contemporary celebrities (Cleon and Socrates, respectively). *Frogs* contains an important element of parody lampooning the tragic playwrights. And generous portions of farce and obscenity are found in nearly all of the eleven extant plays, *Lysistrata* and *Assemblywomen* being prime examples. Bridson found that both the satirical and the farcical elements in *Sweeney Agonistes* left much to be desired compared to the writings of Joyce and Lewis – both of them therefore more recognizably 'Aristophanic' than Eliot.

Yet, there is good reason to take Eliot's reference to Aristophanes seriously, and not to dismiss it, as is often done, as a pretentious way to signal a satire or farce. It is therefore important to understand how the paratextual term 'Aristophanic' operates for Eliot, if it is to tell us something about the role of comedy in Eliot's writing and about the way in which Eliot conceived of the use of the classics for modern literature. Moreover, a precise account of the relationship between *Sweeney Agonistes* and its supposed classical source provides answers to a number of evident questions: why did Eliot look to Greek drama when he turned his attention to the writing of verse plays? And why did he give preference to comedy over tragedy when he considered the Greeks?

Musical drama

Eliot's involvement with Aristophanes was much older than the composition, in 1924 and 1925, of what we now know as *Sweeney Agonistes*. Eliot studied Aristophanes in his second year at Harvard (Crawford 2015: 86) and he was familiar with *A History of Ancient Greek Literature* by Gilbert Murray, whose career, as well as that of other British scholars of ancient Greek, he would follow closely. At the beginning of the 1920s, when *The Waste Land* was given its final shape, Eliot and Pound carried on a parallel conversation about Greek drama. Eliot mentioned 'trying to read Aristophane', to which Pound retorted: 'Aristophanes probably depressing' – his own interest in Greek drama remained with 'Aeschyle' (1988: 504–5).[2] A few years later, Eliot wrote to Leonard Woolf that he wanted to go to a performance of *Birds* at Cambridge University on 1 March 1924, when the idea of a verse play based on Aristophanes had been gestating for a while (2009: 326).

Sweeney Agonistes was only published under that title in 1932, and it is then that the label 'Fragments of an Aristophanic Melodrama' first appeared. However, drafts and partial publications show that the Aristophanic connection was at the forefront of Eliot's mind from the beginning. Both referring to traditional parts of Old Comedy, 'Fragment of a Prologue' and 'Fragment of an Agon' appeared in the *Criterion* in 1926 and 1927 respectively. One of the early drafts of the Prologue even placed Aristophanes in the main title: 'Homage to Aristophanes: Fragment of a Melocomic Minstrelsy'.[3] The word 'homage' conveys great admiration for the literary achievement of the Greek playwright, and suggests that Eliot found his plays not just funny but also important within the European tradition. The play remained unfinished, but the 1932 publication including the reference to Aristophanes indicates that Eliot wished to emphasize the Aristophanic connection, even at this late stage.

But what is an 'Aristophanic melodrama'? Why not the more obvious designation 'comedy'? Aristophanes wrote comedies, surely, and Eliot himself wrote to Pound about having 'mapt out [his] Aristophanic comedy' in 1923 (2009: 209). Carol Smith has observed that the play 'is melodramatic in the older sense of the term, a play combining music and drama' (1963: 58). By using the term 'melodrama', Eliot avoided the terms comedy and tragedy, but still referred to a common feature of all Greek drama: the combination of song and spoken dialogue. The term illustrates the importance Eliot attached to music and especially rhythm in poetic drama. He may also have followed a suggestion of the critic Hugh Gordon Porteus, who in a letter of 1931 compared *Sweeney Agonistes* to Ezra Pound's radio opera *Le Testament de François Villon*, originally announced and promoted as a 'broadcast melodrama' for its experimental use of song, sound effects and rhythm (Eliot 2014: 602).[4] Foregrounding the element of music, and downplaying the association of the term comedy with Victorian moralism and the 'comedy of manners', Eliot aimed for a comic play that could nonetheless have a serious ground or a serious message and a sophisticated form. Such a melodrama, 'perched on the uneasy edge between tragedy and the horribly grotesque' (Crawford 1987: 165), would break away from the realistic theatre of Eliot's time, and give more weight to the music and rhythm of the spoken word. Strikingly, an alternative model for such a stylized, anti-realistic drama somewhere on the edge between tragedy and grotesque horror presented itself: Seneca, possibly the very opposite of a comic writer. The presence of Seneca behind *Sweeney Agonistes* has been recognized by several critics (Chinitz 2003: 110–3; Matthews 2013: 118; Buttram 2009: 182), but the first one to do so was probably Ezra Pound. In the introduction to *Make It New*, Pound distinguished five types of criticism, the fifth and most intense one being 'criticism in new composition': a rare type, but 'the criticism of Seneca by Mr. Eliot's *Agon* is infinitely more alive, more vigorous than in his essay on Seneca' (1935b: 75).[5]

While it is no doubt true that Eliot took his insights about the form of Senecan tragedy on board, the main model for his comic, musical verse play was, from its inception, the Old Comedy of Aristophanes. The question remains: in what sense is *Sweeney Agonistes* Aristophanic? It is obvious that the work is no translation of Aristophanes in the strict sense, but neither can it adequately be described as an adaptation. None of the characters correspond to any of Aristophanes' characters. Insofar as a real plot can be identified, that does not immediately recall any of the extant comedies either. The setting is a brothel, presumably – a place where the characters of Sweeney and Doris had met before, in the poem 'Sweeney Erect'. The two fragments consist of a lot of fast-running dialogue and very little action. The 'Fragment of a Prologue' contains a telephone call, a fortune-telling session with a pack of cards and a scene of mutual introductions when Wauchope, Horsfall, Klipstein and Krumpacker arrive. In the 'Fragment of an Agon', Sweeney teases Doris about life on a desert island, proclaims that 'life is death' and tells a story about the murder of a girl. All of this is punctuated by songs that echo the themes of primitive life, sex and death.

A ritual plot

The play's 'Aristophanicity' lies hidden on another level. Eliot designed *Sweeney Agonistes*, and conceived it as Aristophanic, on the basis of the deep structure of all of Aristophanes' comedies as described by Francis Cornford in *The Origin of Attic Comedy*. Eliot had encountered Cornford's work as a result of his long-standing interest in anthropology, and its accounts of primitive religion and the evolution of civilizations. He used the works of James Frazer and Jessie Weston as inspiration for *The Waste Land*, and in 1920 stated that 'few books are more fascinating than those of Miss [Jane] Harrison, or Mr. [F. M.] Cornford, or Mr. Cooke [sic], when they burrow in the origins of Greek myths and rites' (1961: 49). Harrison, Cornford and Cook formed a group of classics scholars known as the Cambridge Ritualists. Building on the evolutionary anthropology of Edward Tylor, William Robertson Smith and James Frazer, they reconsidered fifth-century Attic drama as an art-form with religious origins: the Dionysiac fertility rite, which shared characteristics with similar vegetation rites across cultures, had over time developed into full-blown drama. Cornford's main thesis was that Old Comedy, like tragedy, having evolved from a superseded ritual drama, displayed a basic structure reminiscent of the traditional elements of the ritual.

When we compare the plays with one another, it is soon evident, in the first place, that nearly all of them end with an incident no less canonical than the *Agon* – a festal procession (*Kômos*) and a union which I shall call a 'Marriage' ... We shall also find in almost every play two other standing incidents which fall between the *Agon* and the final *Kômos* – a scene of Sacrifice and a Feast ... Meanwhile, for the sake of clearness, it will be well to state here the hypothesis we shall offer in explanation of these facts. It is that *this canonical plot-formula preserves the stereotyped action of a ritual or folk drama, older than literary Comedy, and of a pattern well known to us from other sources.*

1934: 2–3[6]

Cornford detected underneath the various themes and plots of the extant comedies a common structure – he calls it a 'plot-formula' – which derives from a ritual or folk drama. Prologue, *parodos*, *agon* and *parabasis* constitute the first part of a play; scenes of sacrifice, feast and marriage the second part. The *agon* and the *parabasis* are the most essential parts: both present a kind of battle or contest between a good and an evil principle, represented in the play by a hero and a villain. The eventual triumph over evil that characterizes comedy was to be traced back, according to Cornford, to the annual ritual killing of the 'old King' and his rebirth as the 'new King', necessary for the fertilization and regeneration of the land and the community.[7]

As Smith and others have pointed out, Eliot's draft outline for *Sweeney Agonistes* shows that he meticulously followed the Old Comedy's structure as described by Cornford and as exemplified by the 'Synopses' of all the extant plays he provided at the end of his book (Smith 1963: 62–72; Crawford 1987: 163–4). Beside the prologue and the *Agon* he published, Eliot planned a *parodos*, a first and a second *parabasis*, a scene of sacrifice and preparations for a dinner. The fragments that we have may not immediately show the signs of a primitive rite, but the same could be said of Aristophanes' own plays. If anything, a highly conventional plot structure with elements of festivity, fertility, and marriage may more readily call to mind New Comedy than Old Comedy, which had after all more varied plots and a strong element of topical, political satire. However, the Cambridge Ritualists precisely de-emphasized the association of New Comedy with ritual (Ackerman 2002: 170–1).[8] For Cornford, the presence of stock characters (soldier, doctor, cook, parasite) even in the political Old Comedy proved his hypothesis of the ritual origin. He assumed a ritual origin even for the parabasis, the most political element of Old Comedy: it supposedly originated in the ritual abuse uttered by *phallophoroi*, bands of Dionysiac revellers. Thus, while Eliot's draft for *Sweeney Agonistes* actually shows his intention to include presumably humorous comments on 'Contemporary Politics' in a parabasis passage (Eliot 2015: I, 792), the play in its published form excludes direct political commentary, giving center stage to ritual elements.

For that reason, many scenes and motifs in the fragments can be read as instances of the ritualistic scenes and elements Cornford had laid bare. A 'myth-and-ritual' oriented reading of the play allows one to see more coherence between the scenes as elements in the Aristophanic structure, while at the same time complicating the interpretation of the play.

The Prologue takes the typical form of how two characters, Dusty and Doris, are in the middle of a discussion (about Doris's dislike of Pereira), when a messenger interrupts them:

TELEPHONE: Ting a ling ling
            Ting a ling ling

116[9]

The telephone does not appear as a stage direction, but as a character in the play, just as a 'real' messenger would. Yet, the central scene of the Prologue is the fortune-telling session that establishes the mythical framework for the play. Eliot had already used cards in *The Waste Land* and connected them to the Frazerian vegetation rite. The same happens here: the first card Doris draws is the King of Clubs. In the vegetation rite, the King stands for the Year Spirit or Year God, who is killed and resurrected. Dusty and Doris debate whether the King refers to Sweeney or Pereira – and it remains somewhat ambiguous whether Sweeney is the good or the evil spirit in this ritual drama: he is an *agonist* rather than being either protagonist or antagonist. Then comes the Queen, who is supposed to be the bride who marries the new King during the *Komos* at the end of the drama. Cornford points out that the marriage in Aristophanic comedy has nothing to do with romantic love, and that the bride is often a courtesan: this points to Mrs. Porter and to Dusty and Doris, who says 'We're all hearts. You can't be sure' (117). But Doris remembers: 'I dreamt of weddings all last night' (117). Other cards, as Dusty explains, symbolize a party and a quarrel: the feast and the fight were 'regular incidents' in Old Comedy's ritual structure, according to Cornford. Finally, the two of spades – 'THAT'S THE COFFIN!!' (117) – stands for a sacrificial death, and is sinisterly related to the wedding Doris mentioned. When all of the ritual elements have thus been announced in this scene, Dusty and Doris discuss the difficulty of interpreting the cards, in a kind of *mise-en-abyme* of the difficulty for the spectator to interpret the play without the key of the ritual drama:

DORIS: Sometimes they'll tell you nothing at all
DUSTY: You've got to know what you want to ask them
DORIS: You've got to know what you want to know

118

The Prologue closes with the arrival and introduction of Sam Wauchope, Captain Horsfall, and Klipstein and Krumpacker (who form the chorus, which means the parodos is in fact integrated in the prologue).[10] As a whole, the Prologue presents Doris as a woman attached to life, fun and human interaction. Doris is someone who talks in terms of what she likes and what she dislikes. She likes Sam and a good laugh: 'I like Sam . . . He's a funny fellow / He's like a fellow once I knew. / *He* could make you laugh' (115). Sam is a gentleman, while Pereira, 'He's no gentleman, Pereira: / You can't trust him!' (115). Doris cannot be bothered with killjoys like Pereira, who deal with dull matters like paying the rent (115). Sam moreover visits Doris in person, while Pereira calls on the phone, which Doris hates: 'Well can't you stop that horrible noise?' (116). Sam lives in

London, a city everyone agrees is a lot of fun: Klipstein and Krumpacker confirm that London is 'swell', 'slick' and 'gay' (120). Pereira's name, by contrast, suggests a foreign origin.

The *Agon* presents the complete opposite of Doris's desires. While her greatest fear is 'THE COFFIN', i.e. to lose her life of sex and the city, Sweeney offers her only boredom and death. First, he fantasizes about a primitive island, where crocodiles and cannibals threaten Doris's life. If she survives, life will be utterly dull:

> There's no telephones
> There's no gramophones
> There's no motor cars
> No two-seaters, no six-seaters,
> No Citroën, no Rolls-Royce.
> Nothing to eat but the fruit as it grows.
> Nothing to see but the palmtrees one way
> And the sea the other way,
> Nothing to hear but the sound of the surf.

> *121*

When Sweeney concludes that in such a seemingly beautiful and unspoiled place life comes down to 'Birth, and copulation, and death. That's all, that's all, that's all, that's all', Doris's simple answer is 'I'd be bored' (122). She is determined to remain in the city: 'I don't like life on your crocodile isle' (123). But then Sweeney declares 'Life is death' (124) to introduce his last story, about a man, *in the city*, who murdered a girl and kept her in a bath of lysol (124). By scattering ritual elements of the fertility myth throughout both his island tale and his city tale – the elements that were *nota bene* predicted by the cards – Sweeney imparts his vision of the meaningless horror of all physical life, however civilized it may seem. Murders take the form of ritual sacrifices: 'I'll convert *you*! / Into a stew!' (121) refers to the figure of the cook in the ritual drama, while the dead girl in the bath is reminiscent of the equally sacrificial 'death by water' of *The Waste Land*. Smaller motifs like eggs and bamboo symbolize fertility, and even the bottle of milk and the milkman (125) take on ritualistic power when we find Cornford describing a ritual in which the 'dying God' was boiled in milk (1934: 89). Thus, Sweeney's city tale ultimately shows how life and death collapse into one another: the murderer is both alive and dead (a living dead man, grown completely lonely and anonymous in the city), while the girl is neither dead nor alive (a comatose body or a perfectly preserved corpse). This is what the myth, and its ritual on which the drama is based, show:

> He didn't know if he was alive
>   and the girl was dead
> He didn't know if the girl was alive
>   and he was dead
> He didn't know if they both were alive

> or both were dead
>
> . . .
>
> Death or life or life or death
> Death is life and life is death

125

On the level of form, this destabilization of the oppositions life/death, fun/boredom, city/island, society/isolation is enacted in the songs. In the *Agon*, the chorus, which is split in two halves as the chorus in Old Comedy typically was, sing minstrel and vaudeville-style songs that elaborate but at the same time sugar-coat Sweeney's message about the less-than-idyllic life on the desert island. When they sing '*We'll gather hibiscus flowers / For it won't be minutes but hours / For it won't be hours but years*' (123), the endless tedium of life is cheerfully hidden behind flowery wallpaper.

It is no surprise that Doris stands off when they suggest a euphemistic 'flirt' under the bamboo tree (123). But what is most striking is the clash between form and content. These songs about primitive life are sung in the styles of ragtime, jazz and the music hall, strongly associated with urban modernity and its lively entertainments.[11] If an element of Aristophanic political commentary is retained in Eliot's comedy, it can be found here. The tunes and rhythms of jazz that are present throughout the play carried distinct racial and political meanings in the interwar period. As Michael Coyle has written, 'jazz came supercharged with anxieties and fantasies about race and expectations of possibly profound shifts in sociocultural reality' (2015: 91). While the music-hall for Eliot exemplified a traditional, authentic working-class form of cultural expression, jazz signified the cosmopolitan mixing of races and cultures by a decadent middle class Eliot dismissed as barbarian.

A new (old) form

The last point indicates that it is important not to lose sight of the form when determining the precise nature of the relationship between *Sweeney Agonistes* and Aristophanic comedy. For the play is, as already stated, clearly not a line-by-line translation, nor an adaptation of the story of any of the Greek plays: it is the formal structure, the framework of Aristophanic comedy as outlined by Cornford that provides the basis for comparison. While Lorna Hardwick offers the term *correspondence* (among a list of options) as an alternative that might be applicable in this case (2003: 9–10), what is going on with *Sweeney Agonistes* seems better captured by the notion of *transposition* or *re-actualization* of an ancient form or genre. Based on the proto-structuralist re-composition of the 'virtual object' (the structural 'simulacrum' in Roland Barthes's parlance) of Old Comedy by Cornford, Eliot produced his very own Aristophanic comedy.[12] Pound's view of *Sweeney Agonistes* as a form of 'criticism in new composition' is therefore quite accurate (we could speak of 'reception in new composition'), even despite the fact that he looked at a different object of criticism (Seneca).

This specific mode of reception accounts for the very existence of *Sweeney Agonistes*. For why did Eliot write a work drawing on Frazerian myth and ritual after *The Waste Land*, which had already done just that? While there are clear thematic analogies between the two works, the *form* is completely different. The importance of this new form clearly emerges from a letter to Richard Aldington, in which Eliot declared *The Waste Land* 'a thing of the past', adding that he was 'feeling toward a new form and style' (Eliot 1988: 596). Verse drama became this new form, and led Eliot to Aristophanes. Despite this crucial difference, the Aristophanic inspiration has often led critics, via Cornford, to a reading of *Sweeney Agonistes* as if it were a second *Waste Land*. Crawford, for instance, states that '[Eliot's] failure in *Sweeney Agonistes* to find anything worthwhile to his personal salvation in all the elaborate investigation of primitive cults resulted in an apparent about-turn in the direction of his thought' (1987: 180–1).[13] It is clear that Crawford's conclusion hinges on Eliot's understanding of the nature of the ritual itself, when he writes: 'The 'Agon' having demonstrated with such force that the core of the rite is not glorious but hideous, there is no point in continuing with the play' (180). Another critic, Martha Carpentier, focuses on the influence of Jane Ellen Harrison and on the religious meaning of the ritual. Reading *Sweeney Agonistes* in relation to the earlier Sweeney poems, she argues that, after his conversion to Anglicanism, 'Eliot's interest has progressed from the horrific violence of sexual relations between man and woman, to the painful, solitary, spiritual purgation or quest that follows matricide' (2013 [1998]: 129).[14] Ronald Schuchard, finally, in another biographical reading (based on the affair between Vivien Eliot and Bertrand Russell), argues that the entire Sweeney universe constitutes Eliot's 'personal myth of sexual betrayal, psychological retribution, and moral regeneration' (91). Like Carpentier, Schuchard also neglects the specific literary form of *Sweeney Agonistes*, placing it on a continuum with the earlier Sweeney poems and *The Waste Land*. At the end of this line, Eliot 'fully ritualize[d] Sweeney's annual visit to Mrs. Porter' (98).[15]

All of these readings are illuminating in themselves, but they ignore that Cornford was more than just a second Frazer (or Weston) and *Sweeney Agonistes* for that reason not simply a second *Waste Land*. Via Cornford, Eliot turned to an existing *literary form*, in this case the dramatic genre of Aristophanic comedy, as an antecedent for a ritual-inspired work. His praise of Joyce's 'discovery' of the 'mythical method' sheds light on his own preoccupation with form: 'In using the myth, in manipulating a continuous parallel between contemporaneity and antiquity, Mr. Joyce is pursuing a method which others must pursue after him' (1975: 177). As Steven Connor has pointed out, it is a stretch to speak of a 'continuous parallel' between the *Odyssey* and *Ulysses*; take the 'Aeolus' chapter, which 'can scarcely be said to employ parallels between characters and events at all' (Connor 2004: 257). Yet, that is probably the point. Eliot adopted precisely that method for *Sweeney Agonistes*, which does not feature any characters or plot elements from Aristophanes. The ancient literary form provided the method, much like the 'mythical method' worked for *Ulysses* 'only because the *Odyssey* is itself a literary compendium, rather than an example of myth in its original or primitive state' (Connor 2004: 258).

The classics and the shock of the old

Eliot's conviction that his 'mythical method' constituted 'a step toward making the modern world possible for art' (1975: 178) accounts for his borrowing of a model from antiquity. It now remains to be figured out why he opted for ancient comedy and not tragedy, and what he hoped to achieve with his own Aristophanic comedy (his reception 'in new composition') in the context of the 1920s. *Sweeney Agonistes* was Eliot's first effort in his project of reinventing a poetic drama for the modern stage. A near-contemporaneous essay lays out the plan:

> Possibly the majority of attempts to confect a poetic drama have begun at the wrong end; they have aimed at the small public which wants 'poetry' ... The Elizabethan drama was aimed at a public which wanted *entertainment* of a crude sort, but would *stand* a good deal of poetry; our problem should be to take a form of entertainment, and subject it to the process which would leave it a form of art. Perhaps the music-hall comedian is the best material.
>
> *1920: 70*

Eliot's mission was to find a popular audience for poetry, reasoning that 'the most direct means of social "usefulness" for poetry, is the theatre' (1975: 94). Poetic drama could only be successful if it could be shared by the culture as a whole, if it was woven out of the social fabric itself – Eliot calls it a 'half-formed *hylè*', defined as 'a habit on the part of the public, to respond to particular stimuli' (1920: 57). In England, this had occurred on the Elizabethan stage, and the only real inheritor of such a native, organic and authentically popular drama was for Eliot the music hall:

> He [the poet] would like to be something of a popular entertainer, and be able to think his own thoughts behind a tragic or a comic mask ... All the better then, if he could have at least the satisfaction of having a part to play in society as worthy as that of the music-hall comedian.
>
> *1975: 95*

A new poetic drama would have to serve the same vital function in society.

According to Eliot, music-hall comedians like Marie Lloyd, Nellie Wallace and Little Tich were capable of effecting the 'Comic Purgation', a sort of comic catharsis that gives the audience pleasure as well as reproof for their moral weakness (Eliot 2006: 142). A 'serious student of the comic spirit' (Schuchard 1999: 88), Eliot was familiar with the theories of comedy by Baudelaire and by Bergson. Baudelaire provided a vision of 'savage comedy', a diabolic, cruel type of comedy typical of English humour and exemplified, for Baudelaire as well as for Eliot, by the Elizabethan dramatists.[16] It is a type of comedy that is to an important extent built on ugliness, horror and tragedy.

The link between *Sweeney Agonistes* and Seneca (mentioned above) helps, paradoxically perhaps, to elucidate Eliot's sense of comedy. While most critics have focused on Eliot's interest in Seneca's rhetoric and style, it is very conceivable that the Roman playwright contributed to Eliot's notion of a violent comedy of grotesque horror. Baudelaire mentions the Elizabethan playwrights as the source of this type of humor, but a major influence on these was of course precisely Seneca, who is often associated with violence and horror to the point of reaching bathos, the effect created – intentionally or not – when the sublime and the lofty suddenly sink to a low point, which can be, for instance, a bad poetic image, but also the intrusion of the vulgar and the obscene (Crangle and Nicholls 2010: 1–6). In Seneca, a tragic situation tends to become so horrible as to seem ludicrous and to provoke laughter.[17] such ludicrous horror informs Baudelaire's notion of the grotesque, which has much in common with bathos – and so does Eliot's view of comedy. Much of the humor of 'The Love Song of J. Alfred Prufrock' can be said to depend on moments of bathos.[18] While this is also true of *Sweeney Agonistes*, the most profound way in which the bathetic produces a comic effect in the play is in how it brings the sublime realms of religious ritual and classical form into complicity with the seedy, vulgar worlds of the brothel and inner-city crime. The result is a grotesque drama that depends on a lot of tragedy in order to become comic.

On the modern stage, music-hall comedians were the only artists still capable of creating authentic comedy out of, essentially, tragedy (Schuchard 1999: 106–7). All of this shaped Eliot's views on comedy and tragedy, expounded explicitly in an essay on Shakespeare:

> For those who have experienced the full horror of life, tragedy is still inadequate. Sophocles felt more of it than he could express, when he wrote *Oedipus the King*; Shakespeare, when he wrote *Hamlet*; and Shakespeare had the advantage of being able to employ his grave-diggers. In the end, horror and laughter may be one – only when horror and laughter have become as horrible and laughable as they can be; and – whatever the conscious intention of the authors – you may laugh or shudder over *Oedipus* or *Hamlet* or *King Lear* – or both at once: then only do you perceive the aim of the comic and the tragic dramatist is the same: they are equally serious … What Plato perceived has not been noticed by subsequent dramatic critics; the dramatic poet uses the conventions of tragic and comic poetry, so far as these are the conventions of his day; there is potential comedy in Sophocles and potential tragedy in Aristophanes, and otherwise they would not be such good tragedians or comedians as they are.
>
> *1960 [1934]: 302*

Comedy and tragedy, if they are to work well as dramatic art, must incorporate comic and tragic elements. As mentioned above, *Sweeney Agonistes* exemplifies this comic-tragic character of poetic drama not only by means of the label 'melodrama', but also by actually enacting the collapse of the opposition between life and laughter (comedy) on the one hand and death and horror (tragedy) on the other. Cornford provided Eliot with ample reasons to choose Aristophanic comedy as a model for this kind of drama. He closes *The Origin of Attic Comedy* by explaining the difference between tragedy and comedy as a mere difference in outlook, because the same incidents of the ritual 'could be given a sad or a happy turn' (1934: 221). A crucial point, however, is that Old Comedy 'keeps nearer to the old ritual outline' (199), because the comic poet is free to invent characters and situations (unlike the tragic poet, who is bound by the material of the myths); 'consequently, the traditional framework of the ritual plot serves well enough' (199), whereas tragedy has to deviate from the ritual plot in order to accommodate the mythic story. Since Eliot was so concerned with finding a literary form for the primal ritual, this characteristic of Old Comedy proved highly alluring.

What the prominence of the ritual guaranteed for the drama was rhythm, a central notion in Eliot's thinking on poetic drama. The rite is after all a pattern of actions processing repeating elements. The vegetation rite, for instance, annually enacts the recurrence of the seasons in a highly structured pattern of actions accompanied by music and dance – it enacts a rhythm and is itself rhythmic. *Sweeney Agonistes* has often been called a jazz play, and it is clear that Eliot placed his stakes on tempo, repetition and on colloquial speech patterns caught in a syncopated rhythm. Looking for the particular 'tune' of humour in Eliot's poetry, Matthew Bevis has insightfully analysed these rhythmic repetitions (often repetitions with a slight variation) in relation to Bergson's idea that people laugh when they see 'something mechanical encrusted upon the living', i.e. when they see machine-like automatism overtake human beings (Bevis 2014: 136).[19] Much of the fun in *Sweeney Agonistes* is indeed derived from how mechanical the characters sound, caught as they are in the speedy rhythm of the dialogue. Here, too, the comic and the tragic converge, when, as Bevis writes, '[t]he sounds of the verse are enamored of the situation they decry' (155). These patterns of mechanical repetition provide comic relief, but also connect the poetry back to the ritual: 'Poetry begins', Eliot said, 'with a savage beating a drum in a jungle' (1975: 95). A vital poetic drama needed to maintain this primal relationship with rhythm.

In an early essay on anthropology, entitled 'War-Paint and Feathers', Eliot wrote that even poetry from very different cultures and from ancient times, can prove relevant for the present. Therefore, 'the poet should know everything that has been accomplished in poetry (accomplished, not merely produced) since its beginnings – in order to know what he is doing himself' (1919: 1036). In Old Comedy, Eliot found a form that had everything to become newly relevant to British culture in the 1920s. By providing the 'mythical method' which made the modern world possible for art, a poetic drama based on this ancient form had the potential to revitalize modern poetry – and with it, modern culture and society as a whole, after the manner of the Elizabethan drama and the music-hall.

Such a project of revitalization also necessarily included an essential 'vitalizing of the Classics' *for* that culture (Eliot 1924: 29). Classical drama was still relevant, but its relevance could only be realized when the plays were read and experienced in performance with the full effect of their fundamental strangeness. Ancient Greek literature lost its relevance when it was domesticated, made familiar by being adapted to contemporary forms and styles. Eliot showed a typically modernist sensitivity to the hermeneutics of reception, when he wrote in his essay on Murray's translation of *Medea* that 'we realize better how different . . . were the conditions of the Greek civilization from ours' (1961: 50). Faulting Murray for turning Euripides into a Victorian poet, Eliot stated: 'Greek poetry will never have the slightest vitalizing effect upon English poetry if it can only appear masquerading as a vulgar debasement of the eminently personal idiom of Swinburne' (48). Since classical literature was 'something that needed to be reinterpreted, retranslated and reordered by every subsequent generation' (Sullivan 2011: 174), Eliot opted for the transposition (and concomitant reactualization and revitalization) of an ancient genre. He turned to the classics not to vulgarize them or adapt them to modern tastes or demands, but to do the exact opposite: to adapt modern culture to a distant classical form. With *Sweeney Agonistes*, he recast modern life in terms of precisely that which was strange and remote and no longer vital in modern culture, i.e. the ritual, the primal rhythm, the savage comedy. If modernism is often characterized in terms of the 'shock of the new', with *Sweeney Agonistes* Eliot resolutely opted for the 'shock of the old'.

CHAPTER 12
'STRAIGHT TALK, STRAIGHT AS THE GREEK!': IRELAND'S OEDIPUS AND THE MODERNISM OF W.B. YEATS

Gregory Baker

'For the last few days I have been longing for the quiet of the boat', declared W.B. Yeats (1865–1939).[1] As Yeats boarded the *R.M.S. Lusitania* for New York on 31 January 1914, he welcomed the journey. The previous month had seen him ridiculed in the English press. George Moore (1852–1933), novelist and his sometime adversary, had published an excerpt from his memoir, *Hail and Farewell*, where he skewered Yeats, recalling a tantrum he had thrown in 1904. Speaking on behalf of Hugh Lane and his exhibition of Impressionist paintings, Yeats then 'instead of talking to us as he used to do about the old stories come down from generation to generation ... began to thunder like Ben Tillett himself against the middle classes, stamping his feet, working himself into a great passion' (Moore 1914: 167). As Yeats sailed from Liverpool, he hoped Moore's story would not dog him across the Atlantic (Yeats [1914] (1972) 269 no. 245).[2] But the crossing brought him little pleasure and less peace. On board, he found the voyage 'villainous' – 'only one calm day yesterday & we are much behind time. I spent three days on my back, not actually sick but sufficiently miserable'.[3] Adding to his misery was his inability to escape discussion of Moore's memoir. Some passengers, however, were sympathetic. One in particular 'a very strange man', he recalled, '. . . came up with a low bow & asked me to write something in his diary for his wife as his wife "thought me the greatest poet in the world".[4] Although pleased by the praise, Yeats soon tired of the man, who seemed one of those people who 'display their personalities at once'.[5] The eager American was Fenton Benedict Turck (1857–1932), a doctor who had recently moved from Chicago to New York City on being appointed director of a medical laboratory financed by the Pearson Research Fund.[6] Thought to have attained a 'position of eminence and authority' in his profession (Garland 1926: 54), Turck was admitted to the practice of medicine in New York without examination. 'And yet,' Turck had little interest in discussing his research with Yeats. Instead, he spoke of his 'one other subject': Greek antiquity.[7] 'When he talks of his science', Yeats told Lady Gregory,

> he is careful & precise but he has one other subject Greece. On that he is a rhetorician of the wildest kind. He talks American journalese, & constantly talks of 'moral uplift' & has the gestures of a public speaker. He sees the whole world as a war between all sorts of evil – in which the Church of Rome is the main sort – & the spirit of Greece ... the moment the restraint of his science was off him he would break out into phrases such as 'Oh all conquering power of love' & ejaculations about 'moral uplift'.[8]

Despite Turck's enthusiasm for defending the Greeks' 'traditions from the barbarians' – 'we must become Greek,' he quipped Yeats felt the doctor was 'incoherent & preposterous', a man who seemed 'to mispronounce every Greek name he uses'.[9]

By the time Yeats boarded the *Lusitania* in 1914, Greek antiquity was a fertile site in his work and imagination, marked not only with his long-standing involvement with the Irish nationalist cause but with a desire to dramatically refashion his poetry following John Synge's death. Throughout the Literary Revival, many Irish writers, including Yeats, had eschewed the use of Greek and Roman mythologies in their work, believing these had become 'worn out and unmanageable' having 'ceased to be a living tradition' (Yeats [1893] 2004a: 210). Instead, their 'resolute purpose' was, as Yeats explained in 1895, to bring the Irish 'literary tradition to perfection' by employing the 'unexhausted and inexhaustible mythology' found in Gaelic folklore (2004b: 287, 281). Synge's death, however, and frustration with more provincial cultural nationalists, prompted a shift in Yeats's approach to the classics. Greek antiquity, specifically the poet's interest in Sophocles' *Oedipus Rex*, slowly but radically transformed his style and politics, a reinvention which would see Yeats become, as Pound wrote, 'at *prise* with things as they are and no longer romantically Celtic' (1914: 68). So it is unsurprising then that Fenton Turck's praise of ancient Greece upset him, and two weeks after the *Lusitania* docked, Yeats savaged Turck's vision of the Greeks in an interview with the *New York Times*. Without naming the doctor, Yeats attacked Turck's phrase, 'moral uplift', arguing that American taste in the literary arts seemed stale and stuck in a bygone age. 'In many ways, in this country', he told the newspaper, 'I think you still live in the Victorian epoch, so far as literature is concerned. Your very phrase "moral uplift," implies it. I think all that sort of thing a misunderstanding of literature'.[10] Using the term 'moral uplift' in descriptions of literature had become prominent in America during the 1890s, especially in debates over the religious character of state-sponsored education. In 1898 the president of Vassar College, James Monroe Taylor (1848–1916), used it to argue that secular education could instil civic morality without specific reference to religious dogma: 'sound education has never been separable from ethical training', he explained, '[b]y a sketch of the principal periods of Greek and Roman education it was shown that the reform movements in education came in connection with moral uplift' (1899: 41). Taylor's desire to see in classical antiquity examples of 'moral uplift' was part of wider practice which stressed what the critic R.W. Livingstone (1880–1960) called the 'moral genius of the Greeks' (1912: 24). As Frank Turner observed, the desire to find in classical antiquity 'prescriptive patterns for a literature of moral uplift and sanity' was widespread at the end of the nineteenth century when the 'metaphor of Greece' had helped to open up, popularly speaking, 'a humanistic path toward the secular', one beyond the turmoil of contemporary social, political and religious disputes (1981: 34–5). The 'selective portrayal of Greece' proved useful in making tangible 'a sense of cultural and ethical confidence about the possibility of a life of dignity, decency, and restraint outside the intellectual and moral boundaries of religion' (ibid.: 35). Surveys of Greek literature from this time were therefore sometimes clotted with 'prescriptions of traditional English humanist values', values directed against 'pluralistic, liberal politics, and subjective morality' (ibid.: 33). As a 'conservative ideological weapon' (ibid.), ancient Greek literature was thus appropriated to consolidate the tastes of an educated middle class, confirming in contemporary readers what Livingstone called 'our moral sympathies' (1912: 167), not 'the morbid pathology and the charming affectations of modern literature' (ibid.: 168). Ancient writers had not been motivated, Livingstone explained, by 'Art for Art's sake', or even 'Intellect for Intellect's sake' (ibid.: 163): they 'do not lead us, like Mr. Yeats, into the bypaths of the human soul, to travel by dark and enchanted ways', but to a consideration of the 'deliberate, laborious, and triumphant battle for virtue' (ibid.: 163, 24).

For Yeats, however, Greek literature's value had little to do with schooling readers in secular virtue, or reinforcing conventional codes of social conduct. Greek poets had explored, he thought, the depths of the human mind without restricting what could be imagined; they refused to 'deny expression to any profound or lasting state of consciousness'.[11] No 'state of consciousness' ever appeared 'morbid and exaggerated' in their literature for the 'Greeks had no exaggerated morbidity of sex, because they were free to express all. They were the most healthy of all peoples. The man who is sex-mad is hateful to me, but he was created by the moralists'.[12] If contemporary poets were to eschew 'morbidity' and exaggeration in their own work, they had to embrace the desire 'to express all' and reject moralism in literature.[13] 'It is', Yeats told the *Times*,

> the history of the more intense states of consciousness that a great artist expounds, and it is necessary to his very existence as an artist that he should be free to make use of all the circumstances necessary for the expression of any permanent state of consciousness; and not only is this necessary to the artist, but to society itself.[14]

During his tour of America that winter, Yeats continued to praise the Greeks as exemplars of artistic freedom while attacking the 'commercial theatre', whose 'damnable system of morals' had brought a 'great deal of money for a great many people' but had sacrificed 'great realistic art' for 'purely topical sentiment' (Yeats [1913] 1971: 68, 70, 68). Yeats's eagerness in defending the freedom of the arts stretched back to bitter disputes he had had with both the Irish press and the country's Catholic hierarchy. Ten years prior, when Synge's play *In the Shadow of the Glen* was vilified as a drama 'no more Irish than the Decameron', a play whose 'libel on womankind' was tantamount to 'staging a lie', Yeats denounced such criticisms (Griffith 1903: 1). 'Extreme politics in Ireland were once the politics of intellectual freedom', he wrote, 'but now, under the influence of a violent contemporary paper, and under other influences more difficult to follow, even extreme politics seem about to unite themselves to hatred of ideas' (Yeats [1903] 1994: 451). As he saw it, the press and pulpit feared giving 'freedom to the imagination of highly-cultivated men, who have begun that experimental digging in the deep pit of themselves, which can alone produce great literature' (Yeats [1903] 1994: 451). Paralysed by the 'enemies of life, the chimeras of the Pulpit and the Press', writers were pressured to produce work 'full of personified averages, partisan fictions, rules of life that would drill everybody into the one posture, habits that are like the pinafores of charity schoolchildren' (Yeats [1903] 1994: 446). Fearing efforts to place Irish theatre under an official censor – perhaps even England's Lord Chamberlain, at the time Edward Hyde

Villiers, 5th Earl of Clarendon (1846–1914) – Yeats hoped to defy the 'rough-and ready-conscience of the newspaper and the pulpit' ([1903] 2003b: 29), to bait any and all who were eager 'to make the bounds of drama narrower' ([1903] 1994: 440).[15] And in what seemed an unlikely place, he discovered a tragedy whose performance might be controversial enough to show that Dublin was indeed 'a place of intellectual excitement – a place where the mind goes to be liberated as it was liberated by the theatres of Greece', in South Bend, Indiana ([1903] 2003a: 26).

While on tour in North America in 1904, Yeats visited the University of Notre Dame, and found, to his surprise, a 'general lack of religious prejudice' among the priests, brothers and students (Yeats [1904] 1994: 520).[16] 'I have been entirely delighted by the big merry priests of Notre Dame – all Irish & proud as lucifer of their success in getting Jews & non-conformists to come to their college' (ibid.: 520). Given the recent maltreatment which Synge's work had received from the Irish 'pulpit', Yeats was shocked to learn that in 1899 the university had urged its undergraduates to translate and stage Sophocles' *Oedipus Rex*.[17] At the time, producing *Oedipus Rex* was censored by the Lord Chamberlain in England, where it was thought the play's frank exploration of incest and parricide could induce viewers to 'gratify' what one advisor to the censor called 'unclean and morbid sentiment'.[18] Sophocles was widely studied at British schools and universities – Matthew Arnold had praised him for showing 'human nature developed in a number of directions, politically, socially, religiously, morally developed – in its completest and most harmonious development' – but *Oedipus* was thought too scandalous, too likely to foment 'a vitiated public taste solely in the cause of indecency'.[19] This reputed indecency, the play's power to scandalize and offend, interested Yeats. Eager to distinguish Ireland's theatre from England's, he returned from America motivated to produce *Oedipus Rex* in Dublin. Yet to bring Sophocles to the Irish stage, Yeats felt *Oedipus* had to be anglicized in a new idiom that could unburden the play of any residual impulse to bowdlerize and censor the Greek's reputedly scandalous nature. The stylistic conventions that scholars 'of the last century' (Yeats [1931] 2000: 221) used to translate Sophocles had produced a language too 'complicated in its syntax for the stage' (Yeats [1933] 2000b: 244), a language which obscured the play's power in a 'Latin mist' ([1933] 2000b: 245). 'I think' those, he wrote,

> who translated Sophocles into an English full of Latinised constructions and Latinised habits of thought, were all wrong – and that the schoolmasters are wrong who make us approach Greek through Latin. Nobody ever trembled on a dark road because he was afraid of meeting the nymphs and satyrs of Latin literature, but men have trembled on dark roads in Ireland and in Greece.

> Yeats [1931] 2000c: 221-2

Because, as Yeats saw it, the kinship of the Irish and the ancient Greek ran deep, deeper even than the bond of Latin with Greek, writers in Ireland were well placed to make men dread once again the κλύδωνα δεινῆς συμφορᾶς of Oedipus (Soph. *OT* 1527). Drawing on the scholarship of the French philologist, Marie Henri d'Arbois de Jubainville

(1827–1910), whose analysis of Greek and Celtic mythologies had alleged that 'an old foundation of Graeco-Celtic legends' existed prior 'to the separation of the two races ... the Hellenes' and the Celts (1903: 69), Yeats believed that Sophoclean tragedy would 'seem at home' in Ireland and at the Abbey (Yeats [1933] 2000b: 245). 'No man has ever prayed to or dreaded one of Vergil's nymphs', he declared, 'but when Oedipus at Colonus went into the Wood of the Furies he felt the same creeping in his flesh that an Irish countryman feels in certain haunted woods in Galway and in Sligo' (ibid.). While the Irish were equipped to modernize Sophocles, to strip *Oedipus* of the 'half Latin, half Victorian dignity' the nineteenth century thrust upon it, Yeats himself, however had little Greek and was a poor student of the language, his headmaster at the Erasmus Smith School in Dublin (a school he attended from 1881–3) once reporting that his 'taking up French and German simultaneously with Latin and Greek' had been 'ruinous' (ibid.: 244).[20] Age had not improved his ability – unable to read classics in the original, Yeats could only gaze 'in useless longing at books that have been, through the poor mechanism of translation, the builders of my soul' (1999: 76).

To remedy this Yeats sought help from ancient Greek scholars and amateur enthusiasts. He first approached Gilbert Murray (1866–1957), then of New College, Oxford, who had recently translated Euripides' *Hippolytus*. 'Will you translate Edipus Rex for us? We can offer you nothing for it but a place in heaven', Yeats told him, 'but if you do, it will be great event ... There is no censor here to forbid it as it has been forbidden in England' ([1905] 2005a: 22–3). In spring 1904 Murray's *Hippolytus* had a successful production under Harley-Granville Barker's direction at London's Lyric Theatre. In England, the production triggered a minor revival of Attic drama Greek tragedy becoming, as Edith Hall and Fiona Macintosh have noted, 'no longer the exclusive preserve of the private theatres' (2005: 496). To Yeats, however, Euripides' success in London exemplified the lack of stylistic daring he associated with English theatre's commercial interests. Thus he pleaded with Murray to 'not ask us to play Euripides instead, for Euripides is rapidly becoming a popular English dramatist, and it is upon Sophocles that we have set our imaginations' (Yeats [1905] 2005a: 23).[21] Staging *Oedipus* would, he assured him, make a greater mark on the public mind in Ireland, persuading the country

> that she is very liberal, abhors censors delights in the freedom of the arts, is prepared for anything. When we have performed Edipus the King, and everybody is proud of having done something which is forbidden in England, even the newspapers will give [up] pretending to be timid.
>
> *Ibid.*

Although he hoped Murray would agree, Yeats underestimated how profoundly the scholar's own aims were shaped by the desire to democratize and popularize the classics. As Christopher Stray has observed, central to Murray's developing 'vision of Hellenism' and its importance for modernity was the notion that study of the classics had 'a reforming and educative mission' (Stray 2007: 3) to maintain 'in an ocean of barbarism' what Murray called 'a large and enduring island of true Hellenic life' (1954: 58). As Murray saw it, Sophocles did not neatly fit this mission, for when considering the tragedian's 'historical growth', Murray noted his 'lack of speculative freedom' and confessed to being 'offended by what seem to be [Sophocles'] inexplicable pieces of conventionalism' (Murray 1897: 203, 239, 203). With no help from Murray, Yeats approached Oliver St John Gogarty (1878–1957) and then his former classmate William Kirkpatrick Magee (1868–1961), better known as John Eglinton. However, before either could complete their versions, Yeats complained about their use of archaisms, insisting that a 'language highly artificial and conscious' might 'not prove vocal' on the Abbey stage.[22]

Though Yeats could not find a scholar ready to translate an unadorned *Oedipus* for Ireland, the prospect of flouting the authority of the Lord Chamberlain remained irresistible, and by late 1911, his plan to stage *Oedipus* began to dovetail with a desire to radically transform his style to move away from what James Longenbach has called 'dreamy languorousness towards concrete vigorousness' (2010: 322). Abandoning the idea of having a scholar complete a translation, Yeats himself set out to adapt Richard Jebb (1841–1905) and A.W. Verrall's (1851–1912) version, *The Oedipus Tyrannus of Sophocles Performed at Cambridge November 22–26, 1887* aided by Walter Nugent Monck (1877–1958), founder of the Norwich Players and later director of the Maddermarket Theatre in Norwich.[23] Though neither had Greek, they began overwriting Jebb and Verrall in January 1912, with a translation of a translation that plunged the polarizing reception of *Oedipus* into the nationalist aspirations of the Abbey Theatre as well as Yeats's desire for a 'manifestly new note' in his poetry (Pound 1914: 65). With *Oedipus* as a testing ground for experiments in 'compression and rhythmical invention' – elements which became 'so characteristic of Modernist verse' – Yeats worked to develop a Sophoclean poetry of 'prose directness' and 'hard light'.[24]

From as early as October 1902, Yeats had professed admiration for 'the regulated declamation of the Greeks', a practice 'we are trying to get back to'.[25] He thought that the 'secret' to the 'greatest of all the arts … the art of speech' had been bequeathed by the Greeks to the civilized nations of Europe, but had been 'lost for centuries'.[26] Without it poetry had drifted into an 'exaggeration of sentiment & sentimental beauty which', he wrote, 'I have come to think unmanly' (Yeats [1904] 1994c: 577). For Yeats, the 'weak' poetry written during the fin de siècle's prevailing 'decadence' exemplified the height of sentimental abstraction and exaggeration (ibid.). Even his 'own early subjective verse', he felt, with its 'shadows and hollow images' had come from a 'region of brooding emotions full of fleshly waters and vapours which kill the spirit & the will' (ibid.). Having grown 'weary of that wild God Dionysius', Yeats insisted he needed 'the Far-Darter', Apollo, instead, and, drawing on a distinction he encountered in Nietzsche's *The Birth of Tragedy* (1872), he rationalized his desire for concrete, formal invention in his poetry and drama as Apollonic (Yeats [1903] 1994d: 372).[27] George Moore observed at this time the aspersions Yeats often cast on the 'Dionysian' character of contemporary poetry, the 'softness, the weakness, the effeminacy of modern literature [which he thought] could be attributed to ideas' (Moore 1911: 348). By contrast, 'Yeats said', Moore recalled, that the ancient writer wrote about things … 'There are no ideas in ancient literature, only things,' and in support of this theory, reference was made to the sagas, to the *Iliad*, to the *Odyssey* … 'It is through the dialect,' he continued, 'that one escapes from abstract words, back to the sensation inspired directly by the thing itself.'

Moore 1911: 348

The longing to see poetry return from the 'region of shadows' to 'the thing itself' prefigured not only Ezra Pound's Imagist doctrines of 1913 – his insistence on the 'direct treatment of the 'thing', whether subjective or objective' – but also T.E. Hulme's belief that 'a classical revival' was afoot in modern poetry, a period marked by 'dry, hard classical verse' wherein writers would again remind man 'that he is mixed up with earth. He may jump, but he always returns back; he never flies away into the circumambient gas.'[28] For Hulme, this 'new classical spirit' differed from the 'strange light' of romanticism, a movement whose view of man as an 'infinite reservoir full of possibilities' had 'debauched us' with 'round metaphors of flight … flying over abysses, flying up into the eternal gases. The word infinite in every other line.'[29] The classical vision, by contrast, accepted the 'sane classical dogma of original sin', and recognized man 'as an extraordinarily fixed and limited animal', an animal which needed 'accurate description', not the 'bringing in of some of the emotions grouped around the word infinite.'[30]

To free his writing from those 'round metaphors of flight', Yeats had looked to Synge, whose use of 'peasant dialect and dialogue' had enacted 'the elemental staging of the primitive, unelaborate stage' at the Abbey.[31] But where Synge had employed Irish Gaelic as a corrective to decorative excess of English aestheticism, Yeats had no such recourse. As he began to adapt Jebb's *Oedipus* in early 1912, he had no Greek, no Irish, nor even Synge himself to rely on. What Yeats did have was the belief that his 'lyric faculty' was finally beginning to return in force (Yeats 1972: 172; cf. Longenbach 1988: 14–15). After publishing his eight-volume *The Collected Works of William Butler Yeats* (1908), the poet had wondered whether his talent could 'ever recover from the heterogeneous labor of these last few years', labour which included advocacy of the Abbey and his involvement in the political disputes of contemporary nationalism (Yeats 1972: 171). However, by the time Yeats turned to Sophocles, his responsibilities at the Abbey had diminished and his recovery was under way, due in part to his collaboration with Ezra Pound (1885–1972). In 1910 it was Pound who suggested that Yeats seemed to have 'come out of the shadows & has declared for life.'[32] His poem 'No Second Troy', with its characterization of Helen as 'beauty like a tightened bow, a kind / That is not natural in an age like this', impressed Pound with its stark vision of Homeric Greece, intimating that a new kind of Hellenic perfection was possible in English (Yeats 1940: 256–7). The poem exemplified, Pound would write, 'the spirit of the new things as I saw them in London.'[33] As he saw it, Yeats was beginning to move away from abstraction, drawn to the *quidditas* of ancient Greek. Articulating in English the 'whatness' of reality, just as the Greeks had expressed things, not ideas in verse, soon became a shared ambition for both writers, one which Pound notably outlined when he told Harriet Monroe (1860–1936) in October 1912 that modern poetry had to be 'objective': 'no slither; direct – no excessive use of adjectives, no metaphors that won't permit examination. It's straight talk, straight as the Greek!'[34] Yeats similarly stressed a desire for naturalness and directness of speech in poetry. In a diary entry dated December 1912, he elaborated on the 'First Principles' guiding his new work:

> Not to find ones art by the analysis of language or amid the circumstances of dreams but to live a passionate life, & to express the emotions that find one thus in simple rhythmical language ~~which never shows the obviously studied vocabulary~~. The words should be the swift natural words that suggest the circumstances out of which they rose ~~of real life~~. One must be both dramatist and actor & yet be in great earnest.[35]

The extent to which Yeats's work on Sophocles helped to clarify these principles is unknown, but it is clear that in the year prior to articulating this rationale Yeats had been adapting Jebb and Verrall's *Oedipus*, convinced that the ancient Greeks had perfected a plain, impassioned speech, a form of writing which spoke of things, and not abstractions, in poetry.

As Yeats saw it, Jebb and Verrall's failure lay in their unspeakable English, an idiom driven by their desire to keep strictly to 'every minutest feature in the Greek structure, every *nuance* of meaning'.[36] They blunted the play's pathos, submerging it in literalism and scholarly abstraction, and so in January 1912 Yeats started to break down their English 'from the point of view of speech', thinking that he could rescue the play's Hellenic character from the 'old, learned, respectable bald heads' of admirable but mistaken scholars.[37] Jebb was, of course, widely regarded as one having 'sympathetic insight' into what Samuel Henry Butcher (1850–1910) once called 'the niceties of Sophoclean language', its 'deflections from ordinary usage' and 'pregnant expressions' (1884: 796).[38] His seven-volume edition of 'perfectly literal' Sophoclean translations, published between 1883 and 1896, provided evidence of

> a remarkable and, and so far as I know, a unique, faculty of infusing poetry into grammar, of leading his readers through particles, moods, and tenses, vividly to realise the dramatic situation and enter into the feelings of the speaker.[39]

But to Yeats, Jebb's literalism made for poor English dialogue and utterly un-Hellenic productions of Sophocles. Jebb set little store by any claims of stylistic or dramatic merit for his versions of Sophocles, once saying of his *Electra* (1870) that nothing was to be 'staked upon it; it pretends to be nothing more than a school & college book, & if it thought useful in that character, it will have fulfilled its purpose' (as printed in Stray 2013: 47).[40] But Yeats desired more than a schoolbook *Oedipus*: he wanted an unmitigated, pure *Oedipus* on the Abbey stage, one which could capture for a modern audience the material passion of the original, spoken Greek. Yeats therefore put 'readers and scholars out of my mind' when retranslating Jebb and Verrall's English, writing his own version 'to be sung and spoken. The one thing I kept in mind was that a word unfitted for living speech, out of its natural order, or unnecessary to our modern technique, would check emotion and tire attention' (1966: 851). Working from manuscripts on which Monck had already made his own revisions during the autumn of 1911, Yeats strove to free Jebb and Verrall of hypotactic constructions, relying on short phrases, repetition, apposition and asyndeton to achieve an 'idiomatic fragmentation … modeled on normal patterns of English speech' (Baker 1967: 94).[41] The end result, though far less experimental and less conversant with the original language, could nonetheless be regarded as a forerunner of modernist bricolage in translation, a form later perfected in Pound's *Homage to Sextus Propertius* (1919) which used collage, emendation and outright mistranslation to upset common conventions of scholarly translation.[42] Where, in the tragedy's opening lines – beginning ὦ τέκνα, Κάδμου τοῦ πάλαι νέα τροφή – Jebb and Verrall had been prolix and literal,

> My children, latest-born to Cadmus who was of old, why are ye set before me thus with wreathed branches of suppliants, while the city reeks with incense, rings with prayers for health and cries of woe? I deemed it unmeet, my children, to hear these things at the mouth of others, and have come hither myself, I, Oedipus renowned of all.
>
> *1887: 1*

Yeats felt their archaizing language awkward, and began compressing their version, making the nominal clause 'latest born to Cadmus who was of old' into the simpler apposition 'descendants of Cadmus'. His earliest revisions, however – those dating from 1912 in the manuscript known as 'Rex 2' – still kept much of Jebb and Verrall's literalism. When compared with the stark and sober questions he used to begin the final version of *King Oedipus* (1928), 'Rex 2' shows Yeats following Jebb and Verrall's precedent (Yeats 1989: 28–34; cf. Arkins 1990: 129).

> My children '} descendants of Cadmus that was of old ~~time,~~ why do you come before ᵐᵉ ~~me thus~~? ʷⁱᵗʰ ~~With~~ the wreathed branches of suppliants, while the city smokes with incense and murmurs ~~with~~ ᵃⁿᵈ cries ~~and prayers~~ of sorrow; ʷⁱᵗʰ prayers for health. I would not ~~hear~~ ˡᵉᵃʳⁿ ~~these~~ from another's mouth, and therefore I have questioned you myself. Answer me, old man.
>
> *Yeats 1989: 189, lines 1–6*

King Oedipus (1928):

> Children, descendants of old Cadmus, why do you come before me, why do you carry the branches of suppliants, while the city smokes with incense and murmurs with prayer and lamentation? I would not learn from any mouth but yours, old man, therefore I question you myself.
>
> *1966: 809, lines 1–6*

Where Sophocles expressed the opening question with a single verb, θοάζετε, Jebb and Verrall rendered the Greek literally, reduplicating the verb and the participle, ἐξεστεμμένοι as 'with wreathed branches of suppliants'. Yeats's 1928 text, by contrast, broke down the original into a vigorous repetition of questions, questions which dissolved the complexity of syntax introduced by the Greek participle, and allowed for a more urgent staccato of short English interrogatives: 'why do you come . . . why do you carry'. According to David Clark and James McGuire's exhaustive account, *The Writing of Sophocles' King Oedipus* (Yeats 1989), it was in part Paul Masqueray's French translation *Oedipe-Roi* (1922) that helped Yeats and Lady Gregory to further alter 'every sentence' of his first revision (Yeats 2000b: 244; Yeats 1989: 37–9). The poet's understanding of certain passages in the French had 'freed' him to use a more idiomatic English (Yeats 1989: 38), and rid his version of anything 'that might not be intelligible on the Blasket Islands' (Yeats 2000b: 245).

The effort, therefore, to atomize Jebb and Verrall's version and reconstitute *Oedipus* in a new form did not come easily. Yeats initially thought *Oedipus* could be ready for production early in 1912 but his progress was slower than expected (1989: 19–33). Though he reportedly completed a draft of the dialogue in February – thinking he had 'made a fine version' of it – he encountered difficulty versifying the choruses, and by early March had to admit to Lady Gregory that '[w]e have put off Oedipus – I thought Monck was getting ill from overwork' (as quoted in Yeats 1989: 29). Moreover, the initial motivating force behind a production – Yeats's interest in defying the English censor – became moot: the Lord Chamberlain had lifted the ban for Max Reinhardt's January 1912 production of Gilbert Murray's *Oedipus, King of Thebes* (1911).[43] Though Murray had hesitated in the task, he finally decided to translate the tragedy into 'English rhyming verse', convinced by what he called 'the fascination of this play, which has thrown its spell on me' (1911: v). *Oedipus* did contain 'a few points of unsophisticated technique', but seemed to him a 'drama of amazing grandeur and power' (ibid: viii). Murray still preferred the 'philosophic reflections', 'subtleties of technique' (ibid.: xi), and 'tremendous choric effects' of Euripides, but he admitted that in 'respect of plot, no Greek play comes near [*Oedipus*]' (ibid.: x). Murray's about-face was indebted, in part, to his 'old master', Francis Storr with whom he had read Sophocles while studying at the Merchant Taylors' School (ibid.: xi). For Yeats, however, the Lord Chamberlain's acquiescence diminished the polemical force he had invested in an Irish *Oedipus*, though he only attributed his loss of interest to the ban's removal in hindsight (Yeats [1931] 2000c: 219–20).[44] The more immediate cause was that his own efforts at making the chorus seem simple and spoken were severely tested by the choral odes' metrical variation and syntactic complexity (Macintosh 2008: 530). As early as 1904, Yeats recognized that these passages would be challenging, reporting to London's *Evening Mail* that the 'greatest difficulty' in performing Greek tragedy lay 'in the management of the chorus' (R.M. 1904: 4). Nonetheless, he remained confident then that 'this little obstacle will be overcome', yet managing the choruses into the kind of 'straight talk' he thought necessary in 1912 proved more troublesome (ibid.).[45] Leaving the choruses unfinished that winter, Yeats did not return again to work on *Oedipus* until February 1926 when, not by coincidence, the spectre of official censorship – new, Irish state-enforced attempts to see that literature provide 'moral uplift' – had re-emerged, casting a shadow over literary endeavors in Ireland.

Declared a dominion within the British Commonwealth in 1922, the Irish Free State effectively took on, as one historian has observed, 'the whole body of British statute law – and English common law tradition – with a few minor exceptions consequent on the terms of the Treaty' (Adams 1968: 13). No exception dealt directly with censorship and so with 'regard to the legislation controlling obscene literature the establishment of the Irish Free State brought no change at all' (ibid.). Various organizations, however, began insisting that it was the duty of new government to 'combat' what the Catholic Truth Society had called 'the pernicious influence of infidel and immoral publications'.[46] 'However we may differ in our political opinions to-day', wrote the Rev. R.S. Devane (1876–1951),

> and however bitter the feelings that have arisen in recent times may be, I think we may truthfully say that Republican and Free Stater, Capitalist and and Worker, Protestant and Catholic, would all rejoice in the re-definition of 'indecency' or 'obscenity,' thereby setting up 'as high a standard as possible,' and so giving a moral lead to other nations.
>
> *1925: 189–90*

In February 1926 the Free State convened a 'Committee of Enquiry on Evil Literature', tasking three academics and two prominent members from the Catholic Church and the Church of Ireland with exploring 'whether it is necessary or advisable in the interest of public morality to extend the existing powers of the State to prohibit or restrict the sale and circulation of printed matter'.[47] After examining the matter, the committee recommended expanding government censorship, proposing the creation of a board 'with a permanent official as Secretary, to advise the Minister of Justice as to any books, newspapers or magazines circulated in the Saorstat that, in the opinion of the Board, are demoralising and corrupting'.[48] As a member of the Irish senate, Yeats often supported the Cosgrave government, but he abhorred the notion that an independent Ireland would curtail intellectual freedom with stricter censorship than under British rule. As Elizabeth Cullingford has observed of the Censorship of Publications Act of 1929:

> The censorship dispute marks a real diminution of Yeats's respect for the Cosgrave Government. It had betrayed its trust by bowing to mob fanaticism ... He left the Senate, then, a disillusioned man. During his term of office he had advocated order, unity, and liberty: the Government had supplied order but had infringed liberty and thus jeopardized unity.
>
> *Cullingford 1981: 193*

In the senate Yeats railed against the legislation, believing that to 'give one man, the Minister of Justice, control over the substance of our thought, for [the] definition of "indecency" and such vague phrases as "subversive of public morality"', would permit him to exclude *The Origin of Species*, Karl Marx's *Capital*, the novels of Flaubert, Balzac, Proust, all of which have been objected to somewhere on moral grounds, half the Greek and Roman Classics, Anatole France and everybody else on the Roman index, and all great love poetry.

Yeats [1928] 2000a: 215

Decades earlier, Yeats had believed that poetry and drama produced in Ireland and for the cause of Irish nationhood, literature modelled on the classics even, might help generate a 'conception of the race as noble as Aeschylus and Sophocles', a reinvention of the freedom of imagination once perfected in Greek tragedy (Yeats 1972: 184). But with the yoke of British rule cast off, forces were conspiring to bring the freedom of the artist 'under a mob censorship' (Yeats [1928] 2000a: 216). And yet, thought embittered by the failures of the Free State, Yeats still joined the national interest of Irish literature to examples from classical antiquity, still speaking, as one scholar has observed, 'of Ireland's future as being allied to the pattern of the Greeks' (Macintosh 1994: 15). His understanding, however, of how that future fit that ancient Greek pattern had evolved during the time it took to complete *King Oedipus*, finally produced at the Abbey Theatre on 7 December 1926. No longer certain that *Oedipus* could persuade the country that 'she is very liberal, abhors censors delights in the freedom of the arts', Yeats elaborated in *Oedipus* a new polemic whose self-critical force was set in tension against the nationalist aims he first envisioned for the tragedy in 1904 (Yeats [1905] 2005a: 23). As he later explained on BBC radio, Oedipus had come to seem 'representative of human genius' (Yeats [1931] 2000c: 221): blinded by his own strength for governing wisely and aggravated by an 'involuntary sin', Oedipus sought the truth so that he might again answer the pleas of his subjects to – ἀνόρθωσον πόλιν (Soph. *OT* 46) – 'Uplift our State' – to save them from the ravages of plague (Yeats 1966: 810). The catastrophe of *Oedipus* lay not in the king's inability to rescue his subjects, but rather in his failure to see that the 'uplift' he could provide was itself compromised, predicated on a severe and lasting cost: exile, blindness and internecine strife. Collective self-deception had reduced the city-state to a wasteland for, in wilful ignorance of Oedipus's history and hidden sin, the Thebans were deceived by a heroic ideal, by a national vision that brought home only plague and ruin. In performing that deception – in staging what Friedrich Hölderlin had once called the undoing of Oedipus's *Allessuchende, Allesdeutende* (1804: 107) – the play seemed no longer to Yeats at least, simply 'the masterpiece of Attic Tragedy' (Jebb 1885: v) but a form rather of 'our new satirical comedy', one whose staging in Dublin had then exposed a 'new Ireland', he wrote, 'so full of curiosity, so full of self-criticism ... sometimes so tolerant, sometimes so bitter in its merriment' (Yeats [1931] 2000c: 223).

RESPONDENT ESSAY 3
MODERNIST TRANSLATIONS AND POLITICAL ATTUNEMENTS
Nancy Worman

The four chapters that make up this final section each focus on different political angles in the works of four modernists, three men and one woman, with each of them construing 'political' in slightly different ways. Both Jessop and Flack take what I would consider more overtly political prospects on their chosen texts: the feminist and anti-war strains in the novels of Laura Riding (in the first instance) and *The Waste Land* and *Ulysses* (in the second). Somers instead looks to ancient ritual to think through Eliot's engagement with Aristophanes in his 'Sweeney' poem and play and thus seems (to me, at any rate) to be working with a more attenuated notion of the political – perhaps something like 'social' or 'communal'. For Baker, in contrast, the political angle is more essentially aesthetic, insofar as he focuses attention on how Yeats makes use of Sophocles to craft a new modernist style that hinges on an ancient 'Greek/Irish' profile. The framing of this section encourages me to extend the discussion by pressing harder on what might constitute the political angles in the authors' readings, and so in what follows I attempt to supplement these lively engagements with some further unfoldings of the strategies, textures and images to which each author directs attention.

Jessop's essay is most concerned with understanding the distinctively gendered qualities of the classical engagements by modernist female writers. While Riding, her featured writer, is best known for her poetry (not to mention her association with Robert Graves), Jessop is more interested in her historical novels *A Trojan Ending* and *Lives of Wives*, both of which seek to rewrite history from a female-centred perspective. That she chose to do so in prose novels is telling; Jessop notes that prose is in fact prosaic, while Riding herself expresses an urge to domesticate and lower the tonal echoes of ancient epic. We may think here as well of Bakhtin's famous formulation of the novelistic mode as more inclusive, multi-vocal and porous than the lyric, which would encourage a recognition that Riding's narrativistic interventions have a political force and revolutionary cast.

As Jessop herself emphasizes, although incremental changes in gender roles helped to shape the modernist movement, it remained centrally male, as well as sustained and celebrated by male literary theorists. Add to this that most modernists' engagements with classical literature centred, implicitly or explicitly, on masculine and heroic modes, and one can begin to discern why female modernists' strategies pursued different ways into the problem of a purportedly shared classical heritage. As Jessop notes, one of Virginia Woolf's strategies was furious confrontation (in *A Room of One's Own* and *Three Guineas*) of a history and classical past not fully available to or inhabitable by women. In her fiction, in some contrast, Woolf took more oblique paths, some of which share with

Riding's novels an imaginative repopulating of ancient forms. While Riding sought to give fuller scope to ancient female characters who linger at the margins of ancient narratives, Woolf chose instead to reinvigorate central female characters, especially those riveting figures from Greek tragedy, in ways that reorient the plots themselves as more fully female-centred and choral.[1] In some ways Woolf's choices are the bolder ones, insofar as she tends to stick close to the heart of the most canonical Greek tales; but Riding's are perhaps the more adventurous in a different mode, as like a learned and clever Hellenistic author she mines the edges of the main stories, illuminating (and often inventing details of) the lives of obscure characters. By means of such details, on Jessop's account, Riding constructs a counter-narrative to male writers' tendencies to trade in romanticized feminine abstractions.

How disappointing and yet inevitable, then, to find that Riding's female characters largely reinforce the compromises forced on women from early on in the historical record: ancillary and domesticated roles, behind-the-scenes manoeuvring and mediating. In seeking to reopen and repopulate ancient tales, Riding is constrained by her chosen genre (historical fiction) and by the tales themselves, as without the full-on gender reversals that no historical genre would countenance, she cannot reinvent a world in which female characters assume full autonomy and operate in manners fundamentally different from the power–knowledge dynamics that have shaped a disastrously misogynistic world history. Jessop does not mention this, perhaps because to do so could appear to undermine Riding's impressive feats of imaginative rewriting, which (as Jessop emphasizes) fiercely reject her male contemporaries' reductive mythologizing of women as, for instance, 'white goddesses' – to invoke the figure and her male invoker closest at hand.

Flack's discussion centres on a political concern that for many female modernists was also a feminist concern: the devastations of war and the seductions of nationalism. Flack focuses her analysis on the backstory of Eliot's *The Waste Land*, which exposes its original commitment to an Odyssean thematics, an anti-*nostos* depicting a chaotic post-war world hedged around by violence and horror. In this world, as earlier manuscript versions show, the Sirens are recast as ancient and three – that is, as more like the three aged Fates of ancient myth than the beautiful singers of Homer's poem. Flack points also to Pound's encouraging Eliot to replace his original epigraph, a quote from Conrad's *Heart of Darkness* that includes the famous exclamation 'The horror! The horror!' by an untranslated one from Petronius's *Satyricon*. The replacement quotation depicts the Cumaean Sibyl, the mantic priestess of Apollo who sits at the entrance to the underworld in Vergil's *Aeneid*, as reduced to a tiny creature in a jar, taunted by schoolboys and wishing to die. The Latin quotation includes its own quotation in Greek, a recursive gesture that reaches back past Virgil to Greek lyric, with the Sibyl's response ἀποθανεῖν θέλω ('I want to die') itself echoing the first line of an ode of Sappho that dramatizes the loss of a beloved friend to marriage (τεθνάκην δ' ᾿αδολῶς θέλω, 'Truly, I want to die', fr. 94).

Petronius's *Satyricon* is itself a latter-day *Odyssey* of sorts, a fact that ought to make the epigraph some kind of compensation for the editing out on which Flack focuses, that of most of the section that repurposes the sea wanderings of the *Odyssey*, 'Death by

Water'. But this compensation is blocked by the quotation itself: an image of the powerful voice of desire, sustained in violent form in Vergil's Sibyl in the *Aeneid*, reduced to a tiny thing in a jar teased by boys, imbedded in a tale told by Trimalchio, a rich and supremely ignorant former slave. The double cipher of untranslated ancient languages thus merely reinforces the mockery of the scene. Or it would do so, for readers who can read these languages. For those who can't, the gesture would be lost, and so the epigraph effects a kind of linguistic feint that the original Conrad would not have. Hence Pound's disdain for it as not weighty enough (read learned and relatively obscure).

As Flack notes, the Conrad quotation points more emphatically to the devastations of empire; the Petronius passage achieves something different, something more elegiac and less implicitly political. While she does not emphasize the sardonically mournful tone of the Sibyl scene, of a culture lost to its inheritors, Flack argues that Eliot's poem itself is elegiac and a response to war, finding in the ultimately suppressed Homeric section 'Death by Water' an echoing of a tradition of poetic expressions of post-war grieving. As Flack explains, again under Pound's influence, Eliot cut almost the entire section, leaving just shy of ten lines, which rendered this Homeric elegy largely lost to the poem's ultimate audience. If we take these editorial choices together we are left with a distinctly different kind of elegiac gesture, one much less political and less overtly aimed, as Flack suggests, at a peaceful confluence of east and west. Instead what is left is, on the one hand, the epigraph with its untranslated ancient languages that mock the undereducated, which in fact reiterates Petronius's own lampoon of Trimalchio. And on the other: the effective elision of the earliest extant post-war mourning song in the western canon, as well as a more accessible means of expressing cultural scepticism and loss.

Flack finds in Joyce an *Odyssey* more keenly attentive to and demonstrative of anti-war and anti-nationalist sentiments, reading in his 'Sirens' episode (11) a rejection of the romance and draw of patriotic songs. While Bloom's resistance to their emotional pull may be, as Flack argues, a refusal of 'Iliadic' pride in nation strength and heroism, it is difficult to see in his slipping away from the singer in the bar and gentle farting at such pretences a positive political message rather than an oblique (and quite funny) solitary disregard. All the less so, then, can I discern such in Eliot, who ultimately edited out much of his Odyssean scene. Not to mention the female voice that in Eliot is encapsulated (literally) and foreclosed and that in Joyce is spurned by the hero. The classical female figures that these modernists re-envision are, after all, powerful and super-human or divine; and while they do not fare much better in the ancient narratives – being always ancillary or menacing (or both) – the modernists reduce their statuses even further, rendering them either opaque or sentimental.

In arguing that Eliot's play *Sweeney Agonistes* can only be read as Aristophanic in the sense of renewing ancient ritual forms, Somers' contribution takes up a much more adumbrated sense of political values imbedded in aesthetic choices than the two preceding chapters. He does not, for instance, address the overtly racialized cast of *Sweeney Agonistes*, although he tracks enough of its details to suggest an additional (and, I think, important) political attunement in relation to Aristophanes' own transmogrifications of social hierarchies. While the ancient dramatist was more concerned with class and gender, as well as human–animal divides, rather than race, these all intersect in telling ways in ancient and modern traditions. That is to say, while Somers focuses on the Cambridge 'ritualist' readings of ancient fertility myths and practices putatively underlying fifth-century Athenian dramatic forms, this focus effectively masks Eliot's use of the Aristophanic frame as a classicizing overlay on a much more contemporary and 'lowbrow' mode: minstrelsy. As scholars have pointed out, Eliot's 'melodrama' toys with blackface modes as a mask for the unsettled modernist self (in Eliot's case American, Southern, expat), and as such both celebrates and targets this 'Other within', to use Mark Bush's phrase for this essentially primitivist appropriation of 'exotics' by modernist writers, who were mostly elite European and North American males.[2]

Eliot's play fragments in fact craft a mash-up of biases, including misogynist and anti-Semitic gestures and those that racialize the Irish namesake of the drama as simian, bestial and thus black-ish. This is already in train in his poem 'Sweeney among the Nightingales', which begins (not so subtly),

Apelike Sweeney spreads his knees
Letting his arms hang down to laugh,
The zebra stripes along his jaw
Swelling to maculate giraffe.

With its epigraph, ὤμοι, πέπληγμαι καιρίαν πληγὴν ἔσω ('Oh me, I am struck by a timely blow within!'), the poem is framed as if it were a 'translation' of Aeschylus's *Agamemnon*, since this is Agamemnon's first shout from inside the palace as his wife Clytemnestra cuts him down (Aesch. *Ag.* 1343). As such the Sweeney poem shares something distinctive with the Sweeney play fragments: a framing gesture towards an ancient dramatic genre, suggesting not mere allusion but rather formal directive. The Sweeney poem should thus in some sense be a 'tragedy', as the Sweeney play should be a 'comedy'. The poem casts a brooding, sardonic eye on a contemporary scene in a cafe, a scene hedged around by debased metonymies for death: while early on Sweeney 'guards the hornèd gate' like a gloomy monkey, at the end the nightingales shit on Agamemnon's shroud. That this is expressed more obliquely – 'let their liquid siftings fall' – calls attention to rather than obscures the defiling of this past, degraded ('stiff, dishonoured') form. So, no tragedy here, or not exactly; the classical references serve as something of a distraction from the racialized, creaturely cast of the café scene, with the apelike Sweeney, 'the silent vertebrate in brown' and Rachel '*née* Rabinovich' snatching at grapes 'with murderous paws'. But it also calls attention to what the modernist turn may do to ancient tragedy, which is to renew it by effectively sullying it, rudely shoving it up next to the sprawl and yawn of the contemporary moment.

Somers, following Carol Smith, solves the problem of how to read *Sweeney Agonistes* as comedy by focusing on the Aristophanic framing and thus looking past its more emphatic racial and sexual inflections to an underlying ritualized form centred on death and rebirth. This may well account for the basic structuring of the play's scenes, as well as shedding light on Eliot's interest in contemporary classicists' work on Dionysiac rites of renewal. But I wonder whether we can also see a similar 'sullying' of the ancient genre at work, though in the case of Attic comedy such defilement would be more in keeping with a genre always ready to shit on itself (cf. all the joking about incontinence). That is, Eliot's introduction of minstrelsy, animality and cannibalism rudely re-visions the ancient mode by re-exposing it to its own violent core: Dionysian *sparagmos*, virginal 'marriage' to death. Thus Sweeney plays cannibal and Doris is threatened with becoming a 'nice little, white little missionary stew' (*CP* 130).

Baker's exploration of Yeats's engagement with Sophocles' *Oedipus the King* reveals a subtext that pivots on gender rather than race. Like Flack's discussion, Baker's focuses on the intersection of 'Greek' aesthetics and nationalist politics. Although the gender subtext is one that he tracks without noting, his contention that Yeats's turn to Greek and to Sophocles in particular invigorated his own writing and drove a stylistic innovating that would change the face of modern poetry raises all sorts of interesting questions about what 'Greek' was for these writers. Yeats's own language in describing his sense of it is not only marked by a scorn for Romantic, Victorian and fin-de-siècle 'decadent' modes; it is also cast in terms of weakness versus strength, languor versus rigor and thus a soft effeminacy versus a hard masculinity. He terms the former poetic styles 'unmanly' and associates them with a Nietzschean version of Dionysus, all fiery emotion and ecstasy, as opposed to Apollonian directness and lucidity. In parallel terms, he calls for a focus on the world of solid things rather than airy ideas – which he finds most perfectly in the Greek language.

But what, exactly, is Yeats's 'Greek'? As Baker highlights, it is not all Greek, nor is it really only Yeats's, influenced as he is by the stylistic high-handedness of none other than Pound; the phrase 'straight as the Greek' that titles Baker's essay is in fact his, not Yeats's. As for the Greek authors themselves, Yeats disdains Euripides along Nietzschean lines, in stark contrast to some of his contemporaries, notably the classicist Gilbert Murray, who instead found fault, at least initially, with the stark themes in Sophocles. Yeats saw things differently, regarding Homer and Sophocles as stylists of brutal clarity and sharp-edged effects that he felt to be very simple, natural – and Irish. Yeats's aesthetic distinctions are thus not only shaded by gender; they also slant towards a romanticization of primitivist aesthetics, a tendency he shares with his pal Pound as well as other modernist writers. If this aesthetic has a texture, it is rough, stony, barren, dusty; across many poems and a few decades, Yeats returns again and again to these 'Greek' materialities, metonymies for a stylistically stringent, tough, heroic age and for his own innovating modes.

Among the poems composed in the early 1930s is *From the 'Antigone'*, presented as if it were a fragment of a lost play; its inclusion in the collection *The Winding Stair and Other Poems* follows on from Yeats's successful mountings of his 'translations' (i.e. reworkings of Jebb's translations) of *King Oedipus* and *Oedipus at Colonus* in 1926 and 1927, the first of which Baker discusses at some length. The poem appears to be a refraction of the ode invoking Eros that the chorus sings before the final entrance of Antigone, after which she and they sing a *kommos* (a lament shared between character[s] and chorus) centred on her 'marriage' to death. Like Yeats's poem, the ode begins with the image of the soft cheeks of a young woman (783–4) and ends with tears (802–3), but the modern poet adds another texture at the end, as 'Oedipus' child / Descends into the loveless dust' (15–16). While in their shared song Antigone and the chorus emphasize instead the rocky tomb to which she has been consigned by Creon, this 'loveless dust' recalls the thin layer of parched earth with which she twice covered her beloved brother Polyneices, as he lay unburied, an enemy of the state by Creon's decree.

In Sophocles' play the messenger's twin descriptions of Antigone's actions centre on this dry cover for his corpse: in the first telling, the guard appointed messenger had described it as strewn on 'thirsty' skin (246–7), the body 'veiled' with this light coating of dust (255–6). In the second, the guards sweep away the dust blanketing the corpse, but then a whirlwind arises, filling the plain with dust, marring the leaves on the trees and choking the air. The guards shut their eyes to the grit, and when after a while the storm passes, they open them to see Antigone, shrieking over her brother's body stripped of its dusty layer (423–4).

We might compare Virginia Woolf's handling of *Antigone* a few years later, when in *The Years* Sara reads her cousin Edward's translation of the play, alone at night in her room and conscious of parties going on elsewhere. The passages that Woolf chooses for Sara's bedtime reading edge towards a strikingly similar conflation; and her renderings of them are also charged with sensory details, in the first instance those surrounding Polyneices's corpse:

> Antigone? She came whirling out of the dust-cloud to where the vultures were reeling and flung white sand over the blackened foot.
>
> *135–6*

Sara then moves on, only half attending, 'picking up a word or two at random' as she gazes out into the garden. She pauses next on the image of Antigone buried alive, in a tomb where there is 'just enough room for her to lie straight out' (136) – which is to say, on the image first introduced in the ode that Yeats reworks. While his gesture towards associating the scenes is fleeting at most, this dust does punctuate his poem's end, its loveless attribute standing in sharp contrast to Antigone's fierce love of her brother, such that she desires to lie 'loving with him beloved' together in the tomb (73).

Dust is, of course, also a favourite modernist metonymy for the fracturing of humanist traditions so celebrated by the Victorians – it is the ultimate thin, desiccated remainder, a mere trace of what has been lost. Classicizing modernists such as Yeats and Woolf would both have been sensitive to the role that dust plays in Homer and tragedy – almost always associated as it is with defeat and death, with a terrible grounded-ness at the edges of human life. Yeats's bold instinct that Sophocles' stringent plays, even filtered through two layers of translating, would resonate with his Irish audiences in particular turns on his notion of Irish nationalism as similarly hedged around with a toughened view of life. It also proved prescient, as Baker points out, to the extent that Irish poets and playwrights would return again and again to the Theban plays, and to *Antigone* especially. And while these later versions may not centre so overtly on this nationalism, the plays remain flashpoints in Ireland for political and more broadly cultural controversies.

In framing my discussion as a meditation on the relations between politics and aesthetics, as well as an extension of the chapters' varied topics in this regard, I hope to urge heightened awareness about how we handle modernist writers in our present moment. The cultural politics of new nationalisms, with their shadings of racism and misogyny, make it all the more urgent that humanists call attention to such shadings in the traditions they study. As Sarah Ahmed has highlighted, these politics have their affects, their emotional attachments and associations, and thus their implicit aesthetic hierarchies (2004). Attending to such concerns can encourage us to recognize, for instance, that Pound's suggestions for editing *The Waste Land* rendered it more classicizing, elitist, and less political, while Eliot's own framing of *Sweeney Agonistes* as Aristophanic drew attention away from its racialized politics and towards ancient aesthetic and ritual practices. And to see too that Yeats's stylistic renewal hinged on a 'manly' version of both classical drama and nationalism, while Riding's less celebrated novels may have been so precisely for their feminism – and even it is constrained by her turn to classical models. Perhaps this is the ultimate challenge of the reception of classical literature: how to engage with and re-inhabit its aesthetics without reproducing its political limitations or using it to promote those of one's own era. All of these essays attend to the political and aesthetic calibrations of modernist writers' choices in this regard, refusing any easy resolutions of the tensions that such intersections inevitably generate.

CHAPTER 13
MODERNIST MIGRATIONS, PEDAGOGICAL ARENAS: TRANSLATING MODERNIST RECEPTION IN THE CLASSROOM AND GALLERY

Marsha Bryant and Mary Ann Eaverly

As the preceding essays show, the relationship between modernism and the classical world is multivalent. Writers have produced literal translations through revision, adaptation and modification – inspired not only by the ancient literary tradition, but also by material culture. For us, the essential definition of translation lies in the Latin word *translatio*. Of the five meanings listed in the *Oxford Latin Dictionary*, only the last is 'translate from one language to another' (Glare 1982). The others describe 'moving (a thing) from one place to another, the transference of ideas from one context to another, the imaginary shift of a situation from one time to another' (19), potentially extending the translation process beyond language and literature. Working together as a literary critic and a classical archaeologist, we explored this process by creating a team-taught, interdisciplinary course, 'Women Writers and Classical Myths', expanding possibilities for pedagogy inside and outside the classroom.

Classically-inspired texts display a rich interplay of crossings, connections and mergings: a dynamic that we term *classical convergences*. More than a linear moving across, these convergences are multimodal – extending across artistic and popular media as well as across time and geography. Thus, we put artworks in conversation with literature through our class's companion exhibition for the Harn Museum of Art, *Classical Convergences: Traditions & Inventions*, co-designed with Carol McCusker (the museum's Curator of Photography). Several modernist artists were forerunners of this convergent practice. For example, H.D.'s pan-Mediterranean epic *Helen in Egypt* (1961) transposes historical epic cinema as well as ancient Greek literature. Salvador Dali's *Colossus of Rhodes* (1954) morphs the legendary classical figure with superheroes and the Statue of Liberty.

Artworks in *Classical Convergences: Traditions & Inventions* (Harn Museum of Art, 16 December 2014–May 2015)

Artefacts

Standing Female Figure	Greek, third century BC, terracotta
Black-Figure Siana Cup (kylix)	Attributed to the Heidelberg Painter Greek, active 560–540 BC

Modern Sculpture

Kore	Anita Huffington, 1991, bronze
Young Narcissus	José de Creeft, 1943, onyx relief

Photography

Nude Male Sculpture	Sommer and Behles, stereograph
Venus rising from the sea, International Exhibition of 1862	The London Stereographic and Photographic Company, stereograph
Mars, Venus and Cupid, International Exhibition of 1862	The London Stereographic and Photographic Company, stereograph
Ange Camilli	Unknown photographer, gelatin silver print postcard
Acropolis caryatids	Albumen print
Great Eleusinian Relief	Photogravure from *En Grece par Monts et par Vaux* (1909)
Male nudes, one holding classical vessel	Len Prince, gelatin silver print
Plate #76 from *Self-Possessed*	Len Prince, gelatin silver print, 2005

Drawings

Venus and the Two Old Men	Jiri Anderle, soft ground, dry point, 1982
Mädchen und Tod	Jiri Anderle, soft ground, dry point, 1983
Cassandra	Jiri Anderle, soft ground, dry point, 1984

Focusing on women, we examined the complex dynamic of their relationships to the largely male-dominated classical literary canon. (Muses inspire male poets, but they do not themselves produce art.) Grounded in modernism as well as classical culture, our syllabus spanned a range of writers that included Homer, Sappho, W.B. Yeats, H.D., Amy Lowell, William Carlos Williams, Robert Graves, W.H. Auden and Stevie Smith, as well as contemporary literature. Like the writers they inherited, our postmodernist poets tapped 'the generative cultural possibilities of translation as a mode of literary production', a phenomenon that Steven Yao has examined in modernist poetry (2002: 209). We also studied ancient, modern and contemporary artworks, which are themselves translations of classical myths. In antiquity, myth appeared not only in literature, but also on objects such as painted vases. (Indeed, some versions of myths appear only in the artistic record.) These artefacts function similarly to the 'cultural composites' Emily Greenwood sees in their literary equivalents (2016: 43); both emerge through the chain of texts and audiences that respond to classical precedents. As we noted in our exhibition statement: 'Male and female artists have different views on how fixed or pliable the classical tradition can be. Some of their classical convergences reinforce traditional gender images and roles. Some take classical figures to new places. And some of them seem to break free from tradition' (2014).

At the beginning of our course, many of our students assumed that women writers and artists who trafficked in classical materials had but two choices: outright rejection or feminist revision. Alicia Suskin Ostriker's influential concept of *revisionist mythmaking* foregrounds women's poems that contest 'gender stereotypes embodied in myth', bringing marginalized female characters centre stage (1986: 216). H.D.'s 'Eurydice' and Stevie Smith's 'Persephone' offer modernist exemplars of this model, indicting myths of female creativity and sexuality along with the traditional trappings of their respective characters.

Yet women writers' convergences with classical materials involve much more than voicing women and reversing power dynamics. Carol Ann Duffy's 'Eurydice' time travels to the present, taking on the publishing industry as well as Orpheus. In Rita Dove's *Mother Love*, an Americanized recreation of the Demeter and Persephone myth, Demeter's and Persephone's voices collide with one another. Margaret Atwood's *Penelopiad* also confounds dualistic models of counter-discourse; here the maids' choral poems intrude and place pressure on Penelope's narrating voice. Ange Mlinko's poem 'Words are the Reverse of Pain' moves beyond a poetics of a woman's voice altogether, refracting myths of Leto and Apollo through World War II. Our students came to learn how individual women writers embraced, questioned, manipulated and reinvented the ancient sources that grounded their art. Focusing on poetry allowed us to address key literary modes such as ekphrasis and epic, as well as tap a wide variety of writers and texts. Elizabeth Bergmann Loizeaux reminds us that ekphrasis has enabled a surprising number of women poets 'from the Greeks through Joanna Baillie to Christina Rossetti, Elizabeth Barrett Browning and Michael Field, and *especially* in the twentieth century' (2009: 121). Neither linear transmission nor counter-discourse can account for this sheer diversity of inventive translations, which includes yet ultimately exceeds traditional ekphrasis *and* modernist juxtaposition.

'Facing three ways': H.D.'s Hermes and modernist migrations

We introduced our course with an early modernist poem that distilled our interdisciplinary approach: H.D's 'Hermes of the Ways'. In effect, we excavated the poem for our students, uncovering its ancient objects as well as its mythic and literary sources (*The Homeric Hymn to Hermes*, Anyte of Tegea's poem in the Greek Anthology, Richard Aldington's English translation). Marsha framed our collaborative presentation with a counterintuitive question: Why is Hermes (rather than a goddess) H.D's preferred portal to the past in her first published poem? Like the Hermetic incarnation H.D. invokes in her *Trilogy* (Hermes Trismegistus), this earlier Hermes 'of the triple path-ways' disrupts dualisms; he is 'Dubious, / facing three ways' (1988).

Hermes was more than just a male Muse for H.D.; he became a queerly generative figure for her creativity. This god of the gateways literally 'stands at the entrance of H.D's poetic career', as Diana Collecott puts it (1999: 259). 'Hermes of the Ways' appeared with a trio of pieces that Pound sent to Harriet Monroe's *Poetry* magazine and signed 'H.D., Imagiste' – a moniker that masked her gender. The poem also plays a pivotal role in H.D's debut volume *Sea Garden* (1916), marking her dynamic reinventions of classical materials. At the beginning of *Tribute to the Angels*, H.D. renders Hermes Trismegistus patron of poets and orators as well as thieves, declaring his domain to be 'thought, / inventive, artful, and curious' (1998). Bringing Hermes into the world of her writing, she embarked on her 'palimpsestic poems' that 'collapse ancient and modern time' while extending gender roles, to borrow from Annette Debo and Lara Vetter's volume on teaching H.D. (2011: 6). The poet's lyric efficiency distills our pedagogical aim of putting Classics, literary studies, and the visual arts in dialogue with one another.

Understanding the complexity of the ancient figure helped students appreciate the choices H.D. made in her evocation of Hermes. Mary Ann presented the god's mythological background and showed how his multiple roles shaped depictions in ancient art. *The Homeric Hymn to Hermes* describes his birth and precocious first day on earth – during which he managed to rustle cattle, slaughter them to make sausage and invent a bow drill to create fire for cooking (among other devious and inventive deeds). Consequently, Hermes becomes the god of tricksters, travellers and thieves as well as messenger to the gods. His physical form varies considerably across the archaeological record and artistic repertoire. Atypically among the male gods, Hermes can appear as both young (beardless) – most famously in the fourth century BC statue by Praxiteles from Olympia – and as a mature man. In this statue, his nude, youthful body exemplifies the ideal perfection of classical male form; he carries the infant Dionysus (the other Greek god who alternates between youthful and mature images). Yet he is bearded in a first-century AD Roman wall painting from Pompeii; he appears wearing a traveller's costume and carrying the caduceus (symbol of heralds).

Artistic renderings of Hermes also span Western constructions of gender and sexuality, including phallic masculinity and androgyny – attributes that also compelled H.D. For example, the ancient Greeks erected herms at crossroads and in front of houses for protection; these were pillars with the bearded head of Hermes and male genitalia. We showed students photographs of the marble herm by Alkamanes (*Hermes Propylaios*, fourth century), as well as vase paintings that depicted people worshipping herms, which were considered containers of the god's essence. Hermaphroditus, Hermes' son with Aphrodite, bends gender identity; he became a fused male/female in response to a scorned nymph's prayers. We see the figure's androgyny in the famous 'sleeping hermaphrodite' statue from the third century BC, now at the Louvre. It depicts a reclining Hermaphroditus who, aside from male genitalia, exhibits the classical female nude form. When H.D. translates Hermes in her poem, she calls upon all these layers of meaning – and the myths and objects behind them. In the context of Mary Ann's presentation, our students could see that these blurred boundaries in H.D.'s poem *continue* classical frameworks as much as contest them.

Androgyny also shapes H.D.'s two-part 'Hermes of the Ways'. Blending her female ancient source (Anyte) with her male modernist translation (Aldington), H.D. sets her poem in a dynamic border zone between land and sea – a 'sensory, whirling, vectored space', as Eileen Gregory describes it (1997: 169). Helen Sword identifies the gender jeopardy H.D. distills in this recurrent scene: 'Do we posit a fluid "female" sea and a rigid "male" land? A passive "female" shore and an active "male" sea?' (1996: 124). Solid and fluid fuse in H.D.'s images of sand grains that are 'hard' yet 'clear as wine', and 'great waves' that 'break' sea and dunes alike. (H.D.'s assonant long *a* sounds also link elements and forces that merge with yet oppose one another: *breaks, grains, great, waves, break*.) Into this windswept place, H.D.'s ungendered speaker calls on Hermes 'of the triple path-ways', sensing his presence.

In discussing part II of 'Hermes of the Ways', Marsha widened the frame of reference to gesture toward H.D.'s position as a woman classical modernist. Rachel Blau DuPlessis has neatly summed up the tradition's challenge for women: 'To enter the classics is to confront the issue of cultural authority, for knowledge of Greek and Latin, formerly barred to women and certain males, was the sigil of knowledge and authority, the main portal of the liberal humanist hegemony' (1986: 17). More recently, Emily Wilson reminds us that 'the works of dead white elite men have largely been translated by living, white elite men' (2017). Yet since H.D. had studied the ancient languages at Bryn Mawr, she has some claim to that domain. Her debut poem turns to face literary tradition, turning towards Hermes to guide the speaker's venture into new creative directions. Again the wind sounds, evoking both artistic inspiration and power for embarking on a quest. If the traditional heroic questing of martial masculinity foiled earlier women writers from participating in epic production, H.D.'s Hermes who beckons 'wayfarers' fuels an alternative voyage. Here H.D.'s imagery often alludes to aspects of Greek mythology the speaker will reject. The apples 'ripened / by a desperate sun' are deemed too 'hard' and 'small' – the poem will provide no golden apples of the Hesperides as there were for Heracles. Moreover, the ambiguous shadow the speaker perceives 'is not the shadow of the mast head / nor of the torn sails' – no buffeted, questing ships will appear. Yet the twists and turns that H.D. weaves into her poem reveal a cunning akin to that of Odysseus:

The boughs of the trees
are twisted
by many bafflings;
twisted are
the small-leafed boughs.

This twisted stanza, a chiasmus, reflects the poem's many crossings of gender and genre boundaries – a fitting figure for the many ways women writers engage the classical past. In the poem's culmination, H.D. crosses boundaries once more: this time by alluding to the birth of Aphrodite ('the great sea foamed'). Shifting from present to past tense in this stanza, the speaker shows persistence and is poised to encounter Hermes, who will propel another kind of odyssey. (Here the poem anticipated our 'Other Odysseys' term paper assignment, in which students explored modern reinventions of epic women characters and assessed the sustainability of classical epic in contemporary culture.)

Musings in the museum

Like the modernists, we sometimes made the museum our classroom. As a space, the Harn Museum disrupted the linearity of syllabus and text, the grid of desks and rows. Our exhibition *Classical Convergences: Traditions & Inventions* disrupted linear models of classical transmission, for museum-goers traverse the galleries in the order they like. They move in their preferred directions, pausing as they see fit and experimenting with angles and distance. We tapped these dynamics in two assignments for our course that drew on artworks in our gallery. McCusker guided us in designing *Classical Convergences* so that it became 'a 3-D visual portrait of classical mythology that reinvigorated the gallery (and collection) with a multivalent conversation – a dynamic mash up of past and present voices and forms' (2017). Modernist translations of classical themes appeared in two pieces: an onyx relief (José de Creeft's *Young Narcissus*, with chiselled lines evoking Picasso's *Les Demoiselles d'Avignon*) and a postcard of body builder Ange Camilli (posing like Myron's ancient statue *Discobolus*, 'Discus Thrower').

Of course, such convergences are not limited to modernist art. Our colleague Mlinko described her model of classical inspiration in her textbox for the exhibit's fifth-century BC, draped terracotta female figure:

> As a poet, I monitor the undertones and overtones of words. Naturally, their histories and etymologies constantly come into play. So I can never forget that 'poetry' comes from a Greek word, as do 'lyric' and 'epic'. The interweaving of Greek and Latin patterns and textures through English verse is mongrel and monstrous in the best sense. When you look at the drapery of something like Standing Female Figure, you get the sense of the kinetic energy trapped in the folds as in the ruffled surface of the sea. That's what I aspire to, as well, in the ruffled surfaces of my verses: energy, beauty, life force.
>
> 2014

Note how Mlinko's response needs neither characters nor stories to converge with the ancient past. This terracotta figurine served as a creative catalyst for her writing – and a fitting entry portal for our students. As Verity Platt points out, artefacts open up the past: 'although they lack voice, such objects nevertheless work to materialize thought: as "vibrant" components of antiquity, they still have the capacity to move and surprise, while inviting their viewers to think beyond the limits of the self' (2016: 77).

Small enough to be held in the hand, *Standing Female Figure* does not monumentalize the classical past – unlike our exhibit's photograph of the large caryatid figures from the Erechtheum on the Acropolis. (Caryatids are female statues which served as columns.) A quotidian object, this type of terracotta figurine served as an individual offering to the gods at domestic shrines and graves, as well as at temples and other public shrines. *Standing Female Figure* emphasizes drapery, in particular the play of folds in the crinkly chiton (and the even finer himation draped over it). Drapery folds became a major component of the classical aesthetic; for example, the Parthenon sculptures epitomize this interest in depicting fabric that both suggests the body beneath and yet also has volume of its own. The figurine in our exhibition resists being co-opted into a 'High Art' construction of the classical past. Because its head is no longer attached, the figurine also evokes the attraction of the fragment or relic for modernist artists – an aesthetic we discussed in class.

Figure 13.1 *Standing Female Figure* (draped female figurine, fifth century BC, Greece). Samuel P. Harn Museum of Art, University of Florida, Gainsville.

Entering the museum with our students also gave us the opportunity to discuss ancient versus modern practices for viewing artworks – especially those depicting deities. We had studied several ekphrastic poems in the classroom, including Charles-René Marie Leconte De Lisle's 'Venus de Milo', Emma Lazarus's 'Venus of the Louvre' and Ranier Maria Rilke's 'Archaic Torso of Apollo'. The reverence and delight people experience in the presence of such artworks may be spiritual, sensual, or aesthetic – or a combination of responses. If the ancients believed that divinity resided within a god's statue, later viewers may perceive a sublime aesthetic or the presence of an artist's genius. Leconte De Lisle addresses the *Venus de Milo* as 'Sacred marble' – a 'symbol of impassive bliss' that can inspire him as he pursues his Parnassian aesthetic. For Lazarus, viewing the same statue elicits tears 'for vanished Hellas and Hebraic pain' as she lays claim to the classical tradition as a Jewish-American woman. John Hollander points out that Lazarus 'addresses the Venus de Milo in its specific Parisian context' (1995: 176), marking the role of the Louvre itself in mediating her cross-cultural encounters with the ancient past. We discussed this poem and Amy Lowell's 'Venus Transiens' in our gallery talk 'Mighty Aphrodites', which brought the general public into our conversations about the artworks in our exhibition.

Classical Convergences: myth, poetry and art in conversation

Inviting our students to explore recurring mythological figures in this gallery, our *Classical Convergences* assignment had them compare two artworks and a poem that depicted either Aphrodite or Persephone. Students had to assess which representation proved most successful in reinventing the ancient figure for contemporary audiences, tracing specific ways the artists and poets translated key elements from the past. How did they create something new while retaining vital elements from the original? To what degree do these versions adhere to the mythic characters and storylines? What original elements had to be maintained for modern audiences to recognize the ancient source? Our students could see how translation inevitably involves omission. Some of them valued examples that veered wildly from classical precedents, claiming that these artworks and poems reflect a liberatory aesthetic. Others argued that such texts ultimately frustrated their readers and viewers. Working with a triptych steered students away from creating dualistic convergences that privileged text over image, or vice versa.

Sample convergence: Aphrodite

Modernist migrations of classical material offer important frameworks for considering the major figure in our museum gallery: Aphrodite. Traditionally, Greek female images were clothed. But Praxiteles broke with this tradition in his statue the *Aphrodite of Knidos* (fourth century BC) – the first large-scale female nude in Greek art. Because of the goddess's strong connection to sexuality as well as to love and beauty, Praxiteles's depiction was deemed acceptable; indeed, it became the prototype for all subsequent representations of Aphrodite. Her iconic pose (right hand over her genitals) reappears across art history. Visitors to our *Classical Convergences* exhibition could see how it inflects the stereograph *Venus Rising from the Sea*, Jiri Anderle's drawing *Mädchen und Tod* and Len Prince's photograph *Plate #76* from *Self-Possessed*. In our 'Mighty Aphrodites' gallery talk, we created a convergence with Prince's image and Lowell's poem 'Venus Transiens', bringing in perspectives from classical mythology and modernist ekphrasis.

Publishing poems with classical allusions was an act of rebellion for Lowell. While her brothers could study Greek and Latin and pursue higher education, she was trained to pursue proper ladyhood – the fitting 'curriculum' for a Boston debutante at that time. Fittingly, Lowell's Latinate title 'Venus Transiens' means more than its English descendant, *transient*; in addition to *crossing over* (which evokes translation), the word signifies *surpassing*. Reinventing Sandro Botticelli's famous painting *The Birth of Venus* (1485), Lowell's poem first appeared in *Poetry* magazine in 1915. The Renaissance painter augmented Aphrodite's pose as Praxiteles sculpted it; Botticelli's Venus covers herself with her hair as well as her hands. Lowell's classical modernism translates Botticelli's alterations into a love poem.

Addressing the beloved directly, the ungendered speaker of 'Venus Transiens' asks a rhetorical question that elevates her higher than Botticelli's serenely graceful goddess.

If the poem's beloved surpasses Aphrodite, then the poet crossing over artistic media may top Botticelli himself:

Tell me,
Was Venus more beautiful
Than you are,
When she topped
The crinkled waves,
Drifting shoreward
On the plaited shell?

The ekphrastic competition between painter and poet is on as Lowell borrows key details from her predecessor: his goddess floats on a pleated clamshell as white as her skin; the goddess is poised between sea and land. Lowell also embellishes Botticelli's painting, adding the strewn flowers the Zephyrs blow with their breath. (Appearing on the left side, they represent the West Wind propelling Aphrodite to shore.) Lowell's speaker asks if these 'painted rosebuds' can rival the poem's tribute in words: 'Was Botticelli's vision / Fairer than mine?' Lowell also alludes to the attendant on the painting's right side, waiting to cloak the goddess when she lands. Instead of fine fabric, the poem offers its beloved 'a gauze / Of misted silver': words to cover her 'too great loveliness – while allowing it to shine through. Melissa Bradshaw notes that Lowell's other love poems from this period share the theme of 'the beloved's blinding beauty, a brightness from which the narrator must seek protection' (2011: 120). Here the poet taps classical precedents for encountering divine loveliness. In addition, Lowell's image of *covering* may mask a taboo desire at the time of the poem's composition – one woman's love for another. Her artistic challenge to Botticelli invites us to see the smitten speaker as the poet herself. Thus 'Venus Transiens' aligns with the practice of 'feminist ekphrasis' that Loizeaux discusses, in which women writers recognize that 'the patterns of power and value implicit in a tradition of male artists and viewers can be exposed, used, resisted and rewritten' (2008: 81). Botticelli's Aphrodite casts her eyes slightly downward, enabling a voyeuristic gaze. But Lowell's figure faces her lover head-on as she moves ashore.

Len Prince's photograph *Plate #76* (from the series *Self-Possessed*, 2005) extends the signifying chain from Praxiteles and Botticelli, creating an Aphrodite that plays on pastoralism as well as the classical tradition. Part of a continuing collaboration with Jessie Mann,[1] this photographic incarnation holds its own in a consumer culture so saturated with the Botticelli Venus that we can buy its likeness on a shower curtain. Retaining the modest arm positions in *The Birth of Venus*, replicating the goddess's fabulous hair with a kitschy wig, Mann confronts the viewer with her 'by-now-familiar thousand-yard stare', to borrow Michael O'Sullivan's characterization (2007). Emerging from the shell of a mass-produced birdbath,[2] she transforms the rural motel courtyard with her extraordinary presence. McCusker sees Mann as 'an Amazonian Venus' because 'her commanding physicality foregrounds her earthly realm, complicating notions of the divine'. The bucolic goat in the background does not react, and the goddess herself appears

Figure 13.2 *Plate #76* from *Jessie Mann: Self-Possessed* (2005), photographed by Len Prince. Samuel P. Harn Museum of Art, University of Florida, Gainsville. © Len Prince.

unaffected by the incongruities. The image astonishes with its artful blend of homage and irony, the mythic and the mundane. Titled with only a plate number, the photograph prompts viewers to imagine their own contexts and titles, as Prince told us. Like Lowell's poem, Prince's photograph invites the audience to participate in the mythmaking process.

Modernism inflects photographic style in several images from the *Self-Possessed* series. Mann poses as Frida Kahlo for one shot, and Prince echoes photographs by Man Ray in others (for example, Mann poses as his Muse figure, Lee Miller). Like Surrealists Ray and Cecil Beaton, Prince often draws from cinema and fashion in creating his striking portraits of artists and celebrities. Famous women Prince has photographed include Deborah Harry, Kathleen Turner, Drew Barrymore and Penélope Cruz.

In *Self-Possessed*, Mann refashions her appearance in each photograph, assuming a range of guises that draw on historical persons and iconic images. In a recent interview for *Bleek Magazine*, Jessie Mann discusses how her extended collaboration with Prince pushes back against gendered conceptions of creativity, including the classical figure of the Muse:

That was one of the main topics I wanted to address with this project, this idea of the tragic muse, the idea that something is being taken from the subject, that the muse is at risk. And all of these conceptions we have about the role of the model, I think are simply because women are most often the subjects in art. It reflects a viewpoint where women are vulnerable, weak, and at risk of being exploited. Why is it so hard for people to conceive of the subject as a willing participant in the art making, as an involved and self-determining agent in the production of the image, or film, or painting, what have you?

Bubich 2016

These images go beyond simply talking back to the Muse. The Mann of *Self-Possessed* is Muse, model and artist simultaneously. She is composed, and she assumes control. The Mann–Prince collaboration disrupts gendered conceptions of artists possessing – or being possessed by – their Muses. Ultimately, *Plate 76* upends incarnations of creativity itself – a key theme in our course. Like the 'twists' of H.D.'s *Hermes of the Ways* and the 'crossing over and surpassing' of Amy Lowell's 'Venus Transiens', the disruptive nature of the Mann–Prince collaboration illustrates the complex and multivalent response of women to the classical tradition.

Migrations, translations, departures

Thus exploring mythology and literature in conjunction with contemporary artworks prompted our students to complicate their understanding of classical characters – and the myths and literary modes through which we traditionally encounter them. They learned that the ancient artefacts and classically inspired artworks were not obdurate objects, but catalysts for convergences. Michael Squire has described the transporting experience of the classical human body in art: 'Standing before us, objects appear as portals that fast-forward past into present: their 'Tardis' or 'Stargate' effect means that images collapse 'antiquity into modernity' in a way that words do not' (2001: xii). In our course, integrating artworks with mythology also drew our students' attention to the fact that women's position in the classical tradition was more complicated than they initially thought. Writing about these objects in conjunction with the literature revealed the writerly nature of reception and translation.

Even the women in epic prove less fixed than we may have imagined they were. Wilson has drawn our attention to the impact that women translators are having on reception, including the first English translation of the *Iliad* by a woman (Caroline Alexander). For Wilson, this outlier position offers advantages: 'The inability to take classical texts for granted is a great gift that some female translators are able to use to shift the canon to a different and unexpected place' (2017). Women artists and writers who rework classical sources can also help us render iconic characters such as Helen and Penelope into more dynamic figures – even prompting us to look back at the ancient originals with new eyes. For example, Homer's *Odyssey* lends some complexity – even volition – to these iconic women. Consider Helen's ability to mimic the voices of the Greek soldiers' wives when she called out to them in their hiding place inside the Trojan horse (Hom. *Od* 4.307–24). She was right about the horse; she was more than her beauty. Recall that Penelope, hailed as a model wife, was cunning; she did more than unravel her daily weaving to fend off suitors. Refusing to take Odysseus at his word, she tests him to verify his identity before embracing him at last (Hom. *Od.* 23.202–32). Selective cultural memory plays a role in translation, as certain parts (and versions) are emphasized or de-emphasized across time. These gaps and inconsistencies open spaces for future writers to fill in.

H.D. was well aware of this process, and her work displays the many possibilities inherent in the Latin word *translatio*. Her late modernist epic *Helen in Egypt* enacts a recovery through reinvention, migrating the classical tradition to a different part of the Mediterranean. She launches the book-length poem by opening up the idea of translation – stressing the textual, geographic and temporal relocations in the process. Invoking her classical predecessor Stesichorus, she situates her most ambitious epic as an act of modernist translation. The framing speaker begins the text by *removing* Helen – and her myth – from their accustomed pages and places: 'According to the *Pallinode*, Helen was never in Troy. She had been transposed or translated from Greece into Egypt' ([1961] 1974: vii). H.D. knew that creativity plays a vital role in translation, which was never a one-way street. Indeed, translation can disrupt older models of cultural literacy and linear transmission. Like transposition in music, the convergent dynamics of adapting classical materials dislocates an older text to another key, another mode, another dimension.

We 'translated' modernism's classical engagement for the postmillennial academy, where students may no longer have a firm footing in either modernist or classical texts. Inheriting postmodern critical approaches and a more diverse canon, these students often discount or even reject the classical tradition as a patriarchal, Eurocentric master narrative – and modernism as *passé*, elitist aesthetic movement. Yet these same students consume a wide spectrum of popular culture shaped by classical motifs, from the Percy Jackson and the Olympians book series to the *Dota 2* online game and the new *Wonder Woman* film. Our course helped deepen our students' appreciation of both the classical tradition and classical modernisms. As teachers in the twenty-first century, we should tap this potentially renewing quality of modernist migrations as we chart new interdisciplinary approaches for a more visually literate generation.

AFTERWORD: MODERNISM GOING FORWARD

J. Alison Rosenblitt

In the rapidly expanding field of classical reception, the world of modernism has received less attention than the world of postmodernist and contemporary writing, art, film and theatre. To be sure, a number of scholars have contributed significant work in the area of modernism and classical reception; however, those of us who work on modernism are numerically far exceeded by our colleagues in postmodern and contemporary areas of study. On a rough count of articles in the flagship *Classical Receptions Journal*, I make out the ratio of articles on postmodern or contemporary topics as against modernist topics higher than 4:1.

A volume such as this one aims primarily to enrich the study of classical reception and modernism in its own right. However, the opportunity to pull threads together in an afterword offers also an opportunity to reach out to the significantly larger number of students and scholars within the classical reception community who work in postmodern and contemporary fields.

One of the contributors to our present volume, Leah Flack, has recently published elsewhere (Flack 2016) about Seamus Heaney's hunt through 'multiple modernisms' (36) in his attempts to negotiate past, present and future, literary tradition and memory in his own poetry. She examines changes in his work as he moved the weight of his modernist engagement away from Eliot and Anglo-American modernism and towards the Russian modernist Osip Mandelstam. Flack's discussion of Heaney highlights ways in which, for Heaney, modernism was still that which must be negotiated with and against.

This same principle holds true for many writers up to and including the present day. Later writers may not embrace an Eliotic version of 'tradition', but their negotiation with modernism necessarily speaks to the ways in which their texts position themselves in relation to earlier texts – not only modernist texts but also other texts, including classical texts, to which modernists themselves respond. Modernism foregrounded claims about tradition and literary alignment. Writers who engage modernism therefore also engage this aspect of modernist claims and expectations. In other words, when writers position themselves vis-à-vis modernism, they are also positioning themselves as receivers, not only because they are 'receiving' modernism but also because the interaction with modernism brings an interaction with its attitudes towards tradition, continuity, rupture and reception. The principle can also operate *vice versa*: a contemporary writer's self-positioning as a receiver of other texts, including classical texts, may shape a self-positioning with respect to modernism. Tessa Roynon makes such a case in her work on Toni Morrison: 'in the readings of her [Morrison's] engagements with the ancient world that follow, I aim to shed new light on her interventions in modernist, postmodernist and feminist aesthetics' (Roynon 2013: 4).[1] For the postmodern and contemporary writers whom I touch upon, however briefly, in this Afterword – Seamus Heaney and Toni Morrison, mentioned just now, and Marlon James, Derek Walcott, Salman Rushdie, Bernard O'Donoghue, Philip Schultz, Jill Bialosky and Vikram Seth (below) – their engagements with classicism and with modernism each activate and implicate the other.

The contributions collected in this volume, with their focus on translation, may justifiably aspire to a particular usefulness in generating a fuller appreciation of the modernist context for work on postmodern and contemporary classical reception. Indeed, this focus on translation is apposite for two reasons: both because – as Steven Yao has shown (2002b) – translation played an important role in modernist self-fashioning and also because translation is an especially direct form of contact with other texts and therefore offers a clear vantage point from which to approach questions of literary 'tradition' and literary self-positioning.[2]

Eliot's 'Tradition and the Individual Talent' (1919), which became the most influential modernist construction of the idea of literary tradition, argues that tradition has an innate coherence. This 'simultaneous order' in which no writer 'has his complete meaning alone' (Eliot [1920] 1997: 41) goes hand in hand with – indeed, facilitates – a modernist fascination with fragmentation, since Eliot's posited simultaneity of the tradition encourages the reading of fragmented interactions with other texts from a position of maximum sensitivity to their intertextual resonances: that is to say, a rich intertextuality flourishes in the belief that, to borrow from Latham and Rogers, a fragment can point within a textual tradition which is 'there' to be activated (Latham and Rogers 2015: 5–6). That fragmented intertextual approach is most famously exemplified and iconicized by the allusive style of *The Waste Land* and its famous line, 'These fragments I have shored against my ruins'.[3] More generally, this 'tension between unity and fragmentation' has been considered 'essential' to the emergence and self-definitions of modernism (Latham and Rogers 2015: 5). Or, as Ioannidou puts it (2017: 132): 'The notion of fragmentation is constitutive of modernity in a twofold way: on the one hand, fragmentation lies at the core of the modern experience, while, on the other hand, modernity is defined through its aspiration to reconstitute this experience in its imagined totality.'

The role of fragmentation in modernist translations from the classics is a theme which emerges strongly from this present volume. H.D. fragments Euripides in translations which are discussed in this volume by Westover, Theis and Hickman and Kozak; fragmentation in H.D.'s *Helen in Egypt* arises in Fyta's contribution. Pound fragments translation of a Homeric passage into his own *Cantos* in such an occlusive mode that it can still prompt such productive debate as generated here between Varsos and Cè, who argue respectively that Canto I shows an exceptional intimacy with the original Homeric text and that it deliberately suppresses the Homeric text in favour of the mediating Latin text of Andreas Divus. Meanwhile, Flack's discussion of *The Waste Land* foregrounds a third mode of modernist fragmentation: that is, the fragmentation of textual relationships engineered by Eliot's and Pound's editorial work on the poem's drafts, which buried at least some of the poem's own formative layers.

I will return to the theme of fragmentation and unity in a moment in order to consider the significance of this particular modernist mode of reception for postmodern and contemporary work. It is, however, far from the only point of connection between modernism and later writing which this volume might illuminate. Vandiver's contribution on the Poets' Translation Series highlights the controversy in the early modernist period over the relative priority of poetics versus scholarship in the work of translation. The most prominent recent effort to produce an anglophone volume of Horace rendered by the collected labours of a number of poets (McClatchy 2002) prompted a comparable debate about what level of classical learning and what familiarity with classical literature or culture might be necessary or desirable in a translator of Horace (see Talbot 2003). Another theme emerging from this volume is investigation of why a translator turns to a given text. This question is raised by several of the contributions here, including Baker on the larger political purposes for which Yeats turned to Sophocles, Somers on how it is that Eliot came to imagine an Aristophanic voice for himself, or Hickman and Kozak on the feminist thinking which governed H.D.'s selection of one play rather than another from within the corpus of Euripides and also guided her process of fragmenting those plays through selective translation of the passages which served her vision. The often self-reflective and consciously politicized nature of current receptions of classical material underlines the ongoing relevance of such questions.

Several of our contributors allude to later writers, and indeed Bryant and Eaverly directly place modernism in dialogue with postmodern and contemporary culture. Bryant and Eaverly, writing from the perspective of pedagogy in higher education, observe that their students often bring an antipathy to modernism and regard its engagement with the classics as inherently patriarchal and Eurocentric. They respond by foregrounding H.D.'s queer, female receptions of the classics. This present volume's rich seam of work on H.D. – with pieces by Fyta, Westover, Theis, and Hickman and Kozak, as well as the reading of 'Hermes of the Ways' in Bryant and Eaverly – will support the blossoming of interest in more recent feminist and queer classical receptions. To the feminist perspective afforded by the contributions on H.D., Jessop adds a consideration of the feminism of Laura Riding. Jessop refers to Riding's 'Lilithian prototype of rebellion and independence', by which she means a turn to the figure of Lilith, the non-canonical wife of Adam, as a term in articulating a challenge to dominant versions of classicism and to dominant constructs of the Western historical narrative. This idea of Lilithian rebellion, which also appears in H.D.'s *Trilogy* (*The Flowering of the Rod*: 33; 1973: 157.1–2), recurs more recently in the work of Marlon James, who has emerged as a major cultural voice over the last few years, and who draws on the figure of Lilith – the name he gives to his central character – in his exploration of rebellion, brutality and classicism in *The Book of Night Women* (2009).

Flack's contribution to this volume addresses another potentially off-putting aspect of high modernism: that is, its seeming delight in the exclusionary deployment of knowledge – including knowledge of the classical tradition and languages – as a barrier against the 'wrong' sort of reader. Flack argues for a version of modernism that is less out of step with later ideals, suggesting that Eliot and Joyce problematize knowledge and the desire for knowledge in ways that scholars have not always recognized. Flack picks up Lawrence Rainey's observation (2006: 75) that the epigraph to *The Waste Land* itself points to a text which ironizes the deployment of knowledge: Trimalchio (in Petronius's *Satyricon*) is giving a garbled version of stories from Greek literature in an attempt to show off his learning. This motif of garbled knowledge is another example of a thread which runs through modernism, postmodernism and contemporary writing. The twists in certain of Pound's translations and quotations, which are explored by Dunton and Tryphonopoulos in this volume, may function partly (as Dunton and Tryphonopoulos admit) to test the reader. On the other hand, misattributions and misquotations from the Latin are used by Ford Madox Ford – as David Scourfield (forthcoming, 2018) explores – perhaps more as a process of the text probing its own characters than testing its readers. Both continuity with and contrast to modernist uses of garbled knowledge can be seen in Derek Walcott's use of misattribution to issue a contemporary, postcolonial challenge. In 'Santa Cruz I' (Doig and Walcott 2016: 53), it is Caesar (not Cato the Elder) who voices the dictum *Delenda est Carthago* ('Carthage must be destroyed'). The transposition of the quotation turns the political position of one particular Roman during particular historical circumstances into a distillation of the destructive impulse of Roman power in the out-of-context voice of its most famous conqueror.[4]

Knowledge which is problematized or distorted allusions to classical texts which are misattributed or misquoted, and ironies, occlusions, and twistings of all sorts characterize many modernist texts and their evasion of a straightforward relationship to antiquity and to classical texts. The more direct mode which characterizes some Decadent and fin-de-siècle receptions of the classics – for example, the way that Sapphic material, imagery and themes are re-imagined in a Sapphic mode and even Sapphic metre in some of Swinburne's poetry – could be contrasted with the questions which Somers encourages us to ask about Eliot's *Sweeney Agonistes*, subtitled 'Fragments of an Aristophanic Melodrama'.[5] Somers' well formulated questions start with 'what is an "Aristophanic melodrama"' (as opposed to the expected term, 'Aristophanic comedy') and thus what exactly is the connection between the plot or structure of Eliot's play and an Aristophanic mode?

Eliot's subtitle, 'Fragments of an Aristophanic Melodrama', also returns us to the theme of fragmentation, together with its implicated counterpart: tradition as the presence of an organic whole. The texts which comprise 'tradition' in a modernist sense thus exercise a presence and weight which may be felt in connection with any new text. In practice, for many modernists, this most especially means the presence and weight of Dante, who – as Cè observes in passing in this volume – has 'conceptual import' even when 'textually . . . excluded'.

The promotion of Dante's *Divina Commedia* into a linchpin of modernist ideas of the literary tradition has itself had a particular role to play in the impact of modernist modes of reception on subsequent receptions of classical epic, of tropes of the classical underworld and (one might even say) simply of the classics full stop. In particular, Derek Walcott's *Omeros* (1990) – a touchpoint for contemporary classical reception – negotiates classical, Dantean and modernist relationships. Walcott works with Homeric material, adopting a loose version of Dante's *terza rima*, and explores issues of centrality and 'hybridity' partly by signalling his willingness to take on the canonical modernists: Joyce appears fleetingly as a character (1990: 201; XXXIX.3), and the book's final chapter refers to the death of Achille (at some point beyond the book's narrative present) as a pointedly

Eliotic 'death by water'.[6] Moreover, while Dante's presence itself continues to infuse later receptions of the classics, that mode of reception – whereby Dante hovers conceptually over other engagements with the classics – has itself been inherited from the modernists, with Joyce now serving in the place of Dante. What Cè says of Dante could be repeated verbatim in description of later writers and Joyce: Joyce is 'conceptually present' even when 'textually excluded' – though, indeed, Joyce is certainly often textually present. Eliot, of course, both recognized and promoted the notion that Joyce defined a new mode of relationship to classical literature and, more specifically, to ancient myth (see Nikopoulos 2016). Joyce's standing as a necessary term entwined with classical receptions appears not only in Walcott, but also, for example, in Siddiqui's assessment of classical metamorphosis in Salman Rushdie's *The Satanic Verses*, where Siddiqui argues that the postcolonial hybridity of Rushdie's novel activates overlapping relationships with Joyce, Ovid and Apuleius.[7]

A few more examples of classical reception in three living poets – Bernard O'Donoghue, Philip Schultz and Jill Bialosky – will show further how contemporary modes of classical reception still respond to the presence of Dante as well as to fragmented modes of modernist receptions, sometimes in connection with the eclecticism which is often said to characterize postmodernism.

In O'Donoghue, we find a poet who has engaged both Dante and Virgil throughout his poetic career and who has translated passages from both the *Divina Commedia* and the *Aeneid*.[8] O'Donoghue's engagements with Virgil – including 'Ter Conatus', the poem which closes *Here Nor There* (1999), and two poems, 'Euryalus' and 'Menoetes', from his most recent volume, *The Seasons of Cullen Church* (2016) – focus notably on the Virgilian underworld and on Virgilian deaths. O'Donoghue's Virgil is a Virgil found through Dante: a poet of death and the underworld – rather than, say, a poet of empire or any of the many other Virgils found by different writers and different eras.[9] For O'Donoghue, as for the modernists, Dante retains a 'conceptual import' regardless of whether the translations of Virgil signal him directly.

Schultz's reception of the classical world in his verse novel *The Wherewithal* (2014) also centres on the underworld. *The Wherewithal* explores the past and the narrative present (in 1968) of a Polish-American character named Henryk Stanislaw Wyrzykowski or Wyrzykowki (he varies his name to avoid the draft). Henryk works as 'head clerk of closed files' in the basement of an administrative building of the California Department of Social Services. There he becomes

> guardian of nobody,
> solicitor of nothing,
> unnatural ferryman lugging a cargo
> of dissolute souls
> from one hostile shore to another
> for no reason other than
> to sustain myself to the next paycheck

Schultz 2014: 7–8

Henryk's basement existence is figured with layers both of Dante and of the classical underworld. Schultz mixes allusions to Dante's Hell, Purgatory and Paradise, and to the classical underworld (including the river Styx), as well as prefacing each of his chapters with a reproduction from Giovanni Battista Piranesi's etchings of a vast prison-world. Schultz's Henryk is enmeshed among the many threads of his life: the translation he is making of his mother's diary, which tells of the atrocities committed in Poland against the Jews and her efforts to save seven Jews hidden in her barn; his own responsibility for an incident which killed his childhood friend; his love affair with the wife of his professor; his attempts to find a job out in California; the Zodiac killings; the draft for the Vietnam war; his job as head clerk of closed files; and his relationship with one of his co-workers, who eventually moves in with him and then leaves him. This enmeshment is aptly reflected in the basement underworld in which references to Dante, to the classical underworld, and to Piranesi forge an imagery not susceptible to separation. Schultz's text jumps abruptly among the threads and time periods of his story, rendering the text and Henryk's life both fragmented and also simultaneous. Schultz's exploration of a post-Holocaust world thus invokes modernism's own understanding of its relationship to fragmentation and order as a response to the chaos of history and the trauma of the Great War (Sherry 2003; Latham and Rogers 2015; Nikopolous 2016).

Finally, in Jill Bialosky's *Subterranean* (2001), Dante acts as a presence which demands acknowledgement even when he is almost intrusive to the collection's initial literary relationships. Bialosky's themes are not obviously Dantean. She draws on the myth of the rape of Persephone and the loss experienced by Demeter as her collection of poems traces the sexual awakening of adolescence, the anticipation of motherhood, the loss of one child and the birth of another. *Subterranean* signals its classical interactions with prefacing quotes taken from Ovid's *Metamorphoses* and from the Homeric Hymn to Demeter. But Dante must still be reckoned with, most explicitly in the poem 'The Circles, the Rings', though there may be hints elsewhere (for instance, in 'the depressed, / twisted trees' of 'The Adolescent Suicide'). S. Connolly, in a review of *Subterranean*, also observes that the final poem of the collection 'ends with a movement upwards, away from the underworld, and like Dante at the close of "Paradiso," facing the stars' (Connolly 2002: 161). Connolly considers 'The Circles, the Rings' one of the stronger poems in the collection, partly because its relationship to Dante 'confound[s] rather than adhere[s] to mythic expectation' (161): an inescapable pressure of Dante for a contemporary receiver of the classics can also become a pressure productive of eclecticism and surprise.

Further thought about the relationship between modernist fragmented modes of classical reception and postmodern eclecticism would have bearing on debates which remain prominent within classical reception studies over the proper remit of the field. In illustration of this, I take one final example: Vikram Seth's verse-novel *The Golden Gate* (1986).[10] In Chapter 1 of *The Golden Gate*, a smattering of classical references, including the classical tag *Eheu fugaces . . .* (1.9, with a reference two lines later to 'siren screams'), situate *The Golden Gate* in dialogue with a *carpe diem* tradition. Seth's occasional allusions to classical texts, images and ideas (which might first of all be considered in connection with *Eugene Onegin* and the classics: see 5.5) also reflect *The Golden Gate*'s self-positioning with respect to modernism, since Chapter 1 could be read as engaging with early Eliot with its focus on economic or work life, its restaurant and café settings, its dry angst and its stifled sexual desire. This classical and modernist positioning is lightly inscribed and, as the book progresses, these engagements recede – although they are mirrored across the book in the character of Janet Hayakawa, a Japanese-American sculptor. Janet's sculptural subjects, which seem pointedly eclectic, include '*Study of Young Man Caught in Eagle's Claws*' (1.13, suggestive of Ganymede). The reviews of Janet's sculptural exhibit are couched in terms which seem to engage modernist ideas of simple and clean forms: her sculpture is first derided for its '*terse aridity*' and then hypocritically praised for its '*tense fluidity / A classic leanness*' (12.19, 13.29). Thus, both the tone of Chapter 1 and the character of Janet show that *The Golden Gate* treats its classical and modernist engagements as intertwined.

The eclecticism of *The Golden Gate* is highlighted on the second page of the main text (1.3) in an introductory sketch of the novel's main character, John, in lines which can easily be read as also bearing a meta-textual import: 'likes to read / Eclectically from Mann to Bede. / (A surrogate, some say, for thinking)'. The classical engagement of *The Golden Gate* is eclectic and not sustained; but it is nonetheless meaningful and challenging. Charles Martindale calls for classical reception studies to confine its enquiries to texts which 'initiate us into a serious or profound dialogue with antiquity', as opposed to superficial engagements with the classical past: 'superficial reception studies do not generate dialogue, do not tell us about the classical (Martindale 2013: 176, 177)'.[11] However, postmodern eclecticism will – at least as it appears in some texts – resist a binary distinction between 'serious and profound dialogue' and superficiality. Indeed, that binary distinction might mislead us into a scholarly hostility which reads eclecticism as a 'surrogate ... for thinking.' Appreciating postmodern and contemporary eclectic modes of reception as part of a response to modernist fragmented modes of reception is a more fruitful road, and one to which I believe this present volume substantially contributes.

This volume's work on modernism and classical reception embraces a move towards plurality – towards multiple modernisms – which can be observed more generally within the field of modernist studies. We recognize the power wielded during the modernist era by the traditionally 'major' modernists and by their literary and critical output: modernism was highly conscious of its own hierarchies. At the same time, we also recognize diversity within the modernist world, and we look to explore spaces – including queer and female spaces – which generated modernisms other than the modernisms of Eliot or Joyce. This approach to modernism multiplies the threads which can be taken forward and multiplies the modernist frames which may be of use to those who work on later receptions of the classics. Moreover, fragmented modernist modes of reception can be approached with renewed sympathy when they do not only mean the rigid hand of Eliot – influential though he is in generating an aesthetic of fragmentation and articulating a critical position which embeds it – but also H.D. and other diverse modernist voices. In sum, the work done by this volume in unfolding modernist relationships to the classics and to translation from classical literature may serve to open up modernist modes of reception to scholars of postmodernism – a move from which those of us in modernist studies will equally benefit. To see what later writers find in modernism makes us better readers of the modernists themselves: for those of us who work in reception, that is, after all, rather the point.

NOTES

INTRODUCTION

1. On the history of classical reception studies, emergent in the early 1990s, see Martindale (2006: 1–13) and a special issue of the *Classical Receptions Journal* (5.2, 2013). For Anglo-American modernism as defined here, see Latham and Rogers (2015) and Levenson (1999).

2. For a recent project addressing this comparative gap, see Brill's *Companion to the Reception of Classics in International Modernism and the Avant-Garde*: while our volume accents Anglo-American modernist literature, Brill's addresses 'international modernism' more generally. In our Afterword, Rosenblitt notes the under-representation of modernism in classical reception studies on twentieth century work: 'in the . . . *Classical Receptions Journal* . . . the ratio of articles on postmodern or contemporary topics as against modernist topics [is] higher than 4:1'. More broadly, of some 170 articles in the *CRJ* between the journal's inception in 2009 and 2018, only three feature early twentieth-century Anglo-American modernists foregrounded in this volume.

3. See Hooley (1988: 16–20).

4. See Adler (2016: 3; Chapter 2).

5. Like Gregory and Collecott, our volume foregrounds modernist work responsive to Ancient Greek literature, but the 1990s also saw publication on modernism and Latin literature such as Hooley's *The Classics in Paraphrase* (1988) and Ziolkowski's *Virgil and the Moderns* (1993). Ziolkowski has followed with work on Ovid and the moderns (2004).

6. See Hooley (1988: 14), for an encapsulation of the modernists' engagements with classical literature.

7. See Sullivan (1964: 5–6): in response to *Homage to Sextus Propertius* in 1919, W.G. Hale of the University of Chicago accused Pound of 'pervert[ing] the flavor of a consciously artistic, almost academic, original', concluding, 'If Mr. Pound were a professor of Latin, there would be nothing left for him but suicide.' For 'irreverence' informing Pound's and other modernists' reception of the classics, see Gillespie (2011: 16).

8. Praising H.D. for 'interpretive genius' for her *Choruses from the Iphigenia in Aulis*, classicist J.W. Mackail also suggested that 'Whether from perversity or . . . some defect of scholarship', H.D. 'sometimes quite misinterprets the original, or reads into it something quite illegitimate' (1916: 2010).

9. See Dendinger (1981).

10. See Hulme (1924, 'Romanticism and Classicism': 73–140).

11. Rich (1972: 18).

12. For an excellent theoretical meditation on translation understood in a capacious sense akin to those of the modernists, through diverse metaphors, see Reynolds (2011).

13. Hooley (1988) notes that 'for the sheer number and stylistic variety of its classical translations, the first half of [the twentieth] century ranks with the Renaissance and the age of Pope' (18). Hooley likewise accents 'translation', construed in a wide sense, as an activity epitomizing modernist reception of classical material.

14. On translation as a favoured, capaciously used term in the modernist lexicon, see Pound on his 'The Seafarer' (1911), whose non-traditional rendering of the Anglo-Saxon poem he framed as 'A Translation' and insisted on calling 'as nearly literal . . . as any translation can be' (quoted in Ruthven 1969: 213). His *Cathay* (1915) was likewise presented as 'Translations . . . from the Chinese'. H.D.'s *Choruses from the Iphigenia in Aulis and the Hippolytus of Euripides* (1919) was subtitled as 'translations by H.D.'. Even H.D.'s first published Imagist verse was introduced in *Poetry* as 'Verses, Translations, and Reflections, from "The Anthology"'.

1 'SEEKING BURIED BEAUTY': THE POETS' TRANSLATION SERIES

1. Two copies of the prospectus survive as enclosures in an unpublished letter from Richard Aldington to Amy Lowell, June 9, 1919; MS Lowell 19 (9), folder 5, letter 77; Houghton Library, Harvard University. The prospectus went out in the 3 July 1919 issue of *The Egoist*.

2. For the importance of translation in the formative stages of H.D.'s and Aldington's work, see also Zilboorg (1991b), especially her illuminating reading of H.D.'s 'Heliodora' as reflecting the couple's early collaborative translational work (134–6). On the PTS, see also Carr (2009: 794–6).

3. Aldington uses the term 'literary-literal' again, in the inverted form 'literal-literary', in a letter of 27 November 1920 to the editor of *The Nation*, defending Storer's translation of Asklepiades, where he identifies it as 'the best modern practice [,] . . . that of France' (Aldington 1920b).

4. Bryher Papers, General Collection, Beinecke Rare Book and Manuscript Library, Yale University; Box 1, Folder 23; partially quoted in Zilboorg (2003: 123 n. 1).

5. In fact, none of Bryher's translations from Greek appeared in the PTS. On Shorter, see Zilboorg (1989).

6. For an account of the different translators' connections with Aldington and H.D., see Zilboorg (1991a); Carr (2009: 794–5).

7. 'H.D.'s knowledge of Greek remains a subject of considerable scholarly debate' (Yao 2002b: 12). Scholars have tended to assume, incorrectly, that Aldington was fully competent in Latin and Greek; see, e.g., Kittredge (1976: 17–21, 33–4). For Aldington's background and schooling, see Whelpton (2014: 41–3); Carr (2009: 409–17).

8. While assuming that Aldington's and H.D.'s novels are straightforwardly autobiographical is fraught with danger, so much of 'Julia's' description of her early life with 'Rafe' parallels H.D.'s experience with Aldington that this comment seems likely to reflect fact.

9. Jacobs' full edition of the Anthology is thirteen volumes; Zilboorg surmises that Aldington here refers to a 'one-volume edition of selections with literal translations which appeared in 1826' (1991b: 128 n. 8).

10. Whitall's account must be the ultimate source of Pondrom's assertion that Aldington actually translated Leonidas, with assistance from Whitall and H.D. (2012: 40). Pondrom cites Zilboorg, who writes, 'Aldington shared with Whitall the plan for the Poets' Translation Series in its earliest stages, and both Whitall and H.D. helped him to translate *The Poems of Leonidas of Tarentum*' (2003: 76 n. 11). The likeliest explanation is that Zilboorg wrote 'Whitall' here by mistake for 'Aldington', and the 'him' should refer to Whitall: 'both **Aldington** and H.D. helped him [Whitall] to translate . . .'. Certainly there is no other indication anywhere that Aldington 'ghosted' Leonidas for Whitall.

11. On the distinction between 'sense' and 'meaning', see Bajaj (2009: 206, 224).

12. H.D. sent her translation of the *Hippolytus* choruses to Aldington in early December 1918 (Zilboorg 2003: 146–7), so she had clearly begun work on them long before Aldington broached the idea of renewing the PTS. One suspects that she had little interest in working closely with Aldington on the second series and simply allowed him to use work she had already completed.

13. Whelpton refers to his 'obsessive plans for the P.T.S.' (2014: 200).

14. Undoubtedly the same as the *Rustic Letters* advertised in 1916. The usual English title of this work is *Letters of Farmers*.

15. The confident listing of the Columella, Claudian, Aelian and Musaeus volumes as 'in preparation' has misled even very careful scholars into assuming these translations actually appeared; see, e.g., Gates (1992: 19 n. 4); Yao (2002b: 4, 249 n. 9).

16. Aldington alerted Flint to the existence of de Mirmont's 'magnificent variorum edition' in a letter of 14 September 1915. He gave Flint a copy of Stoer's 1608 'pocket' edition of Ausonius but advised him to consult de Mirmont in the British Museum as well (Gates 1992: 18).

17. Gregory says that Mackail was H.D.'s 'bible for the Greek text ... of poems within the Greek Anthology' (1997: 169); see also Brinkman and Brinkman (2016: 44–5). Nisbet sees Mackail's book as 'perhaps the key text' of Imagism as a movement (2013: 285).

18. Aldington derives ἀγόνας from ἄγονος, *agonos*, sterile, rather than taking the word as the Aeolic form of ἀγανός, *aganos*, 'gentle'. For an explanation of Aldington's idiosyncratic use of 'sterile' to mean 'pure', see Zilboorg (2003: 103 n. 8).

19. Aldington's Anyte translation uses very short paragraphs, often only two lines, but these do not correspond with either line or couplet breaks in the Greek original.

20. This may have been in response to a very negative review in *The New Age*, which sneered at Storer's lines: 'To turn Sappho's precise forms into Imagist *vers libres* shows little metrical tact, even if the result were rhythmically beautiful, which to our ears it is not' ('Review' 1915). Whether Storer considered his lines to be *vers libre* or not is unclear.

21. On this, see Vandiver (forthcoming).

22. It is noteworthy that, although the prospectus for the first series says that it will include translations of prose works, in fact both sets of the PTS translated only poetry.

23. The bibliography on Murray is substantial; Morwood (2007) is one starting point. Eliot ([1918] 1932) was quite atypical at the time in its criticism of Murray's translations.

24. See Yao (2002a: 99).

25. Hickman comments that this introduction does not sound like H.D., who admired Murray's work, and suggests that Aldington may have been the author (personal communications, 4 and 19 August 2016). In any case, H.D. was apparently willing to let the implied barb against Murray be printed in her name.

26. H.D.'s interest in Euripides was crucial to her work from the earliest stages; Gregory (1997: 140–7); Yao (2002a: 82–100). It seems plausible that she was not interested in turning aside from her ongoing work on Euripides to translate a less-known, more self-contained author for the PTS. Zilboorg's suggestion that the first PTS was 'designed at least in part to showcase the third number' (H.D.'s *Iphigeneia* choruses) seems unlikely, given the overall statement of purpose for the series. It is particularly striking that it was Aldington, not H.D., who translated Anyte, since H.D.'s 'Hermes of the Ways' incorporates and expands on Anyte's poem that Aldington translates under that same title; see Gregory (1997: 169); Babcock (1995: 203–6); Yao (2002a: 89–92). (H.D.'s 'Hermes of the Ways' incorporates elements from several poems in Mackail's edition of the *Anthology*, including one anonymous poem to which Mackail gave the title 'Hermes of the Ways'; Babcock 1995: 206.) Although H.D.'s first contributions to *Poetry*

(January 1913) were printed under the overall title 'Verses, Translations, and Reflections from the "Anthology"', she never thereafter referred to any of her poems as 'translations' or even 'versions' of poets from the Anthology nor did she ever undertake a complete translation of any lyric poet. Babcock suggests the title may have been added to the poems by Harriet Monroe, who also 'added a note to H.D.'s poems insisting that they were not to be considered translations' (1995: 203). Gregory agrees that the title 'was probably … assigned … by Pound or Harriet Monroe' (1997: 276 n. 17). See also Varney (2010b).

27. E.g. Wescott (1921). Eliot's praise for the PTS is qualified, and one suspects exists primarily to contrast with his dislike of Murray (Eliot 1916; Eliot [1918] 1932: 50).

28. Unpublished letter, 22 June 1916; Amy Lowell Correspondence, 1883–1927 (MS Lowell 19-19.4), Houghton Library, Harvard University. Aldington also wrote to Lowell in 1919 that 'people admit our translations are well done' (Gates 1992: 46). F.S. Flint presented the review as wholly positive in a 29 January 1917, letter to J. C. Squire; Copp (2009: 117).

29. Many modern H.D. scholars still imply that Mackail's review offered unqualified praise; e.g. Carr (2009: 796); Gregory (1997: 25, 261 n. 25); Pondrum (1969: 570, 2012: 40).

30. Aldington mentions in a letter to Charles Bubb, dated 8 February 1918, that he used Preisendanz's 1912 Teubner edition (Keller 1988: 43). This small volume would be easily portable.

31. The previous edition of this collection, Aldington (1921), leaves the errors uncorrected.

32. For a different view of Aldington's attitude to his audience, see Rohrbach (1996: 187–8).

33. The *locus classicus* for such criticism of Pound's 'Homage' is Hale (1919). Ironically, Aldington makes an error of his own in his correction of Pound's rendering of *nocte canes* as 'night dogs'; the words mean 'thou singest by night', Aldington says (1941: 138). But the tense of *canes* is future, not present.

34. For a summary of Pound's disavowal of the term 'translation' for his Propertius, see Yao (2002b: 57–59).

2 OUT OF HOMER: GREEK IN POUND'S *CANTOS*

1. My thanks to Brian Neville, friend and colleague, with whom I have closely read and discussed my text.

2. Apart from numerous specialized studies on Pound's relations to specific languages (especially Latin and Chinese) there are a number of works of a more general scope that have convincingly argued for the poetic significance of Pound's translation strategies. Kenner (1971) is paramount in many respects, and puts systematic emphasis on the role of Greek in Pound's poetry. Apter (1984) methodically defines the distinctness of Pound's translation principles. Xie (1999) provides a thorough overview insisting on the literary and conceptual creativity of Pound's translations; Pym (1995) makes an analogous point from the perspective of translation theory; Venuti (1995: 187–205) examines more critically the dialectics between foreignizing and domesticating effects in Pound's case; Yao (2002b) projects modernist translation strategies onto various other fields of modernist discourse.

3. The suggestion refers, specifically, to Aeschylus but it is part of a broader discussion as indicated by the exact title of the essay, 'Translators of Greek: Early Translators of Homer', first published in 1920 but composed of a number of earlier essays.

4. My approach also bears on Pound's poetic work with other ancient languages, especially with Chinese in *Cathay* or in the *Cantos*, which cannot be considered here.

5. Affinities between Pound and Benjamin have been widely noted, starting with Steiner, who states that Benjamin's work is 'very obviously akin to the collage and montage-aesthetic in the poetry of Ezra Pound and T.S. Eliot and in the prose of Joyce' (1998: 21–2). Pérez-Villalon (2003) and Hatlen (2003) examine these relations mostly on a general level of cultural history including the role of translation therein. Rabaté (2016) offers analogous passing remarks. Focusing on more concrete aspects of how translation works with respect to the question of meaning, I will mainly be discussing Benjamin's *The Task of the Translator* (1968a), first published in 1923. I will also refer to a shorter essay entitled *On the Mimetic Faculty* (Benjamin 1986), composed some ten years later and published only posthumously.

6. See, for example, his emphatic 'Damn ideas anyhow. An idea in only an imperfect induction from fact', in his essay on the translators of Homer (Pound 1954a: 267).

7. In a different context, Fenollosa's configuration of the Chinese ideogram, which had a determinant influence on Pound's conception of the linguistic sign, also implies considerable tension between precise contours and sweeping movement. Nature, for instance, is seen as 'a vast storehouse of forces' in which relations are more real and more important than the things which they relate'; furthermore, 'the type of sentence in nature is a flash of lightning' in which 'the act is the very substance of the fact denoted' (Fenollosa 1962: 152, 148, 142).

8. For an overview of the history of these translations see Steiner (1996).

9. For a more detailed discussion of Homeric indeterminacy in the case of the hexameter and of how modern translations deal with it, see Varsos (2014).

10. See the very characteristic case of the relations between Pound and W.H.D. Rouse, whose prose translation of the *Odyssey* adopts colloquial tones without integrating more radical aspects of modernist poetic writing (Flack 2015).

11. Pound comments extensively on and quotes long passages from Divus's translation in his essay on Homer's translators (1954a: 259–64), which I use as a source for my own quotations from Divus's version.

12. His translation of the *Odyssey* was completed by 1615.

13. Greek citations are from Homer (1984).

14. We can only briefly compare this to other translations of Homer tending towards domestication in ways characteristic of their times. Pope's dramatic amplification (the *Odyssey*, translated with collaborators, appeared in 1725) can be seen as adjusting Homer to Virgilian as well as modern epic registers:

> Now to the shores we bend, a mournful train,
> Climb the tall bark, and launch into the main:
> At once the mast we rear, at once unbind
> The spacious sheet, and stretch it to the wind:
> Then pale and pensive stand, with cares opprest,
> And solemn horrour saddens every breast.
>
> *Homer 1967b: 377–9*

Butcher and Lang (translation published in 1879) mark the elegancy of their prose by a repetitive syntax with biblical overtones that constitute the ground of their domestication strategies:

> Now when we had gone down to the ship and to the sea, first of all we drew the ship unto the fair salt water, and placed the mast and sails in the black ship, and took those sheep and put them therein, and ourselves too climbed on board, sorrowing, and shedding big tears.
>
> *Homer 1900: 172*

Lattimore's long line (translation published in 1965) owes a lot to this prose precedent but is even more strongly marked by a syntactic parataxis that may be seen as somewhat estranging:

> Now when we had gone down again to the sea and our vessel,
> first of all we dragged the ship down into the bright water,
> and in the black hull set the mast in place, and set sails,
> and took the sheep and walked them aboard, and ourselves also,
> embarked, but sorrowful, and weeping big tears.

Homer 1965: 168

15. Pope is quite obscure in his 'And hellward bending, o'er the beach [we] descry / The dolesome passage to th' infernal sky' (Homer 1967b: 380); Butcher and Lang's 'we held on our way along the stream of Oceanus, till we came to the place' (Homer 1900: 172) is quite unequivocal; and so is, more recently, Lattimore's 'and ourselves walked along by the stream of the Ocean / until we came to that place' (Homer 1965: 168).

16. Chapman is morphologically close to Pound with his 'weake-neckt dead' and also semantically with his archaic 'prease of shadows' (for the *amenēnà kárēna* of lines 29 and 49 respectively). He domesticates quite clearly, however, with his 'Soules of the deceast' (for line 37 of the original). Versions from other translations, all of them more clearly descriptive, are: Pope's impressively/ metaphorical expressions: 'the wan shades we hail, th'infernal Gods [...]/ Thin airy shoals of visionary ghosts;/ [...] gore untasted flows' (Homer 1967: 381, 383, for lines 29, 37 and 49 of the original respectively); Butcher and Lang's almost literal 'the strengthless heads of the dead' (Homer 1900: 173, the same for lines 29 and 49) and 'the spirits of the dead that be departed' (Homer 1900: 173, for line 37); Lattimore's enjambments: 'the strengthless heads of the perished/ dead' (Homer 1965: 169, for lines 29 and 49) but also, not avoiding the notion of soul, 'the souls / of the perished dead' (Homer 1965: 169, for line 37).

17. Odysseus closes his conversation with Elpenor's soul by promising that he will 'do and accomplish' (τελευτήσω τε και ἔρξω, *Od.* 11.80) what his comrade has asked for, that is, according to Pound's version of Elpenor's request, a 'tomb by sea-bord' for '*A man of no fortune, and with a name to come*' (Pound 1986: 4).

18. For exegetical comments see Terrell (1980: 3–4). For ὀρειχάλκου and Ἀργειφόντης see Homer (1982: 426, 414). For Dartona's Latin version of the second Hymn see Pound (1954a: 266).

19. Commentators have clarified connections to Porphyry as well as to the Renaissance Neoplatonist scholar Marsilio Ficino. See Terrell (1980: 92) and especially Liebregts (2004: 117–18). I suggest that the corresponding phrase of the Greek original could be: πολλὰ γάρ ἐστιν ὁ νοῦς (Πορφύριος 1907, 41).

20. The exegetical details of the passage have been amply clarified by Terrell (1980: 93–4). For an insightful interpretation of the passage in connection to the Homeric *Nekuia* and especially Herakles' *katabasis* to Hades see Tryphonopoulos (1992: 127).

21. Terrell (1980: 92) refers us to Johannes Schweighaeuser's 1801–7 bilingual edition of Ἀθηναίου Ναυκρατικοῦ Δειπνοσοφισταί: *Athenaei Naucratitae Deipnosophistarum: libri quindecim* as the source for the Greek and the Latin passage that Pound quotes with minor adaptations.

22. There are other possible configurations of the issue. With respect to Pound, Xie (1999: 220) talks of 'universals' that would be 'by necessity disruptive, distorting and transformative'. Further theoretical and figural transpositions can lead us to Deleuze's description of books as rhizomatic assemblages, very much reminiscent of almost any page in Pound's *Cantos*: 'In a book, as in all things, there are lines of articulation or segmentarity, strata and territories; but also lines of flight, movements of deterritorialization and destratification' (1987: 3).

23. 'Ideas as it were tremble at the edge of expression,' as Davie has succinctly put it (1964: 218).

24. This also draws near to how Steiner relativizes translation antinomies: 'Good translation, on the contrary, can be defined as that in which the dialectic of impenetrability and ingress, of intractable alienness and felt "at-homeness" remains unresolved, but expressive' (1975: 413).

25. The tension is clearly echoed by the oscillation in Canto CXVI between the ironically regretful 'And I am not a demigod / I cannot make it cohere' and the rather obstinate, but perhaps equally ironic 'i.e. it coheres all right / even if my notes do not cohere' (Pound 1986: 796, 797).

3 TRANSLATING THE *ODYSSEY*: ANDREAS DIVUS, OLD ENGLISH AND EZRA POUND'S CANTO I

1. *LE* = Pound (1954a: 249–75, at 259–67). The relevant section on Divus was first published in the September 1918 issue of *The Egoist* (Riikonen 2008: 139).

2. *LE* 259.

3. Divus's preface proves Pound's tentative suggestion that Divus's translation is based on the Aldine edition of the Homeric poems (*Odyssea* 1524) – first printed in Venice in a two-volume set in 1504 (Wilson 2017: 160) – when, after identifying himself as the author of a previous *Iliad* translation, he states that 'as for the individual spreads, their numeration, pages and lines, here [i.e. in my *Odyssey* translation] everything is the same as in the Greek Homer in the Aldine edition (*ex aeditione Aldina*)' (f. 2r).

4. On the fragmentation of epic language enacted here, see Flack (2015: 43).

5. Pound's *Venerandam* (*Cantos* I.72) is the first word of *Hom. Hymn* 6 and *with the golden crown, Aphrodite* translates the second part of the same line, only omitting the epithet *pulchram* ('beautiful'); the following two lines (73–4) consist of selective tags and translations drawn from the rest of *Hom. Hymn* 6 (Terrell 1993: 3). The Latin phrase underlying Pound's *Bearing the golden bough of Argicida* (75), by contrast, derives from the much longer *Hom. Hymn* 5, where it may have suggested itself to Pound on account of being repeated within five lines (117 *habens auream virgam Argicida* ~ 121 *auream virgam habens Argicida* 'the slayer of Argus [i.e. Mercury] holding the golden wand').

6. The *Cantos* are quoted by poem and line number (*Cantos* I = Pound 1995: 3–5); 'Divus' refers to Divus's *Odyssea Latina* (1538), lines 1–104 of which are transcribed by Pound himself (*LE* 259–62); 'Od.' refers to the Greek text of the *Odyssey*, quoted from the Oxford edition (1922). The one-line discrepancy between Homer and Divus starting at Divus 11.92 (~ *Od.* 11.93) is the result of the Aldine edition's omission of the formulaic address to Odysseus at *Od.* 11.92.

7. *A Draft of XVI Cantos* (Pound 1925). In Ur-Canto III, composed in late 1915 and published in *Poetry* in August 1917, the *Odyssey* translation, while itself longer, played a structurally less prominent role; the decisive shift towards the now canonical version came with the 'interpolation' published in *The Future* in April 1918 (Bush 1976: 190–3).

8. = 67 of the poem's total of 76 lines. Moreover, *Cantos* I.68–9 mention the edition and the authors of the source text, Homer and Divus, and 70–1 refer to one of Odysseus's future adventures, the Sirens and his more imminent return to Circe.

9. For a representative recent articulation of Canto I's multi-layeredness see Flack (2015: 14): 'Pound initiates his poetic voyage in *The Cantos* in Odysseus' voice, layered in the resonant echoes of history from Homer's Greek through Divus's Latin and the cadences of Anglo-Saxon English'. See also Cookson (2001: 4) and Boitani (1994: 17).

10. Terrell (1993: 1–4) and Robaey (1989), while being attuned to numerous points of philological detail, stop short of positing any systematic patterns.

11. Dante provides an important third literary context to the *Cantos*, whose Inferno constitutes an attractive analogue for the Homeric *Nekuia* and offers an interpretation of Odysseus as an adventurer comparable to the Poundian narrator. But despite the *Commedia*'s undeniable conceptual import for Canto I, Pound's poem textually excludes Dante and therefore does not feature in the present investigation into Canto I's poetics of translation. Cf. Bush 1976: 133; Sicari 1991; Wilmer 1996; Flack 2015: 37.

12. *LE* 264. Again, Pound's intuition is confirmed by Divus's preface (Wolfe 2015: 52 n. 163; Kenner 1971: 350).

13. Some characteristic instances of where the Latin language falls short of providing a close equivalent for the Greek construction include: Greek denominative adjectives where Latin needs to use a nominal periphrasis (πυγούσιος ~ *cubiti mensura*, *Od.* 11.25); Greek compound adjectives and verbs that require a separate adverb or object in Latin (πολύτλητοι ~ *multa passi*, *Od.* 11.38); and conjunctions that govern the infinitive in Greek but the subjunctive in Latin (πρὶν Τειρεσίαο πυθέσθαι ~ *antequam Tiresiam audirem*, *Od.* 11.50).

14. Divus's version was from the beginning 'designed to be read with the Greek text', as Sowerby (1996: 171) notes, even if the first bilingual Greek–Latin edition of the *Odyssey* based on Divus's translation was only published in 1567 by Jean Crespin (Johannes Crispinus) (177).

15. Found very rarely in Latin poetry, e.g. Vergil, *Aeneid* 4.219–21.

16. Vergil's epithets for *mare* include *placidum, purpureum, velivolum, magnum, altum*.

17. Exceptions consist in clusters of particles where commonly one of the particles goes untranslated: e.g. ῥα at *Od.* 11.1, ἄρ at 11.2 and δέ at 11.4.

18. On tmesis in Latin literature see Bernard (1960).

19. Pound explicitly remarks on this Grecism, in classical Latin virtually restricted to the technical register: 'it is *illepidus* to chuck Latin nominative participles about in such profusion ... Romans did not use *habentes* as the Greeks used ἔχοντες, etc'. (*LE* 264).

20. Armstrong (2014). See also Sowerby (1996).

21. Both Robaey (1989) and Flack (2015) often pair Homer and Divus. I was unable to consult Whittaker (1970).

22. The metaphor of 'evasion' has been suggested to me by the editors.

23. When Pound began engaging Divus (late 1915, cf. n. 7 above), he had just published *Cathay*, a collection for whose translations he equally relied on an intermediary crib, consisting in 'meticulous word-for-word glosses in English and stilted interlinear renderings' (Yao 2002b: 26). This use of cribs, from a practical point of view, by 'decoupling literary translation from an operative requirement of semantic comprehension' (27) allowed what Steven Yao has labelled a radical reformulation of translation practices in English (27).

24. The Hellenistic grammarian Dionysius Thrax illustrates his definition of synonymy by giving a list consisting of ἄορ ξίφος μάχαιρα σπάθη φάσγανον (*Grammatici Graeci* I.i, pp. 36.5–6(7) Uhlig, cf. Hainsworth 1993: 13).

25. In the wake of Milman Parry's insights into the formulaic character of Homeric epic, the two phrases can moreover be seen as metrical alternatives – one beginning with a vowel (ἄορ, cf. *Il.* 21.173, *Od.* 10.321), the other with a consonant (ξίφος, cf. *Od.* 9.300, 10.126, 294, 535) – for expressing the same 'essential idea' (Parry 1971: 272) of 'drawing the sharp sword from the thigh'; a third alternate, beginning with the trisyllabic φάσγανον, occurs at *Il.* 1.190. Such a formulaic interpretation, while unavailable to Divus himself, provides retrospective support for his practice of synonymic translation.

26. The former option is favoured by the weight of the evidence, consisting especially in Pound's pervasive focus on Divus's text in his explicit remarks on the composition of his *Nekuia*

rendering (*LE* 259–67 *passim*) and in his modest command of Greek, as suggested by explicit statements, such as 'I do not imagine I am the sole creature who has been … very ill-taught his Greek' (*LE* 249), and the complete absence of Greek from Pound's college and graduate school curricula (for which see Moody 2007: 19, 27–8). The latter option, first suggested to me by Samuel Meister, in addition to its inherent interest gains some plausibility from the comparative brevity of the passage, which would have allowed Pound plenty of time to familiarize himself with the Greek; if Pound used either of the English translations he references at *LE* 249, Chapman has simplicity ('sword' twice), Pope, variety ('sword … falchion').

27. Raffaello Maffei, for instance, retains Homer's lexical diversity by varying between *ad mare* and *in altum* at *Od*. 11.1–2.

28. 'Salt flood' is a 'frequent' synonym for 'sea' in Middle English poetry (*OED s.v.* 'salt, adj.' 1a) and is also found twice in Shakespeare (*RJ* III.v.134, *Tim* V.i.214) and, more recently, in Bryant's *Odyssey* translation (Bryant 1871) at *Od*. 5.552; Pound himself uses 'deep' as a noun twice in Canto XCI.

29. For another example concerning the two colour-adjectives μέλας ('black') and κύανος ('dark-blue') used to describe ships in the Homeric passage see Robaey (1989: 68 n. 12).

30. On the first two lines of Canto I as an example of 'condensation' see Moody (2007: 314–15).

31. Robaey (1989).

32. E.g. Robaey (1989: 69, 78).

33. *Odysseus* (*Cantos* I.65) rather than *Ulysses* (Divus 99 *Ulysse* [vocative]) and *Kimmerian* (12) for *Cimmeriorum* (14).

34. One lexical example of such direct transmission is Divus's *pyram* (11.31) from Homer's πυρήν (*Cantos* I.26 *pyre*) and, in light of Divus's translation practice, Homeric word order is also continued in the Latin version.

35. As Jones (2006: 43–4) shows, Pound had a long-standing interest in 'forging a synthesis' between the poetries of the North and the South and considered the English language to be intrinsically suited to that purpose. For Pound's famous dictum, '*dichten* = condensare', playing on the double meaning in the German word for poetry (*Dichtung*), see Robaey (1989: 68).

36. This combination of radical syntactical changes with an emphatic word-by-word literalism amounts to parody, as suggested to me by Samuel Meister.

37. The diminutive form *pitkin* is how Pound himself translates at *Cantos* I.21 the first occurrence of *fossa* (Divus 11.25).

38. On the shift in contemporary aesthetic preferences epitomized by Keats's 1816 sonnet 'On First Looking into Chapman's Homer', see Richards (1980). Pound shared the Romantics' enthusiasm for Chapman, describing him as 'the best English 'Homer'' (*LE* 249; Pound's assessment, mostly positive, of Pope is at *LE* 250), but his Homeric translations, despite their frequent use of archaic diction and syntactical distortion, were evidently not radical enough for Pound's project, perhaps due to their mechanical rhyme scheme (AA BB CC etc.) and predictable iambic pattern (his *Iliad* is in heptameters, his *Odyssey* in pentameters throughout).

39. See also Ahearn (2003: 32–3). Walter Pater refers to the 'composite experience of all the ages' (Pater 1868: 307, quoted by Martindale 2006: 7).

40. Pound 1971: 87 (with Jones 2006: 31). Pound makes a similar remark in the subscript to *Future* Canto III.

41. Following Jones's practice, I use quotation marks ('The Seafarer') for Pound's poem and italics (*The Seafarer*) for the original.

42. See also Haynes (2003: 42), who proposes a parallel distinction between *actual* ('Anglo-Saxon', 'Latin') and *perceived* ('Saxon', 'Latinate') features of a particular linguistic tradition.

43. Jones (2006: 46). A notable exception is *Cantos* I.6 *Bóre us out ónward with béllying cánvas*, where the two alliterating syllables are unstressed.

44. Ibid.

45. Ibid. On alliteration in Latin poetry see Coleman (1999: 47–8).

46. A comparable, if more complex, case of a Latinate word ('sepulchre') contained within a Germanic alliterative phrase appears in *Unwept, unwrapped in sepulchre* (45).

47. Jones (2006: 36).

48. With a falling rhythm begin *Cantos* I.3–7, 9–13, 15–16 and 19.

49. Jones, more conservatively, observes that '[a]pproximately half the lines start with a stressed syllable' (2006: 45).

50. *LE* 6.

51. For the change from *swarthy* to *swart* see Robaey (1989: 68 n. 8). On the opening *and* of Canto I and 'the impossibility of starting anywhere but *in medias res*' see Jones (2006: 41).

52. Terrell (1993: 1).

53. Pound (1934: 115) comments on 'dreory' 'orig. Sax. means *bloody*' (Jones 2006: 46 n. 76). The word first appears at *Beowulf* 1417 *Wæter under stod dreorig ond gedrefed* 'The water stood under, gory and stirred up'.

54. 'mid' in this sense occurs three times in 'The Seafarer': ''mid burghers', ''mid the English' and ''mid the doughty'.

55. In Canto I those are *sun-rays* (v. 14), *bell-sheep* (v. 27), *lance heads* (v. 32), *nape-nerve* (v. 53) and *sea-bord* (v. 55).

56. Canto I has *day's end* (v. 9) and *death's heads* (v. 24).

57. The first nine lines of Pound's 'Seafarer' alone contain the noun-compounds *breast-cares*, *sea-surge*, and *nightwatch* and the genitive-compounds *song's truth*, *journey's jargon*, *care's hold*, and *ship's head*.

58. Haynes (2003: 104–37) lists the compound epithets alongside negative adjectives and certain meters as Hellenizing features.

59. *Pace* Jones (2006: 45–6). Note that even the two elements 'trim' and 'coif' are derived from opposite traditions.

60. Subject–verb inversion occurs here: *then sat we* (8), *came we then* (11, 17), *here did they rites* (19), *poured we* (22), *then prayed I* (24).

61. Omitting articles and verbs is also common, e.g. in *Sun to his slumber* (*Cantos* I.10), which stands for 'The sun went to his slumber', or *shadows o'er all the ocean* (ibid.), where 'there were' or 'spread' must be supplied. Like the subject–verb inversions, such omissions commonly serve to underpin the falling rhythm typical of Anglo-Saxon poetry.

62. See Flack (2015: 36–7) and Kahane (1999: 815–16).

63. For epiphany as a poetic technique see Flack (2015: 43).

64. Plato, *Ion* 536b4, b5; 542a4; Porphyry, *Quaestiones Homericae ad Iliadem* 297.16–17 Schrader.

65. Morgan (1999: 32–9).

66. These 'polemical' interpretations of 'out of' have been suggested to me by the editors and George Varsos, respectively.

67. I owe this suggestion to James Taylor.

68. *Pace* Liebregts 2011 and others who prefer to emphasize Pound's 'self-identification' with Homer (87).

69. Reference in Jones (2006: 47 and n. 80). Cf. Gunn (1994: 98), cited by Jones (2006: 19).

70. *LE* 264.

71. Kenner (1971: 350); Haynes (2010: 104).

72. Alexander (1997: 26).

73. *Od.* 11.29b = 11.49b νεκύων ἀμενηνὰ κάρηνα 'powerless heads of the dead'.

74. Jones (2006: 42) suggests a similar welding together of the Germanic and Graeco-Roman traditions for Pound's characterization of Homer in Saxonist terms as the poet with an 'Ear, ear for the sea-surge' at the beginning of Canto II (*Cantos* II.14).

4 TO TRANSLATE OR NOT TO TRANSLATE? POUND'S PROSODIC PROVOCATIONS IN *HUGH SELWYN MAUBERLEY*

1. The translation here comes from Richard Sieburth (2003), who cites the original line in *Odyssey* 12 as taken 'from the sirens' song' (1308 n. 549.13).

2. Adams explains: 'Quantitative meters in English are wholly artificial: were it not for the prestige of Greek and Latin, they would certainly never have been attempted. "Quantity" refers to the time allotted to the pronunciation of vowel sounds, long or short. But in English, we simply do not attend to the length of time given to vowel sounds in our speech; long and short do not figure into the meaning, as they do in the classical languages' (1997: 66).

3. 'Perhaps the commonest quantitative models in English', Adams writes, 'are the lyric quatrains, the stanzas called "Sapphic" and "Alcaic." The Sapphic quatrain consists of three lines like this, with the options indicated:

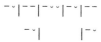

followed by a shorter one like this (called an Adonic): ‾ ˘ ˘ | ‾ ˘' (1997: 67).

4. This is a term of reference coined by Demetres Tryphonopoulos, who has introduced the concept elsewhere, emphasizing the under-evaluated significance of prosodic play in Poundian and modernist studies. Two of his conference presentations that address prosodic allusion are: (i) '"For three years he strove to maintain / The sublime in the old sense": Sublimity and Ecstasy in Longinus and Pound', delivered at the 2003 Twentieth-Century Literature Conference at the University of Louisville; and (ii) '"ἴδμεν γάρ τοι πάνθ᾽ ὅσ᾽ ἐνὶ Τροίῃ εὐρείῃ": Teaching Ezra Pound's Subtle Allusiveness', presented at the Modernism's Legacies Conference, held at Western University in 2014.

5. An excellent example of Pound's practice of textual transmission appears in the closing six lines of Canto I, where Pound enacts a reading of an original Latin text in the same way he has translated Sappho's stanza into a prosodically identical stanza of his own that enacts a quantitative meter in English.

6. The full stanza from *Mauberley* reads: 'The "age demanded" chiefly a mould in plaster / Made with no loss of time, / A prose kinema, not, not assuredly, alabaster / Or the "sculpture" of rhyme' (I.2.29–32).

7. In Canto 105, Pound includes a series of verses that allude to the 'fragmentary' nature of his poetry, includes an untranslated line of Greek text, and then prompts his readers: 'I shall have to learn a little greek to keep up with this / but so will you, drratt you' (1996: 770).

8. As the name implies, a 'pure' dactylic hexameter line would be made up of six (hexa-) dactyls:

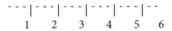

Note the last foot: the last syllable is anceps; there will never be a full dactyl in the last foot, only a spondee or a trochee.

9. Pound refers to Peisistratus and alludes to his role in this stanza from *Mauberley*: 'All men, in law, are equals. / Free of Peisistratus, / We choose a knave or an eunuch / To rule over us' (I.3.53–6).

10. See also Adams's excellent commentary on Pound's role as innovator of free verse and the free verse epic 'The Metrical Contract of *The Cantos*' published in the summer 1988 issue of the *Journal of Modern Literature*.

11. Pound continues with this commentary on his research process: 'My pawing over the ancients and semi-ancients has been one struggle to find out what has been done, once for all, better than it can ever be done again, and to find out what remains for us to do, and plenty does remain, for if we still feel the same emotions as those which launched the thousand ships, it is quite certain that we come on these feelings differently, through different manners, through different nuances, by different intellectual gradations' (ibid.).

12. Espey cites these colourful descriptors found in Pound's letters to Iris Barry, written in the summer of 1916, found in *Selected Letters*, page 91.

13. See endnote 4.

14. This is Leonard Diepeveen's term; see *Changing Voices: The Modern Quoting Poem* (1993).

15. Pound provides a hint of how to read this section in a letter on 8 July 1922 to Felix E. Schelling: 'The meter in *Mauberley* is Gautier and Bion's "Adonis"; or at least those are the two grafts I was trying to flavour it with. Syncopation from the Greek; ...' (1971: 181).

16. Bion's dactylic hexameters come closer to Callimachus's rather than to Homer's. J.D. Reed offers this explication: 'Bion's work survives in 214 hexameters (two of them incomplete), enough to permit general observations about his metrical style ... A cursory look at this metre will reveal a cultivation of the refined hexameter technique associated especially with Callimachus ... The metre and prosody of Theocritus' bucolic poetry are in many respects closer to Homeric than to Callimachean practice' (1997: 36).

17. In Canto 1, for example, Pound integrates the Adonic foot into the metric pattern, particularly in the opening ten lines. His gesture is somewhat obscured by his feat of translation: here Pound takes a passage from an ancient Latin translation of Book II of the *Odyssey*, then translates it into English. Later, in Canto 17, which picks up directly from Canto 1, Pound borrows from the Classical rhetoric of the *Odyssey*, writing a lyric passage about the Cave of Nerea, but he presents it in free-verse form, emphasizing innovation with experimental line length and layout, but somehow still re-creating the tone of Homer's work.

RESPONDENT ESSAY 1: RINGING TRUE: POUNDIAN TRANSLATION AND POETIC MUSIC

1. Pound ([1917] 1968: 232). The form of this assertion recalls Matthew Arnold's argument about the relation of Criticism and Culture, in *Culture and Anarchy* ([1869] 2009). Used by permission of New Directions Publishing Corp.

5 TRANSLATION AS MYTHOPOESIS: H.D.'S *HELEN IN EGYPT* AS META-PALINODE

1. The tradition on Helen's elusiveness reaches beyond the Aeschylean Helen. See Hdt. 2.112–20; Stes. 28; cf. Pl. *Phdr.* 243a–b; *Rep.* 9.586c.

2. H.D.'s interest in the Attic dramatist Euripides began in 1903 at the University of Pennsylvania when she watched Ezra Pound perform during a staging of *Iphigeneia in Tauris*. H.D. sustained a lifelong connection with the Greek poet and playwright by translating a series of his choral odes (*Iphigeneia at Aulis, Hippolytus, Hecuba, Orestes, Electra* and *Ion*), choral poems, prose-choros texts based on other extant Euripidean plays and entire plays (*Hippolytus Temporizes, Ion* and *Helen in Egypt*). Euripides helped H.D. to realize 'the inter-relatedness between choral poetry, dramatic monody, and choral performance' (Fyta 2015: 23), to accept her organic connection to a timeless mythic body and unravel the trajectories of her poetic matrix.

3. I am indebted to Prof. Demetres Tryphonopoulos for this semantic pointer pivotal to my argument. The palinode, as its etymology suggests, aims at re-enacting a figural gesture of homecoming. This gesture stems from a desire for *nostos* to its beginnings.

4. A challenging reading of H.D.'s poem could interpret it as a allegorization of space where – according to Paul de Man – the prevalence of allegory

   > always corresponds to the unveiling of an authentically temporal destiny. This unveiling takes place in a subject that has sought refuge against the impact of time in a natural world to which, in truth, it bears no resemblance [...] In the world of the symbol it would be possible for the image to coincide with the substance [...] Their relationship is one of simultaneity, which, in truth, is spatial in kind, and in which the intervention of time is merely a matter of contingency, whereas, in the world of allegory, time is the originary constitutive category.
   >
   > *1983: 203*

   Egypt with its mythic and historic connotations reinforces notions of human finitude and temporality, regardless of the poem's attempts at restoring this seeming contradiction. De Man's phrasing of the 'veiled' temporal destiny correlates with several scenes depicting the veiled Helen shifting in time and space.

5. Patricia Philippy argues that Stesichorus's and Plato's central concerns are Helen's associations to love poetry, 'Thus, the palinode sets the grounds upon which the struggle between poetic rivals and philosophy is carried out' (1995: 33).

6. See Woodbury (1967: 166); Jenkins (1999: 216) and Constantinidou (2008: 166–7).

7. William Allan defines the notion 'protean' from a socio-cultural perspective as one suiting 'the needs and purposes of the ever-changing society that produces them [myths]' (Euripides 2008: 18).

8. I purposely use the verb 'correct' to establish the direct alignment between palinode and meta-palinode; in other words, both have a corrective intent.

9. H.D. herself 'corrected' and annotated in 1954 her 1919 essay on Helen. The marginal, hand-written comments and endnotes on the typescript show that she was shocked by the extent of her own misunderstanding and misappraisal Helen's implications in poetic writing. It stands then to reason that *Helen in Egypt* should amend the former misconceptions and recant H.D.'s former disapprobation.

10. H.D. refers to Pound's influence in her autobiographical scrapbook *End to Torment* (1979: 41). Norman Holmes Pearson would write about them as her 'Cantos', the apex of her poetic powers

(1997: 121). In a letter to Pearson dated 3 February 1955, H.D. also defines the verse parts in *Helen in Egypt* as 'cantos' introduced by 'captions or short descriptive paragraphs, as introductions to cantos' (177).

11. Barbour's 2011 essay on the origins of prose captions in H.D.'s *Helen in Egypt* offers insightful readings of its compositional process and its uses of prose and oral textuality. Additionally, Susan Gubar's essay 'Sapphistries' locates the use of prose or stage instructions in H.D.'s poetics as early as the epithalamic, Sapphic poem 'Hymen' from H.D.'s 1921 poetry collection of the same name (1984: 43–62).

12. Written in 412 BC, *Helen* is Euripides' third play after *Trojan Women* and *Orestes*, whose approach to the myth comes closer to the Homeric version about Helen. At the end of *Electra*, the Dioskouroi predict her future passage to Egypt under the protection of Proteus, king of Egypt and presage the coming, rectified version of the myth. In his *Encomium of Helen*, written before the Euripidean play, the sophist Gorgias subjects the traditional logos to persuasion and argument and exonerates Helen from blame (Euripides 2004: n. 11, 177). The story that Euripides has used in his Palinode of Helen was already known 'to Herodotus (2.113–17), who had it from the Egyptian priests but believed that Homer knowingly suppressed it [...] Homer's account of some other parts of Helen's life does not quite cohere at all points, and it is conceivable that Herodotus was right and the *Iliad* and the *Odyssey* contain two different versions of the story' (Woodbury 1967: 165). A.W. Verall misinterprets the dramatic type of *Helen* in his *Four Essays on Euripides*, noting that the play must be a capricious', 'non-sensical' romantic comedy on a par with *A Midsummer Night's Dream* (1905: 47). In *The Rise of the Greek Epic*, Gilbert Murray depicts Helen as a Jungian-like archetypical figure (1907: 224). J.D. Conacher pinpoints the singularity of the Euripidean play: 'Homer, Cyclic epic, Stesichorus, and Herodotus: however different their versions, Euripides appears to have adopted elements from each [...] and in the end to have produced a version of the Helen myth quite different from any which had gone before' (1967: 288). This information is quite crucial for H.D.'s critical and textual reception for the origins and making of *Helen in Egypt*. The scholarly majority still stresses the impact of the Iliadic *Odyssey* when considering H.D.'s intertextuality and excludes other sources involving Euripides' reception of the myth.

13. Euripides must have also known Herodotus's variant in which Paris was sent away from Egypt after his elopement with Helen from Sparta (Arnott 1990: 3). *Helen* reiterates a challenge to the epic world by demonstrating with irony the impossibility of escaping fully from the traditional myth (77). R. Lattimore classifies Euripides among the philosophical poets (2003: 123–4). In the dialogues between his characters and between characters and chorus members, Euripides frequently adopts 'the Socratic method in order to come closer to reality. He pretends, like Socrates did, that he does not know the truth, until it comes into the light by the means of the reversal of fortune and *catharsis*' (Athanasopoulou 2008: 76).

14. Among Euripides' predecessors, Stesichorus seems to be the first to introduce in his Palinode the trope of the *Eidolon* in the developing myth of Helen: 'The innovation in the Homeric myth that can be definitely attributed to the archaic age is the introduction of the phantom. This may have occurred in some Hesiodic work and was certainly in Stesichorus' (Woodbury 1967: 165). Stesichorus provides a more politically nuanced reading of Helen and Euripides follows suit. Isocrates and Plato claim that the palinode was the result of Stesichorus's attempt to be redeemed for his unfavourable portrayal of Helen.

15. In her memoir *Compassionate Friendship* (1955), H.D. mentions that the readings triggered in her a kind of out-of-body experience. Listening to her voice, she had found her alter ego or double: 'This is myself, Helen out of the body, in another world, the *eidolon* of the legend' (quoted in Connor 2004: 84).

16. There are further references to Helen as well, including allusions to the existence of two Palinodes in Dio Chrysostom's work, though it is not certain that H.D. had read or knew about them. According to Ruby Blondell, the first palinode was a severe critique of Hesiod's accusations against Helen while the second also condemned Homer's censure of Helen since, in reality, she never went to Troy, and legitimately married Paris (2013: 247).

17. See William Allan, introduction to Euripides' *Helen* (2008: 15). H.D. has assimilated references both from Pausanias's *Descriptions of Greece*, Books 2 and 3 and from L.R. Farnell's printed lectures titled *Greek Hero Cults and Ideas on Immortality* about Helen as a cultic figure and goddess of fertility. Both works are part of her library in the Beinecke.

18. In the *Astral H.D.*, Matte Robinson approaches the figures of the 'Many-Names' and many forms in Proteus also named Formalhaut, a misspelling of the star in the night in H.D.'s *Helen in Egypt*. In the dream world, conflations of space and name are not uncommon: 'Fomalhaut', writes Robinson, 'another aspect of the "Large Star" from Chaboseau, becomes "Formalhaut" in *Helen in Egypt*, who stands for "the Nameless-of-the-Many-Names" Proteus, echoing the Protean figure of the dreams in *the Hirslanden Notebooks* [...], [Formalhaut's temple] is the same Amen temple, at all times, in all places, at all plains of existence' (2016: 212). 'This temple is thus the astral form of the temple, proper to the dimension to which she finds herself [in *Helen in Egypt*], the Platonic form of the temple behind all the other temples' (2016: 136).

19. Presaging Robinson's work, Demetres Tryphonopoulos outlines Pound, and H.D.'s poetic affiliations to the occult tradition, in his groundbreaking paper 'Fragments of a Faith Forgotten': '[In H.D.'s *Trilogy* the] transcription of old texts, adaptation, erasure, allusion, quotation, and re-making are the functions of the occultist' (2003b: 239). H.D. clearly continues these practices in *Helen in Egypt* as well.

20. H.D.'s reference to the veil of Cytherea highlights the inextricable bond between Pandora, Aphrodite and Helen, iconic female figures, arbiters of desire and destruction. The veil they wear confers upon them invisibility and αἰδώς, or modesty.

21. For H.D. the sounds of bombs exploding during the Blitz in London are memories that could easily resurface and seem to haunt the speaker of these lines.

22. I refer to H.D.'s translations from 'The *Iphigeneia in Aulis* of Euripides', published in 1916, the choral sequences from 'From *Electra-Orestes*' (1932) and the monodies of Electra and Orestes in 'Orestes Theme' (1934).

23. Addressing H.D.'s classical intertextuality, Eileen Gregory views *Helen in Egypt* as a 'Euripidean refiguration of Greek mythology' (1997: 221).

24. Theonoe (Θεονόη) is the prophetess, sister of Theoclymenus, villainous king of Egypt and daughter to Proteus. In Euripides' play she saves the lives of Helen and Menelaus. Her *agōn*, the philosophical exchange she has with Helen on metaphysics is crucial, and her 'pronouncements resolve the structural crisis of the play' (Marshall 2014: 261).

25. This story is repeated in Herodotus. His second book of *Histories* has determined the Western reception of Egypt for many centuries. His work remains an important historical source 'due to a powerful rhetoric of otherness as much as it is to richness of detail, narrative sophistication' (Vasunia 2001: 76).

26. Tracing H.D.'s classical intertextuality in *Helen in Egypt*, Gregory argues that H.D. intended for the poem to become the last in the cycle of the lost oracle plays. This information most likely stems from H.D.'s endnotes in *Notes on Euripides*. Situated at the site of a temple, *Iphigenia among the Taurians*, *Helen* and *Ion* involve the return to Greece of a 'lost or exiled [royalty or] goddess' after the completion of a Persephonian descent into the underworld. Gregory adds that aided for this reading by Henri Grégoire's commentaries and translations,

H.D. may have been influenced by his 'very compelling account of the role of Theonoe in the *Helen* as a regal and wise precursor of Socrates' Diotima, interpreting the divine *nous*' (224).

27. Euripides must have constructed the excerpt of Theonoe's speech and its connections to the divine *nous* from Anaxagoras; *ether* is the source of life, the personification of the upper air and the good realm where gods dwell.

> Just as we control our bodies by our thoughts, so the cosmos is controlled by *nous*; we may be unclear about the details, but the results are obvious to us. One fundamental point about Anaxagoras's theory of mind is that nowhere in the extant material does he identify mind with a divine principle or god. In fragment 1018 and in *Trojan Women* (886) [I would include the above-mentioned lines from Theonoe's dialogue with Helen], Euripides connects the necessity of the universe with Zeus and mind (Ζεύς, εἴτ' ἀνάγκη φύσεως εἴτε νοῦς βροτῶν). Although later testimonial reports in Aëtius and Iamblichus say that Anaxagoras connected *nous* and god, there are many more reports of his denial of divinity to the heavenly bodies and his alleged atheism.
>
> *Online Stanford Encyclopedia of Philosophy*

See also Anaxagoras frag. 12, 13, 9, 14, in Kirk et al. (1984: 362–5).

It is no coincidence that H.D. relates the essence of 'God' as etheric and those who penetrate into this etheric realm as initiates akin to those of the Eleusinian Mysteries.

6 REPRESSION, RENEWAL AND 'THE RACE OF WOMEN' IN H.D.'S *ION*

1. I am grateful to the editors for their recommendations for improving this essay and to Ruth Salter for encouraging me to begin it.

2. Ion may be less crystalline than Gregory suggests. In H.D.'s translation, he addresses Apollo in a prayer in his first speech (2003:157). In the Greek, however, Ion describes the god in third person, then addresses the priests directly. H.D. changed all of Ion's dialogue into direct address. Her translation intensifies the reader's sense of Ion's devotion to Apollo and of his ignorance about his ancestry.

3. References to Euripides's *Ion* are from the edition by A.S. Owen (1939). For arguments that translators should focus on the general meaning of a text instead of its specific words, see Humboldt (Schulte and Biguenet 1992: 55) and Arnold (Schulte and Biguenet 1992: 5).

4. H.D. relied on the French prose rendering by Leconte de Lisle to prepare her English translation of Euripides' play (Friedman 529).

5. On 14 August 1935, H.D. wrote to Bryher, 'if I get this Ion done, it will break the backbone of my H.D. repression' (Friedman 2002: 528).

6. H.D. emphasizes this need when Ion tells Kreousa, 'O, I envy you' because of her Athenian provenance (2003: 173). H.D.'s diction strays from the meaning of the verb θαυμάζω (*thaumázō*) at line 263. By contrast, Leconte de Lisle follows the Greek closely, translating it as '*combien je t'admire!*' (408). H.D.'s rendering of Ion's words echo a repeated line in her poems 'Fragment Sixty-eight' and 'Envy' (1983: 187–9; 319–21).

7. In a letter, H.D. links a basket she uses to nurse a fallen bird with her memory of pregnancy and the translation of *Ion* (Friedman 531).

8. In a note to her *Ion*, H.D. identifies the parts of the play she leaves out of her translation (2003: 149).

7 BRAVING THE ELEMENTS: H.D. AND JEFFERS

1. See Robert Zaller's *Robinson Jeffers and the American Sublime*.

2. See William Shakespeare's *As You Like It*.

3. See H.D's papers at Yale University, 'Notes on Euripides, Pausanius, and Greek Lyric Poets', Box 43.

4. Both H.D. and Jeffers adapt Euripides' Hippolytus–Phaedra story into *Hippolytus Temporizes* (1927) and *Cawdor* (1928).

5. Counter-modern should not be confused with anti-modern. Both H.D. and Jeffers are modernists but since they work in streams running alongside or adjacent to currents of traditional modernism, I view their endeavours as *countering* alternatives to the major flows of modernism.

6. See *The Emancipated Spectator*. Jacques Rancière similarly advocates for a theatrical text that generates its own spectatorship: 'An emancipated community is a community of narrators and translators' (2011: 22).

7. See Gaston Bachelard's *Psychoanalysis of Fire*.

8. In *Piercing Together the Fragments*, Josephine Balmer (2013) argues that H.D.'s antagonism to classical scholarship frees the poet to pursue her own idiosyncratic methods of translation, even inserting practitioner's statements into fictional works like *Bid Me to Live*.

9. For further consideration, see Eileen Gregory's insightful chapter in *H.D. and Hellenism* (1997) called 'Euripides: Dream Time and Dream Work'.

10. See Simon Goldhill's chapter 'Genre and Transgression', in *Reading Greek Tragedy* (1986).

11. See 'Notes on Euripides', where H.D. writes, 'I know we need scholars to decipher and interpret the Greek, but we also need: poets and mystics and children to re-discover this Hellenic world, to see through the words; the words being but the outline, the architectural structure of that door or window, through which we are all free, scholar and unlettered alike, to pass.'

12. Jonathan Culler's term from his *Theory of the Lyric* (2015).

13. The same can be said of Jeffers' treatment in his poetry of taboo subjects, like rape and incest, often in long, complex narrative forms.

14. See Michel Serres' *The Parasite* for additional reading regarding productive noise, interference and systems of order.

15. See Jonathan Lear's seminal essay 'Katharsis' (1992), where he defines catharsis as a condition more akin to being receptive to the experience of tragic possibility, where we never forget our role as audience members. Lear goes on to assert, 'tragedy is not rhetoric, it is poetry' (322).

8 REINVENTING *EROS*: H.D.'S TRANSLATION OF EURIPIDES' *HIPPOLYTUS*

1. See Gregory (1997: 25): during the war years, in addition to the *Iphigenia in Aulis* and the *Hippolytus*, H.D. also began, and abandoned, work on the *Rhesos* (then attributed to Euripides) and *Ion*, work on which she would continue later in her career. Later, she would also engage with Euripides' *Hecuba*, the *Bacchae*, the *Andromache*, the *Electra*, the *Orestes* and *Helen* (Gregory 1997: 219).

2. See Gregory (1990: 142). H.D.'s remarks are from 'Delia Alton', 221.

3. From engagement with the Hippolytus myth, H.D. also develops 'Hippolytus Temporizes', 'Phaedra', 'She Contrasts with Herself Hippolyta' and 'She Rebukes Hippolyta', all appearing in *Hymen* (1924). Other poems published 1924–7 – 'Leucadian Artemis' (1924) and 'Songs from Cyprus' (1925) – were partially integrated into the play. Gregory also names 'All Mountains' (1925) and 'Calliope' as related material (Gregory 1990, 134).

4. See Østermark-Johansen (2017).

5. See Pater (1910, 152–86: 183).

6. For a discussion of recuperating shame as a resource towards making new identities, see Sedgwick (2002, esp. Ch. 1).

7. See Hickman and Kozak (forthcoming 2018).

8. In 'Notes on Euripides', H.D. says of both Euripides and the work of 'Greek poets' generally that they allow us to 'emerge from our restricted minds … into a free … vibrant, limitless realm' (133).

9. We use the edition of Sappho which H.D. used: see Wharton (1887).

10. Hickman addresses the 'Romantic sublime' in H.D.'s thought as marked by the word 'shattering' (Hickman 2012: 15).

11. 'Lexical mind' is our own methodological term for what our approach charts.

12. Gregory references Hillman on initiatory process as relevant to what H.D. seeks to show through wounds: 'the wound that is so necessary to initiation ceremonies ends the state of innocence as it opens one in a new way at another place, making one suffer from openness, bringing one close to the world as wonder' (Hillman, 'Puer Wounds' as quoted in Gregory 1990: 153).

13. Hickman (2012: 14).

14. Ibid.: 15.

15. H.D. begins to read *eros* as a force for opening the perspective beyond what she calls 'our restricted minds' (H.D. 1986: 133). Carson's *Eros the Bittersweet* captures H.D.'s line of thought:

> As Sokrates tells it, your story begins the moment Eros enters you. That intersection is the biggest risk of your life. How you handle it is an index of the quality, wisdom, and decorum of the things inside you. As you handle it you come into contact with what is inside you, in a sudden and startling way. You perceive what you are, what you lack, what you could be … A mood of knowledge floats out over your life. You seem to know what is real and what is not. Something is lifting you toward an understanding so complete and clear it makes you jubilant. This mood is no delusion, in Sokrates' belief. It is a glance into time, at realities you once knew, as staggeringly beautiful as the glance of your beloved.
>
> *Carson 1986: 152–3*

16. As H.D.'s narrator meditates in *Bid Me to Live*, 'It might be all right for men, but for women … there was a biological catch and … danger. You dried up and were an old maid, danger. You drifted into the affable hausfrau, danger. You let her rip and had operations in Paris … danger' (H.D. 2011: 82). H.D.'s work with the *Hippolytus* allows her to register the ideological danger *eros* can pose for males as well.

17. H.D. writes this during the years she maintains a friendship with D.H. Lawrence.

18. 'robes' (Halleran 1995), 'fine-spun cloths' (Kovacs 1995). In H.D.'s moment, Murray uses 'raiment' (Murray 1908), E.P. Coleridge (1910), 'a thin veil'; as does Way from 1912 ('dainty-woven veil'). Here, where 'veil' is not the only evident choice for such fabric, H.D.'s choice suggests her interest in shame and modesty.

19. As Zeitlin notes, 'evidence is strong that the [first] play outraged its audience by the shamelessness of its Phaedra, who openly declared her guilty passion to Hippolytus and when rebuffed, just as brazenly confronted her husband ... and ... accused Hippolytus of sexual assault' (Zeitlin 1996: 219).

20. As she does with several translations, H.D. excerpts the *Hippolytus* so as to feature the choros. The choros exerted ongoing fascination for H.D., for ethical reasons – in *Ion*, she notes, 'The choros is, as it were, an outside voice .... It is the play's collective conscience' (H.D. 1982: 24). By featuring the choral voice in her *Hippolytus* (she engages with all five choral odes), H.D. implicitly critiques and displaces the form of collective judgement that would brand Phaedra's desire as shameful – featuring an alternative site of judgement, a choros sympathetic to the suffering of both Phaedra and Hippolytus.

21. As Zeitlin notes, 'The image of a nexus or knot is a leading idea, both literal and metaphorical, in the workings of the drama' (1996: 225): Hippolytus's name means 'loosener of horses', and Phaedra's asks how to 'loosen' the 'knot' of the 'logos'. Through her ethical interventions, H.D. seeks to 'loosen' the knots of the discursive rope that kills both Phaedra and Hippolytus.

22. Murray's 1908 translation, which H.D. likely knew, also frequently uses 'evil' (we count twenty instances).

23. Addressing Pater's influence on the early H.D., Gregory's comments surface why the limits of the Paterian are germane to the line of H.D.'s thought we follow: 'What appears to be missing from Pater's aesthetics of the crystal ... is a sufficient sense of the *matrix* .... Though ... Pater acknowledges a place in feeling for the virginal mother, he has consistent difficulty in confronting the dark aspects of feeling and desire' (1997: 88) – and we would suggest, female desire.

24. As Collecott (1999) notes, the adjective *poikilos*, sometimes translated as 'many coloured', occurs in Campbell, Fragment 39, to which H.D. alludes in 'Thetis' and 'The Wise Sappho'.

25. This imagery registers H.D.'s developing partnership with Annie Winifred Ellerman, or Bryher, starting in 1918–19.

RESPONDENT ESSAY 2: H.D. AND EURIPIDES: GHOSTLY SUMMONING

1. Meditating on the Sapphic fragments in 'The Wise Sappho' (1920), H.D. says: '[R]eading deeper we are inclined to visualize these broken sentences and unfinished rhythms as rocks – perfect rock shelves and layers of rock ...' (H.D. 1982: 58). See also the stratigraphic mapping of historical and literary events in 'Hipparchia', the first segment of *Palimpsest* (Gregory 1997: 60).

2. In this primal scene of classical reception as the moment of summoning ghosts, H.D. clearly has much in common with her cohort Ezra Pound. Pound's translation in Canto I from the Nekyia of the *Odyssey* is a kind of primal text of modernism. The analogue for this moment in H.D.'s writing is her summoning not of Homer, but of Euripides' Homer, in *Choruses from the Iphigeneia at Aulis*. Her translation of these choruses, but especially the first, where the women of Chalkis behold the arrayed ships of the Greeks, is also a Nekyia, a summoning of the ancient text at a moment of danger. In this she shares with Pound the deathly context of war, and, implicitly, a version of his heroic ambition for cultural renewal. They each achieve a sense of temporal estrangement and otherness through language – Pound in his deliberate archaism, H.D. in her startling directness and spareness. However, as moments of classical reception that participate in 'a circuit of reproposal and interpretation', they differ in

fundamental ways – Pound's Odysseus speaking from within a male heroic cohort, H.D.'s women from within a female cohort marginal to the public enterprise. And this basic difference implies many others in the moment of reception, in terms of both questioning and interpretation.

3. For instances of this complex literary mediation see the 'Descriptive Catalogue by Poem' in Gregory (1997: 234–52). Laity especially elaborates H.D.'s engagement with Victorian writers, e.g. Pater, D.G. Rossetti and Swinburne. With regard to classical scholarship and archaeology, see chapters in Gregory on Walter Pater (1997: 75–107) and Jane Ellen Harrison (1997: 108–25).

4. The translation of the *Ion* follows soon upon the completion of H.D.'s sessions with Freud, which took place in a Vienna already marked by Fascist presence, with Freud's own home singled out for vandalism. H.D. indicates in her notebook to *Helen in Egypt* her awareness of the possibility of the contemporary threat of atomic war.

5. Recent critics to give H.D.'s translation this kind of careful analysis are Jenkins (2007); Varney (2010a); and Hickman and Kozak (2018).

6. Critics, beginning with early reviewers, have seen the early *Choruses from the Iphigeneia at Aulis* in terms of imagism. For recent explorations of the chorus-sequence and the choral voice see Hickman and Kozak (2018); and Barbour (2012). Many critics have engaged the generic hybridity of *Helen in Egypt*, beginning with Friedman's analysis in terms of a revision of Homeric epic (1981: 253–72), and subsequently Gregory's emphasis on its ground in Euripidean drama (1997: 218–22). For more recent treatments of this question see House (2014) and Flack (2015). In terms of formal hybridity, many critics have noted how the prose captions work in tension with lyrics and complicate any clear emerging certitude or closure. See, for instance, Hokanson (1992: 338–42); and Barbour (2012).

9 'UNTRANSLATABLE' WOMEN: LAURA RIDING'S CLASSICAL MODERNIST FICTION

1. Many male modernists inserted misogynist pronouncements into manifestoes and creative work, including Ezra Pound, T.S. Eliot, Henry James, Wyndham Lewis and F.T. Marinetti. In *A Room of One's Own*, Virginia Woolf observes:

> For here again we come within range of that very interesting and obscure masculine complex which has had so much influence upon the woman's movement; that deep-seated desire, not so much that *she* shall be inferior as that *he* shall be superior, which plants him wherever one looks, not only in front of the arts, but barring the way to politics too, even when the risk to himself seems infinitesimal and the suppliant humble and devoted.
>
> *1929: 57*

2. Examples of this ambivalence include Charlotte Perkins Gilman's *The Yellow Wallpaper* (1891), Kate Chopin's *The Awakening* (1899), Edith Wharton's *The House of Mirth* (1905) and D. H. Lawrence's *Women in Love* (1920).

3. Hoberman identifies the period between the two World Wars as particularly productive for women's fiction engaging 'issues of power, gender, and narrative authority' (1997: 2).

4. I read *A Trojan Ending* in ways different from Hoberman, who sees Riding's Cressida as a 'textual monster' who 'terrifies because she defies coherence' (1997: 65). I disagree: I find her Cressida to be both coherent and rational, and thereby Riding counters the literary Cressida's reputation.

5. Many of the *Epilogue* essays reflect a preoccupation with reading modernity against the classical: for example, Rimbaud against Catullus ('The Cult of Failure'); Tacitus on the German character ('Germany'); the ancient Greek philosophers and tragedians on civil infractions and social transgression ('Crime').

6. Graves continued his work in classical studies and mythology. Other works include *The Golden Fleece* (1944), *Hercules, My Shipmate* (1945), *Homer's Daughter* (1955), *The Greek Myths* (1955) and *The Siege and Fall of Troy* (1962); as well as translations, including *The Anger of Achilles: The Iliad* (1959).

7. Riding's novels were less successful than Graves's, earning reviews like 'untiring, pointless and boring' (*New Statesman*) and 'sometimes a little stifled by an academic attitude and prose style almost too plain' (*Book of the Month*). For more information, see Elizabeth Friedmann's *A Mannered Grace* (2005: 297).

8. Murray (2006: 328–9). Graves's quotation includes my expansion of the passage, quoted by Murray, from *The White Goddess* (2006: 440). Graves's *The White Goddess* has received a great deal of attention from feminist scholars over the years, several of whom are cited in Murray's article, including Lillian Feder's *Ancient Myths in Modern Poetry* (1971); Germaine Greer's *Slip-shod Sibyls: Recognition, Rejection and the Woman Poet* (1995); Katherine McAlpine and Gail White's *The Muse Strikes Back: A Poetic Response by Women to Men* (1997); Efrossini Spentzou and Don Fowler's *Cultivating the Muse: Struggles for Power and Inspiration in Classical Literature* (2002).

9. Hoberman discusses Riding's later feud with Graves during the 1970s, when Riding claims that Graves stole and then misrepresented her ideas about the feminine as expressed in the manuscript 'The Word "Woman"'. According to Hoberman, 'Riding's notion of woman as articulate moral agent becomes Graves's "white goddess", a muse dependent on human, generally male poets to give her voice' (1997: 61). See also Amber Vogel's 'Not Elizabeth to His Ralegh: Laura Riding, Robert Graves, and Origins of the White Goddess' (2007).

10. The modernist period is otherwise characterized as a 'crisis of representation', pressured by debates problematizing self, society, empire and, of course, history. Most glaringly, for women writers the modernist crisis of representation begged the question of little to no representation.

11. Additionally, classical reception studies reinstate women working and publishing in the classics and history, more generally, at the turn of the twentieth century: examples include Jane Harrison's *Prolegomena to the Study of Greek Religion* (1903); Jessie Weston's *From Ritual to Romance* (1920); Margaret Smith's *Studies in Early Mysticism in the Near Middle East* (1931); Grace Harriet Macurdy's *Hellenistic Queens: A Study of Woman-Power in Macedonia, Seleucid Syria, and Ptolemaic Egypt* (1932).

12. In 'Their Last Interview', in *Experts Are Puzzled* (Riding 1930), Lilith Outcome engages in a lengthy conversation with God. In the short work 'Eve's Side of It', Riding writes: 'I have sometimes thought of Lilith as my mother . . . It is true that Lilith made me, but I had no father' (1993: 160).

13. Many of the stories in *Experts Are Puzzled* feature women characters that resonate with the Lilith myth (for example, 'Mademoiselle Comet' is 'a creature of pure pleasure' notable for her 'long bright dead hair'). Riding's valuation of the gender system and social power relations, in works like 'The Damn Thing' (*Anarchism Is Not Enough*), which critiques heterosexual sex, and 'The Word "Woman"', predate Simone de Beauvoir's *The Second Sex* by two decades.

14. In 'The Metaphysics of Modernism', Michael Bell notes:

> Modernist writers were almost obsessively concerned with history in a double sense: they were concerned both about what was happening in their world and the nature of historical

understanding as such. The mythopoeic basis of history has several very different aspects but it importantly includes an underlying recognition of the projective nature of all historical meaning. Insofar as myth is an affirmation of values it may be a form of historical motivation: as it proves to be, through the retrospective understanding of the poet.

2011: 14–15

15. Riding, *Lives of Wives* (1939: 327–8). In the early project, *Voltaire: A Biographical Fantasy*, Riding found her authority for her historical subject on imaginative and subjective knowing: 'To know *about* a life requires much learning. To *know* it needs only a partisan fancy … My facts cannot be challenged, for I have none; nor can my fancy be questioned, since it is proved by its own deviations wherever it goes' (1927: 3).

16. In Riding's novel, Odysseus and Aeneas are scoundrels.

17. Cressida is a compilation of several obscure historical women (Chryseis and Briseis) conflated by medieval and Renaissance authors to create a literary character. For a comprehensive accounting of Riding's use of Homer's *Iliad* in the construction of her novel, see Peter Christensen's 'Historical Truth in Laura Riding's *A Trojan Ending*' (1991a).

18. Christensen compares *A Trojan Ending* to Jean Giraudoux's play *La Guerre de Troie n'aura pas lieu* (1935) – a contemporaneous example of the use of classical setting for the critique of current events (in this case, an anti-war argument).

19. According to Christensen, Riding's sources for the Persian emperor Cyrus the Great (though with little attention paid to Amytis) derive from Greek accounts, instead of the Persian, to include Herodotus's *The Histories*, Xenophon's *Cyropedia*, Ctesias's *Persica* and the *Old Testament*. Depictions of Olympias, the wife of the Greek king of Macedonia, Philip the Great and mother to Alexander the Great, were more available, to include Grace Harriet Macurdy's contemporaneous *Hellenistic Queens: A Study of Woman-Power in Macedonia, Seleucid Syria, and Ptolemaic Egypt* (1932) in addition to Plutarch's *The Lives of the Nobel Grecians and Romans*. Riding most likely developed her version of the life of Pythias, wife of Aristotle, from Diogenes Laertius's *Lives of the Eminent Philosophers* (Book V). Notably, Riding paints Aristotle in an extremely negative light, depicting him as more calculated than intelligent and a social poseur. Histories of Herod's rule of Judea – and thereby Mariamne's life – were available in translations of two early sources: Josephus's *The Jewish War* and *Jewish Antiquities*. According to Christensen, Riding works to emphasize the 'credibility' of her accounts when she inserts Nicolaus of Damascus, historian in Herod's court – a name that the knowledgeable would correlate with Josephus's works. Finally, Cleopatra's notoriety was well established from ancient sources through her literary representations across time.

20. In the same monograph, *Translating Words, Translating Cultures*, Hardwick notes: 'the icons of Troy, Helen and Achilles already had a special significance in providing critical and ironic foils for early twentieth-century poets' (2000b: 49).

10 LOST AND FOUND IN TRANSLATION: THE GENESIS OF MODERNISM'S SIREN SONGS

1. Here and in what follows, I am citing the translation by Lattimore (Homer, 1965).

2. On the Sirens in relation to the Iliadic Muses, also see Segal (1983: 40) and Doherty (1995).

3. In particular, see Pogorzelski (2016), Rosenblitt (2016) and Flack (2015). Elizabeth Vandiver's (2010) significant study might be included here, but she also goes out of her way to state that her study is not a study of modernism.

11 'TRYING TO READ ARISTOPHANE': *SWEENEY AGONISTES*, RECEPTION AND RITUAL

1. The review originally appeared in *New English Weekly* 2 (12 January 1933): 304.

2. On a different occasion, Pound expressed a certain measure of interest in Aristophanes, writing to Iris Barry that 'Aristophanes parodies some of the tragic verse very nicely, at least I believe so' (Pound 1971: 94).

3. In this draft, the same epigraph from the *Oresteia* as the one in the published version appears in French, taken from the translation by Paul Mazon. Mazon, who happened to be one of the greatest Aristophanes specialists in France, also published *Extraits d'Aristophane* in Greek (1902) and in French (1906). The use of Mazon's translations may have prompted the French names of Aristophane and Aeschyle in the correspondence between Eliot and Pound. For a detailed textual history of *Sweeney Agonistes*, see Eliot (2015: II, 449–53).

4. For more about Pound's understanding of the term 'melodrama,' see Fisher (2002: 24–32).

5. The essay is entitled 'Date Line' and first appeared in *Make It New* in 1934. Pound's other categories of criticism are: (1) criticism by discussion, (2) by translation, (3) by exercise in the style of a given period, and (4) via music.

6. All quotations from Cornford are taken from the 1934 re-issue of *The Origin of Attic Comedy*. The book was first published in 1914, and Eliot probably read it between 1916 and 1920.

7. Jane Ellen Harrison and Gilbert Murray, close associates of Cornford, speak in this regard of the *Eniautos-Daimon*, the Year-King or Year-Spirit, analogous to Frazer's Corn-Spirit or Vegetation-Spirit. He is the incarnation of 'the whole world-process of decay, death, renewal', and was annually re-enacted in a *dromenon*, a rite with magical intent, which in Greek culture took the form of the Dionysian dithyramb, predecessor of ancient drama (Ackerman 2002: 125–35).

8. Ackerman (2002: 170) points out that while Gilbert Murray long considered New Comedy a turn away from ritual, he later revised this view in a text that was published a long time after *Sweeney Agonistes*, explaining how recurring elements in New Comedy plays add up to 'the general terms of a ritual' as well. See Murray (1943).

9. Citations from *Sweeney Agonistes* are all from Eliot (2015), vol. 1.

10. Wauchope and Horsfall are war veterans, and their friends, Klipstein and Krumpacker, are 'American gentlemen here on business' (119). Their background suggests a direct link with Aristophanes' *Acharnians*, where the chorus, a group of old men from Acharniae, are war veterans and charcoal merchants. They staunchly defend the war effort against Sparta, a stance echoed in Klipstein's 'Yes we did our bit, as you folks say, I'll tell the world we got the Hun on the run' (119). There is evidence that Eliot studied *Acharnians* closely (Eliot 2015: I, 787). *Acharnians* perhaps attracted Eliot because, being the earliest extant play of the Old Comedy, it had supposedly preserved its ritual structure better than later plays – it is interesting in that respect also because it integrates a sacrifice to Dionysus in its plot.

11. To complicate matters further, these types of music were at the time precisely viewed as so-called 'primitive' or 'folk' styles elevated to the level of art. Another entertainment form present in *Sweeney Agonistes* is the minstrel show: the minor characters Swarts and Snow (their names signal racial ambiguity) serve as 'Tambo' and 'Bones', traditional minstrel figures. The song 'Under the Bamboo Tree' is based on a real song from 1902 written by James Weldon Johnson, later to become a seminal figure in the Harlem Renaissance. David Chinitz explains that Johnson 'was striving to transform the "coon song" by ameliorating its stereotyped portrayal of African Americans. To this end Johnson strove to portray the black characters in his songs as essentially no different from his white listeners' (2003: 116).

12. I call Cornford a 'proto-structuralist' only for the sake of the argument. He was of course in no way a structuralist in the sense we give to the term when we discuss Lévi-Strauss or Barthes: as a classical anthropologist, he was primarily interested in the *origins* of cultural phenomena. His aim is therefore not to lay bare the ahistorical 'grammar' of literary comedy, but to reconstruct, from evidence in the surviving plays, the older, ritual drama from which literary comedy supposedly evolved. For a structuralist, by contrast, the very notion of an origin would be unthinkable.

13. The idea that Eliot considered *Sweeney Agonistes* a failure is defensible, because it remained unfinished; on the other hand, the fragments were later re-issued separately and in the *Collected Poems*.

14. Eliot's official conversion to the Anglican faith happened in 1927. While this is the same year in which the 'Fragment of an Agon' was published, the play had been planned and plotted long before.

15. Schuchard's comments on *Sweeney Agonistes* are from a chapter entitled 'The Savage Comedian' – his discussion of Eliot as a 'serious student of the comic spirit' is very enlightening (1999: 88).

16. In 'On the Essence of Laughter', Baudelaire writes:

> Laughter is satanic; it is therefore profoundly human. In man it is the consequence of his idea of his own superiority; and in fact, since laughter is essentially human, it is essentially contradictory, that is to say it is at one and the same time a sign of infinite greatness and of infinite wretchedness.
>
> *1981: 148*

17. Seneca's taste for cruelty and bloodshed is the main reason why he fell out of favor after the Renaissance and up to the late nineteenth century, when his drama was still accused of barbarism (Fleming and Grant 2013: 7–8).

18. It has repeatedly been argued that bathos held special appeal to modernist and avant-grade writers in the twentieth century. See for instance Sell (1984) and Crangle (2010). Sell explicitly points to Seneca as a source of twentieth-century bathos.

19. Bevis does not neglect to mention Wyndham Lewis's inversion of Bergson's definition: 'The root of the Comic is to be sought in the sensations resulting from the observations of a *thing* behaving like a person' (quoted in Bevis 2014: 146). The best example is perhaps to be found precisely in *Sweeney Agonistes*, when the telephone speaks the lines 'Ting a ling ling / Ting a ling ling' (Eliot 2015: I, 116).

12 'STRAIGHT TALK, STRAIGHT AS THE GREEK!': IRELAND'S OEDIPUS AND THE MODERNISM OF W.B. YEATS

1. W.B. Yeats, 'To Lady Gregory' (31 January 1914). *The Collected Letters of W.B. Yeats*. Intelex Past Masters, Entry no. 2394.

2. 1914 indicates the original year Yeats wrote the entry, 1972 the publication by Donoghue, 269 the page number therein, and no. 245, the designated number Yeats himself originally used to mark the entry.

3. W.B. Yeats, 'To Lady Gregory' (5 February 1914). *The Collected Letters of W.B. Yeats*. Intelex Past Masters, Entry no. 2396.

4. Ibid.

5. Ibid.

6. Passenger Manifest for the *R.M.S. Lusitania*, sailing from Liverpool to New York City, 31 January–7 February 1914, p. 4, line #29. On Turck's reputation, see Hamlin Garland (1926).

7. Yeats, 'To Lady Gregory' (5 February 1914).

8. Ibid.

9. Ibid.

10. '"American Literature Still in Victorian Era" – Yeats', *New York Times* (22 February 1914), SM10.

11. Ibid.

12. Ibid.

13. Ibid.

14. Ibid.

15. Since the Licensing Act of 1737 and the subsequent Theatre Regulation Act of 1843 – a law that adapted censorship's authority to serve 'the taste of the emergent Victorian bourgeoisie' – theatrical productions across England were required to seek a formal licence from the government. The Lord Chamberlain retained the right to alter the title, dialogue, or general character of scripts submitted for review. Yeats saw the practical effect of this requirement as manufacturing theatre stained by commercial interest and marred with a 'pretended hatred of vice'. In Ireland, by contrast, stage production had remained outside English jurisdiction and free from review. 'We are better off so far as the law is concerned than we would be in England', Yeats wrote in 1904, for 'the theatrical law of Ireland was made by the Irish Parliament, and ... we must be grateful that the ruling caste of free spirits, that being free themselves, they left the theatre in freedom. Nevertheless, 'the prevailing standards for acceptable stage productions in Ireland drew heavily', as one scholar has suggested, 'upon the British model, especially ... in prohibiting obscenity and blasphemy. Many plays performed in Ireland at the end of the nineteenth century were works licensed by the Lord Chamberlain.' See Green and Karolides (2005: 568; Yeats 2003d: 45; Dean 2004: 11), as well as Fowell and Palmer (1913: 373–4).

16. On Yeats's North American tour of 1904, see Strand (1978: 9–85).

17. The performance at Notre Dame was given on 15 May 1899 and commemorated with the publication of *The Oedipus Tyrannus of Sophocles, Translated and Presented by the Students of Notre Dame University*. The book contained the Greek text of the play alongside the English translation made by the students. Introducing the tragedy, the students were keen to note that in translating *Oedipus* 'nothing should be farther from our minds than idolatry or superstition. Although we will introduce you, next Monday, into a pagan temple, in the very hour of sacrifice, we beg that our actions and our sayings be not considered, in any way, idolatrous.

   We do not mean to pray to pagan gods,
   And if we swear in Greek, the harm is less'.

18. Stanley Buckmaster, Member of the Advisory Board on Stage Plays, Letter to the Lord Chamberlain, Charles Spencer (23 November 1910). Lord Chamberlain's Plays Correspondence File: *Oedipus Rex* 1910/814, British Library Archive.

19. Matthew Arnold (1961: 28); Sir John Hare, Member of the Advisory Board on Stage Plays, Letter to the Lord Chamberlain, Charles Spencer (21 November 1910). Lord Chamberlain's Plays Correspondence File: *Oedipus Rex* 1910/814, British Library Archive.

20. As quoted in Murphy (1978: 133); on Yeats's knowledge of Greek, see Arkins (1990: 3–4); Liebregts (1993: 9–21), as well as Foster (1997: 33–4).

21. It is likely that Yeats's distaste for Euripidean tragedy emerged from Nietzsche's condemnation of 'frevelnder Euripides' in *The Birth of Tragedy* (1872). Euripides was, Nietzsche insisted, 'the poet of aesthetic Socratism', a 'murderous principle' by which 'the old tragedy' of Sophocles and Aeschylus had been destroyed. See Nietzsche (1901: 4).

22. Gogarty ([1905] 1971: 88); Yeats ([1906] 2005b: 509).

23. See *The Oedipus Tyrannus of Sophocles: As arranged for performance at Cambridge, November 1887.* R.C. Jebb and A.W. Verrall, trans. (Cambridge, 1887); Clark and McGuire (1989) 19.

24. Yao (2002b: 135); Pound (May 1914, 66, 67). In his poem 'Xenia', Pound insisted that his own 'songs' seek 'ever to stand in the hard Sophoclean light / And take your wounds from it gladly'. Pound, 'Xenia'. *Poetry* 3.2 (November 1913) 60.

25. *Freeman's Journal* (31 October 1902, 4).

26. *Freeman's Journal* (31 October 1902, 4).

27. Yeats's interest in Nietzsche's analysis of Greek tragedy was reported on in the *Daily Chronicle* of 13 May 1903. P.G.W. 'Daily Chronicle Office, Wednesday Morning', *Daily Chronicle* (13 May 1903, 7).

28. Yeats ([1904] 1994c: 577); Pound (1918: 95); Hulme (1924: 113, 133, 120). Yeats echoed Hulme's sentiment in the 1914 interview, '"American Literature Still in Victorian Era" – Yeats' *New York Times* (22 February 1914), SM10.

29. Hulme (1924: 113, 127, 117, 116, 127, 120).

30. Ibid. (117, 116, 127).

31. Ibid. (120); J.M. Synge, Letter to Spencer Bodney (10, 12 December 1907), as quoted in Synge (1966: 47); Yeats, as quoted in *Weekly Freeman* (23 May 1903, 9).

32. '16: Ezra Pound to Margaret Craven' (30 June 1910), in Pound (1988: 41).

33. '23: Ezra Pound to Margaret Craven' (27 November 1910), in Pound (1988: 61).

34. Ezra Pound, '7: To Harriet Monroe' (October 1912), in Pound (1971: 11); cf. Yeats, 'Letter to Gordon Bottomley' (8 January 1910). *The Collected Letters of W. B. Yeats.* Intelex Past Masters, Entry no. 1263.

35. W.B. Yeats, 'First Principles'. Maud Gonne Xmas Notebook, 1912 (NLI 30, 358). Yeats Archive, Box 88.2, SUNY Stony Brook.

36. Review of R.C. Jebb, *Sophocles: The Plays and Fragments, with Critical Notes, Commentary, and Translation*, in *Journal of Education* 178 (1 May 1884, 180).

37. Yeats, 'To Lady Gregory' (6 January 1912). *The Collected Letters of W.B. Yeats.* Intelex Past Masters, Entry no. 1794; Yeats, 'The Scholars' (1940: 337).

38. S.H. Butcher, 'Sophocles'. *The Fortnightly Review* 205 (1 June 1884, 796).

39. Review of R.C. Jebb, *Sophocles: The Plays and Fragments, with Critical Notes, Commentary, and Translation* (Cambridge, 1883) in *The Athenaeum* 2948 (26 April 1884, 531); Butcher (1 June 1884, 796–7).

40. Jebb, as printed in Stray (2013: 47).

41. On Yeats's desire 'to make the language of poetry coincide with passionate, normal speech', see Earle (1988: 19–48), Parkinson (1964: 181–231), and Arkins (1994: 3–26). See also Yeats, 'To Lady Gregory' (7 January 1912). *The Collected Letters of W.B. Yeats.* Intelex Past Masters, Entry no. 1796.

42. On the *Homage* see Sullivan (1964); Bush (1983: 61–79); Hooley (1988); Rudd (1994: 117–58) as well as Thomas (1983: 39–58) and Willett (2005: 173–220).

43. On Max Reinhardt's production, see Hall and Macintosh (2005: 538–54) as well as Purdom (1955: 129–31).

44. Yeats was undeterred that winter despite having seen Max Reinhardt's production in London late that January. See Yeats (1989: 29–33).

45. When Yeats finally returned to working on 'the material version of a chorus for a version of *Oedipus*' in February 1926, he would reiterate that his verse had 'more and more adopted – seemingly without any will of mine – the syntax and vocabulary of common personal speech'. Yeats, Letter to H.J.C. Grierson (21 February [1926]), in Yeats (1955: 710).

46. A description of the Society's aims was advertised in the entry for the 'Catholic Truth Society of Ireland' in *The Irish Catholic Directory and Almanac for 1920* (1920: 207).

47. *Report of the Committee on Evil Literature* (1927: 3).

48. *Report of the Committee on Evil Literature* (1927: 18).

RESPONDENT ESSAY 3: MODERNIST TRANSLATIONS AND POLITICAL ATTUNEMENTS

1. I am thinking here of *Mrs Dalloway*, *To the Lighthouse* and *The Waves* in particular (see, e.g., Spiropoulou 2002; Dalgarno 2006, 2012).

2. See, e.g., North (1992); Blau duPlessis (1995); Bush (2005).

13 MODERNIST MIGRATIONS, PEDAGOGICAL ARENAS: TRANSLATING MODERNIST RECEPTION IN THE CLASSROOM AND GALLERY

1. Mann is familiar to followers of American photography, as she appeared in her mother Sally Mann's photography during her childhood.

2. In an email to the authors, Len Prince shared the detail about purchasing the birdbath from Walmart (16 June 2017).

AFTERWORD: MODERNISM GOING FORWARD

1. As an example of what is gained from bearing in mind the modernist context, see also Ioannidou (2017), who positions her study of postmodern engagement with Greek tragedy against the modernist backdrop.

2. Our volume takes 'translation' in a wide sense, as does other recent work on modernism and translation, e.g. Parker and Mathews (2011).

3. *The Waste Land*, l. 430; Ziolkowski (1993: 121–3); Martindale (2013: 171, Eliot fragmenting Petronius); Latham and Rogers (2015: 5–6). I use 'iconicized' with reference to the arguments made about *The Waste Land* by Rainey (1998).

4. See Burnett (2000: 73) for discussion of Walcott and Roman imperialism and an earlier use of the same phrase in his poetry.

5. I make this point about contrast with the Decadent era but I acknowledge the limits of such contrasts in view of Laity's arguments (Laity 1996, 2004) about the constructed and gendered nature of the modernists' own claims to a clean break with Decadent writing.

6. Walcott (1990: 320, LXIV.1), from Eliot's *The Waste Land*. The fact that the phrase is Eliot's must be relevant to any attempt to read this point in Walcott's text as a Homeric engagement, e.g. McConnell (2013: 114–15). On the role of Dante in the poem's 'hybridity', see McConnell (2013: 107–54); see also Burkitt (2007) for a discussion of Walcott's self-positioning and extensive further bibliography in McConnell (2013).

7. Siddiqui (2014). I also note that Flack's discussion of Heaney (Flack 2016), to which I referred at the outset, considers a change in Heaney's relationship to Dante as a facet of Heaney's move from engagement with an Eliot-focused modernism to a Mandelstam-focused modernism.

8. Overt Dantean engagements and translations appear scattered throughout most of O'Donoghue's published collections; the list includes 'The Nth Circle' (*The Weakness*, 1991), 'Nel Mezzo del Cammin' (*Gunpowder*, 1995), 'Fra Alberigo's Bad Fruit' (*Outliving*, 2003), 'Amicitia' (*Farmers Cross*, 2011) and 'The Mantuans' (*The Seasons of Cullen Church*, 2016).

9. Ziolkowski (1993) explores the many Virgils whom the modernists themselves found.

10. *The Golden Gate* falls within the 'New Formalism'; its relationship to eclecticism is postmodern. For another way of looking at postmodern fragmentation in a reception context, see Ioannidou (2017: 131–66).

11. Rood (2013) explores some of the problems with Martindale's approach and points out that Martindale's vision of a classical reception studies, which is predicated on aesthetic response, excludes political and ethical dimensions to acts of classical reception and to the study of classical reception.

WORKS CITED

Ackerman, R. (2002), *The Myth and Ritual School: J.G. Frazer and the Cambridge Ritualists*, New York: Routledge.

Adams, M. (1968), *Censorship: The Irish Experience*, Dublin: Scepter Publishers Ltd.

Adams, S. (1977), 'Pound's Quantities and "Absolute Rhythm"', *Essays in Literature* 4: 95–109.

Adams, S. (1997), *Poetic Designs: An Introduction to Meters, Verse Forms, and Figures of Speech*, Peterborough: Broadview.

Adler, E. (2016), *Classics, the Culture Wars, and Beyond*, Ann Arbor: University of Michigan Press.

Ahearn, B. (2003), '*Cathay*: What Sort of Translation?', in Z. Qian (ed.), *Ezra Pound and China*, 31–48, Ann Arbor: University of Michigan Press.

Ahmed, S. (2004), *The Cultural Politics of the Emotions*, New York: Routledge.

Aji, H. (2003), 'Translation as Vortex: A Foreword', in H. Aji (ed.), *Ezra Pound dans le vortex de la traduction, Annales du monde anglophone* 16: 9–14, Paris: L'Harmattan.

Aldington, R. (1913), 'To Atthis', *The New Freewoman* 6 (1): 114.

Aldington, R. (1915a), 'The Poets' Translation Series. Announcement', *The Egoist* 2 (8): 45–6 = *The Little Review* 2 (6): 45–6.

Aldington, R., trans. (1915b), *The Poems of Anyte of Tegea*, London: Ballantyne.

Aldington, R., trans. (1915c), *A Choice of the Latin Poets of the Italian Renaissance*, London: Ballantyne.

Aldington, R. (1916), 'The Poets' Translation Series (Second Prospectus)', *The Egoist* 3 (1): 15.

Aldington, R. (1918), 'Letters to an Unknown Woman', *The Dial* 64: 226–7.

Aldington, R. (1919a), 'The "Lament for Adonis"', *The Egoist* 6 (1): 10–11.

Aldington, R. (1919b), 'The Poets' Translation Series', London: The Egoist Press.

Aldington, R., trans. (1919c), *Greek Songs in the Manner of Anacreon*, London: The Egoist Press.

Aldington, R., trans. (1919d), *The Latin Poets of the Renaissance*, London: The Egoist Press.

Aldington, R., trans. (1920a), *The Poems of Meleager of Gadara*, London: The Egoist Press.

Aldington, R. (1920b), Letter to the editor, *The Nation*, 27 November: 310.

Aldington, R., trans. (1921), *Medallions in Clay*, New York: Alfred A. Knopf.

Aldington, R., trans. (1930), *Medallions,* London: Chatto & Windus.

Aldington, R. (1941), *Life for Life's Sake: A Book of Reminiscences*, New York: The Viking Press.

Aldington, R., and E. Storer, trans. (1919), *The Poems of Anyte of Tegea*, trans. R. Aldington, *Poems and Fragments of Sappho*, trans. E. Storer, London: The Egoist Press.

Alexander, M. (1997), 'Ezra Pound as Translator', *Translation and Literature* 6 (1): 23–30.

Apter, R. (1984), *Digging for Treasure: Translation after Pound*, New York: Peter Lang.

Arkins, B. (1990), *Builders of My Soul: Greek and Roman Themes in Yeats*, Savage: Barnes & Noble.

Arkins, B. (1994), 'Passionate Syntax: Style in the Poetry of Yeats', *Yeats: An Annual of Critical and Textual Studies*, Ann Arbor: University of Michigan Press, 12: 3–26.

Armstrong, R. (2014), 'Homer, Translation', in G. Giannakis (ed.), *Encyclopedia of Ancient Greek Language and Linguistics: Volume 2*, 175–82, Leiden: Brill.

Arnold, M. ([1869] 2009), *Culture and Anarchy*, J. Garnett (ed.), Oxford: Oxford University Press.

Arnold, M. ([1870]), 'On Translating Homer', J. Lynch (ed.): http://andromeda.rutgers.edu/~jlynch/Texts/translating.html

Arnold, M. (1961), 'On the Modern Element in Literature', (14 November 1857), in R.H. Super (ed.), *The Complete Prose Works of Matthew Arnold. Volume I: On the Classical Tradition*, 18–37, Ann Arbor: University of Michigan Press.

Works Cited

Arnott, W.G. (1990), 'Euripides' Newfangled *Helen*', *Antichthon* 24: 1–18.

Athanasopoulou, E.N. (2008), 'The Motif of Love in the *Helen* and the *Alcestis* of Euripides', PhD thesis, Department of Greek Studies, University of Johannesburg Press.

Austin, N. (1994), *Helen of Troy and Her Shameless Phantom*, Ithaca: Cornell University Press.

Babcock, R.G. (1995), 'Verses, Translations, and Reflections from "The Anthology": H.D., Ezra Pound, and the Greek Anthology', *Sagetrieb* 14: 201–16.

Bajaj, B. (2009), 'Meaning' and 'Sense', in J. Munday (ed.), *The Routledge Companion to Translation Studies*, Rev. edn., 206, 224, London: Routledge.

Baker, W. E. (1967), 'The Strange and the Familiar', *18, Perspectives in Criticism, Syntax in English Poetry, 1870-1930*, 84–106, Berkeley, CA: University of California Press.

Balmer J. (2013), *Piecing Together the Fragments*, Oxford: Oxford University Press.

Baran, H., Halsall, A.W. and Watson, A. (2012), 'Aposiopesis', in R. Greene and S. Cushman (eds.), *Princeton Encyclopedia of Poetry and Poetics*, 4th edn., Princeton: Princeton University Press.

Barbour, S. (2012), 'The Origins of the Prose Captions in H.D.'s *Helen in Egypt*', *RES* 63: 466–90.

Baudelaire, C. (1981), *Selected Writings on Art and Artists*, trans. P.E. Charvet, Cambridge: Cambridge University Press.

Beecroft, A.J. (2006), '"This is not a True Story": Stesichorus' *Palinode* and the Revenge of the Epichoric', *TAPA* 136: 47–70.

Bell, M. (2011), 'The Metaphysics of Modernism', in *The Cambridge Companion to Modernism*, M. Levenson (ed.), 9–32, New York: Cambridge University Press.

Benjamin, W. (1968a), 'The Task of the Translator', in H. Arendt (ed.), *Illuminations*, trans. H. Zohn, 69–82, New York: Schocken Books.

Benjamin, W. (1968b), 'Theses on the Philosophy of History', in H. Arendt (ed.), *Illuminations*, trans. H. Zohn, 253–64, New York: Schocken Books.

Benjamin, W. (1986), 'On the Mimetic Faculty', in P. Demetz (ed.), *Reflections*, trans. E. Jephcott, 333–6, New York: Schocken Books.

Bernard, E. (1960), *Die Tmesis der Präposition in lateinischen Verbalkomposita*, Winterthur: P. G. Keller.

Bevis, M. (2014), 'Eliot Among the Comedians', *Literary Imagination* 16: 135–56.

Bibb, A. (2010), 'Vision, Paranoia and the Creative Power of Obsessive Interpretation', *Journal for Cultural and Religious Studies* 10: 99–116.

Bion. ([n.d.] 1977), *Lament for Adonis*, trans. J.M. Edmonds, in *The Greek Bucolic Poets*, 387, Cambridge, MA: Harvard University Press.

Blanchot B. (1980), *The Writing of the Disaster*, Lincoln: University of Nebraska Press.

Blondell, R. (2013), *Helen of Troy: Beauty, Myth, Devastation*, New York: Oxford University Press.

Boitani, P. (1994), *The Shadow of Ulysses: Figures of a Myth*, trans. A. Weston, Oxford: Oxford University Press.

Bowen, Z.R. (1974), *Musical Allusions in the Works of James Joyce: Early Poetry through Ulysses*, New York: SUNY.

Bowra, C.M. (1961), *Greek Lyric Poetry*, 2nd edn., Oxford: Clarendon Press.

Bradshaw, M. (2011), *Amy Lowell: Diva Poet*, New York: Ashgate.

Brinkman, B. and B. Brinkman (2016), 'Educating the "Perfect Imagist": Greek Literature and Classical Scholarship in the Poetry of H.D.', in A. J. Goldwyn and J. Nikopoulous (eds.), *Brill's Companion to the Reception of Classics in International Modernism*, 38–52, Leiden: Brill.

Brogan, T.V.F. (2012), 'Anadiplosis' in R. Greene and S. Cushman (eds.), *Princeton Encyclopedia of Poetry and Poetics*, 4th edn., Princeton: Princeton University Press.

Brown, H. and Halsall, A.W. (2012), 'Anacoluthon' in R. Greene and S. Cushman (eds.), *Princeton Encyclopedia of Poetry and Poetics*, 4th edn., Princeton, NJ: Princeton University Press.

Bryant, M., Eaverly, M. A. and McCusker, C. (2014), Exhibition. Classical Convergences: Traditions and Reinventions. Harn Museum of Art, University of Florida, Gainesville, FL. 16 Dec., 2014–May 2015.

Bubich, O. (2016), 'Interview with Jessie Mann', *Bleeker Magazine*, 14 November: bleek-magazine. com/interviews/jessie-mann/

Budgen, F. ([1934] 1972), *James Joyce and the Making of* Ulysses, London: Grayson & Grayson.

Burkert, W. ([1962] 1972), *Lore and Science in Ancient Pythagoreanism*, trans. Edwin L. Minar, Jr., Cambridge, MA: Harvard University Press.

Burkert, W. (2001), *Savage Energies: Lessons of Myth and Ritual in Ancient Greece*, trans. Peter Bing, Chicago: University of Chicago Press.

Burkitt, K. (2007), 'Epic Proportions: Post-Epic Verse-Novels and Postcolonial Critique', PhD Diss., University of Salford.

Burnett, P. (2000), *Derek Walcott: Politics and Poetics*, Gainesville: University Press of Florida.

Bush, C. (2005), 'The Other of the Other? Cultural Studies, Theory, and the Location of the Modernist Signifier', *Comparative Literature Studies* 42 (2): 162–80.

Bush, R. (1976), *The Genesis of Ezra Pound's Cantos*, Princeton: Princeton University Press.

Bush, R. (1983), 'Gathering the Limbs of Osiris: The Subject of Pound's Homage to Sextus Propertius', in D. Hoffman (ed.), *Ezra Pound and William Carlos Williams: The University of Pennsylvania Conference Papers*, 61–79, Philadelphia: University of Pennsylvania Press.

Bush, R. (1996), 'The Modernist under Siege', in J. Allison (ed.), *Yeats's Political Identities, Selected Essays*, 325–33. Ann Arbor: University of Michigan Press.

Butcher, S.H. (1884), 'Sophocles.' *The Fortnightly Review* 205 (1 June) 794–811.

Butler, S. (2016), 'Introduction: On the Origin of "Deep Classics"', in S. Butler (ed.), *Deep Classics: Rethinking Classical Reception*, 1–19, London: Bloomsbury.

Buttram, C. (2009) '*Sweeney Agonistes*: A Sensational Snarl', in D.E. Chinitz (ed.), *A Companion to T. S. Eliot*, 179–90, Malden: Wiley-Blackwell.

Campbell, D. (1991), ed. and trans. *Greek Lyric III*, Cambridge, MA: Harvard University Press.

Carne-Ross, D.S. (1985), *Pindar*, New Haven: Yale University Press.

Carpentier, M.C. ([1998] 2013), *Ritual, Myth, and the Modernist Text: The Influence of Jane Ellen Harrison on Joyce, Eliot, and Woolf*, London: Taylor & Francis.

Carr, H. (2009), *The Verse Revolutionaries: Ezra Pound, H.D., and the Imagists*, London: Jonathan Cape.

Carson, A. (1986), *Eros the Bittersweet*, Princeton: Princeton University Press.

'Catholic Truth Society of Ireland' (1920), *The Irish Catholic Directory and Almanac for 1920*, 207, Dublin: James Duffy and Co.

Chinitz, D.E. (2003), *T.S. Eliot and the Cultural Divide*, Chicago: University of Chicago Press.

Christensen, P. (1991a), 'Historical Truth in Laura Riding's *A Trojan Ending*', *Focus on Robert Graves and His Contemporaries* 1: 1–17.

Christensen, P. (1991b), 'Women as a Spiritual Force in Laura Riding's *Lives of Wives*', *Focus on Robert Graves and His Contemporaries* 1: 18–35.

Coleman, R.G.G. (1999), 'Poetic Diction, Poetic Discourse and the Poetic Register', in J.N. Adams and R.G. Mayer (eds.), *Aspects of the Language of Latin Poetry*, 21–96, Oxford: Oxford University Press.

Collecott, D. (1999), *H.D. & Sapphic Modernism 1910–1950*, Cambridge: Cambridge University Press.

Committee on Evil Literature (1927), *Report of the Committee on Evil Literature*, Dublin: Stationery Office.

Conacher, D.J. (1967), *Euripidean Drama: Myth, Theme and Structure*, Toronto: University of Toronto Press.

Connolly, S. (2002), 'Review: Short Reviews', *Poetry* 181 (2): 160–69.

Connor, R. (2004), *H.D. and the Image*, Manchester: Manchester University Press.

Connor, S. (2004), 'Modernity and Myth', in L. Marcus and P. Nicholls (eds.), *The Cambridge History of Twentieth-Century English Literature*, 251–68, Cambridge: Cambridge University Press.

Works Cited

Constantinidou, S. (2008), *Logos into Mythos: The Case of Gorgias' Encomium*, Athens: Institut de Livre A. Kardamitsa.

Cookson, W. (2001), *A Guide to the Cantos of Ezra Pound*, 2nd edn., London: Anvil Press.

Copp, M., ed. (2009), *Imagist Dialogues: Letters between Aldington, Flint and Others*, Cambridge: Lutterworth.

Coyle, M. (2015), 'Popular Culture', in D. Chinitz and G. McDonald (eds.), *A Companion to Modernist Poetry*, 81–94, Oxford: Wiley-Blackwell.

Cornford, F. M. (1934), *The Origin of Attic Comedy*, Cambridge: Cambridge University Press.

Crangle, S. and P. Nicholls (2010), 'Introduction: On Bathos', in S. Crangle and P. Nicholls (eds), *On Bathos*, 1–6, London: Continuum.

Crangle, S. (2010), 'Dada IS Bathos! Or: of the Hobbyhorse Endlessly Rocking', in S. Crangle and P. Nicholls (eds.), *On Bathos*, 27–48, London: Continuum.

Crawford, R. (1987), *The Savage and the City in the Work of T.S. Eliot*, Oxford: Clarendon Press.

Crawford, R. (2015), *Young Eliot: From St. Louis to* The Waste Land, London: Jonathan Cape.

Culler, J. (2015), *Theory of the Lyric*, Cambridge: Harvard University Press.

Cullingford, E. (1981), *Yeats, Ireland and Fascism*, New York: New York University Press.

Cunliffe, R. J. (1963), *A Lexicon of Homeric Dialect*, London: University of Oklahoma, London.

Dalgarno, E. (2006), 'Virginia Woolf: Translation and Iterability', *Yearbook of English Studies* 36 (1): 145–56.

Dalgarno, E. (2012), *Virginia Woolf and the Migrations of Language*, Cambridge: Cambridge University Press.

Davie, D. (1964), *Ezra Pound: Poet as Sculptor*, New York: Oxford University Press.

Dean, J.F. (2004), 'Theatrical Censorship and Disorder in Ireland', *Riot and Great Anger: Stage Censorship in Twentieth-century Ireland*, 11–33, Madison: University of Wisconsin Press.

Debo, A. and L. Vetter (2011), *Approaches to Teaching H.D.'s Poetry and Prose*, New York: MLA.

DeKoven, M. (2011), 'Modernism and Gender', in *The Cambridge Companion to Modernism*, M. Levenson (ed.), 212–31, Cambridge: Cambridge University Press.

Deleuze G. and Guattari F. (1986), *Kafka: Toward a Minor Literature*, Minneapolis: University of Minnesota Press.

Deleuze G. and Guattari F. (1987), *A Thousand Plateaus: Capitalism and Schizophrenia*, Minneapolis: University of Minnesota Press.

De Man, P. (1983), *Blindness and Insight*, 2nd rev. edn., Minneapolis: University of Minnesota.

De Mirmont, H. de la Ville, ed. and trans. (1889), *D. M. Ausonii Mosella: La Moselle d'Ausone*, Paris: Alphonse Lemerre.

Dendinger, L.N., ed. (1981), *E.E. Cummings: The Critical Reception*, New York: Burt Franklin & Co., Inc.

Derrida, J. ([1972] 1981), *Dissemination*, trans. Barbara Johnson, Chicago: Chicago University Press.

Devane, Rev. R. S. (1925), 'Indecent Literature: Some Legal Remedies', *Irish Ecclesiastical Record* 5th ser. 25: 182–204.

Diepeveen, L. (1993), *Changing Voices: The Modern Quoting Poem*, Ann Arbor: University of Michigan Press.

Doherty, L. (1995), *Siren Songs: Gender, Audiences, and Narrators in the* Odyssey, Ann Arbor: University of Michigan Press.

Doig, P. and D. Walcott (2016), *Morning, Paramin*, London: Faber and Faber.

Duncan, R. (2011), *The H.D. Book*, M. Boughn and V. Coleman (eds.), Berkeley: University of California Press.

DuPlessis, R.B. (1986), *H.D.: The Career of That Struggle*, Bloomington: Indiana University Press.

DuPlessis, R.B. (1995), 'HOO, HOO, HOO: Some Episodes in the Construction of Modern Whiteness', *American Literature* 67 (4): 667–700.

Earle, R.H. (1988), 'Questions of Syntax, Syntax of Questions: Yeats and the Topology of Passion', *Yeats: An Annual of Critical and Textual Studies*, vol. 6, 19–48, Ann Arbor: University of Michigan.

Easterling, P.E. (1987), 'Women in Tragic Space', *BICS* 34: 15–26.

Eliot, T.S. (1916), 'Classics in English', *Poetry* 9 (2): 101–4.

Eliot, T.S. ([1918] 1932), 'Euripides and Professor Murray', *Selected Essays 1917–1932*, 46–50, New York: Harcourt, Brace and Co.

Eliot, T.S. (1919), 'War-Paint and Feathers: Review of *The Path on the Rainbow*, ed. by George W. Cronyn', *The Athenaeum*, 17 October: 1036.

Eliot, T.S. ([1919] 1975), 'Tradition and the Individual Talent', in *Selected Prose of T.S. Eliot*, F. Kermode (ed.), 37–44, New York, Harcourt.

Eliot, T.S. ([1920] 1997), *The Sacred Wood: Essay on Poetry and Criticism*, London: Methuen.

Eliot, T.S. ([1929] 2015), 'Dante', in F. Dickey, J. Formichelli and R. Schuchard (eds.), *The Complete Prose of T.S. Eliot: The Critical Edition*, 700–45, Baltimore: Johns Hopkins University Press.

Eliot, T.S. ([1934] 1960), 'Shakespeare Criticism I: From Dryden to Coleridge', in H. Granville-Barker and G.B. Harrison (eds.), *A Companion to Shakespeare Studies*, 287–99, Garden City, NY: Anchor Books – Doubleday & Co.

Eliot, T.S. (1961), *Selected Essays*, London: Faber & Faber.

Eliot, T.S. (1965), *To Criticize the Critic*, New York: Farrar.

Eliot, T.S. (1971), *The Waste Land: A Facsimile and Transcript of the Original Drafts Including the Annotations of Ezra Pound*, V. Eliot (ed.), Orlando: Harcourt.

Eliot, T.S. (1975), '*Ulysses*, Order, and Myth', *Selected Prose of T.S. Eliot*, F. Kermode (ed.), 175–8, New York: Harcourt Brace and Company.

Eliot, T.S. (1988), *The Letters of T.S. Eliot, Vol. 1: 1898–1922*, V. Eliot (ed.), London: Faber & Faber.

Eliot, T.S. (2006), *The Annotated* Waste Land *with Eliot's Contemporary Prose*, Lawrence Rainey (ed.), 2nd edn., New Haven: Yale University Press.

Eliot, T.S. (2009), *The Letters of T.S. Eliot, Vol. 2: 1923–1925*, V. Eliot and H. Haughton (eds.), London: Faber & Faber.

Eliot, T.S. (2014), *The Letters of T.S. Eliot, Vol. 5: 1930–1931*, V. Eliot and J. Haffenden (eds.), London: Faber & Faber.

Eliot, T.S. (2015), *The Poems of T.S. Eliot*. 2 vols, C. Ricks and J. McCue (eds.), London: Faber & Faber.

Ellmann, R. (1982), *James Joyce*, New York: Oxford.

Espey, J. (1955), *Ezra Pound's* Mauberley: *A Study in Composition*, London: Faber.

Euripides (n.d.), Ἡρακλεῖδαι, Ἰφιγένεια ἐν Αὐλίδι, Ἰφιγένεια ἐν Ταύροις, P. Lekatsas and Th. Stavrou (eds.), Ι. Ζαχαρόπουλος, Athens.

Euripides (1910), *Hippolytus*, E.P. Coleridge (trans.): http://sacred-texts.com/cla/eurip/hippol.htm.

Euripides (1915), *Hippolytus: Translated into English Rhyming Verse with Explanatory Notes by G. Murray*, London: George Allen & Unwin.

Euripides ([1939] 1969), *Ion*, A.S. Owen (ed.), Oxford: Oxford University Press.

Euripides (1970), *Ion*, trans. A. Pippin Burnett, Englewood Cliffs, Prentice-Hall, 1970.

Euripides (1995a), *Children of Heracles, Hippolytus, Andromache, Hecuba*, D. Kovacs (ed. and trans.), Loeb Classical Library 484, Cambridge, MA: Harvard University Press.

Euripides (1995b), *Hippolytos*, with an Introduction, Translation and Commentary by M.R. Halleran, Warminster: Aris & Philips.

Euripides (1996), *Ion*, trans. W.S. DiPiero, New York: Oxford University Press.

Euripides (1999), *Trojan Women, Iphigenia among the Taurians*, trans. and ed. D. Kovacs, Loeb Classical Library 10, Cambridge, MA: Harvard University Press.

Euripides (2002a), *Bacchae, Iphigenia at Aulis, Rhesus*, trans. and ed. D. Kovacs, Loeb Classical Library 6, Cambridge, MA: Harvard University Press.

Euripides (2002b), *Helen, Phoenician Women, Orestes*, trans. and ed. D. Kovacs, Loeb Classical Library 5, Cambridge, MA: Harvard University Press.

Works Cited

Euripides (2004), *Helen*, trans. and ed. A.M. Dale, Oxford University Press, Bristol Classical Press, Oxford.

Euripides (2005), *Εκάβη*, trans. and ed. Κ. Synodinou, *Μετάφραση, Σχόλια, Σημειώσεις, τομ,* τομ. 1 και 2, *Δαίδαλος,* Athens.

Euripides (2008) *Helen*, trans. and ed. W. Allan, Cambridge: Cambridge University Press.

Euripides (2011), *The Complete Euripides: Vol. 5: Medea and Other Plays*, Peter Burian (ed.), New York: Oxford University Press.

Evans, R.O. and T.V.F. Brogan, (2012), 'Antonomasia' in R. Greene and S. Cushman (eds.), *Princeton Encyclopedia of Poetry and Poetics*, 4th edn., Princeton: Princeton University Press.

Fairhall, J. (1990), '*Ulysses*, the Great War, and the Easter 1916 Rising', in David Bevan (ed.), *Literature and War*, 25–38, Amsterdam: Rodopi.

Fairhall, J. (1995), *James Joyce and the Question of History*, Cambridge: Cambridge University Press.

Farnell, L.R. (1921), *Greek Hero Cults and Ideas of Immortality*, Oxford: Clarendon Press.

Fenollosa, E. (1962), 'The Chinese Written Character as a Medium for Poetry', in K. Shapiro (ed.), *Prose Keys to Modern Poetry*, 136–155, New York: Harper & Row.

Fisher, M. (2002), *Ezra Pound's Radio Operas: The BBC Experiments, 1931–1933*, Cambridge, MA: MIT.

Flack, L.C. (2015), '"The News in the Odyssey Is Still News": Ezra Pound, W.H.D. Rouse, and a Modern *Odyssey*', *Modernism/Modernity* 22 (1): 105–24.

Flack, L.C. (2016), 'Whatever is Given/Can Always Be Reimagined': Seamus Heaney's Indefinite Modernism', in P. Reynolds (ed.), *Modernist Afterlives in Irish Literature and Culture*, 35–48, London: Anthem.

Fleming, K. and T. Grant (2013), 'Introduction: Seneca in the English Tradition', Canadian Review of Comparative Literature 40 (1): 7-15.

Flint, F.S., trans. ([1916]), *The Mosella of Decimus Magnus Ausonius*, London: Spottiswoode.

Foley, H. (2003), 'Choral Identity in Greek Tragedy', *CPh* 98: 1–30.

Ford, A. (1992), *Homer: The Poetry of the Past*, Ithaca: Cornell University Press.

Foster, R.F. (1997), *W.B. Yeats, A Life. Volume I. The Apprentice Mage, 1865–1914*, Oxford: Oxford University Press.

Fowell, F. and F. Palmer (1913), *Censorship in England*, London.

Friedmann, E. (2005), *A Mannered Grace: The Life of Laura (Riding) Jackson*, New York: Persea Books.

Friedman, S.S. (1981), *Psyche Reborn: The Emergence of H.D.*, Bloomington: Indiana University Press.

Friedman, S.S. (1990), *Penelope's Web: Gender, Modernity, H.D.'s Fiction*, Cambridge: Cambridge University Press.

Freud, S. ([1914] 1950), 'Remembering, Repeating, and Working-Through', in *The Standard Edition of the Complete Psychological Works of Sigmund Freud*, J. Strachey (ed. and trans.), Volume 12: 145–57, London: Hogarth.

Freud, S. ([1920] 1961), *Beyond the Pleasure Principle*, trans. J. Strachey, New York: W.W. Norton.

Friedman, S.S., ed. (2002), *Analyzing Freud: Letters of H.D., Bryher, and Their Circle*, New York: New Directions.

Fussell, P. (1975), *The Great War and Modern Memory*, Oxford: Oxford University Press.

Fyta, A. (2015) *H.D.'s poetics and Euripidean Drama*, PhD Diss., University of Ioannina.

Gamel, M.-K. (2001), '"Apollo Knows I Have No Children": Motherhood, Scholarship, Theatre', *Arethusa* 34 (1): 153–71.

Garland, H. ed., (1926), *Nature's Alchemy, Special Bulletin of the Turck Foundation for Biological Research*, New York.

Gates, N. T., ed. (1992), *Richard Aldington: An Autobiography in Letters*, University Park: Pennsylvania State University Press.

Geffcken, J., ed. (1896), *Leonidas von Tarent*, Leipzig: Teubner.

Gilbert, S. M. (1999), '"Rats' Alley": The Great War, Modernism, and the (Anti) Pastoral Elegy', *New Literary History* 30: 179–201.

Gillespie, S. (2011), *English Translation and Classical Reception: Towards a New Literary History*, Malden: Wiley-Blackwell.

Glare, P.G.W., ed. (1982), *Oxford Latin Dictionary*, Oxford: Oxford University Press.

Glissant, E. (1990), *Poétique de la relation*, Paris: Gallimard.

Godard, B. (1990), 'Theorizing Feminist Discourse/Translation', in *Translation, History and Culture*, S. Bassnett and A. Lefevere (eds.), 87–96, New York: Pinter.

Goff, B. (1995), 'The Women of Thebes', *CJ* 90 (4): 353–65.

Gogarty, O. St. John ([1905] 1971), *Many Lines to Thee – Letters to G. K. A. Bell*, J. F. Carens (ed.), Dublin: Dolmen.

Goldhill, S. (1986), *Reading Greek Tragedy*, Cambridge: Cambridge University Press.

Goldwyn, A. and J. Nikopoulos, (eds.) (2016), *Brill's Companion to the Reception of Classics in International Modernism and the Avant-Garde*, Boston: Brill.

Grant, M. (ed.) (1982), *T.S. Eliot: The Critical Heritage, Vol. 1*, London: Routledge.

Graves, R. ([1948] 1997) *The White Goddess*, London: Faber and Faber.

Graziosi, B. and E. Greenwood, (eds.) (2007), *Homer in the Twentieth Century: Between World Literature and the Western Canon*, Oxford: Oxford University Press.

Green, J. and N.J. Karolides (2005), 'Theatre Regulation Act (U. K.) (1843)', *The Encyclopedia of Censorship, New Edition*, 568, New York: Facts on File.

Greenwood, E. (2016), 'Reception Studies: The Cultural Mobility of Classics', *Daedalus: Journal of the American Academy of Arts & Sciences*, Spring: 41–9.

Gregory, E. (1990), 'Virginity and Erotic Liminality: H.D.'s *Hippolytus Temporizes*', *Contemporary Literature* 31 (2): 133–60.

Gregory, E. (1997), *H.D. and Hellenism: Classic Lines*, Cambridge: Cambridge University Press.

Gregory, E. (2012), 'H.D. and Translation', in N.J. Christodoulides and P. Mackay eds. *The Cambridge Companion to H.D.*, 143–56, Cambridge: Cambridge University Press.

Griffith, A. (1903), 'All Ireland.' *United Irishman* (17 October), 1.

Groden, M. (1977), *Ulysses in Progress*, Princeton: Princeton University Press.

Gubar, S. (1984), 'Sapphistries', *Signs*, 10: 43–62.

Guest, B. (1984), *Herself Defined: The Poet H.D. and Her World*, Garden City: Doubleday.

Gunn, T. (1994), *Shelf Life: Essays, Memoirs and an Interview*, London: Faber.

Hall, E. and F. Macintosh (2005), *Greek Tragedy and the British Theatre 1660–1914*, Oxford: Oxford University Press.

Hardwick, L. (2000), 'Translation as Critique and Intervention', in *Translating Words, Translating Cultures*, London: Duckworth.

Hardwick, L. (2000), *Translating Words, Translating Cultures*, London: Duckworth.

Hardwick, L. (2003), *Reception Studies*, Oxford: Oxford University Press.

Haynes, K., ed. (2010), *Classics and Translation: Essays by D.S. Carne-Ross*, Lewisburg: Bucknell University Press.

H.D., trans. ([1915]), *Choruses from Iphigeneia in Aulis*, London: Ballantyne.

H.D., trans. (1919), *Choruses from the Iphigeneia in Aulis and the Hippolytus of Euripides*, London: The Egoist Ltd.

H.D. (1920), *Notes on Euripides, Pausanius and Greek Lyric Poets,* H.D. Papers. Beinecke Rare Book and Manuscript Library, Box 43: Folder 1111, New Haven: Yale University Press.

H.D. ([1926] 1968), *Palimpsest*, Carbondale: Southern Illinois University Press.

H.D. ([1927] 2003), *Hippolytus Temporizes & Ion: Adaptations of Two Plays by Euripides*, New York: New Directions.

H.D. ([1956] 1974 (2012)), *Tribute to Freud*, New York: New Directions.

H.D. (1960), *Bid Me to Live (A Madrigal)*, New York: Dial. H.D.

Works Cited

H.D. (1974), *Helen in Egypt*, intro. H. Gregory, New York: New Directions.

H.D. (1979), *End to Torment: A Memoir of Ezra Pound*, N.H. Pearson and M. King (eds.), New York: New Directions.

H.D. (1981), *HERmione*, New York: New Directions.

H.D. (1982), *Notes on Thought and Vision and The Wise Sappho*, San Francisco: City Lights.

H.D. (1983), *Collected Poems, 1912–1944*, Louis L. Martz (ed.), New York: New Directions.

H.D. (1986), 'Notes on Euripides', *Ion: A Play After Euripides*, 132–3, New York: Black Swan Books.

H.D. (1987/8), 'Responsibilities', *Agenda* 25 (3–4): 51–3.

H.D. (1988), *Selected Poems*, Louis L. Martz (ed.), New York: New Directions.

H.D. (1992), *Paint It To-day*, edited and with an Introduction by C. Laity, New York: New York University Press.

H.D. (1998), *Trilogy*. Introduction and Readers' Notes by A. Barnstone, New York, New Directions.

H.D. (2011), *Bid Me to Live*, C. Zilboorg (ed.), Gainsville: University Press of Florida.

H.D. (2012), *Magic Mirror, Compassionate Friendship, Thorn Thicket: A Tribute to Erich Heydt*, N. Christodoulides (ed.), Victoria, BC: ELS Editions.

Hainsworth, J.B. (1993), *The Iliad: A Commentary. Volume III: Books 9–12*, Cambridge: Cambridge University Press.

Hale, W.G. (1919), 'Pegasus Impounded', *Poetry* 14 (1): 52–5.

Harrison, J. E. ([1908] 1975), *Prolegomena to the Study of Greek Religion*, New York: Arno.

Hatlen, B. (2003), 'Pound and/or Benjamin', in H. Aji (ed.), *Ezra Pound and Referentiality*, 69–82, Paris: Universitaires de Paris-Sorbonne.

Haynes, K. (2003), *English Literature and Ancient Languages*, Oxford: Oxford University Press.

Haynes, K. (2007), 'Modernism', in C.W. Kallendorf (ed.), *A Companion to the Classical Tradition*, 101–14, Oxford: Blackwell.

Helmreich S. (2015), 'Transduction', in D. Novak and M. Sakakeeny (eds.), *Keywords in Sound*, Durham: Duke University Press.

Hesiod (2006), *Theogony, Works and Days, Testimonia*, G.W. Most (ed. and trans.), Cambridge, MA: Harvard University Press.

Heuving, J. (2016), *The Transmutation of Love and Avant-Garde Poetics*, Tuscaloosa: Alabama University Press.

Hickman, M. (2005), *The Geometry of Modernism: The Vorticist Idiom in Lewis, Pound, H.D. and Yeats*, Austin: University of Texas Press.

Hickman, M. (2012) '"Uncanonically Seated": H.D. and Literary Canons', in N.J. Christodoulides and P. Mackay (eds.), *The Cambridge Companion to H.D.*, 9–22, Cambridge: Cambridge University Press.

Hickman, M. and L. Kozak (forthcoming 2018), "Poppies, Scarlet Flowers, This Beauty": H.D.'s *Choruses from the Iphigeneia in Aulis* and the First World War', *Classical Receptions Journal*.

Hoberman, R. (1997), *Gendering Classicism: The Ancient World in Twentieth-Century Women's Historical Fiction*, Albany: State University of New York.

Hokanson, R. O'Brien, (1992), '"Is it all a Story?": Questioning Revision in H.D.'s *Helen in Egypt*', *American Literature* 64 (2): 331–46.

Hölderlin, F. (1804), 'Anmerkungen zum Oedipus', *Die Trauerspiele des Sophokles*, 97–108, Frankfurt.

Hollander, J. (1981), *The Figure of Echo: A Mode of Allusion in Milton and After*, Berkeley: University of California Press.

Hollander, J. (1995), *The Gazer's Spirit: Poems Speaking to Silent Works of Art*, Chicago: University of Chicago.

Hollenberg, D.K., ed. (1997), *Between History and Poetry: The Letters of H.D. and Norman Holmes Pearson*, Iowa City: Iowa University Press.

Homer (1524) *Odyssea. Ὀδύσσεια. Βατραχομυομαχία. Ὕμνοι λβ': Ulyssea. Batrachomyomachia. Hymni XXXII*, 3rd edn., Venice: Aldus Manutius.

Homer (1538) *Homeri Odyssea ad verbum translata, Andrea Divo Iustinopolitano interprete. Eiusdem Batrachomyomachia, id est ranarum et murium pugna, Aldo Manutio interprete. Eiusdem Hymni Deorum XXXII, Georgio Dartona Cretense interprete*, Paris: Christianus Wechelus.

Homer (1871), *The Odyssey of Homer: Translated into English Blank Verse*, trans. W. C. Bryant, Boston: Houghton, Mifflin and Company.

Homer (1900), *The Odyssey of Homer*, trans. S.H. Butcher and A. Lang, London: Macmillan & Co.

Homer (1922), *Homeri Opera*, T.W. Allen and D.B. Monro eds. 2nd edn., Oxford: Oxford University Press.

Homer (1965), *The Odyssey of Homer,* trans. R. Lattimore, New York: Harper & Row.

Homer (1967a), *Chapman's Homer: The Odyssey and the Lesser Homerica*, A. Nicoll (ed.), Princeton: Princeton University Press.

Homer (1967b), *The Odyssey: Books I–XII*, trans. A. Pope, ed. M. Mack, London, Methuen & Co.

Homer (1982), 'The Homeric Hymns' in *Hesiod, the Lesser Hymns and Homerica*, trans. H.G. Evelyn-White, 285–463, Cambridge, MA: Harvard University Press.

Homer (1984), *The Odyssey,* ed. A.T. Murray, v. 1, Cambridge, MA: Harvard University Press.

Homer (1995), *The Odyssey, Books 1–12*, trans. A.T. Murray, Cambridge, MA: Harvard University Press.

Homer (1996), *The Odyssey*, trans. R. Fagles, New York: Penguin.

Homer (2011), *The Iliad*, trans. R. Lattimore, Chicago: University of Chicago Press.

Hooley, D. (1988), *The Classics in Paraphrase: Ezra Pound and Modern Translations of Latin Poetry*, Selinsgrove: Susquehanna University Press.

House, V. (2014), 'H.D.'s Revision of Kleos Culture in *Helen in Egypt*', *Medea's Chorus: Myth and Women's Poetry Since 1950*, 1–25, New York: Peter Lang.

Huffington, A. (n.d.), 'Artist's Statement', www.anitahuffington.com

Hulme, T.E. (1924), 'Romanticism and Classicism', in *Speculations: Essays on the Humanism and the Philosophy of Art*, H. Read (ed.), 73–140, London: Kegan Paul, Trench, Trubner & Co.

Ioannidou, E. (2017), *Greek Fragments in Postmodern Frames: Rewriting Tragedy 1970–2005. Classical Presences*, Oxford: Oxford University Press.

Jackson, L. (Riding) (1993), *The Word 'Woman' and Other Related Writings*, E. Friedmann and A.J. Clark (eds.), New York: Persea Books.

Jebb, R.C. (1885), *The Oedipus Tyrannus Edited for the Syndics of the University Press*, Cambridge: Cambridge University Press.

Jebb, R.C. (1887), *The Oedipus Tyrannus of Sophocles Performed at Cambridge November 22–26, 1887, with a Translation in Prose by Richard Claverhouse Jebb and a translation of the songs of the Chorus in verse adapted to the music of C. Villiers Stanford by Arthur Woolgar Verall*, Cambridge: Cambridge University Press.

Jeffers, R. (1928), 'The Women on Cythaeron', *Poetry* 31(4): 175–80.

Jeffers, R. (1988, 1991, 2000), 'To the Stone-Cutters', 'Thurso's Landing', 'A Humanist's Tragedy', and 'Foreword: The Selected Poetry of Robinson Jeffers [1938]', in T. Hunt (ed.), *The Collected Poetry of Robinson Jeffers*, Volumes One, Three, and Four, Stanford: Stanford University Press.

Jeffers R. (2011), 'April 24, 1934', in J. Karman (ed.), *The Collected Letters Robinson Jeffers with The Selected Letters of Una Jeffers, Volume Two, 1931–1939*, Stanford: Stanford University Press.

Jenkins, T.E. (1999), 'Homeros Ekainopoiese', in Merrian Carlisle and Olga Levaniouk (eds.), *Nine Essays on Homer*, 207–26, Lanham: Rowman & Littlefield.

Jenkins, T.E. (2007), 'The "Ultra-Modern" Euripides of Verrall, H.D. and MacLeish', *Classical and Modern Literature* 27 (1): 121–45.

Jenkyns, R. (2007), 'United Kingdom', in C.W. Kallendorf (ed.), *A Companion to the Classical Tradition*, 265–78, Malden: Wiley-Blackwell.

Works Cited

Jones, C. (2006), *Strange Likeness: The Use of Old English in Twentieth-Century Poetry*, Oxford: Oxford University Press.

Joyce, J. (1957), *Selected Letters*, R. Ellmann (ed.), New York: Viking.

Joyce, J. (1959), *The Critical Writings of James Joyce*, E. Mason and R. Ellmann (eds.), London: Faber and Faber.

Joyce, J. (1984), *Ulysses*, New York: Garland.

Jubainville, H. d'Arbois de (1903), *The Irish Mythological Cycle & Celtic Mythology*, trans. Richard Irvine Best, Dublin: Hodges, Figgis and Co.

Kahane, A. (1999), 'Blood for Ghosts? Homer, Ezra Pound, and Julius Africanus', *New Literary History* 30 (4): 815–36.

Karman, J. (1995), *Robinson Jeffers: Poet of California*, Brownsville: Story Line.

Karman, J. (2001), *Stone of the Sur*, Stanford: Stanford University Press.

Kaufman, M.E. (1992), 'T.S. Eliot's New Critical Footnotes to Modernism', in K. Dettmar (ed.), *Rereading the New: A Backward Glance at Modernism*, Ann Arbor: University of Michigan Press.

Keller, D.H. (1988), *'Bubb Booklets': Letters of Richard Aldington to Charles Clinch Bubb*, Francestown: Typographeum.

Kenner, H. (1951), *The Poetry of Ezra Pound*, Norfolk: New Directions.

Kenner, H. (1968), 'The Muse in Tatters', *Arion* 7 (2): 212–33.

Kenner, H. (1971), *The Pound Era*, Berkeley: University of California Press.

Kenner, H. (1985), 'Pound and Homer', in George Bornstein (ed.), *Ezra Pound among the Poets*, 112, Chicago: University of Chicago.

Kirk, G.S., Raven, J.E. and Schofield, M., eds. (1984), *The Presocratic Philosophers*, 2nd edn, Cambridge: Cambridge University Press.

Kittredge, S.B. (1976), *The Literary Career of Richard Aldington*, PhD diss., New York University Press.

Laity, C. (1996), *H.D. and the Victorian Fin de Siècle: Gender, Modernism, Decadence*, Cambridge: Cambridge University Press.

Laity, C. (2004), 'T.S. Eliot and A.C. Swinburne: Decadent Bodies, Modern Visualities, and Changing Modes of Perception', *Modernism/Modernity* 11 (3): 425–48.

Latham, S. and G. Rogers, eds. (2015), *Modernism: Evolution of an Idea*, London: Bloomsbury.

Lattimore, R. (1947), 'A Note on Pindar and His Poetry', in *The Odes of Pindar*, v–xii, Chicago: University of Chicago Press.

Lawrence, K. (1981), *The Odyssey of Style in* Ulysses, Princeton: Princeton University Press.

Lear, J. (1992), 'Katharsis', in A.O. Rorty (ed.), *Aristotle's Poetics*, Oxford: Princeton University Press.

Leconte de Lisle (1884), *Euripide*, tome seconde, Paris: Alphonse Lemerre.

Levenson, M., ed. (1999), *The Cambridge Companion to Modernism*, Cambridge: Cambridge University Press.

Liddell, H.G. and R. Scott, eds. (1878) *Greek-English Lexicon*, 6th edn., New York: Harper Brothers.

Liebregts, P. (1993), *Centaurs in the Twilight: W. B. Yeats's Use of the Classical Tradition*, Amsterdam: Rodopi.

Liebregts, P. (2004), *Ezra Pound and Neoplatonism*, Madison: Fairleigh Dickinson University Press.

Liebregts, P. (2010), 'The Classics', in I. Nadel (ed.), *Ezra Pound in Context*, 171–80, Cambridge: Cambridge University Press.

Liebregts, P. (2011), '"Bricks Thought into Being Ex Nihil": Ezra Pound and Creation', in J. Gery and W. Pratt eds. *Ezra Pound, Ends and Beginnings: Essays and Poems from the Ezra Pound Conference Venice, 2007*, 81–96, New York: AMS.

Livingstone, R.W. (1912), *The Greek Genius and its Meaning to Us*, Oxford: Clarendon Press.

Lloyd-Jones, H. (1975). *Females of the Species: Semonides on Women*, Park Ridge: Noyes.

Logue, C. (2001), *War Music*, London: Faber and Faber.

Loizeaux, E.B. (2008), *Twentieth-Century Poetry and the Visual Arts*, Cambridge: Cambridge University Press.

Longenbach, J. (1988), *Stone Cottage: Pound, Yeats and Modernism*, Oxford: Oxford University Press.

Longenbach, J. (2010), 'Modern Poetry', in D. Holdeman and B. Levitas (eds.), *Yeats in Context*, 320–29, Cambridge: Cambridge University Press.

Loraux, N. (1993), *The Children of Athena: Athenian Ideas about Citizenship and the Division between the Sexes*, C. Levine (trans.), Princeton: Princeton University Press.

[Louÿs, Pierre], trans. (1893), *Les poésies de Méléagre*, Paris: [Mercure de France].

Lusty, N. (2008), 'Sexing the Manifesto: Mina Loy, Feminism and Futurism', *Women: A Cultural Review* 19 (3): 245–60.

Machacek, G. (2007), 'Allusion', *PMLA* 122 (2): 522–36.

Macintosh, F. (1994), 'The Irish Literary Revival and the Classical Tradition', *Dying Acts: Death in Ancient Greek and Modern Irish Tragic Drama*, 1–18, Cork: Cork University Press.

Macintosh, F. (2008), 'An Oedipus for Our Times? Yeats's Version of Sophocles' *Oedipus Tyrannus*', in M. Revermann and P. Wilson (eds.), *Performance, Iconography, Reception: Studies in Honour of Oliver Taplin*, 524–47, Oxford: Oxford University Press.

Mackail, J.W., trans. (1890), *Select Epigrams from the Greek Anthology*, London: Longmans, Green and Co.

[Mackail, J.W.] (1916), 'A Note of the Classical Revival', *Times Literary Supplement*, 4 May: 210.

[Mackail, J.W.] (1919), 'Poets' Translations', *Times Literary Supplement*, 20 November: 666.

MacNair, H.F., ed. (1945), *Florence Ayscough & Amy Lowell: Correspondence of a Friendship*, Chicago: University of Chicago Press.

Marshall, C.W. (2014), *The Structure and Performance of Euripides' Helen*, Cambridge: Cambridge University Press.

Martin, R.P. (1989), *The Language of Heroes: Speech and Performance in the Iliad*, G. Nagy, preface, Ithaca: Cornell University Press.

Martindale, C. (1993), *Redeeming the Text: Latin Poetry and the Hermeneutics of Reception*, Cambridge: Cambridge University Press.

Martindale, C. (2006), 'Introduction: Thinking through Reception', in C. Martindale and R.F. Thomas eds. *Classics and the Uses of Reception*, 1–13, Malden: Blackwell.

Martindale, C. (2013), 'Reception: A New Humanism? Receptivity, Pedagogy, the Transhistorical', *Classical Receptions Journal* 5 (2): 169–83.

Matthews, S. (2013), *T.S. Eliot and Early Modern Literature*, Oxford: Oxford University Press.

Mayer, J.T. (1989), *T.S. Eliot's Silent Voices*, Oxford: Oxford University Press.

McApline, K. and G. White (eds.) (1997), *The Muse Strikes Back: A Poetic Response by Women to Men*, Brownsville: Story Line.

McClatchy, J.D., ed. (2002), *Horace, The Odes: New Translations by Contemporary Poets*, Princeton: Princeton University Press.

McConnell, J. (2013), *Black Odysseys: The Homeric Odyssey in the African Diaspora since 1939*, Oxford: Oxford University Press.

McGann, J.J. (2006), '"The Grand Heretics of Modern Fiction": Laura Riding, John Cowper Powys, and the Subjective Correlative', *Modernism/modernity* 13: 309–23.

Mills, J. (2014), *Virginia Woolf, Jane Ellen Harrison, and the Spirit of Modernist Classicism*, Columbus: Ohio State University Press.

Mlinko, A. (2014), Textbox for Classical Convergences: Traditions and Reinventions. Harn Museum of Art, University of Florida, Gainesville, FL. Dec. 2014–May 2015.

Moody, A.D. (2007), *Ezra Pound: Poet. A Portrait of the Man and His Work. I: The Young Genius 1885-1920*, Oxford: Oxford University Press.

Moore, G. (1911), *Hail and Farewell! Ave*, London: William Heinemann.

Moore, G. (1914), 'Yeats, Lady Gregory, and Synge', *The English Review* 16: 167–70.

Morgan, L. (1999), *Patterns of Redemption in Virgil's* Georgics, Cambridge: Cambridge University Press.

Morris, A. (2003), *How to Live/What to Do: H.D.'s Cultural Poetics*, Champaign-Urbana: University of Illinois Press.

Morwood, J. (2007), 'Gilbert Murray's Translations of Greek Tragedy', in Christopher Stray, (ed.), *Gilbert Murray Reassessed: Hellenism, Theatre, and International Politics*, 133–44, Oxford: Oxford University Press.

Moyer, P. (1997), 'Getting Personal about Euripides', in *Compromising Traditions: The Personal Voice in Classical Scholarship*, J.P. Hallett and T. Van Nortwick (eds.), 102–19, London: Routledge.

Murnaghan, S. (2007), 'The Memorable Past: Antiquity and Girlhood in the Works of Mary Butts and Naomi Mitchison', in *Remaking the Classics: Literature, Genre and Media in Britain 1800-2000*, C. Stray (ed.), 125–39, London: Duckworth.

Murphy, W.M. (1978), *Prodigal Father: The Life of John Butler Yeats (1839–1922)*, Ithaca: Cornell University Press.

Murray, G. (1897), *A History of Ancient Greek Literature*, New York: D. Appleton and Co.

Murray, G. (1907), *The Rise of the Greek Epic*, Oxford: Oxford University Press.

Murray, G. (1911), *Oedipus, King of Thebes*, New York: Oxford University Press.

Murray, G. (1954), *Hellenism and the Modern World*, Boston: Beacon Press.

Murray, P. (2006), 'Reclaiming the Muse', in *Laughing with Medusa*, V. Zajko and M. Leonard (eds.), 327–54, Oxford: Oxford University Press.

Nicholls, P. (2010), 'The Elusive Allusion: Poetry and Exegesis', in N. Marsh and P. Middleton (eds.), *Teaching Modernist Poetry*, 10–24, Basingstoke: Palgrave Macmillan.

Nietzsche, F. (1901), *Nietzsche as Critic, Philosopher, Poet and Prophet*, T. Common (trans.), London: Grant Richards.

Nikopoulos, J. (2016), 'The Wisdom of Myth: Eliot's "Ulysses, Order, and Myth"', in A. Goldwyn and J. Nikopoulos (eds.), *Brill's Companion to the Reception of Classics in International Modernism and the Avant-Garde, Brill's Companions to Classical Reception Volume 9*, 292–311, Leiden: Brill.

Nisbet, G. (2013), *Greek Epigram in Reception: J. A. Symonds, Oscar Wilde, and the Invention of Desire, 1805-1929*, Oxford: Oxford University Press.

North, M. (1992), 'The Dialect in/of Modernism: Pound and Eliot's Racial Masquerade', *American Literary History* 4 (1): 56–76.

Østermark-Johansen, L. (2017), 'Pater's 'Hippolytus Veiled': A Study from Euripides?', *Pater the Classicist: Classical Scholarship, Reception, and Aestheticism*, 183–99, Oxford: Oxford University Press.

Ostriker, A.S. (1986), *Stealing the Language: The Emergence of Women's Poetry in America*, Boston: Beacon.

O'Sullivan, M. (2007), WP article on *Self-Possessed*: www.washingtonpost.com/wp-dyn/content/article/2007/01/25/AR2007012500556.html.

Oswald, A. (2011), *Memorial: An Excavation of the Iliad*, London: Faber and Faber.

Padel, R., (1974), 'Images of the Elsewhere: Two Choral Odes of Euripides', *CQ* 24: 227–41.

Parker, J. and T. Matthews, eds. (2011), *Tradition, Translation, Trauma: The Classic and the Modern. Classical Presences*, Oxford: Oxford University Press.

Parkinson, T. (1964), *W.B. Yeats: The Later Poetry*, Berkeley: University of California.

Parry, M. (1971), *The Making of Homeric Verse: The Collected Papers of Milman Parry*, A. Parry (ed.), Oxford: Clarendon Press.

Pater, W. (1868), *Westminster Review* 90 (October): 300–12.

Pater, W. (1910), 'Hippolytus Veiled.' *Greek Studies*, 152–86, London: Macmillan & Co.

Pérez-Villalon, F. (2003), 'Pound/Benjamin: Translation as Departure and Redemption' in H. Aji (ed.), *Ezra Pound dans le vortex de la traduction, Annales du monde anglophone*, 15–24, Paris: L'Harmattan.

Perysinakis, I. (2016), 'The Motif of Wealth in Aristophanes' *Ploutos* and Herodotus' *Historiae*', unpublished paper, University of Ioannina.

P.G.W. (1903), 'Daily Chronicle Office, Wednesday Morning', *Daily Chronicle* (13 May) 7.

Philippy, P.B. (1995), *Love's Remedies: Recantation and Renaissance Lyric Poetry*, London: Bucknell University Press.

Pindar ([n.d.] 1947), 'Olympia 2 [Second Olympian Ode]', R. Lattimore (trans.), *The Odes of Pindar*, 5–8, Chicago: University of Chicago.

Plato (2002), *Πολιτεία*, Ν.Μ. Σκουτερόπουλος (επ. και μετφ.), Αθήνα: Εκδόσεις Πόλις.

Plato (2012), *Phaedrus*, Harvey Yunis (ed.), Cambridge: Cambridge University Press.

Platt, V. (2016), 'The Matter of Classical Art History', *Daedalus: Journal of the American Academy of Arts & Sciences*, Spring: 69–78.

Pogorzelski, R. (2016), *Virgil and Joyce: Nationalism and Imperialism in the* Aeneid *and* Ulysses, Madison: University of Wisconsin.

Pondrom, C.N. (1969), 'Selected Letters from H.D. to F.S. Flint: A Commentary on the Imagist Period', *Contemporary Literature* 10 (4): 557–86.

Pondrom, C.N. (2012), 'H.D. and the "Little Magazines"', in N.J. Christodoulides and P. Mackay (eds.), *The Cambridge Companion to H.D.*, 37–50, Cambridge: Cambridge University Press.

Πορφύριος (1907), *Αφορμαί προς τα νοητά*, B. Mommert (ed.), Lipsiae: Teubner.

Pound, E. ([1910] 2005), *The Spirit of Romance*, R. Sieburth (ed.), New York: New Directions.

Pound, E. (1912), *Ripostes*, London: Stephen Swift.

Pound, E. (1913) 'Xenia', *Poetry* 3 (2): 60.

Pound, E. (1914), 'The Later Yeats', *Poetry* 4 (2): 64–9.

Pound, E. (1915), *Cathay*, London: Elkin Mathews.

Pound, E. (1918), A Retrospect', *Pavannes and Divisions*, 95–111, New York: Alfred Knopf.

Pound, E. ([1917] 1968), 'Notes on Elizabethan Classicists', in T.S. Eliot (ed.), *Literary Essays of Ezra Pound*, 227–48, New York: New Directions.

Pound, E. ([1920] 2010), '*Hugh Selwyn Mauberley: Life and contacts*' in R. Sieburth (ed.), *New Selected Poems and Translations*, 109–23, New York: New Directions.

Pound, E. (1925), *A Draft of XVI Cantos*, Paris: Three Mountains.

Pound, E. ([1932] 1937), 'Harold Monro', *The Criterion* 11 (45), in *Polite Essays*, London: Faber and Faber.

Pound, E. ([1934] 1951), *ABC of Reading*, London: Faber and Faber.

Pound, E. ([1934] 2010), *The ABC of Reading*, M. Dirda (ed.), New York: New Directions.

Pound, E. (1935a), 'Cavalcanti', in *Literary Essays of Ezra Pound*, T.S. Eliot (ed.), 149–200, New York: New Directions.

Pound, E. (1935b), *Make It New*, New Haven: Yale University Press.

Pound, E. ([1950] 1971), *Selected Letters of Ezra Pound, 1907–1941*, D.D. Paige (ed.), New York: New Directions.

Pound, E. ([1938] 1952), *Guide to Kulchur*, London: Peter Owen.

Pound, E. (1954a), *Literary Essays*, T.S. Eliot (ed.), London: Faber and Faber.

Pound, E. ([1918] 1954b), 'A Retrospect', *Literary Essays*, T.S. Eliot (ed.), 3–14, London: Faber and Faber.

Pound, E. ([1962] 1978), *Love Poems of Ancient Egypt*, N. Stock (ed.), New York: New Directions.

Pound, E. (1967), *Pound/Joyce: The Letters of Ezra Pound to James Joyce, with Pound's Essays on Joyce*, F. Read (ed.), New York: New Directions.

Pound, E. (1970), *The Translations of Ezra Pound*, H. Kenner (ed.), New York: New Directions.

Works Cited

Pound, E. (1971), *Selected Letters of Ezra Pound 1907–1941*, D.D. Paige (ed.), New York: New Directions.

Pound, E. (1986), *The Cantos*, London: Faber and Faber.

Pound, E. (1988), *Ezra Pound and Margaret Cravens: A Tragic Friendship, 1910–1912*, O. Pound and R. Spoo (eds.), Durham: Duke University Press.

Pound, E. (1995 [1996]), *The Cantos*, 13th printing, New York: New Directions.

Pound, E. (2003), *Ezra Pound: Poems and Translations*, R. Sieburth (ed.), New York: Library of America.

Prins, Y. (1999), *Victorian Sappho*, Princeton: Princeton University Press.

Prins, Y. (2017), *Ladies' Greek: Victorian Translations of Tragedy*, Princeton: Princeton University Press.

Pucci, P. (1987), *Odysseus Polutropos: Intertextual Readings in the* Odyssey *and the* Iliad, Ithaca: Cornell University Press.

Pucci, P. (1998), *Song of the Sirens: Essays on Homer*, Oxford: Rowman & Littlefield.

Purdom, C.B. (1955), *Harley Granville Barker, Man of the Theatre, Dramatist, and Scholar*, London: Rockliff.

Pym, A. (1995), 'Resistant Translation Strategies in Robert Lowell's *Imitations* and Ezra Pound's *Cantos*', in *Cross-Words: Issues and Debates in Literary and Non-Literary Translating*, Chr. Pagnoulle and I. Mason (eds.), Liège: University of Liège, 159–71.

Rabaté, J.-M. (2016), 'Ezra Pound and the Globalization of Literature' in P. Stazi and J. Parks (eds.), *Ezra Pound in the Present*, 107–34, New York: Bloomsbury.

Rabinowitz, N.S. (1993), *Anxiety Veiled: Euripides and the Traffic in Women*, Ithaca: Cornell University Press.

Rainey, L. (1998), *Institutions of Modernism: Literary Elites and Public Culture*, New Haven: Yale University Press.

Rainey, L., ed. (2006), *The Annotated Waste Land with Eliot's Contemporary Prose*, New Haven: Yale University Press.

Rancière J. (2011), *The Emancipated Spectator*, New York & London: Verso.

Reed, J.D. (1997), *Bion of Smyrna: The Fragments and the Adonis*, Cambridge: Cambridge University Press.

Review of R.C. Jebb (1884), *Sophocles: The Plays and Fragments, with Critical Notes, Commentary, and Translation*, in *Journal of Education* 178: 180–1.

Review of R. C. Jebb, *Sophocles: The Plays and Fragments, with Critical Notes, Commentary, and Translation* (Cambridge 1883) in *The Athenaeum* 2948 (26 April 1884): 531–32.

Review of *Poems and Fragments of Sappho*, E. Storer (trans.) (1915), *The New Age*, 21 October: 601.

Review of *Sophocles: The Plays and Fragments*, R.C. Jebb. (ed.), *The Athenaeum* 3056 (22 May 1886): 674–5.

Rich, A. 'When We Dead Awaken: Writing as Re-vision', *College Teachers of English* 34 (1) (1972): 18–30.

Richards, M.R. (1980), 'Pope, Chapman, and the Romantics', *Keats–Shelley Journal* 29: 11–21.

Ricks, D. (1989), *The Shade of Homer: A Study of Modern Greek Poetry*, Cambridge: Cambridge University Press.

Riding, L. (1927), *Voltaire: A Biographical Fantasy*, London: The Hogarth Press.

Riding, L. (1930), *Experts Are Puzzled*, London: Jonathan Cape.

Riding, L. (1935), *Progress of Stories*, London: Seizin/Constable.

Riding, L. (1937), *A Trojan Ending*, London: Seizin/Constable.

Riding, L. (1939), *Lives of Wives*, London: Cassell.

Riding, L. (1993), 'Eve's Side of It', in *The Word 'Woman' and Other Related Writings*, New York: Persea Books.

Riding, L. and R. Graves. (1927), *A Survey of Modernist Poetry*, London: William Heinemann.

Riikonen, H.K. (2008), 'Andreas Divus, Ezra Pound and the Fate of Elpenor', *Interlitteraria* 13: 138–47.

R.M. (1904), 'The National Theatre Society, Its Work and Ambitions, A Chat with Mr. W.B. Yeats', *Evening Mail* (Dublin) 27 December: 4.

Robaey, J. (1989), 'Pound traduttore di Omero: "Canto I" e 'Odissea XI'", *Quaderni Urbinati di Cultura Classica* 33 (3): 65–92.

Robinson, J.S. (1982), *H.D. The Life and Work of an American Poet*, Boston: Houghton Mifflin.

Robinson, M. (2013), 'H.D.'s *Ion*: The Door Swings Both Ways', in *Americans and the Experience of Delphi*, P. Lorenz and D. Roessel (eds.), 263–79, Boston: Somerset Hall.

Robinson, M. (2016), *The Astral H.D. Occult and Religious Sources and Contexts for H.D.'s Poetry and Prose*, New York: Bloomsbury Academic.

Rohrbach, E. (1996), 'H.D. and Sappho: "A Precious Inch of Palimpsest"', in E. Greene (ed.), *Re-reading Sappho: Reception and Transmission*, 184–98, Berkeley: University of California Press.

Rood, T. (2013), 'Redeeming Xenophon: Historiographical Reception and the Transhistorical', *Classical Receptions Journal* 5 (2): 199–211.

Rosenblitt, J.A. (2016) *E.E. Cummings' Modernism and the Classics*, Oxford: Oxford University Press.

Rudd, N. (1994), 'Pound and Propertius: Two Former Moderns' with 'Appendix: Professor Hales and Homage as a Document of Cultural Transmission', *The Classical Tradition in Operation*, 117–58, Toronto: University of Toronto Press.

Ruthven, K.K. (1969), *A Guide to Ezra Pound's Personae* (1926), Los Angeles: University of California Press.

Saussy, H. (2005), 'Chiasmus', *Comparative Literature* 57 (3): 234–38.

Scafuro, A. (1990), 'Discourses of Sexual Violation in Mythic Accounts and Dramatic Versions of "The Girl's Tragedy"', *Differences: A Journal of Feminist Cultural Studies* 2 (1): 125–59.

Schein, S. (2008), '"Our Debt to Greece and Rome": Canon, Class and Ideology', in *A Companion to Classical Receptions*, L. Hardwick and C. Stray (eds.), 75–85, Malden: Blackwell.

Schuchard, R. (1999), *Eliot's Dark Angel: Intersections of Life and Art*, New York: Oxford University Press.

Schulte, R. and J. Biguenet, eds. (1992), *Theories of Translation*, Chicago: University of Chicago Press.

Schultz, P. (2014), *The Wherewithal*, New York: W.W. Norton and Company.

Scourfield, J.H.D. (2018), 'Classical In/stabilities: Virginia Woolf, Ford Madox Ford, and the Great War', *Classical Receptions Journal*.

Sedgwick, E.K. (2002), *Touching, Feeling: Affect, Pedagogy, Performativity*, Durham, NC: Duke University Press.

Segal, C. (1983), '*Kleos* and Its Ironies in the *Odyssey*', *Classical Antiquity* 52: 22–47.

Segal, C. (1999), 'Euripides' *Ion*: Generational Passage and Civic Myth', in *Rites of Passage in Ancient Greece: Literature, Religion, Society*, M.W. Padilla (ed.), *Bucknell Review* 43 (1): 67–108, Lewisburg: Bucknell University Press.

Sell, R. (1984), 'The Comedy of Hyperbolic Horror: Seneca, Lucan and Twentieth-Century Grotesque', Neohelicon 11 (1): 277–300.

Semonides (1995). 'Women', trans. D. A. Svarlien, *Diotima*: www.stoa.org/diotima/anthology/sem_7.shtml

Serres, M. (2007), *The Parasite*, L.R. Schehr (trans.)., Minneapolis: University of Minnesota Press.

Seth, V. (1986), *The Golden Gate*, New York: Random House.

Sherry, V. (2003), *The Great War and the Language of Modernism*, Oxford: Oxford University Press.

Works Cited

Sicari, S. (1991), *Pound's Epic Ambition: Dante and the Modern World*, Albany: State University of New York Press.

Siddiqui, A. (2014), '"Gods into bulls, men into wolves, women into spiders": Classical metamorphosis in *The Satanic Verses*', *Classical Receptions Journal* 6 (3): 426–45.

Simon, E. (1983), *Festivals of Attica*, Madison: University of Wisconsin.

Smith, C.H. (1963), *T.S. Eliot's Dramatic Theory and Practice: From* Sweeney Agonistes *to* The Elder Statesman, Princeton: Princeton University Press.

Sophocles (1899), *The Oedipus Tyrannus of Sophocles, Translated and Presented by the Students of Notre Dame University*, Notre Dame: Notre Dame University Press.

Sowerby, R. (1996), 'The Homeric *Versio Latina*', *Illinois Classical Studies* 21: 161–202.

Spiropoulou, A. (2002), '"On Not Knowing Greek": Virginia Woolf's Spatial Critique of Authority', *Interdisciplinary Literary Studies* 4 (1): 1–19.

Spoo, R. (1986), '"Nestor" and the Nightmare: The Presence of the Great War in *Ulysses*', *Twentieth Century Literature* 32: 137–54.

Squire, M. (2001), *The Art of the Body*, London: I.B. Tauris.

Steiner, G. (1966), *The Penguin Book of Modern Verse Translation*, London: Harmsworth.

Steiner, G. (1975), *After Babel: Aspects of Language and Translation*, Oxford: Oxford University Press.

Steiner, G. (1996), *Homer in English*, London: Penguin Books.

Steiner, G. (1998), 'Introduction', in W. Benjamin, *The Origin of the German Baroque Drama*, trans. J. Osborne, 7–24, London: Verso.

Stesichorus (1991), *Greek Lyric, Vol. III*, Loeb Classical Library, No. 476, Cambridge, MA: Harvard University Press.

Storer, E., trans. (1915), *Poems and Fragments of Sappho*, London: Ballantyne.

Storer, E., trans. (1920), *The Windflowers of Asklepiades and the Poems of Poseidippos*, London: The Egoist Press.

Strand, K. (1978), 'W.B. Yeats's American Lecture Tours', PhD diss., Northwestern University Press.

Stray, C. (1998), *Classics Transformed: Schools, Universities, and Society in England, 1830–1960*, Oxford: Clarendon Press.

Stray, C. (2007), 'Jebb's Sophocles: An Edition and Its Maker', in *Classical Books, Scholarship and Publishing in Britain Since 1800*, 75–96, London: Institute of Classical Studies, University of London.

Stray, C., ed. (2013), *Sophocles' Jebb: A Life in Letters. Cambridge Classical Journal, Supplement, 38*, Cambridge: Cambridge Philological Society.

Sullivan, H. (2011), 'Classics', in J. Harding (ed.), *T.S. Eliot in Context*, 169–79, Cambridge: Cambridge University Press.

Sullivan, J.P. (1964), *Ezra Pound and Sextus Propertius: A Study in Creative Translation*, Austin: University of Texas.

Susanetti, D. (2016), 'Circulation of Spectres: Ghosts and Spells', *Deep Classics: Rethinking Classical Reception*, Shane Butler (ed.), 255–68, London: Bloomsbury.

Sword, H. (1996), *Engendering Inspiration: Visionary Strategies in Rilke, Lawrence, and H.D.*, Ann Arbor: University of Michigan Press.

Synge, J.M. (1966), *Collected Works, Volume II: Prose*, Alan Price (ed.), London: Oxford University Press.

Talbot, J. (2003), 'Twenty-first Century Horace and the End of a Shared Culture', *Arion* 11 (2): 149–92.

Tarlo, H. (2012), 'An Insurmountable Chasm? Re-visiting, Re-imagining and Re-writing Classical Pastoral through the Modernist Poetry of H.D.', *Classical Receptions Journal* 4 (2): 235–60.

Taylor, J.M. (1899), 'Should the State teach Morals in its Schools?' (10 December 1898), *The Schoolmasters' Association of New York and Vicinity 1898-1899*, 39–42, Newark: Baker Printing Co.

Terrell, C. ([1980] 1993), *A Companion to* The Cantos *of Ezra Pound,* Berkeley: University of California.

Thomas, R. (1983), *The Latin Masks of Ezra Pound*, Ann Arbor: UMI Research.

Tryphonopoulos, D. (1992), *The Celestial Tradition: A Study of Ezra Pound's* The Cantos, Waterloo: Wilfrid Laurier University Press.

Tryphonopoulos, D. (2003a), '"For three years he strove to maintain / The sublime in the Old sense": Sublimity and Ecstasy in Longinus and Pound', paper presented at the Twentieth-Century Literature conference at the University of Louisville, Louisville, 27 February–3 March.

Tryphonopoulos, D. (2003b), '"Fragments of a Faith Forgotten": Ezra Pound, H.D. and the Occult Tradition', *Paideuma* 32: 229–244.

Tryphonopoulos, D. (2005), '"With usura hath no man a house of good stone" (Pound, Canto 45): An interview with Leon Surette', *English Studies in Canada* 31 (2): 273–91.

Tryphonopoulos, D. (2014), '"ἴδμεν γάρ τοι πάνθ᾽ ὅσ᾽ ἐνὶ Τροίη εὑρείη": Teaching Ezra Pound's Subtle Allusiveness', invited paper presented at the Modernism's Legacies conference (Department of English and Writing Studies colloquium series 2013–14) at Western University Press, London, 10 April.

Turner, F.M. (1981), *The Greek Heritage in Victorian Britain*, New Haven: Yale University Press.

Vandiver, E. (2010), *Stand in the Trench, Achilles: Classical Receptions in British Poetry of the Great War*, Oxford: Oxford University Press.

Vandiver, E. (forthcoming), '"A group of Ardent Hellenists": The Imagists, Greek Meter, and Making It New', in P. Tambakaki (ed.), *Brill's Companion to Classical Reception and Modern World Poetry*, Leiden: Brill.

Varney, J. (2010a). 'The Imagist Poet as Cultural Mediator: H.D. and the Translation of the Classics', in T. Naaijkens (ed.), *Event or Incident: On the Role of Translation in the Dynamics of Cultural Exchange*, 71–106, Bern: Peter Lang.

Varney, J. (2010b), 'The "Wobbling" Translation: H.D. and the Transmission of the Classics', *The Translator* 16 (1): 1–18.

Varsos, G. (2007), 'The Disappearing Medium: Remarks on Language in Translation', *Intermédialités* 10: 165–79.

Varsos, G. (2014), 'Rhythmic Indeterminacy: On the Translations of the Homeric Hexameter into English and French', in Chr. Raguet and M.N. Karsky (eds.) *Tension rythmique et traduction / Rhythmic Tension and Translation*, 13–51, Montréal: Éditions québécoises de l'œuvre.

Vasunia, P. (2001), *The Gift of the Nile: Hellenizing Egypt from Aeschylus to Alexander*, Berkeley, University of California.

Vendler H. (1995), 'Huge Pits of Darkness, Huge Peaks of Light: Robinson Jeffers', in *Soul Says, On Recent Poetry*, 52–62, Cambridge: Harvard University Press.

Venuti, L. (1995), *The Translator's Invisibility: A History of Translation*, London: Routledge.

Venuti, L., ed. (2000), *The Translation Studies Reader*, New York: Routledge.

Verrall, A.W. (1905), *Essays on Four Plays of Euripides: Andromache, Helen, Heracles, and Orestes*, Cambridge: Cambridge University Press.

Vogel, A. (2007), 'Not Elizabeth to His Ralegh: Laura Riding, Robert Graves, and Origins of the White Goddess', in M. Stone and J. Thompson (eds.), *Literary Couplings: Writing Couples, Collaborators, and the Construction of Authorship*, 229–39, Madison: University of Wisconsin.

Walcott, D. (1990), *Omeros*, London: Faber and Faber.

Works Cited

Weare, J. (2012), 'Anaphora', in R. Greene and S. Cushman (eds.), *Princeton Encyclopedia of Poetry and Poetics*, 4th edn., Princeton: Princeton University Press.

Wenthe, W. (1995), '"The Hieratic Dance": Prosody and the Unconscious in H.D.'s Poetry', *Sagatrieb* 14: 113–40.

Wescott, G. (1921), 'Classics in English', *Poetry* 18 (5): 284–8.

Wharton, H., ed. and trans. (1887), *Sappho: Memoir, Text, Selected Renderings, and A Literal Translation*, 2nd edn., London: David Stott; Chicago: A. C. McClurg.

Whelpton, V. (2014), *Richard Aldington: Poet, Soldier and Lover, 1911–1929*, Cambridge: Lutterworth.

Whitall, J., trans. ([1916]), *Poems of Leonidas of Tarentum*, London: Ballantyne Press.

Whitall, J. (1936), *English Years*, London: Jonathan Cape.

Whitbeck, C.N. (2013), *The Palinodic Strain,* PhD thesis, Department of Classics, University of Pennsylvania.

Whittaker, B.M. (1970), 'Stylistic Analysis and Poetic Translation: Pound's Canto I', PhD diss., York University Press, Toronto.

Willett, S.J. (2005), 'Reassessing Ezra Pound's *Sextus Propertius*', *Syllecta Classica* 16: 173–220.

Wilmer, C. (1996), 'Pound, Dante and the Homeric Underworld', *Agenda* 34 (3): 135–44.

Wilson, E. (2017), 'Found in Translation: How Women Are Making the Classics Their Own.' *The Guardian*, 7 July (https://www.theguardian.com/books/2017/jul/07/women-classics-translation-female-scholars-translators).

Wilson, N.G. (2017), *From Byzantium to Italy: Greek Studies in the Italian Renaissance*, 2nd edn, London: Bloomsbury.

Winter, J. (1998), *Sites of Memory, Sites of Mourning: The Great War in European Cultural History*, Cambridge: Cambridge University Press.

Wolfe, J. (2015), *Homer and the Question of Strife from Erasmus to Hobbes*, Toronto: University of Toronto.

Woodbury, L. (1967), 'Helen and the Palinode', *Phoenix* 21: 157–76.

Woolf, V. (1929), *A Room of One's Own*, New York: Harcourt Brace and World.

Wright, M. (2005), *Euripides' Escape-Tragedies: A Study of Helen, Andromeda, and Iphigenia Among the Taurians*, Oxford: Oxford University Press.

Xie, M. (1999), 'Pound as Translator', in I. Nadel (ed.), *The Cambridge Companion to Ezra Pound*, 204–23, Cambridge: Cambridge University Press.

Yao, S.G. (2002a), 'From Greece to Egypt': Translation and the Engendering of H.D.'s Poetry', *Translation and the Languages of Modernism*, 79–114, New York: Palgrave Macmillan.

Yao, S.G. (2002b), *Translation and the Languages of Modernism: Gender, Politics, Language*, New York: Palgrave Macmillan.

Yeats, W.B. *The Collected Letters of W.B. Yeats*, Intelex Past Masters Database.

Yeats, W.B. *Maud Gonne Xmas Notebook 1912*, NLI 30, 358. Yeats Archive, Box 88.2. SUNY Stony Brook.

Yeats, W.B. ([1902] 1961), 'Speaking to the Psaltery', in *Essays and Introductions*, 13–27, London: Palgrave Macmillan.

Yeats, W.B. ([1903] 1994a), 'To the Editor of the *United Irishman*, 10 October 1903', in R. Schuchard and J. Kelly (eds.), *The Collected Letters of W.B. Yeats, Volume 3*, 440–5, Oxford: Clarendon Press.

Yeats, W.B. ([1903] 1994), 'To the Editor of the *United Irishman*, 24 October 1903', in R. Schuchard and J. Kelly (eds.), *The Collected Letters of W.B. Yeats, Volume 3*, 451–3, Oxford: Clarendon Press.

Yeats, W.B. ([1904] 1994b), 'To Lady Augusta Gregory, 18 January 1904', in R. Schuchard and J. Kelly (eds.) *The Collected Letters of W.B. Yeats, Volume 3*, 520–2, Oxford: Clarendon Press.

Yeats, W.B. ([1904] 1994c), 'To George Russell (AE), April 1904', in R. Schuchard and J. Kelly (eds.), *The Collected Letters of W.B. Yeats, Volume 3*, 576–8, Oxford: Clarendon Press.

Yeats, W.B. ([1903] 1994d), 'To John Quinn, 15 May 1903', in R. Schuchard and J. Kelly (eds.), *The Collected Letters of W.B. Yeats, Volume 3*, 372–3, Oxford: Clarendon Press.

Yeats, W.B. ([1906] 2005) 'To John Millington Synge, 3 October 1906', *The Collected Letters of W.B. Yeats, Volume 4: 1905–1907*, J. Kelly and R. Schuchard (eds.), 508–10, Oxford: Oxford University Press.

Yeats, W.B. ([1913] 1971), 'The Theatre and Beauty' (c. December 1913). Transcribed in R. O'Driscoll, 'Two lectures on the Irish theatre by W.B. Yeats', in R. O'Driscoll (ed.), *Theatre and Nationalism in Twentieth-century Ireland*, 66–88, Toronto: University of Toronto.

Yeats, W.B. ([1928] 2000a), 'The Irish Censorship' (29 September 1928), in Colton Johnson (ed.), *The Collected Works of W.B. Yeats. Volume X: Later Articles and Reviews*, 214–18, New York: Scribner Press.

Yeats, W.B. (1940), *The Variorum Edition of the Poems of W.B. Yeats*, P. Allt and R.K. Alspach (eds.), New York: Macmillan.

Yeats, W.B. (1955), *The Letters of W. B. Yeats*, Allan Wade (ed.), New York: Macmillan.

Yeats, W.B. (1966), 'Sophocles' *King Oedipus*, A Version for the Modern Stage', in R.K. Alspach (ed.), *The Variorum Edition of the Plays of W.B. Yeats*, 809–51, New York: Macmillan.

Yeats, W.B. (1972), *Memoirs*, Denis Donoghue (ed.), New York: Macmillan.

Yeats, W.B. (1989), *The Writing of Sophocles' King Oedipus*, D.R. Clark and J.B. McGuire (eds.) Philadelphia: The American Philosophical Society.

Yeats, W.B. (1999), *The Collected Works of W. B. Yeats. Volume III: Autobiographies*, W. H. O'Donnell and D. N. Archibald (eds.), New York: Scribner.

Yeats, W.B. ([1928] 2000a), 'The Irish Censorship', in *The Collected Works of W.B. Yeats. Volume X: Later Articles and Reviews*, Colton Johnson (ed.), 214–18, New York: Scribner.

Yeats, W.B. ([1933] 2000b), 'Plain Man's *Oedipus*', in *The Collected Works of W.B. Yeats. Volume X: Later Articles and Reviews*, Colton Johnson (ed.), 244–5, New York: Scribner.

Yeats, W.B. ([1931] 2000c), 'Oedipus the King' (8 September 1931), in *The Collected Works of W. B. Yeats. Volume X: Later Articles and Reviews*, Colton Johnson (ed.), 219–23, New York: Scribner.

Yeats, W.B. (2003a), '*Samhain*: 1903 – The Reform of the Theatre', *The Collected Works of W.B. Yeats. Volume VIII: The Irish Dramatic Movement*, M. Fitzgerald and R. J. Finneran (eds.), 26–8. New York: Scribner.

Yeats, W.B. (2003b) '*Samhain*: 1903 – Moral and Immoral Plays', *The Collected Works of W.B. Yeats. Volume VIII: The Irish Dramatic Movement*, M. Fitzgerald and R.J. Finneran (eds.), 29–31, New York: Scribner.

Yeats, W.B. (2003c), '*Samhain*: 1903 – The Theatre, The Pulpit and the Newspapers', *The Collected Works of W.B. Yeats. Volume VIII: The Irish Dramatic Movement*, M. Fitzgerald and R. J. Finneran (eds.), 36–39, New York: Scribner.

Yeats, W.B. (2003d), '*Samhain*: 1904 – The Dramatic Movement', *The Collected Works of W.B. Yeats. Volume VIII: The Irish Dramatic Movement*, M. Fitzgerald and R.J. Finneran (eds.), 40–51, New York: Scribner.

Yeats, W.B. ([1893] 2004a), 'The Message of the Folk-lorist' (19 August 1893), in *The Collected Works of W.B. Yeats. Volume IX: Early Articles and Reviews*, J.P. Frayne and M. Marchaterre (eds.), 209–13, New York: Scribner.

Yeats, W.B. ([1895] 2004b), 'Irish National Literature, III' (September 1895), *The Collected Works of W.B. Yeats. Volume IX: Early Articles and Reviews*, J.P. Frayne and M. Marchaterre (eds.), 280–7, New York: Scribner.

Yeats, W.B. ([1905] 2005) 'To Gilbert Murray, 24 January 1905', in J. Kelly and R. Schuchard (eds.), *The Collected Letters of W.B. Yeats, Volume 4: 1905–1907*, 22–4, Oxford: Oxford University Press.

Yip, W. (1969), *Ezra Pound's* Cathay, Princeton: Princeton University Press.

Works Cited

Zaller, R. (2012), *Robinson Jeffers and the American Sublime*, Redwood City: Stanford University Press.

Zeitlin, F.I. (1996), *Playing the Other: Gender and Society in Classical Greek Literature*, Chicago: University of Chicago Press.

Zeitlin, F.I. (2010), 'The Lady Vanishes: Helen and Her Phantom in Euripidean Drama', in *Allusion, Authority and Truth: Festschrift for Pietro Pucci*, P. Mitsis and C. Tsagalis (eds.), 263–82, Berlin: Walter de Gruyter.

Zilboorg, C. (1989), 'A New Chapter in the Lives of H.D. and Richard Aldington: Their Relationship with Clement Shorter', *Philological Quarterly* 68 (2): 241–62.

Zilboorg, C. (1991a), 'Joint Venture: Richard Aldington, H. D. and the Poets' Translation Series', *Philological Quarterly* 70 (1): 67–98.

Zilboorg, C. (1991b), '"Soul of My Soul": A Contextual Reading of H.D.'s "Heliodora"', *Sagetrieb* 10 (3): 121–38.

Zilboorg, C., ed. (2003), *Richard Aldington & H.D.: Their Lives in Letters, 1918–1961*, Manchester: Manchester University Press.

Ziolkowski, T. (1993), *Virgil and the Moderns*, Princeton: Princeton University Press.

Ziolkowski, T. (2004), *Ovid and the Moderns*, Ithaca: Cornell University Press.

INDEX

Page numbers in *italics* indicate photographs, while **bold** marks tables.

Index

Index

'Hipparchia', 123
Hippolytus Temporizes, 106–7, 117
as *Imagiste*, 66, 93, 98–99
Latin/Greek fluency, 9, 210n7
and mysticism, 91
and New Womanhood, 108
Notes on Euripides, 66
Notes on Thought and Vision, 92
Paint it To-day, 107, 114, 116, 119
Palimpsest, 87
Sea Garden, 96, 114–15
'The Wise Sappho', 117–18
Tribute to Freud, 82–83
Trilogy, 78–79, 83, 86
See also *Helen in Egypt* (H.D.); *Hippolytus*
   (H.D.); *Ion* (H.D.); *Iphigenia in Aulis* (H.D.)
Heaney, Seamus, 201–2
Heart of Darkness (Conrad), 148, 182
Helen in Egypt (H.D.), 65–67, 87, 89, 125–26, 189,
   200, 221n9, 224n26
   audio recording of, 68–69
   Eidolon, 74–75
   'Leuké', 69–74
   as meta-palinode, 65, 71, 73–75
   palinodic nature of, 65–66
   'Pallinode', 65, 71
   theatricality of, 66
Helen of Troy, 65, 69, 87, 199–200
   in *A Trojan Ending*, 138
   phantom nature of, 68
Hellenism, and modernist writers, 5, 18
hermeneutic tools
   intertextuality, 51
   prosidy as, 46–47
Hermes, 191–92
'Hermes of the Ways' (H.D), 191–93, 199
HERmione (H.D.), 106, 114–16
Hesiod, 90
   Theogony, 78, 87–88
Heuving, Jean, 71, 126
Hickman, Miranda, 23, 31, 126–7, 202–3, 211n25
'Hipparchia' (H.D.), 123
Hippolytus (H.D.), 12, 78, 88, 115, 211n12, 227n20
   Aphrodite in, 112–13
   Artemisian eroticism, 110, 112
   and eros, 110, 112
   evil in, 112–13
   and feminism, 108
   misogyny in, 107, 115–16
   Phaedra in, 106, 109, 115, 117
Hippolytus Temporizes (H.D.), 106–7, 117
'Historial Truth' (Christensen), 139
historical fiction, Riding's, 136–38, 141
history
   and poetry, 31, 154
   as study of men, 131–32, 135

and women writers, 135
   See also historical fiction
Hoberman, Ruth, 139
   Gendering Classicism, 132–33
'Homage to Sextus Propertius' (Pound), 17, 58, 209n7
Homer
   accusations of bias, 139
   audience of, 58
   Pound on, 52
   scholarly editions of, 49
   translations of, 24
Homeri Odyssea ad verbum translata (Divus), 33, 42
   See also Divus, Andreas
Homeric epithets, 40
Homeric Hymn to Aphrodite (2nd), 26–27
   Pound's allusions to, 24
Homeric Hymn to Hermes, 192
the Homeric Question, 23
'How to Read' (Pound), 22
Hugh Selwyn Mauberley (Pound). See *Mauberley*
   (Pound)
Hulme, T.E., 2
human languages, and pure language, 29

imagists, 60, 175
   and ancient poetry, 13
   editors of PTS as, 9
   and translations, 4
'Immerso nell'acqua frangosa', 70
interpretive paraphrasing, in Pound's works, 21
Ion (H.D.), 78, 88–89
   Apollo in, 79, 82
   baskets/boxes in, 81
   H.D.'s translation, 85, 92–93, 121
   Ion in, 83, 224n2
   Kreousa, 77–78, 80–84, 88, 121–22
   secrets in, 78–79
   use of prose in, 78, 89, 99–100
Iphigenia among the Taurians (Euripides), 71
Iphigenia in Aulis (H.D.), 15, 67, 78–79, 105–6, 112
Ireland, 150–51, 179
Irish Free State, 179–80
Irish nationalism, 170, 186

Jebb, Richard, *The Oedipus Tyrannus of Sophocles*,
   174, 176
Jeffers, Robinson, 91–93, 96, 98, 125
   'Songs of the Dead Men to the Three Dancers',
   96–97
   'The Humanist's Tragedy', 97
   'Thurso's Landing', 93
Jenkins, Thomas, 82, 121
Jones, Chris, 38, 40
Joyce, James, 155
   and the Sirens, 143–44
   Ulysses, 144, 149–54, 163

Index

music, 157
    and poetry, 61–62
music-hall comedians, 165

Nagy, Gregory, 65
narrators, and Homer, 42
nationalism, 187
    See also Irish nationalism
Nekuia episode, 24, 33, 35, 41
Neoplatonic traditions, 22–23, 27
New York Times, 170
Newman, F.W., 58
Nicholls, Peter, 45, 47
Nietzsche, Friedrich, 155
nineteenth century
    historicism, 59–60
    views on translation, 3
nonsensuous similarities, 29–30
nostos, 65, 146
Notes on Euripides (H.D.), 66
Notes on Thought and Vision (H.D.), 92
nous, 22–23

O'Donoghue, Bernard, 205
Odysseus
    as 'no one', 28
    and the Sirens, 48–51, 143, 151
the *Odyssey*, 163, 199–200
    Chapman's translation, 25
    Divius's translation, 25, 42
    and Joyce, 150
    See also Canto I (Pound)
Oedipus Rex
    and censorship, 172
    Yeats's fascination with, 170, 184
The Oedipus Tyrannus of Sophocles (Jebb and
    Verrall), 174, 176
Old Comedy, 158–59, 162, 166
Old English, and alliteration, 25
Old English poetry, 38
    See also The Seafarer
'On the Mimetic Facility' (Benjamin), 60
'On Translation' (Benjamin), 60
orichalchi, 27
The Origin of Attic Comedy (Eliot), 166
Ostriker, Alicia Suskin, 190
'out of Homer' phrase, 26, 33, 41–42
'out of' phrase, 59
Oxford English Dictionary, 37

Padel, Ruth, 75
Paint it Today (H.D.), 107, 114, 116, 119
palimpsest, vs. palinode, 66–68
Palimpsest (H.D.), 87
palinodes, 5, 66, 73, 126–27
Penelope, 191, 199–200

personae/masks, used by Pound, 50
Perysinakis, Ioannis, 65
Petronius, *Satyricon*, 182–83, 203–4
Pindar, 52–53
    difficulties with, 9
    Pound on, 28, 55
    Second Olympian Ode, 46, 52
Poems: 1909-1925 (Eliot), 145–46
Poems and Translations (Sieburth), 62
poetic material history, 59
poetic music, 61–62
poetry
    Eliot on, 164, 166–67
    and form, 8–9
    Greek, 171
    mystic views of, 17
    Pound on, 48
    vs. scholarship, 8–9, 17–18
    Yeats on, 174–76
Poets Translation Series (PTS), 5, 7–9, 11, 17, 203
    corrections, 16
    Mackail on, 1, 14–16
    prose translations, 12–14
    reviews of, 14–15
Porphyry, 42
Porteus, Hugh Gordon, 157
post-millennial students, 200, 203
Pound, Ezra
    and the 2nd *Homeric Hymn to Aphrodite*, 24
    'A Few Don'ts by an Imagiste', 39
    'A Retrospect', 48, 51
    ABC of Reading, 51–52
    'Apparuit', 45
    Cathay, 38, 58, 216n23
    on Cavalcanti, 23
    collaborating with Yeats, 175, 185
    critical prose of, 51
    critiques of, 2, 17, 209n7
    'Early Translators of Homer', 33–34
    editing Eliot's work, 144–46, 149, 182–83, 187
    expectations of readers, 45–9, 52, 56, 61, 204
    fluency of, 53
    Guide to Kulchur, 22
    on his own works, 21
    'Homage to Sextus Propertius', 17, 58, 209n7
    'How to Read', 22
    on Joyce, 155
    'Lament for Adonis', 46
    Love Poems of Ancient Egypt, 62
    omissions by, 46, 49
    poetic strategies, 48, 53
    on poetry, 48
    on *Sweeney Agonistes*, 162
    on translation and language, 22, 58
    translation methods, 27–29, 43, 58
    use of allusions, 46–47, 55–56, 61

262

Index